DATE DUE

An Introduction to
THE STUDY OF THE
MAYA HIEROGLYPHS

SYLVANUS GRISWOLD MORLEY

With a New Introduction and Bibliography by
J. ERIC S. THOMPSON
Formerly on the Staff of the Carnegie Institution
of Washington

Dover Publications, Inc., New York

Published in Canada by General Publishing Company, Ltd., 30 Lesmill Road, Don Mills, Toronto, Ontario.
Published in the United Kingdom by Constable and Company, Ltd., 10 Orange Street, London WC 2.

This Dover edition, first published in 1975, is an unabridged republication of the work originally published by the Government Printing Office, Washington, D. C., 1915, as Bulletin 57 of the Bureau of American Ethnology, Smithsonian Institution. Plates 3 and 27 through 32 originally appeared in color. A new introduction and bibliography have been prepared specially for the present edition by J. Eric S. Thompson.

International Standard Book Number: 0-486-23108-9
Library of Congress Catalog Card Number: 74-82503

Manufactured in the United States of America
Dover Publications, Inc.
180 Varick Street
New York, N. Y. 10014

INTRODUCTION TO THE DOVER EDITION

"To Sylvanus Griswold Morley, 'The little friend of all the world'" was the affectionate dedication of a book by Thomas Gann, medical officer in British Honduras (now Belize) at the turn of the century, who in his spare time excavated Maya mounds and presumably read Kipling. "That small, near-sighted, dynamic bundle of energy" was a description of Morley by another very old friend and colleague.

"Vay," as everyone from Maine to Guatemala called him, was certainly pint-size; his exuberant personality was a very important factor in increasing and popularizing knowledge of the Maya.

Born in Chester, Pa., in 1883, he graduated from Pennsylvania Military College in 1904 with a degree in civil engineering, but even before high school days he had been deeply interested in archaeology, particularly that of Egypt, and it was with the intention of entering that field that he went next to Harvard. There, F. W. Putnam, then director of the Peabody Museum of Archaeology and Ethnology, deflected his interest to the Maya, pointing out the far greater opportunities in that then near-virgin field.

Morley, still an undergraduate and off his own bat, made his first archaeological visit to Yucatan and other parts of Mexico in 1907. Subsequent work at Pueblo ruins in New Mexico stimulated his interest in archaeology but did not lessen his new-found love for the Maya. His opportunity came when Edgar L. Hewett, director of the School of American Archaeology in Santa Fe, New Mexico, and Morley's boss in those excavations in the Southwest, obtained a concession to dig at the important Maya site of Quirigua, Guatemala, and sent Morley to work there then and again in the subsequent seasons of 1911, 1912 and 1914. That experience, together with two long expeditions in search of new hieroglyph texts, whetted his interest in epigraphy.

This bore fruit in *An Introduction*, which he submitted (in longhand and even in pencil!) to the Bureau of American Ethnology late in 1912. Luckily for him and for us he had made there two friends of considerable influence, Frederick Hodge, head of the Bureau, and Charles Walcott, Secretary of the Smithsonian Institution, of which the Bureau was a part. The work appeared in 1915.

Morley had established his reputation in his field, but prospects for a successful career were bleak. There was no future with the impoverished School of American Archaeology, which was in no position to finance a long-term program of excavation in the Maya area. The only other possibility was the Peabody Museum at Harvard, which had been involved in Maya research for the past two decades. Unfortunately, Vay had antagonized a colleague or, rather, an influential senior statesman of Maya research at Harvard, a very rare occurrence in his long career.

Charles P. Bowditch, a wealthy and peppery Bostonian, had largely financed Peabody Museum expeditions to the Maya area, and, following publication of the reports, privately printed his elucidation of the epigraphic material thus brought to light. One such report, published in 1908, included the site of Naranjo with a rich harvest of hieroglyphic texts. Morley, without consulting Bowditch, published the following year his own commentary on those inscriptions, and labeled the paper as being in partial fulfillment of the requirements for a Ph.D. at Harvard. Bowditch saw to it that Vay did not get his degree and was determined the Peabody Museum should never support his work.

Rescue came in the shape of the Carnegie Institution of Washington, which was considering involvement in anthropology. Morley, again with friends at court, was one of three men invited to outline projects. He submitted a report proposing excavation at the great Maya site of Chichen Itza, in the north of the Peninsula of Yucatan.

There cannot be much doubt that the proposal outlined by W. H. R. Rivers, outstanding British ethnologist, was of considerably more merit than Morley's. Rivers' plan was for intensive ethnological research in the Pacific on the grounds that the native Polynesian and Melanesian cultures were disintegrating before the advance of western civilization. If these were not thoroughly investigated in the very near future, there would soon be little left to salvage. Archaeological ruins, on the other hand, would not suffer appreciably if left for a few more decades beneath the ground. Another point, perhaps not then so evident: improving techniques in archaeology would recover far fuller data if excavation were postponed. As one who worked in those early days at Chichen Itza, I realize how much more information we would have recovered had excavation been postponed. The importance of potsherds for working out chronology and trade contacts, now one of the great tools of the archaeologist, was hardly realized in those days, and, of course, then, before the great discovery of the Carbon-14 method of dating, we just threw away ash and chunks of carbonized wood as valueless.

Because of his contagious enthusiasm, persuasive tongue and friends at court, Vay won the day and his plan was accepted despite the opposition of the President of the Carnegie Institution —one of the very rare occasions, one imagines, in which a president of that institution was outvoted by an executive committee he chaired. However, chaotic conditions in Mexico following the 1910 revolution made work at Chichen Itza impossible. Morley's substitute plan on Maya chronology was approved (by then he had won over the President of the Carnegie Institution). The original plan was to record all known Maya inscriptions in one volume. In fact, the first publication—*The Inscriptions at Copan* —covering that one site, ran to 655 pages.

To gather new epigraphic data, Morley undertook a series of expeditions mainly to the forests at Peten in northern Guatemala; these were to continue without break from 1915 to 1923 (he had been on similar trips from 1910 to 1914).

That first expedition under Carnegie auspices was typical. It involved, as a first leg, journeying up the Belize river in what was then British Honduras, to the limits of navigation, and thence through the forests of Peten, Guatemala, to the ruins of La Honradez, which yielded a nice crop of Maya dates. Back to Belize, and thence by ship, rail and mule to Copan, in the Republic of Honduras.

The final leg of the itinerary was by boat and mule from Puerto Barrios, up the Golfo Dulce, and overland to Cajabon in the Alta Verapaz. From there on there were not even mule trails; Vay and his assistant slogged it on foot for seven days with Indian porters to carry their equipment to the Maya ruins of Cancuen. Dismissing their porters, the two white men took a dugout down the Pasión river and thence proceeded by mule and river boat back to Belize. That last journey was one of over 1,000 miles, largely through inhospitable country. For Morley it was well worth while. Those four months of exploration added seven "cities" to the nineteen with decipherable dates previously known, a really good bag.

Nowadays, archaeological camps in the Maya forest are seldom without a refrigerator and fresh food to stock it brought in daily by plane from the nearest city. Anyone taken ill can be in a city hospital in a few hours, the sundowner is iced and there is radio communication with the city. In Morley's day, travel was exclusively by mule through the roadless rain forests of the Peten, almost without inhabitants save for gatherers of chicle (raw product of chewing gum), who were in scattered camps during the rainy season, when the sap of the sapodilla tree flows. It was from them that Morley learned of undiscovered sites they came across when cruising for stands of the sapodilla.

Narrow, winding trails opened by the chicle gatherers were the only means of communication. It was a question of jogging hour after hour, day after day, along those monotonous trails. There is little romance in the forest and little of the beauty of travel agencies' brochures. The exotic flowers are invisible for they seek the sunlight at treetop level, 150 to 200 feet above the traveler, who can stare only at dull-hued tree trunks, lianas and bromelias when he is not ducking to avoid being caught up, like Absalom, in the branch of a tree, or watching that his mule does not scrape him against the thorns of the *cuum* palm.

Each night one camps, sweaty, unwashed and tick-bitten, at some abandoned chicle-gatherers' camp, where often water is not to be had in the dry season. Mules get loose, causing long delays before the cavalcade can get under way next morning. Vay, who appreciated the comforts of life, hated every minute of it, but he endured it, for only thereby—as he put it—could he bring home the epigraphic bacon obtained from sculptured stone monuments, still erect or half-buried, which bestrewed the forest-covered courts of some hitherto unknown site.

Then, mules unloaded and camp made, the gang would be set to felling trees to let in light for photography and to bring out the faint detail of what were only too often eroded glyphs. Only then could Vay set to work drawing the glyphs, a handkerchief around each wrist to keep sweat from trickling on his sketchbook—as I have seen him—ruler in one hand to measure each carved glyph and drive off mosquitoes; pencil in the other.

There could be danger. In 1916, returning from the discovery of Uaxactun, in the very heart of the Peten, which had yielded the then earliest known Maya date, Morley came very close to death. His party was ambushed on the trail by Guatemalan soldiers who opened fire, believing them to be a party of revolutionaries operating in the neighborhood. The guide and a doctor with the expedition, who were at the head of the mule train, were instantly killed; the rest of the party escaped unharmed and next morning succeeded in reaching the safety of British Honduras territory.

Morley, as was his custom, had been riding in second place, immediately behind the guide, but some minutes before the attack he chanced to drop his eyeglasses. By the time he had retrieved them and remounted, he was next to last in the file; the doctor had taken his place immediately behind the guide. Losing his glasses undoubtedly saved Morley's life.

When the United States entered the First World War, Morley

was recruited for U.S. Intelligence and spent some time making a reconnaissance of the Atlantic coasts of Honduras and Nicaragua. He took his intelligence work seriously but it was curious how that work led him to such nests of German intrigue and espionage as the Maya ruins of Copan, Quirigua, Tulum, Chichen Itza, Uxmal, etc.

By 1923 Mexico had largely recovered from its revolutionary fever and the time was auspicious for initiating work at the great site of Chichen Itza, as conceived nine years earlier. But the situation was delicate. The Mexican authorities were well aware that large quantities of very valuable objects, dredged from the Well of Sacrifice at that same site, had been illegally smuggled out of the country to a leading museum in the United States. Furthermore—and this was a sore point with Mexicans —the United States government had not recognized General Obregón as president of Mexico.

I doubt that Mexico would have granted the concession had it not been for Vay's very friendly relations with everyone in the country from the Governor of Yucatan and the leading Mexican archaeologists down to the humblest peon. No Mexican could resist his stories—he had an incredible fund of them and was a born raconteur—translated from English into Vay's "Spanish." His Spanish was atrocious; his vocabulary was extensive, but his pronunciation and grammar, almost bereft of tenses and genders, were a standing joke all over Middle America. As the great Mexican archaeologist Alfonso Caso once remarked with a perceptible twinkle in his eye at the conclusion of an archaeological meeting, "These sessions have been memorable. We have listened to speeches in three languages, Spanish, English and Morley."

Morley's handling of the representatives of the Carnegie Institution of Washington and the Mexican authorities was superb and the concession was duly signed in an atmosphere of goodwill. I have wondered what President Obregón thought of him. Obregón had a dry, almost macabre sense of humor, very different from Vay's bubbling exuberance. Relations between the United States and Mexico would surely have been much better had Morley been the American ambassador in Mexico in those far-off, troubled years.

Excavation started at Chichen Itza under Morley's direction in 1924 and continued until 1937. Even after that the Carnegie Institution continued to use its headquarters there (in the old hacienda buildings) as a center for operations throughout the Yucatan Peninsula. For many years the labor force, comprising Maya from neighboring villages and masons from Mérida, exceeded sixty. The Temple of the Warriors, with the Chac Mool temple beneath, the Caracol, the Temple of the Three Lintels and the Temple of the Wall Panels, now leading attractions for tens of thousands of visitors to Chichen Itza, were excavated and restored under Morley's direction—*Si monumentum requiris, circumspice.*

Archaeologists of the Mexican government were similarly engaged on restoration of other buildings at that and other sites in Yucatan.

Morley also initiated excavation by the Carnegie Institution at other Maya sites, principally Copan, his first love, and Uaxactun, then thought to have been the first "city" to erect dated stelae.

I joined the staff at Chichen Itza in 1926. I had written asking for a job, saying that I could read the calendar glyphs (largely through diligent reading of *An Introduction*). That subject was, of course, Vay's great love, and as specialists in that field were scarce as hen's teeth, I got the job.

I reached Chichen Itza one morning in January—the train from Mérida left, I think, at 5:30 A.M. and there was a twenty-mile drive from the nearest station. Morley had gone to visit an outlying group of ruins, and I went part way to meet him. Long before he became visible, I heard his voice, high-pitched and with a nasal accent—Pennsylvanian it was said, but I've never heard another son of the Quaker state talk that way. The *chachalacas,* those Roman geese of the New World, screamed their alarm. Then round a bend in the trail came the little man, wearing a huge Mexican sombrero. A line halfway between the ground and the peak of the sombrero would have passed not much below the brim of the hat. That was the beginning of a friendship broken only by his death.

On his lecture tours from coast to coast of the United States, "selling the Maya to the American public," which he did extremely well, he would visit us, first in Chicago, later in the village of Harvard, Mass. We would invite friends to meet him. Vay, often cross-legged on the floor, would discuss some abstruse problem, such as the order in which some Maya monuments had been set up, something which one would think of interest only to a specialist, yet our visitors who had hardly heard of the Maya were enthralled. It was a gift the gods confer on few.

Life at Chichen Itza was very comfortable, yet at the drop of a hat Vay would be off to investigate reports of newly discovered ruins. Sceptical of my claim to have found Classic-period texts at Coba (in the thinking of those days, they had no right to be there), he insisted on returning with me to that remote site in

Quintana Roo to check my findings. Indeed, he wanted to start the next morning, but with backside still sore from much riding, I persuaded him to wait three or four days. Later, on getting news of a large site in a distant corner of the State of Campeche dripping with hieroglyphic monuments, he hastily abandoned the fleshpots of Chichen Itza to visit that site of Calakmul. The trip paid off; Calakmul had more stelae than any other Maya site. As late as 1944, when he was on the wrong side of sixty and not in good health, for the tropics had not spared him, he and I, with our wives, reaped a rich epigraphic harvest at Toniaa, in the state of Chiapas. It was a tough trip.

When Chichen Itza finally closed down, Morley rented a small hacienda on the outskirts of Mérida, and it was there and in Santa Fe that he wrote his best seller, *The Ancient Maya*.

In 1947, on the verge of retirement from the Carnegie Institution, after 33 years of field work for them, he took over the directorship of the School of American Archaeology (by then changed to The School of American Research) on the death of its director, Edgar L. Hewett, under whom Morley had had his first archaeological experience in the Southwest and, later, in the Maya area.

Santa Fe had been Vay's American home for nearly forty years. He had a great affection for the place and had campaigned hard to preserve and reintroduce its adobe architecture of the Spanish period. It was appropriate that he should die there. His constitution undermined by those early years of living rough, he succumbed to a heart attack in August 1948.

Morley was not an intellectual. He was content to amass data, but showed little interest in using them to interpret Maya civilization. His energies were directed to deciphering the calendrical dates—his ability to wrest a date from a badly weathered stela was phenomenal—but his concern for noncalendrical glyphs was so small that usually he did not trouble to draw them.

The results of his many years of exploration were published in *The Inscriptions at Copan*, already mentioned, and *The Inscriptions of Peten*, 1937–38, comprising four volumes of text, one of plates and another of maps. In this encyclopedia every known date in that region is discussed in detail and there are descriptions and plans of each site.

Morley's indifference to interpretation is very evident in his popular book, *The Ancient Maya*, 1946. In that book can be detected Vay's greatness and his weakness. He was able to imbue his reader or his hearer with his enthusiasm and he did not hide his conviction that the Maya were a race of supermen. He applied to Maya civilization that bubbling zeal which had stood him in such good stead in his personal relations. The book was a sort of Hallelujah chorus. Fact was piled on fact, but there was hardly a whisper of a why.

Nevertheless, the book served its purpose. By and large, archaeologists are cloistered creatures, content to write for one another, but archaeology depends on public support. Vay had the ability to communicate his ardor to the public, and in this book and in his many public lectures he did an outstanding job along those lines, thereby insuring that funds for research flowed in.

In *An Introduction to the Study of the Maya Hieroglyphs* Morley's factual approach is combined with a marked weakness, but to the advantage of the book. He was extremely repetitive and prolix; he would take three pages to say what could be stated in one longish paragraph. The factual approach is that of the high school teacher: "That is so," not "Why is that so?" On the other hand, by repetition one drives home the point to the pupil, and after all, readers of *An Introduction* are on high school level so far as the Maya calendar is concerned.

For those reasons, this book is still, after sixty years, the best presentation of the subject. It should, however, be noted that the title is a misnomer; the contents cover only that part of the glyphs, important as it is, pertaining to the calendar.

It is extraordinary how little dated the book is. Naturally, the years have added to our knowledge of the mechanics of that most intricate calendar. Using material Morley had gathered and published in a comparative presentation—*The Supplementary Series in the Maya Inscriptions,* 1916—John Teeple was able to work out the Maya system of lunar recording. The sequence of the Lords of the Nights was recognized largely from the texts Morley had amassed. With typical generosity he made all his unpublished data on those glyphs available to me. Glyphs which the Maya used to indicate whether a count from one date to another was backward or forward were recognized, and slowly the meanings of the passages which accompany those dates are being established.

Those were additions to knowledge; in no way do they detract from Morley's original publication, still without rival in its field. Three or four pages of Maya history in Chapter I are no longer acceptable; the rest stands. Few textbooks written in the infancy of a field of research have more than antiquarian interest; *An Introduction* is a rare exception.

J. ERIC S. THOMPSON

PRINCIPAL WRITINGS OF S. G. MORLEY

1909   The inscriptions of Naranjo, northern Guatemala. *American Anthropologist*, 11: 543–62.
1913   Excavations at Quirigua, Guatemala. *National Geographic Magazine*, 24: 339–61. (First of a number of articles popularizing the Maya in this and other magazines.)
1915   An introduction to the study of the Maya hieroglyphs. Bureau of American Ethnology, Bulletin 57. Washington, D.C.
1916   The supplementary series in the Maya inscriptions. *In* Holmes Anniversary Volume presented . . . in honor of his seventieth birthday, pp. 366–96. Washington, D.C.
1917   The hotun as the principal chronological unit of the old Maya empire. *Proceedings 19th International Congress of Americanists*, 1915, pp. 195–201. Washington, D.C. (Periodicity of Maya monuments, an important contribution.)
1920   The inscriptions at Copan. Carnegie Institution of Washington, Publication 219. Washington, D.C.
1937–38 The inscriptions of Peten. Carnegie Institution of Washington, Publication 437, 6 vols. Washington, D.C.
1946   The ancient Maya. Stanford University Press, Stanford.
1949   (With A. Barrera Vásquez). The Maya chronicles. Carnegie Institution of Washington, Publication 585, Contribution no. 48. Washington, D.C.

WRITINGS ABOUT S. G. MORLEY

KIDDER, A. V.   Sylvanus Griswold Morley, 1883–1948. *El Palacio*, 55: 267–74. Santa Fe, N.M. 1948.
ROYS, R. L., and M. W. HARRISON.   Sylvanus Griswold Morley, 1883–1948. *American Antiquity*, 14: 215–21. 1949.
THOMPSON, J. E. S.   Sylvanus Griswold Morley, 1883–1948. *American Anthropologist*, 51: 293–97. 1949.
LONG, BOAZ (editor).   Morleyana. A collection of writings in memoriam Sylvanus Griswold Morley, 1883–1948. The School of American Research, Santa Fe, N.M. 1950.
LISTER, R. H., and F. C. LISTER.   In search of Maya glyphs. From the archaeological journals of Sylvanus G. Morley. Museum of New Mexico Press, Santa Fe. 1970.
BRUNHOUSE, R. L.   Sylvanus G. Morley and the world of the ancient Mayas. University of Oklahoma Press, Norman. 1971.

ADVANCES IN DECIPHERMENT SINCE "AN INTRODUCTION"

THOMPSON, J. E. S.   Maya hieroglyphic writing: an introduction. University of Oklahoma Press, Norman. 1960.
——   Maya hieroglyphs without tears. British Museum, London. 1972.

LETTER OF TRANSMITTAL

SMITHSONIAN INSTITUTION,
BUREAU OF AMERICAN ETHNOLOGY,
Washington, D. C., January 7, 1914.

SIR: I have the honor to submit the accompanying manuscript of a memoir bearing the title "An Introduction to the Study of the Maya Hieroglyphs," by Sylvanus Griswold Morley, and to recommend its publication as a bulletin of the Bureau of American Ethnology.

The hieroglyphic writing developed by the Maya of Central America and southern Mexico was probably the foremost intellectual achievement of pre-Columbian times in the New World, and as such it deserves equal attention with other graphic systems of antiquity.

The earliest inscriptions now extant probably date from about the beginning of the Christian era, but such is the complexity of the glyphs and subject matter even at this early period, that in order to estimate the age of the system it is necessary to postulate a far greater antiquity for its origin. Indeed all that can be accepted safely in this direction is that many centuries must have elapsed before the Maya hieroglyphic writing could have been developed to the highly complex stage where we first encounter it.

The first student to make any progress in deciphering the Maya inscriptions was Prof. Ernst Förstemann, of the Royal Library at Dresden. About 1880 Professor Förstemann published a facsimile reproduction of the Dresden codex, and for the next twenty years devoted the greater part of his time to the elucidation of this manuscript. He it was who first discovered and worked out the ingenious vigesimal system of numeration used by the Maya, and who first pointed out how this system was utilized to record astronomical and chronological facts. In short, his pioneer work made possible all subsequent progress in deciphering Maya texts.

Curiously enough, about the same time, or a little later (in 1891), another student of the same subject, Mr. J. T. Goodman, of Alameda, California, working independently and without knowledge of Professor Förstemann's researches, also succeeded in deciphering the chronological parts of the Maya texts, and in determining the values of the head-variant numerals. Mr. Goodman also perfected some tables, "The Archaic Chronological Calendar" and "The Archaic Annual Calendar," which greatly facilitate the decipherment of the calculations recorded in the texts.

It must be admitted that very little progress has been made in deciphering the Maya glyphs except those relating to the calendar and chronology; that is, the signs for the various time periods (days and months), the numerals, and a few name-glyphs; however, as these known signs comprise possibly two-fifths of all the glyphs, it is clear that the general tenor of the Maya inscriptions is no longer concealed from us. The remaining three-fifths probably tell the nature of the events which occurred on the corresponding dates, and it is to these we must turn for the subject matter of Maya history. The deciphering of this textual residuum is enormously complicated by the character of the Maya glyphs, which for the greater part are ideographic rather than phonetic; that is, the various symbols represent ideas rather than sounds.

In a graphic system composed largely of ideographic elements it is extremely difficult to determine the meanings of the different signs, since little or no help is to be derived from varying combinations of elements as in a phonetic system. In phonetic writing the symbols have fixed sounds, which are unchanging throughout, and when these values have once been determined, they may be substituted for the characters wherever they occur, and thus words are formed.

While the Maya glyphs largely represent ideas, indubitable traces of phoneticism and phonetic composition appear. There are perhaps half a dozen glyphs in all which are known to be constructed on a purely phonetic basis, and as the remaining glyphs are gradually deciphered this number will doubtless be increased.

The progress which has been made in deciphering the Maya inscriptions may be summarized as follows: The Maya calendar, chronology, and astronomy as recorded in the hieroglyphic texts have been carefully worked out, and it is unlikely that future discoveries will change our present conception of them. There remains, however, a group of glyphs which are probably non-calendric, non-chronologic, and non-astronomic in character. These, it may be reasonably expected, will be found to describe the subject matter of Maya history; that is, they probably set forth the nature of the events which took place on the dates recorded. An analogy would be the following: Supposing, in scanning a history of the United States, only the dates could be read. We would find, for example, July 4, 1776, followed by unknown characters; April 12, 1861, by others; and March 4, 1912, by others. This, then, is the case with the Maya glyphs—we find dates followed by glyphs of unknown meaning, which presumably set forth the nature of the corresponding events. In a word, we know now the chronologic skeleton of Maya history; it remains to work out the more intimate details which alone can make it a vital force.

The published writings on the subject of the Maya hieroglyphs have become so voluminous, and are so widely scattered and inaccessible, that it is difficult for students of Central American archeology to become familiar with what has been accomplished in this important field of investigation. In the present memoir Mr. Morley, who has devoted a number of years to the study of Maya archeology, and especially to the hieroglyphs, summarizes the results of these researches to the present time, and it is believed that this *Introduction to the Study of the Maya Hieroglyphs* will be the means of enabling ready and closer acquaintance with this interesting though intricate subject.

Very respectfully,

F. W. HODGE,
Ethnologist-in-Charge.

Dr. CHARLES D. WALCOTT,
    Secretary of the Smithsonian Institution,
        Washington, D. C.

PREFACE

With the great expansion of interest in American archeology during the last few years there has grown to be a corresponding need and demand for primary textbooks, archeological primers so to speak, which will enable the general reader, without previous knowledge of the science, to understand its several branches. With this end in view, the author has prepared An Introduction to the Study of the Maya Hieroglyphs.

The need for such a textbook in this particular field is suggested by two considerations: (1) The writings of previous investigators, having been designed to meet the needs of the specialist rather than those of the beginner, are for the greater part too advanced and technical for general comprehension; and (2) these writings are scattered through many publications, periodicals as well as books, some in foreign languages, and almost all difficult of access to the average reader.

To the second of these considerations, however, the writings of Mr. C. P. Bowditch, of Boston, Massachusetts, offer a conspicuous exception, particularly his final contribution to this subject, entitled "The Numeration, Calendar Systems, and Astronomical Knowledge of the Mayas," the publication of which in 1910 marked the dawn of a new era in the study of the Maya hieroglyphic writing. In this work Mr. Bowditch exhaustively summarizes all previous knowledge of the subject, and also indicates the most promising lines for future investigation. The book is a vast storehouse of heretofore scattered material, now gathered together for the first time and presented to the student in a readily accessible form. Indeed, so thorough is its treatment, the result of many years of intensive study, that the writer would have hesitated to bring out another work, necessarily covering much of the same ground, had it not been for his belief that Mr. Bowditch's book is too advanced for lay comprehension. The Maya hieroglyphic writing is exceedingly intricate; its subject matter is complex and its forms irregular; and in order to be understood it must be presented in a very elementary way. The writer believes that this primer method of treatment has not been followed in the publication in question and, furthermore, that the omission of specimen texts, which would give the student practice in deciphering the glyphs, renders it too technical for use by the beginner.

Acknowledgment should be made here to Mr. Bowditch for his courtesy in permitting the reproduction of a number of drawings from his book, the examples of the period, day and month glyphs figured being derived almost entirely from this source; and in a larger sense for his share in the establishment of instruction in this field of research at Harvard University where the writer first took up these studies.

In the limited space available it would have been impossible to present a detailed picture of the Maya civilization, nor indeed is this essential to the purpose of the book. It has been thought advisable, however, to precede the general discussion of the hieroglyphs with a brief review of the habitat, history, customs, government, and religion of the ancient Maya, so that the reader may gather a general idea of the remarkable people whose writing and calendar he is about to study.

CONTENTS

List of Tables

ILLUSTRATIONS

BIBLIOGRAPHY

AGUILAR, SANCHEZ DE. 1639. Informe contra idolorum cultores del Obispado de Yucatan. Madrid. (Reprint in *Anales Mus. Nac. de Mexico*, VI, pp. 17-122, Mexico, 1900.)

BOWDITCH, CHARLES P. 1901 a. Memoranda on the Maya calendars used in the Books of Chilan Balam. *Amer. Anthr.*, n. s., III, No. 1, pp. 129-138, New York.

—— 1906. The Temples of the Cross, of the Foliated Cross, and of the Sun at Palenque. Cambridge, Mass.

—— 1909. Dates and numbers in the Dresden Codex. *Putnam Anniversary Volume*, pp. 268-298, New York.

—— 1910. The numeration, calendar systems, and astronomical knowledge of the Mayas. Cambridge, Mass.

BRASSEUR DE BOURBOURG, C. E. 1869-70. Manuscrit Troano. Études sur le système graphique et la langue des Mayas. 2 vols. Paris.

BRINTON, DANIEL G. 1882 b. The Maya chronicles. Philadelphia. (No. 1 of *Brinton's Library of Aboriginal American Literature.*)

—— 1894 b. A primer of Mayan hieroglyphics. *Pubs. Univ. of Pa.*, Ser. in Philol., Lit., and Archeol., III, No. 2.

BULLETIN 28 of the Bureau of American Ethnology, 1904: Mexican and Central American antiquities, calendar systems, and history. Twenty-four papers by Eduard Seler, E. Förstemann, Paul Schellhas, Carl Sapper, and E. P. Dieseldorff. Translated from the German under the supervision of Charles P. Bowditch.

COGOLLUDO, D. L. 1688. Historia de Yucathan. Madrid.

CRESSON, H. T. 1892. The antennæ and sting of Yikilcab as components in the Maya day-signs. *Science*, XX, pp. 77-79, New York.

DIESELDORFF, E. P. *See* BULLETIN 28.

FÖRSTEMANN, E. 1906. Commentary on the Maya manuscript in the Royal Public Library of Dresden. *Papers Peabody Mus.*, IV, No. 2, pp. 48-266, Cambridge. *See also* BULLETIN 28.

GATES, W. E. 1910. Commentary upon the Maya-Tzental Perez Codex, with a concluding note upon the linguistic problem of the Maya glyphs. *Papers Peabody Mus.*, VI, No. 1, pp. 5-64, Cambridge.

GOODMAN, J. T. 1897. The archaic Maya inscriptions. (Biologia Centrali-Americana, Archæology, Part XVIII. London.) [*See* Maudslay, 1889-1902.]

—— 1905. Maya dates. *Amer. Anthr.*, n. s., VII, pp. 642-647, Lancaster, Pa.

HEWETT, EDGAR L. 1911. Two seasons' work in Guatemala. *Bull. Archæol. Inst. of America*, II, pp. 117-134, Norwood, Mass.

HOLMES, W. H. 1907. On a nephrite statuette from San Andrés Tuxtla, Vera Cruz, Mexico. *Amer. Anthr.*, n. s., IX, No. 4, pp. 691-701, Lancaster, Pa.

LANDA, DIEGO DE. 1864. Relacion de las cosas de Yucatan. Paris.

LE PLONGEON, A. 1885. The Maya alphabet. Supplement to *Scientific American*, vol. XIX, Jan. 31, pp. 7572-73, New York.

MALER, TEOBERT. 1901. Researches in the central portion of the Usumatsintla valley. *Memoirs Peabody Mus.*, II, No. 1, pp. 9-75, Cambridge.

—— 1903. Researches in the central portion of the Usumatsintla valley. [Continued.] *Ibid.*, No. 2, pp. 83-208.

—— 1908 a. Explorations of the upper Usumatsintla and adjacent region. *Ibid.*, IV, No. 1, pp. 1-51.

MALER, TEOBERT. 1908 b. Explorations in the Department of Peten, Guatemala, and adjacent region. Ibid., No. 2, pp. 55–127.

—— 1910. Explorations in the Department of Peten, Guatemala, and adjacent region. [Continued.] Ibid., No. 3, pp. 131–170.

—— 1911. Explorations in the Department of Peten, Guatemala. Tikal. Ibid., v, No. 1, pp. 3–91, pls. 1–26.

MAUDSLAY, A. P. 1889–1902. Biologia Centrali-Americana, or contributions to the knowledge of the flora and fauna of Mexico and Central America. Archæology. 4 vols. of text and plates. London.

MORLEY, S. G. 1910 b. Correlation of Maya and Christian chronology. Amer. Journ. Archeol., 2d ser., XIV, pp. 193–204, Norwood, Mass.

—— 1911. The historical value of the Books of Chilan Balam. Ibid., XV, pp. 195–214.

PONCE, FRAY ALONZO. 1872. Relacion breve y verdadera de algunas cosas de las muchas que sucedieron al Padre Fray Alonzo Ponce, Comisario General en las provincias de Nueva España. Colección de documentos inéditos para la historia de España, LVII, LVIII. Madrid.

ROSNY, LEON DE. 1876. Essai sur le déchiffrement de l'écriture hiératique de l'Amérique Centrale. Paris.

SAPPER, CARL. See BULLETIN 28.

SCHELLHAS, PAUL. See BULLETIN 28.

SELER, EDUARD. 1901 c. Die alten Ansiedelungen von Chaculá im Distrikte Nenton des Departements Huehuetenango der Republik Guatemala. Berlin.

—— 1902–1908. Gesammelte Abhandlungen zur amerikanischen Sprach- und Alterthumskunde. 3 vols. Berlin.

See also BULLETIN 28.

SPINDEN, H. J. 1913. A study of Maya art, its subject-matter and historical development. Memoirs Peabody Mus., VI, pp. 1–285, Cambridge.

STEPHENS, J. L. 1841. Incidents of travel in Central America, Chiapas, and Yucatan. 2 vols. New York.

—— 1843. Incidents of travel in Yucatan. 2 vols. New York.

THOMAS, CYRUS. 1893. Are the Maya hieroglyphs phonetic? Amer. Anthr., VI, No. 3, pp. 241–270, Washington.

VILLAGUTIERRE, SOTOMAYOR J. 1701. Historia de la conquista de la provinzia de el Itza, reduccion, y progressos de la de el Lacandon y otras naciones de el reyno de Guatimala, a las provincias de Yucatan, en la America septentrional. Madrid.

An Introduction to
THE STUDY OF THE
MAYA HIEROGLYPHS

PLATE 1

THE MAYA TERRITORY, SHOWING LOCATIONS OF PRINCIPAL CITIES

Chapter I. THE MAYA

Habitat

Broadly speaking, the Maya were a lowland people, inhabiting the Atlantic coast plains of southern Mexico and northern Central America. (See pl. 1.) The southern part of this region is abundantly watered by a network of streams, many of which have their rise in the Cordillera, while the northern part, comprising the peninsula of Yucatan, is entirely lacking in water courses and, were it not for natural wells (*cenotes*) here and there, would be uninhabitable. This condition in the north is due to the geologic formation of the peninsula, a vast plain underlaid by limestone through which water quickly percolates to subterranean channels.

In the south the country is densely forested, though occasional savannas break the monotony of the tropical jungles. The rolling surface is traversed in places by ranges of hills, the most important of which are the Cockscomb Mountains of British Honduras; these attain an elevation of 3,700 feet. In Yucatan the nature of the soil and the water-supply not being favorable to the growth of a luxuriant vegetation, this region is covered with a smaller forest growth and a sparser bush than the area farther southward.

The climate of the region occupied by the Maya is tropical; there are two seasons, the rainy and the dry. The former lasts from May or June until January or February, there being considerable local variation not only in the length of this season but also in the time of its beginning.

Deer, tapirs, peccaries, jaguars, and game of many other kinds abound throughout the entire region, and doubtless formed a large part of the food supply in ancient times, though formerly corn was the staple, as it is now.

There are at present upward of twenty tribes speaking various dialects of the Maya language, perhaps half a million people in all. These live in the same general region their ancestors occupied, but under greatly changed conditions. Formerly the Maya were the van of civilization in the New World,[1] but to-day they are a dwindling

---

[1] All things considered, the Maya may be regarded as having developed probably the highest aboriginal civilization in the Western Hemisphere, although it should be borne in mind that they were surpassed in many lines of endeavor by other races. The Inca, for example, excelled them in the arts of weaving and dyeing, the Chiriqui in metal working, and the Aztec in military proficiency.

race, their once remarkable civilization is a thing of the past, and its manners and customs are forgotten.

HISTORY

The ancient Maya, with whom this volume deals, emerged from barbarism probably during the first or second century of the Christian Era; at least their earliest dated monument can not be ascribed with safety to a more remote period.[1] How long a time had been required for the development of their complex calendar and hieroglyphic system to the point of graphic record, it is impossible to say, and any estimate can be only conjectural. It is certain, however, that a long interval must have elapsed from the first crude and unrelated scratches of savagery to the elaborate and involved hieroglyphs found on the earliest monuments, which represent not only the work of highly skilled sculptors, but also the thought of intensively developed minds. That this period was measured by centuries rather than by decades seems probable; the achievement was far too great to have been performed in a single generation or even in five or ten.

It seems safe to assume, therefore, that by the end of the second century of the Christian Era the Maya civilization was fairly on its feet. There then began an extraordinary development all along the line. City after city sprang into prominence throughout the southern part of the Maya territory,[2] each contributing its share to the general progress and art of the time. With accomplishment came confidence and a quickening of pace. All activities doubtless shared in the general uplift which followed, though little more than the material evidences of architecture and sculpture have survived the ravages of the destructive environment in which this culture flourished; and it is chiefly from these remnants of ancient Maya art that the record of progress has been partially reconstructed.

This period of development, which lasted upward of 400 years, or until about the close of the sixth century, may be called per-

---

[1] The correlation of Maya and Christian chronology herein followed is that suggested by the writer in "The Correlation of Maya and Christian Chronology" (*Papers of the School of American Archæology*, No. 11). See Morley, 1910 b, cited in BIBLIOGRAPHY, pp. XV, XVI. There are at least six other systems of correlation, however, on which the student must pass judgment. Although no two of these agree, all are based on data derived from the same source, namely, the Books of Chilan Balam (see p. 3, footnote 1). The differences among them are due to the varying interpretations of the material therein presented. Some of the systems of correlation which have been proposed, besides that of the writer, are:

1. That of Mr. C. P. Bowditch (1901 a), found in his pamphlet entitled "Memoranda on the Maya Calendars used in The Books of Chilan Balam."

2. That of Prof. Eduard Seler (1902–1908): I, pp. 588–599). See also *Bulletin 28*, p. 330.

3. That of Mr. J. T. Goodman (1905).

4. That of Pio Perez, in Stephen's Incidents of Travel in Yucatan (1843: I, pp. 434–459; II, pp. 465–469) and in Landa, 1864: pp. 366–429.

As before noted, these correlations differ greatly from one another, Professor Seler assigning the most remote dates to the southern cities and Mr. Goodman the most recent. The correlations of Mr. Bowditch and the writer are within 260 years of each other. Before accepting any one of the systems of correlation above mentioned, the student is strongly urged to examine with care The Books of Chilan Balam.

[2] It is probable that at this early-date Yucatan had not been discovered, or at least not colonized.

haps the "Golden Age of the Maya"; at least it was the first great epoch in their history, and so far as sculpture is concerned, the one best comparable to the classic period of Greek art. While sculpture among the Maya never again reached so high a degree of perfection, architecture steadily developed, almost to the last. Judging from the dates inscribed upon their monuments, all the great cities of the south flourished during this period: Palenque and Yaxchilan in what is now southern Mexico; Piedras Negras, Seibal, Tikal, Naranjo, and Quirigua in the present Guatemala; and Copan in the present Honduras. All these cities rose to greatness and sank again into insignificance, if not indeed into oblivion, before the close of this Golden Age.

The causes which led to the decline of civilization in the south are unknown. It has been conjectured that the Maya were driven from their southern homes by stronger peoples pushing in from farther south and from the west, or again, that the Maya civilization, having run its natural course, collapsed through sheer lack of inherent power to advance. Which, if either, of these hypotheses be true, matters little, since in any event one all-important fact remains: Just after the close of Cycle 9 of Maya chronology, toward the end of the sixth century, there is a sudden and final cessation of dates in all the southern cities, apparently indicating that they were abandoned about this time.

Still another condition doubtless hastened the general decline if indeed it did no more. There is strong documentary evidence [1] that about the middle or close of the fifth century the southern part of Yucatan was discovered and colonized. In the century following, the southern cities one by one sank into decay; at least none of their monuments bear later dates, and coincidently Chichen Itza, the first great city of the north, was founded and rose to prominence. In the absence of reliable contemporaneous records it is impossible to establish the absolute accuracy of any theory relating to times so

---

[1] This evidence is presented by The Books of Chilan Balam, "which were copied or compiled in Yucatan by natives during the sixteenth, seventeenth, and eighteenth centuries, from much older manuscripts now lost or destroyed. They are written in the Maya language in Latin characters, and treat, in part at least, of the history of the country before the Spanish Conquest. Each town seems to have had its own book of Chilan Balam, distinguished from others by the addition of the name of the place where it was written, as: The Book of Chilan Balam of Mani, The Book of Chilan Balam of Tizimin, and so on. Although much of the material presented in these manuscripts is apparently contradictory and obscure, their importance as original historical sources can not be overestimated, since they constitute the only native accounts of the early history of the Maya race which have survived the vandalism of the Spanish Conquerors. Of the sixteen Books of Chilan Balam now extant, only three, those of the towns of Mani, Tizimin, and Chumayel, contain historical matter. These have been translated into English, and published by Dr. D. G. Brinton [1882 b] under the title of "The Maya Chronicles." This translation with a few corrections has been freely consulted in the following discussion."—MORLEY, 1910 b: p. 193.

Although The Books of Chilan Balam are in all probability authentic sources for the reconstruction of Maya history, they can hardly be considered contemporaneous since, as above explained, they emanate from post-Conquest times. The most that can be claimed for them in this connection is that the documents from which they were copied were probably aboriginal, and contemporaneous, or approximately so, with the later periods of the history which they record.

remote as those here under consideration; but it seems not improbable that after the discovery of Yucatan and the subsequent opening up of that vast region, the southern cities commenced to decline. As the new country waxed the old waned, so that by the end of the sixth century the rise of the one and the fall of the other had occurred.

The occupation and colonization of Yucatan marked the dawn of a new era for the Maya although their Renaissance did not take place at once. Under pressure of the new environment, at best a parched and waterless land, the Maya civilization doubtless underwent important modification.[1] The period of colonization, with the strenuous labor by which it was marked, was not conducive to progress in the arts. At first the struggle for bare existence must have absorbed in a large measure the energies of all, and not until their foothold was secure could much time have been available for the cultivation of the gentler pursuits. Then, too, at first there seems to have been a feeling of unrest in the new land, a shifting of homes and a testing of localities, all of which retarded the development of architecture, sculpture, and other arts. Bakhalal (see pl. 1), the first settlement in the north, was occupied for only 60 years. Chichen Itza, the next location, although occupied for more than a century, was finally abandoned and the search for a new home resumed. Moving westward from Chichen Itza, Chakanputun was seized and occupied at the beginning of the eighth century. Here the Maya are said to have lived for 260 years, until the destruction of Chakanputun by fire about 960 A. D. again set them wandering. By this time, however, some four centuries had elapsed since the first colonization of the country, and they doubtless felt themselves fully competent to cope with any problems arising from their environment. Once more their energies had begun to find outlet in artistic expression. The Transitional Period was at an end, and The Maya Renaissance, if the term may be used, was fully under way.

The opening of the eleventh century witnessed important and far-reaching political changes in Yucatan. After the destruction of Chakanputun the horizon of Maya activity expanded. Some of the fugitives from Chakanputun reoccupied Chichen Itza while others established themselves at a new site called Mayapan. About this time also the city of Uxmal seems to have been founded. In the year 1000 these three cities—Chichen Itza, Uxmal, and Mayapan—formed a confederacy,[2] in which each was to share equally in the government of the country. Under the peaceful conditions which

---

[1] As will appear later, on the calendric side the old system of counting time and of recording events gave place to a more abbreviated though less accurate chronology. In architecture and art also the change of environment made itself felt, and in other lines as well the new land cast a strong influence over Maya thought and achievement. In his work entitled "A Study of Maya Art, its Subject Matter and Historical Development" (1913), to which students are referred for further information, Dr. H. J. Spinden has treated this subject extensively.

[2] The confederation of these three Maya cities may have served as a model for the three Nahua cities, Tenochtitlan, Tezcuco, and Tlacopan, when they entered into a similar alliance some four centuries later.

followed the formation of this confederacy for the next 200 years the arts blossomed forth anew.

This was the second and last great Maya epoch. It was their Age of Architecture as the first period had been their Age of Sculpture. As a separate art sculpture languished; but as an adjunct, an embellishment to architecture, it lived again. The one had become handmaiden to the other. Façades were treated with a sculptural decoration, which for intricacy and elaboration has rarely been equaled by any people at any time; and yet this result was accomplished without sacrifice of beauty or dignity. During this period probably there arose the many cities which to-day are crumbling in decay throughout the length and breadth of Yucatan, their very names forgotten. When these were in their prime, the country must have been one great beehive of activity, for only a large population could have left remains so extensive.

This era of universal peace was abruptly terminated about 1200 A. D. by an event which shook the body politic to its foundations and disrupted the Triple Alliance under whose beneficent rule the land had grown so prosperous. The ruler of Chichen Itza, Chac Xib Chac, seems to have plotted against his colleague of Mayapan, one Hunnac Ceel, and in the disastrous war which followed, the latter, with the aid of Nahua allies,[1] utterly routed his opponent and drove him from his city. The conquest of Chichen Itza seems to have been followed during the thirteenth century by attempted reprisals on the part of the vanquished Itza, which plunged the country into civil war; and this struggle in turn paved the way for the final eclipse of Maya supremacy in the fifteenth century.

After the dissolution of the Triple Alliance a readjustment of power became necessary. It was only natural that the victors in the late war should assume the chief direction of affairs, and there is strong evidence that Mayapan became the most important city in the land. It is not improbable also that as a result of this war Chichen Itza was turned over to Hunnac Ceel's Nahua allies, perhaps in recognition of their timely assistance, or as their share in the spoils of war. It is certain that sometime during its history Chichen Itza came under a strong Nahua influence. One group of buildings in particular[2] shows in its architecture and bas-reliefs that it was undoubtedly inspired by Nahua rather than by Maya ideals.

According to Spanish historians, the fourteenth century was characterized by increasing arrogance and oppression on the part of the rulers of Mayapan, who found it necessary to surround themselves with Nahua allies in order to keep the rising discontent of their sub-

---

[1] By Nahua is here meant the peoples who inhabited the valley of Mexico and adjacent territory at this time.

[2] The Ball Court, a characteristically Nahua development.

jects in check.[1] This unrest finally reached its culmination about the middle of the fifteenth century, when the Maya nobility, unable longer to endure such tyranny, banded themselves together under the leadership of the lord of Uxmal, sacked Mayapan, and slew its ruler.

All authorities, native as well as Spanish, agree that the destruction of Mayapan marked the end of strongly centralized government in Yucatan. Indeed there can be but little doubt that this event also sounded the death knell of Maya civilization. As one of the native chronicles tersely puts it, "The chiefs of the country lost their power." With the destruction of Mayapan the country split into a number of warring factions, each bent on the downfall of the others. Ancient jealousies and feuds, no longer held in leash by the restraining hand of Mayapan, doubtless revived, and soon the land was rent with strife. Presently to the horrors of civil war were added those of famine and pestilence, each of which visited the peninsula in turn, carrying off great numbers of people.

These several calamities, however, were but harbingers of worse soon to come. In 1517 Francisco de Cordoba landed the first Spanish expedition[2] on the shores of Yucatan. The natives were so hostile, however, that he returned to Cuba, having accomplished little more than the discovery of the country. In the following year Juan de Grijalva descended on the peninsula, but he, too, met with so determined a resistance that he sailed away, having gained little more than hard knocks for his pains. In the following year (1519) Hernando Cortez landed on the northeast coast but reembarked in a few days for Mexico, again leaving the courageous natives to themselves. Seven years later, however, in 1526, Francisco Montejo, having been granted the title of Adelantado of Yucatan, set about the conquest of the country in earnest. Having obtained the necessary "sinews of war" through his marriage to a wealthy widow of Seville, he sailed with 3 ships and 500 men for Yucatan. He first landed on the island of Cozumel, off the northeast coast, but soon proceeded to the mainland and took formal possession of the country in the name of the King of Spain. This empty ceremony soon proved to be

---

[1] One authority (Landa, 1864: p. 48) says in this connection: "The governor, Cocom—the ruler of Mayapan—began to covet riches; and for this purpose he treated with the people of the garrison, which the kings of Mexico had in Tabasco and Xicalango, that he should deliver his city [i. e. Mayapan] to them; and thus he brought the Mexican people to Mayapan and he oppressed the poor and made many slaves, and the lords would have killed him if they had not been afraid of the Mexicans."

[2] The first appearance of the Spaniards in Yucatan was six years earlier (in 1511), when the caravel of Valdivia, returning from the Isthmus of Darien to Hispaniola, foundered near Jamaica. About 10 survivors in an open boat were driven upon the coast of Yucatan near the Island of Cozumel. Here they were made prisoners by the Maya and five, including Valdivia himself, were sacrificed. The remainder escaped only to die of starvation and hardship, with the exception of two, Geronimo de Aguilar and Gonzalo Guerrero. Both of these men had risen to considerable prominence in the country by the time Cortez arrived eight years later. Guerrero had married a chief's daughter and had himself become a chief. Later Aguilar became an interpreter for Cortez. This handful of Spaniards can hardly be called an expedition, however.

but the prelude to a sanguinary struggle, which broke out almost immediately and continued with extraordinary ferocity for many years, the Maya fighting desperately in defense of their homes. Indeed, it was not until 14 years later, on June 11, 1541 (old style), that, the Spaniards having defeated a coalition of Maya chieftains near the city of Ichcanzihoo, the conquest was finally brought to a close and the pacification of the country accomplished. With this event ends the independent history of the Maya.

MANNERS AND CUSTOMS

According to Bishop Landa,[1] who wrote his remarkable history of Yucatan in 1565, the Maya of that day were a tall race, active and strong. In childhood the forehead was artificially flattened and the ears and nose were pierced for the insertion of earrings and nose-orna-ments, of which the people were very fond. Squint-eye was consid-ered a mark of beauty, and mothers strove to disfigure their children in this way by suspending pellets of wax between their eyes in order to make them squint, thus securing the desired effect. The faces of the younger boys were scalded by the application of hot cloths, to prevent the growth of the beard, which was not popular. Both men and women wore their hair long. The former had a large spot burned on the back of the head, where the hair always remained short. With the exception of a small queue, which hung down behind, the hair was gathered around the head in a braid. The women wore a more beautiful coiffure divided into two braids. The faces of both sexes were much disfigured as a result of their religious beliefs, which led to the practice of scarification. Tattooing also was common to both sexes, and there were persons in almost every community who were especially proficient in this art. Both men and women painted themselves red, the former decorating their entire bodies, and the latter all except their faces, which modesty decreed should be left unpainted. The women also anointed themselves very freely with fragrant gums and perfumes. They filed their teeth to sharp points, a practice which was thought to enhance their beauty.

The clothing of the men was simple. They wore a breechclout wrapped several times around the loins and tied in such a way that one end fell in front between the legs and the other in the correspond-

---

[1] Diego de Landa, second bishop of Merida, whose remarkable book entitled "Relacion de las Cosas de Yucatan" is the chief authority for the facts presented in the following discussion of the manners and customs of the Maya, was born in Cifuentes de l'Alcarria, Spain, in 1524. At the age of 17 he joined the Franciscan order. He came to Yucatan during the decade following the close of the Conquest, in 1549, where he was one of the most zealous of the early missionaries. In 1573 he was appointed bishop of Merida, which position he held until his death in 1579. His priceless *Relacion*, written about 1565, was not printed until three centuries later, when it was discovered by the indefatigable Abbé Brasseur de Bourbourg in the library of the Royal Academy of History at Madrid, and published by him in 1864. The *Relacion* is the standard authority for the customs prevalent in Yucatan at the time of the Conquest, and is an invaluable aid to the student of Maya archeology. What little we know of the Maya calendar has been derived directly from the pages of this book, or by developing the material therein presented.

ing position behind. These breechclouts were carefully embroidered by the women and decorated with featherwork. A large square cape hung from the shoulders, and sandals of hemp or leather completed the costume. For persons of high rank the apparel was much more elaborate, the humble breechclout and cape of the laboring man giving place to panaches of gorgeously colored feathers hanging from wooden helmets, rich mantles of tiger skins, and finely wrought ornaments of gold and jade.

The women sometimes wore a simple petticoat, and a cloth covering the breasts and passing under the arms. More often their costume consisted of a single loose sacklike garment called the *hipil*, which reached to the feet and had slits for the arms. This garment, with the addition of a cloth or scarf wrapped around the shoulders, constituted the women's clothing a thousand years ago, just as it does to-day.

In ancient times the women were very chaste and modest. When they passed men on the road they stepped to one side, turning their backs and hiding their faces. The age of marriage was about 20, although children were frequently affianced when very young. When boys arrived at a marriageable age their fathers consulted the professional matchmakers of the community, to whom arrangements for marriage were ordinarily intrusted, it being considered vulgar for parents or their sons to take an active part in arranging these affairs. Having sought out the girl's parents, the matchmaker arranged with them the matter of the dowry, which the young man's father paid, his wife at the same time giving the necessary clothing for her son and prospective daughter-in-law. On the day of the wedding the relatives and guests assembled at the house of the young man's parents, where a great feast had been prepared. Having satisfied himself that the young couple had sufficiently considered the grave step they were about to take, the priest gave the bride to her husband. The ceremony closed with a feast in which all participated. Immediately after the wedding the young husband went to the home of his wife's parents, where he was obliged to work five or six years for his board. If he refused to comply with this custom he was driven from the house, and the marriage presumably was annulled. This step seems rarely to have been necessary, however, and the mother-in-law on her part saw to it that her daughter fed the young husband regularly, a practice which betokened their recognition of the marriage rite.

Widowers and widows married without ceremony, it being considered sufficient for a widower to call on his prospective wife and eat in her house. Marriage between people of the same name was considered an evil practice, possibly in deference to some former exogamic law. It was thought improper to marry a mother-in-law or an aunt by marriage, or a sister-in-law; otherwise a man could marry whom he would, even his first cousin.

The Maya were of a very jealous nature and divorces were frequent. These were effected merely by the desertion of the husband or wife, as the case might be. The parents tried to bring the couple together and effect a reconciliation, but if their efforts proved unsuccessful both parties were at liberty to remarry. If there were young children the mother kept them; if the children were of age the sons followed the father, the daughters remaining with their mother. Although divorce was of common occurrence, it was condemned by the more respectable members of the community. It is interesting to note that polygamy was unknown among the Maya.

Agriculture was the chief pursuit, corn and other grains being extensively cultivated, and stored against time of need in well-appointed granaries. Labor was largely communal; all hands joined to do one another's work. Bands of twenty or more each, passing from field to field throughout the community, quickly finished sowing or harvesting. This communal idea was carried to the chase, fifty or more men frequently going out together to hunt. At the conclusion of these expeditions the meat was roasted and then carried back to town. First, the lord of the district was given his share, after which the remainder was distributed among the hunters and their friends. Communal fishing parties are also mentioned.

Another occupation in high favor was that of trade or commerce. Salt, cloth, and slaves were the chief articles of barter; these were carried as far as Tabasco. Cocoa, stone counters, and highly prized red shells of a peculiar kind were the media of exchange. These were accepted in return for all the products of the country, even including the finely worked stones, jades possibly, with which the chiefs adorned themselves at their fetes. Credit was asked and given, all debts were honestly paid, and no usury was exacted.

The sense of justice among the Maya was highly developed. If a man committed an offense against one of another village, the former's lord caused satisfaction to be rendered, otherwise the communities would come to blows. Troubles between men of the same village were taken to a judge, who having heard both sides, fixed appropriate damages. If the malefactor could not pay these, the obligation extended to his wife and relatives. Crimes which could be satisfied by the payment of an indemnity were accidental killings, quarrels between man and wife, and the accidental destruction of property by fire. Malicious mischief could be atoned for only by blows and the shedding of blood. The punishment of murder was left in the hands of the deceased's relatives, who were at liberty to exact an indemnity or the murderer's life as they pleased. The thief was obliged to make good whatever he had stolen, no matter how little; in event of failure to do so he was reduced to slavery. Adultery was punishable by death. The adulterer was led into the courtyard of the chief's house, where all had assembled, and after being tied to a stake, was turned over to the mercies of the outraged husband, who either pardoned him or crushed his head with a heavy rock. As for the guilty woman, her infamy was deemed sufficient punishment for her, though usually her husband abandoned her.

The Maya were a very hospitable people, always offering food and drink to the stranger within their gates, and sharing with him to the last crumb. They were much given to conviviality, particularly the lords, who frequently entertained one another with elaborate feasts, accompanied by music and dancing, expending at times on a single occasion the proceeds of many days' accumulation. They usually sat down to eat by twos or fours. The meal, which consisted of vegetable stews, roast meats, corn cakes, and cocoa (to mention only a few of the viands) was spread upon mats laid on the ground. After the repast was finished beautiful young girls acting as cupbearers passed among the guests, plying them industriously with wine until all were drunk. Before departing each guest was presented with a handsome vase and pedestal, with a cloth cover therefor. At these orgies drinking was frequently carried to such excess that the wives of the guests were obliged to come for their besotted husbands and drag them home. Each of the guests at such a banquet was required to give one in return, and not even death could stay the payment of a debt of this kind, since the obligation descended to the recipient's heirs. The poor entertained less lavishly, as became their means. Guests at the humbler feasts, moreover, were not obliged to return them in kind.

The chief amusements of the Maya were comedies and dances, in both of which they exhibited much skill and ingenuity. There was a variety of musical instruments—drums of several kinds, rattles, reed flutes, wooden horns, and bone whistles. Their music is described as having been sad, owing perhaps to the melancholy sound of the instruments which produced it.

The frequent wars which darken the final pages of Maya history doubtless developed the military organization to a high degree of efficiency. At the head of the army stood two generals, one hereditary and the other elective (*nacon*), the latter serving for three years. In each village throughout the country certain men (*holcanes*) were chosen to act as soldiers; these constituted a kind of a standing army, thoroughly trained in the art of war. They were supported by the community, and in times of peace caused much disturbance, continuing the tumult of war after war had ceased. In times of great stress when it became necessary to call on all able-bodied men for military service, the holcanes mustered all those available in their respective districts and trained them in the use of arms. There were but few weapons: Wooden bows strung with hemp cords, and arrows tipped with obsidian or bone; long lances with sharp flint points; and metal (probably copper) axes, provided with wooden handles. The defensive armor consisted of round wicker shields strengthened with deer hide, and quilted cotton coats, which were said to have extraordinary resisting power against the native weapons. The highest chiefs wore wooden helmets decorated with brilliant plumes, and cloaks of "tiger" (jaguar) skin, thrown over their shoulders.

With a great banner at their head the troops silently stole out of the city, and moved against the enemy, hoping thus to surprise them. When the enemies' position had been ascertained, they fell on them suddenly with extraordinary ferocity, uttering loud cries. Barricades of trees, brush, and stone were used in defense, behind which archers stood, who endeavored to repulse the attack. After a battle the victors mutilated the bodies of the slain, cutting out the jawbones and cleaning them of flesh. These were worn as bracelets after the flesh had been removed. At the conclusion of their wars the spoils were offered in sacrifice. If by chance some leader or chief had been captured, he was sacrificed as an offering particularly acceptable to the gods. Other prisoners became the slaves of those who had captured them.

The Maya entertained an excessive and constant fear of death, many of their religious practices having no other end in view than that of warding off the dread visitor. After death there followed a prolonged period of sadness in the bereaved family, the days being given over to fasting, and the more restrained indulgence in grief, and the nights to dolorous cries and lamentations, most pitiful to hear. Among the common people the dead were wrapped in shrouds; their mouths were filled with ground corn and bits of worked stone so that they should not lack for food and money in the life to come. The Maya buried their dead inside the houses [1] or behind them, putting into the tomb idols, and objects indicating the profession of the deceased—if a priest, some of his sacred books; if a seer, some of his divinatory paraphernalia. A house was commonly abandoned after a death therein, unless enough remained in the household to dispel the fear which always followed such an occurrence.

In the higher walks of life the mortuary customs were more elaborate. The bodies of chiefs and others of high estate were burned and their ashes placed in large pottery vessels. These were buried in the ground and temples erected over them.[2] When the deceased

---

[1] The excavations of Mr. E. H. Thompson at Labna, Yucatan, and of Dr. Merwin at Holmul, Guatemala, have confirmed Bishop Landa's statement concerning the disposal of the dead. At Labna bodies were found buried beneath the floors of the buildings, and at Holmul not only beneath the floors but also lying on them.

[2] Examples of this type of burial have been found at Chichen Itza and Mayapan in Yucatan. At the former site Mr. E. H. Thompson found in the center of a large pyramid a stone-lined shaft running from the summit into the ground. This was filled with burials and funeral objects—pearls, coral, and jade, which from their precious nature indicated the remains of important personages. At Mayapan, burials were found in a shaft of similar construction and location in one of the pyramids.

was of very high rank the pottery sarcophagus took the form of a human statue. A variant of the above procedure was to burn only a part of the body, inclosing the ashes in the hollow head of a wooden statue, and sealing them in with a piece of skin taken from the back of the dead man's skull. The rest of the body was buried. Such statues were jealously preserved among the figures of the gods, being held in deep veneration.

The lords of Mayapan had still another mortuary practice. After death the head was severed from the body and cooked in order to remove all flesh. It was then sawed in half from side to side, care being taken to preserve the jaw, nose, eyes, and forehead in one piece. Upon this as a form the features of the dead man were filled in with a kind of a gum. Such was their extraordinary skill in this peculiar work that the finished mask is said to have appeared exactly like the countenance in life. The carefully prepared faces, together with the statues containing the ashes of the dead, were deposited with their idols. Every feast day meats were set before them so they should lack for nothing in that other world whither they had gone.

Very little is known about the governmental organization of the southern Maya, and it seems best, therefore, first to examine conditions in the north, concerning which the early authorities, native as well as Spanish, have much to say. The northern Maya lived in settlements, some of very considerable extent, under the rule of hereditary chiefs called *halach uinicil*, or "real men," who were, in fact as well as name, the actual rulers of the country. The settlements tributary to each *halach uinic* were doubtless connected by tribal ties, based on real or fancied blood relationship.

During the period of the Triple Alliance (1000–1200 A. D.) there were probably only three of these embryonic nations: Chichen Itza, Uxmal, and Mayapan, among which the country seems to have been apportioned. After the conquest of Chichen Itza, however, the halach uinic of Mayapan probably attempted to establish a more autocratic form of government, arrogating to himself still greater power. The Spanish authorities relate that the chiefs of the country assembled at Mayapan, acknowledged the ruler of that city as their overlord, and finally agreed to live there, each binding himself at the same time to conduct the affairs of his own domain through a deputy.

This attempt to unite the country under one head and bring about a further centralization of power ultimately failed, as has been seen, through the tyranny of the Cocom family, in which the office of halach uinic of Mayapan was vested. This tyranny led to the overthrow of the Cocoms and the destruction of centralized government, so that when the Spaniards arrived they found a number of petty chieftains, acknowledging no overlord, and the country in chaos.

The powers of the halach uinic are not clearly understood. He seems to have stood at the apex of the governmental organization, and doubtless his will prevailed just so far as he had sufficient strength to enforce it. The *batabs*, or underchiefs, were obliged to visit him and render him their homage. They also accompanied him in his tours about the country, which always gave rise to feasting back and forth. Finally they advised him on all important matters. The office would seem to have been no stronger in any case than its incumbent, since we hear of the halach uinic of Mayapan being obliged to surround himself with foreign troops in order to hold his people in check.

Each batab governed the territory of which he was the hereditary ruler, instructing his heir in the duties of the position, and counseling that he treat the poor with benevolence and maintain peace and encourage industry, so that all might live in plenty. He settled all lawsuits, and through trusted lieutenants ordered and adjusted the various affairs of his domain. When he went abroad from his city or even from his house a great crowd accompanied him. He often visited his underchiefs, holding court in their houses, and meeting at night in council to discuss matters touching the common good. The batabs frequently entertained one another with dancing, hunting, and feasting. The people as a community tilled the batab's fields, reaped his corn, and supplied his wants in general. The underchiefs were similarly provided for, each according to his rank and needs.

The *ahkulel*, the next highest official in each district, acted as the batab's deputy or representative; he carried a short thick baton in token of his office. He had charge of the localities subject to his master's rule as well as of the officers immediately over them. He kept these assistants informed as to what was needed in the batab's house, as birds, game, fish, corn, honey, salt, and cloth, which they supplied when called on. The ahkulel was, in short, a chief steward, and his house was the batab's business office.

Another important position was that of the *nacon*, or war-chief. In times of war this functionary was second only to the hereditary chief, or batab, and was greatly venerated by all. His office was elective, the term being three years, during which he was obliged to refrain from intercourse with women, and to hold himself aloof from all.

An important civil position was that held by the *ahholpop*, in whose keeping was the *tunkul*, or wooden drum, used in summoning people to the dances and public meetings, or as a tocsin in case of war. He had charge also of the "town hall" in which all public business was transacted.

The question of succession is important. Bishop Landa distinctly states in one passage "That when the lord died, although his oldest son succeeded him, the others were always loved and served and even regarded as lords." This would seem to indicate definitely that descent was by primogeniture. However, another passage suggests that the oldest son did not always succeed his father: "The lords were the governors and confirmed their sons in their offices if they [the sons] were acceptable." This suggests the possibility, at least, that primogeniture could sometimes be set aside, particularly when the first-born lacked the necessary qualifications for leadership. In a somewhat drawn-out statement the same authority discusses the the question of "princely succession" among the Maya:

If the children were too young to be intrusted with the management of their own affairs, these were turned over to a guardian, the nearest relation. He gave the children to their mothers to bring up, because according to their usage the mother has no power of her own. When the guardian was the brother of the deceased [the children's paternal uncle] they take the children from their mother. These guardians give what was intrusted to them to the heirs when they come of age, and not to do so was considered a great dishonesty and was the cause of much contention. . . . If when the lord died there were no sons [ready, i. e., of age] to rule and he had brothers, the oldest or most capable of his brothers ruled, and they [the guardians] showed the heir the customs and fetes of his people until he should be a man, and these brothers, although the heir were [ready] to rule, commanded all their lives, and, if there were no brothers the priests and principal people selected a man suitable for the position.[1]

The foregoing would seem to imply that the rulers were succeeded by their eldest sons if the latter were of age and otherwise generally acceptable; and that, if they were minors when their fathers died, their paternal uncles, if any, or otherwise some capable man selected by the priests, took the reins of government, instructing the heir in the duties of the position which he was to occupy some day; and finally that the regent did not lay down his authority until death, even though the heir had previously attained his majority. This custom is so unusual that its existence may well be doubted, and it is not at all improbable that Bishop Landa's statement to the contrary may have arisen from some misapprehension. Primogeniture was not confined to the executive succession alone, since Bishop Landa states further that the high priest *Ahau can mai* was succeeded in his dignity by his sons, or those next of kin.

Nepotism doubtless prevailed extensively, all the higher offices of the priesthood as well as the executive offices being hereditary, and in all probability filled with members of the halach uinic's family..

The priests instructed the younger sons of the ruling family as well as their own, in the priestly duties and learning; in the computation of years, months, and days; in unlucky times; in fetes and ceremonies; in the administration of the sacraments; in the practices of prophecy and divination; in treating the sick; in their ancient history; and finally in the art of reading and writing their hieroglyphics, which was taught only to those of high degree. Genealogies were carefully preserved, the term meaning "of noble birth" being *ah kaba*, "he who has a name." The elaborate attention given to the subject of lineage, and the exclusive right of the *ah kaba* to the benefits of education, show that in the northern part of the Maya territory at least govern-

---

[1] Landa, 1864: p. 137.

DIAGRAM SHOWING PERIODS OF OCCUPANCY OF PRINCIPAL SOUTHERN CITIES

ment rested on the principle of hereditary succession. The accounts of native as well as of Spanish writers leave the impression that a system not unlike a modified form of feudalism prevailed.

In attempting to gain an approximate understanding of the form of government which existed in the southern part of the Maya territory it is necessary in the absence of all documentary information to interpret the southern chronology, architecture, and sculpture—practically all that remains of the older culture—in the light of the known conditions in the north. The chronology of the several southern cities (see pl. 2) indicates that many of them were contemporaneous, and that a few, namely, Tikal, Naranjo, Palenque, and Copan were occupied approximately 200 years, a much longer period than any of the others.[1] These four would seem to have been centers of population for a long time, and at least three of them, Tikal, Palenque, and Copan, attained considerable size. Indeed they may well have been, like Chichen Itza, Uxmal, and Mayapan, at a later epoch in the north, the seats of halach uincil, or overlords, to whom all the surrounding chiefs were tributary. Geographically considered, the country was well apportioned among these cities: Tikal dominating the north, Palenque, the west, and Copan, the south.

The architecture, sculpture, and hieroglyphic writing of all the southern centers is practically identical, even to the borrowing of unessential details, a condition which indicates a homogeneity only to be accounted for by long-continued and frequent intercourse. This characteristic of the culture, together with the location and contemporaneity of its largest centers, suggests that originally the southern territory was divided into several extensive political divisions, all in close intercourse with one another, and possibly united in a league similar to that which later united the principal cities of the north. The unmistakable priestly or religious character of the sculptures in the southern area clearly indicates the peaceful temper of the people, and the conspicuous absence of warlike subjects points strongly to the fact that the government was a theocracy, the highest official in the priesthood being at the same time, by virtue of his sacerdotal rank, the highest civil authority. Whether the principle of hereditary succession determined or even influenced the selection of rulers in the south is impossible to say. However, since the highest offices, both executive and priestly, in the north were thus filled, it may be assumed that similar conditions prevailed in the south, particularly as the northern civilization was but an outgrowth of the

[1] As the result of a trip to the Maya field in the winter of 1914, the writer made important discoveries in the chronology of Tikal, Naranjo, Piedras Negras, Altar de Sacrificios, Quirigua, and Seibal. The occupancy of Tikal and Seibal was found to have extended to 10.2.0.0.0; of Piedras Negras to 9.18.5.0.0; of Naranjo to 9.19.10.0.0; and of Altar de Sacrificios to 9.14.0.0.0. (This new material is not embodied in pl. 2.)

southern. There is some ground for believing that the highest office in the south may have been elective, the term being a *hotun*[1] (1,800 days), and the choice restricted to the members of a certain family. The existence of this restriction, which closely parallels the Aztec procedure in selecting rulers,[2] rests on very slender evidence, however, so far as the Maya are concerned and is mentioned here simply by way of suggestion.

The religion of the ancient Maya was polytheistic, its pantheon containing about a dozen major deities and a host of lesser ones. At its head stood Itzamna, the father of the gods and creator of mankind, the Mayan Zeus or Jupiter. He was the personification of the East,

the rising sun, and, by association, of light, life, and knowledge. He was the founder of the Maya civilization, the first priest of the Maya religion, the inventor of writing and books, and the great healer. Whether Itzamna has been identified with any of the deities in the ancient Maya picture-writings is uncertain, though there are strong reasons for believing that this deity is the god represented in figure 1. His characteristics here are: The aged face, Roman nose, and sunken toothless mouth.

Fig. 1. Itzamna, chief deity of the Maya Pantheon (note his name glyphs, below).

Scarcely less important was the great god Kukulcan, or Feathered Serpent, the personification of the West. It is related of him that he came into Yucatan from the west and settled at Chichen Itza, where he ruled for many years and built a great temple. During his sojourn he is said to have founded the city of Mayapan, which later became so important. Finally, having brought the country out of war and dissension to peace and prosperity, he left by the same way he had entered, tarrying only at Chakanputun on the west coast to build a splendid temple as an everlasting memorial of his residence among the people. After his departure he was worshipped as a god because of what he had done for the public good. Kukulcan was the Maya counterpart of the Aztec Quetzalcoatl, the Mexican god of light, learning, and culture. In the Maya pantheon he was regarded as having been the great organizer, the founder of cities, the framer of laws, and the teacher of their new calendar. Indeed, his attributes

[1] As will be explained in chapter V, the writer has suggested the name *hotun* for the 5 tun, or 1,800 day, period.

[2] Succession in the Aztec royal house was not determined by primogeniture, though the supreme office, the *tlahtouani*, as well as the other high offices of state, was hereditary in one family. On the death of the tlahtouani the electors (four in number) seem to have selected his successor from among his brothers, or, these failing, from among his nephews. Except as limiting the succession to one family, primogeniture does not seem to have obtained; for example, Moctezoma (Montezuma) was chosen tlahtouani over the heads of several of his older brothers because he was thought to have the best qualifications for that exalted office. The situation may be summarized by the statement that while the supreme ruler among the Aztec had to be of the "blood royal," his selection was determined by personal merit rather than by primogeniture.

and life history are so human that it is not improbable he may have been an actual historical character, some great lawgiver and organizer, the memory of whose benefactions lingered long after death, and whose personality was eventually deified. The episodes of his life suggest he may have been the recolonizer of Chichen Itza after the destruction of Chakanputun. Kukulcan has been identified by some as the "old god" of the picture-writings (fig. 2), whose characteristics are: Two deformed teeth, one protruding from the front and one from the back part of his mouth, and the long tapering nose. He is to be distinguished further by his peculiar headdress.

FIG. 2. Kukulcan, God of Learning (note his name glyph, below).

The most feared and hated of all the Maya deities was Ahpuch, the Lord of Death, God "Barebones" as an early manuscript calls him, from whom evil and especially death were thought to come. He is frequently represented in the picture-writings (fig. 3), usually in connection with the idea of death. He is associated with human sacrifice, suicide by hanging, death in childbirth, and the beheaded captive. His characteristics are typical and unmistakable. His head is the fleshless skull, showing the truncated nose, the grinning teeth, and fleshless lower jaw, sometimes even the cranial sutures are portrayed. In some places the ribs and vertebræ are shown, in others the body is spotted black as if to suggest the discoloration of death. A very constant symbol is the stiff feather collar with small bells attached. These bells also appear as ornaments on the head, arms, and ankles. The to us familiar crossbones were also another Maya death symbol. Even the hieroglyph of this god (fig. 3) suggests the dread idea for which he stood. Note the eye closed in death.

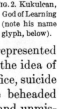

FIG. 3. Ahpuch, God of Death (note his name glyphs, below).

Closely associated with the God of Death is the God of War, who probably stood as well for the larger idea of death by violence. He is characterized (fig. 4) by a black line painted on his face, sometimes curving, sometimes straight, supposed to be symbolical of war paint, or, according to others, of his gaping wounds. He appears in the picture-writings as the Death God's companion. He presides with him over the body of a sacrificial victim, and again follows him applying torch and knife to the habitations of man. His hieroglyph shows as its characteristic the line of black paint (fig. 4).

FIG. 4. The God of War (note his name glyph, below).

Another unpropitious deity was Ek Ahau, the Black Captain, also a war god, being represented (fig. 5) in the picture-writings as armed

with a spear or an ax. It was said of him that he was a very great
and very cruel warrior, who commanded a band of seven black-
amoors like himself. He is characterized by his black color, his
drooping lower lip, and the two curved lines at the right of his eye.
His hieroglyph is a black eye (fig. 5).

Contrasted with these gods of death, violence, and destruction was the Maize God, Yum Kaax, Lord of the
Harvest Fields (fig. 6). Here we have one of the most
important figures in the whole Maya pantheon, the god
of husbandry and the fruits of the earth, of fertility and
prosperity, of growth and plenty. The Maize God was
as well disposed toward mankind as Ahpuch and his
companions were unpropitious. In many of the picture-writings Yum Kaax is represented as engaged in
agricultural pursuits. He is portrayed as having for
his head-dress a sprouting ear of corn surrounded by
leaves, symbolic of growth, for which he stands. Even
the hieroglyph of this deity (fig. 6) embodies the same
idea, the god's head merging into the conventionalized ear of corn
surrounded by leaves.

FIG. 5. Ek Ahau,
the Black Cap-
tain, war deity
(note his name
glyph, below).

Another important deity about whom little or nothing is known
was Xaman Ek, the North Star. He is spoken of as the "guide of
the merchants," and in keeping with that character is associated in
the picture-writings with symbols of peace and plenty.
His one characteristic seems to be his curious head,
which also serves as his name hieroglyph (fig. 7).

Other Maya deities were: Ixchel, the Rainbow,
consort of Itzamna and goddess of childbirth and
medicine; Ixtab, patroness of hunting and hanging;
Ixtubtun, protectress of jade cutters; Ixchebelyax,
the inventress of painting and color designing as applied to fabrics.

Although the deities above described represent only
a small fraction of the Maya pantheon, they include,
beyond all doubt, its most important members, the
truly great, who held the powers of life and death,
peace and war, plenty and famine—who were, in short, the arbiters
of human destiny.

FIG. 6. Yum Kaax,
Lord of the Har-
vest (note his name
glyph, below).

The Maya conceived the earth to be a cube, which supported the
celestial vase resting on its four legs, the four cardinal points. Out
of this grew the Tree of Life, the flowers of which were the immortal
principle of man, the soul. Above hung heavy clouds, the fructi-
fying waters upon which all growth and life depend. The religion
was dualistic in spirit, a constant struggle between the powers of

light and of darkness.   On one side were arrayed the gods of plenty,
peace, and life; on the other those of want, war, and destruction;
and between these two there waged an unending strife for the control
of man.   This struggle between the powers of light and darkness is
graphically portrayed in the picture-writings.   Where
the God of Life plants the tree, Death breaks it in
twain (fig. 8); where the former offers food, the latter
raises an empty vase symbolizing famine; where one
builds, the other destroys.   The contrast is complete,
the conflict eternal.

The Maya believed in the immortality of the soul
and in a spiritual life hereafter.   As a man lived in this
world so he was rewarded in the next.   The good and
righteous went to a heaven of material delights, a
place where rich foods never failed and pain and sor-
row were unknown.   The wicked were consigned to a
hell called Mitnal, over which ruled the archdemon

Fig. 7. Xaman Ek,
the North Star God
(note his name
glyph, below).

Hunhau and his minions; and here in hunger, cold, and exhaustion they
suffered everlasting torment.   The materialism of the Maya heaven
and hell need not surprise, nor lower our estimate of their civilization.
Similar realistic conceptions of the hereafter have been entertained
by peoples much higher in the cultural scale than the Maya.

Worship doubtless was the most important feature of the Maya
scheme of existence, and an endless succession of rites and ceremonies

was considered necessary to retain the
sympathies of the good gods and to pro-
pitiate the malevolent ones.   Bishop
Landa says that the aim and object of
all Maya ceremonies were to secure three
things only: Health, life, and sustenance;
modest enough requests to ask of any
faith.   The first step in all Maya religious rites was the expulsion of the evil

Fig. 8. Conflict between the Gods of Life
and Death (Kukulcan and Ahpuch).

spirits from the midst of the worshipers.   This was accomplished
sometimes by prayers and benedictions, set formulæ of proven
efficacy, and sometimes by special sacrifices and offerings.

It would take us too far afield to describe here even the more
important ceremonies of the Maya religion.   Their number was liter-
ally legion, and they answered almost every contingency within the
range of human experience.   First of all were the ceremonies dedicated to special gods, as Itzamna, Kukulcan, and Ixchel.   Probably
every deity in the pantheon, even the most insignificant, had at least
one rite a year addressed to it alone, and the aggregate must have
made a very considerable number.   In addition there were the annual
feasts of the ritualistic year brought around by the ever-recurring

seasons. Here may be mentioned the numerous ceremonies incident to the beginning of the new year and the end of the old, as the renewal of household utensils and the general renovation of all articles, which took place at this time; the feasts of the various trades and occupations—the hunters, fishers, and apiarists, the farmers, carpenters, and potters, the stonecutters, wood carvers, and metal workers—each guild having its own patron deity, whose services formed another large group of ceremonials. A third class comprised the rites of a more personal nature, those connected with baptism, confession, marriage, setting out on journeys, and the like. Finally, there was a fourth group of ceremonies, held much less frequently than the others, but of far greater importance. Herein fall the ceremonies held on extraordinary occasions, as famine, drought, pestilence, victory, or defeat, which were probably solemnized by rites of human sacrifice.

The direction of so elaborate a system of worship necessitated a numerous and highly organized priesthood. At the head of the hierarchy stood the hereditary high priest, or *ahaucan mai*, a functionary of very considerable power. Although he had no actual share in the government, his influence was none the less far-reaching, since the highest lords sought his advice, and deferred to his judgment in the administration of their affairs. They questioned him concerning the will of the gods on various points, and he in response framed the divine replies, a duty which gave him tremendous power and authority. In the ahuacan mai was vested also the exclusive right to fill vacancies in the priesthood. He examined candidates on their knowledge of the priestly services and ceremonies, and after their appointment directed them in the discharge of their duties. He rarely officiated at sacrifices except on occasions of the greatest importance, as at the principal feasts or in times of general need. His office was maintained by presents from the lords and enforced contributions from the priesthood throughout the country.

The priesthood included within its ranks women as well as men. The duties were highly specialized and there were many different ranks and grades in the hierarchy. The *chilan* was one of the most important. This priest was carried upon the shoulders of the people when he appeared in public. He taught their sciences, appointed the holy days, healed the sick, offered sacrifices, and most important of all, gave the responses of the gods to petitioners. The *ahuai chac* was a priest who brought the rains on which the prosperity of the country was wholly dependent. The *ah macik* conjured the winds; the *ahpul* caused sickness and induced sleep; the *ahuai xibalba* communed with the dead. At the bottom of the ladder seems to have stood the *nacon*, whose duty it was to open the breasts of the sacrificed victims. An important elective office in each community was that held by the *chac*, or priest's assistant. These officials, of which there were four, were elected from the *nucteelob,* or village wise men. They served for a term of one year and could never be reelected. They aided the priest in the various ceremonies of the year, officiating in minor capacities. Their duties seem to have been not unlike those of the sacristan in the Roman Catholic Church of to-day.

In closing this introduction nothing could be more appropriate than to call attention once more to the supreme importance of religion in the life of the ancient Maya. Religion was indeed the very fountain-head of their civilization, and on its rites and observances they lavished a devotion rarely equaled in the annals of man. To its great uplifting force was due the conception and evolution of the hieroglyphic writing and calendar, alike the invention and the exclusive property of the priesthood. To its need for sanctuary may be attributed the origin of Maya architecture; to its desire for expression, the rise of Maya sculpture. All activities reflected its powerful influence and all were more or less dominated by its needs and teachings. In short, religion was the foundation upon which the structure of the Maya civilization was reared.

The inscriptions herein described are found throughout the region formerly occupied by the Maya people (pl. 1), though by far the greater number have been discovered at the southern, or older, sites. This is due in part, at least, to the minor rôle played by sculpture as an independent art among the northern Maya, for in the north architecture gradually absorbed in its decoration the sculptural activity of the people which in the south had been applied in the making of the hieroglyphic monuments.

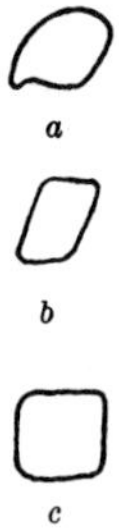

The materials upon which the Maya glyphs are presented are stone, wood, stucco, bone, shell, metal, plaster, pottery, and fiber-paper; the first-mentioned, however, occurs more frequently than all of the others combined. Texts have been found carved on the wooden lintels of Tikal, molded in the stucco reliefs of Palenque, scratched on shells from Copan and Belize, etched on a bone from Wild Cane Key, British Honduras, engraved on metal from Chichen Itza, drawn on the plaster-covered walls of Kabah, Chichen Itza, and Uxmal, and painted in fiber-paper books. All of these, however, with the exception of the first and the last (the inscriptions on stone and the fiber-paper books or codices) just mentioned, occur so rarely that they may be dismissed from present consideration.

FIG. 9. Outlines of the glyphs: *a, b,* In the codices; *c,* in the inscriptions.

The stones bearing inscriptions are found in a variety of shapes, the commonest being the monolithic shafts or slabs known as *stelæ.* Some of the shaft-stelæ attain a height of twenty-six feet (above ground); these are not unlike roughly squared obelisks, with human figures carved on the obverse and the reverse, and glyphs on the other faces. Slab-stelæ, on the other hand, are shorter and most of them bear inscriptions only on the reverse. Frequently associated with these stelæ are smaller monoliths known as "altars," which vary greatly in size, shape, and decoration, some bearing glyphs and others being without them.

The foregoing monuments, however, by no means exhaust the list of stone objects that bear hieroglyphs. As an adjunct to architecture inscriptions occur on wall-slabs at Palenque, on lintels at Yaxchilan and Piedras Negras, on steps and stairways at Copan, and on piers and architraves at Holactun; and these do not include the great number of smaller pieces, as inscribed jades and the like. Most of the glyphs in the inscriptions are square in outline except for rounded corners (fig. 9, *c*). Those in the codices, on the other hand, approximate more nearly in form rhomboids or even ovals (fig. 9, *a, b*). This difference in outline, however, is only superficial in significance and involves no corresponding difference in meaning between other-

22

wise identical glyphs; it is due entirely to the mechanical dissimilarity
of the two materials.   Disregarding this consideration as unessential,
we may say that the glyphs in both the inscriptions and the codices
belong to one and the same system of writing, and if it were possible
to read either, the other could no longer withhold its meaning from us.

In Maya inscriptions the glyphs are arranged in parallel columns,
which are to be read two columns at a time, beginning with the uppermost glyph in the left-hand column, and then from left to right and
top to bottom, ending with the lowest glyph in the second column.
Then the next two columns are read in the same order, and so on.
In reading glyphs in a horizontal band, the order is from left to right
in pairs.   The writer knows of no text in which the above order of
reading is not followed.

A brief examination of any Maya text, from either the inscriptions
or the codices, reveals the presence of certain elements which occur
repeatedly but in varying combinations.   The apparent multiplicity
of these combinations leads at first to the conclusion that a great
number of signs were employed in Maya writing, but closer study will

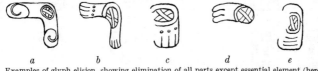

a   b   c   d   e

FIG. 10.   Examples of glyph elision, showing elimination of all parts except essential element (here, the
crossed bands).

show that, as compared with the composite characters or glyphs
proper, the simple elements are few in number.   Says Doctor
Brinton (1894 b: p. 10) in this connection: "If we positively knew the
meaning . . . of a hundred or so of these simple elements, none of
the inscriptions could conceal any longer from us the general tenor
of its contents."   Unfortunately, it must be admitted that but little
advance has been made toward the solution of this problem, perhaps
because later students have distrusted the highly fanciful results
achieved by the earlier writers who "interpreted" these "simple
elements."

Moreover, there is encountered at the very outset in the study of
these elements a condition which renders progress slow and results
uncertain.   In Egyptian texts of any given period the simple phonetic elements or signs are unchanging under all conditions of composition.   Like the letters of our own alphabet, they never vary and
may be recognized as unfailingly.   On the other hand, in Maya texts
each glyph is in itself a finished picture, dependent on no other for
its meaning, and consequently the various elements entering into it
undergo very considerable modifications in order that the resulting
composite character may not only be a balanced and harmonious de-

sign, but also may exactly fill its allotted space. All such modifications probably in no way affect the meaning of the element thus mutilated.

The element shown in figure 10, *a–e* is a case in point. In *a* and *b* we have what may be called the normal or regular forms of this element. In *c*, however, the upper arm has been omitted for the sake of symmetry in a composite glyph, while in *d* the lower arm has been left out for want of space. Finally in *e* both arms have disappeared and the element is reduced to the sign (*), which we may conclude, therefore, is the essential characteristic of this glyph, particularly since there is no regularity in the treatment of the arms in the normal forms. This suggests another point of the utmost importance, namely, the determination of the essential elements of Maya glyphs. The importance of this point lies in the fact that great license was permitted in the treatment of accessory elements so long as the essential element or elements of a glyph could readily be recognized as such. In this way may be explained the use of the so-called

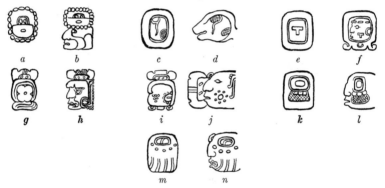

a   *b*   *c*   *d*   *e*   *f*

g   *h*   *i*   *j*   *k*   *l*

m   *n*

Fig. 11.   Normal-form and head-variant glyphs, showing retention of essential element in each.

"head" variants, in which the outline of the glyph was represented as a human or a grotesque head modified in some way by the essential element of the intended form. The first step in the development of head variants is seen in figure 11, *a*, *b*, in which the entire glyph *a* is used as a headdress in glyph *b*, the meaning of the two forms remaining identical. The next step is shown in the same figure, *c* and *d*, in which the outline of the entire glyph *c* has been changed to form the grotesque head *d*, though in both glyphs the essential elements are the same. A further development was to apply the essential element (**) of *e* to the head in *f*, giving rise to a head variant, the meaning of which suffered no corresponding change. The element (†) in figure 11, *g*, has been reduced in size in *h*, though the other two essential elements remain unchanged. A final step appears in *i* and *j*, where in *j* the position of one of the two essential elements of *i* (††) and the form of the other (‡) have been changed. These variants are puzzling enough when the essential characteristics and meaning of a glyph have been determined, but when both are unknown the problem is indeed knotty.   For example, it would seem as a logical deduction from the foregoing examples, that *l* of figure 11 is a "head" variant of *k;* and similarly *n* might be a "head" variant of *m*, but here we are treading on uncertain ground, as the meanings of these forms are unknown.

Nor is this feature of Maya writing (i. e., the presence of "head variants") the only pitfall which awaits the beginner who attempts to classify the glyphs according to their appearance.   In some cases two entirely dissimilar forms express exactly the same idea.   For example, no two glyphs could differ more in appearance than *a* and *b*, figure 12, yet both of these forms have the same meaning.   This is true also of the two glyphs *c* and *d*, and *e* and *f*.   The occurrence of forms so absolutely unlike in appearance, yet identical in meaning, greatly complicates the problem of glyph identification.   Indeed, identity in both meaning and use must be clearly established before we can recognize as variants of the same glyph, forms so dissimilar as the examples above given.   Hence, because their meanings are unknown we are unable to identify *g* and *h*, figure 12, as synonyms,

a   b   c   d   e   f   g   h

FIG. 12.   Normal-form and head-variant glyphs, showing absence of common essential element.

notwithstanding the fact that their use seems to be identical, *h* occurring in two or three texts under exactly the same conditions as does *g* in all the others.

A further source of error in glyph identification is the failure to recognize variations due merely to individual peculiarities of style, which are consequently unessential.   Just as handwriting differs in each individual, so the delineation of glyphs differed among the ancient Maya, though doubtless to a lesser extent.   In extreme cases, however, the differences are so great that identification of variants as forms of one and the same glyph is difficult if indeed not impossible.   Here also are to be included variations due to differences in the materials upon which the glyphs are delineated, as well as those arising from careless drawing and actual mistakes.

The foregoing difficulties, as well as others which await the student who would classify the Maya glyphs according to form and appearance, have led the author to discard this method of classification as unsuited to the purposes of an elementary work.   Though a problem of first importance, the analysis of the simple elements is far too complex for presentation to the beginner, particularly since the greatest diversity of opinion concerning them prevails among those who have studied the subject, scarcely any two agreeing at any one point; and finally because up to the present time success in reading Maya writing has not come through this channel.

The classification followed herein is based on the general meaning of the glyphs, and therefore has the advantage of being at least self-explanatory. It divides the glyphs into two groups: (1) Astronomical, calendary, and numerical signs, that is, glyphs used in counting time; and (2) glyphs accompanying the preceding, which have an explanatory function of some sort, probably describing the nature of the occasions which the first group of glyphs designate.

According to this classification, the great majority of the glyphs whose meanings have been determined fall into the first group, and those whose meanings are still unknown into the second. This is particularly true of the inscriptions, in which the known glyphs practically all belong to the first group. In the codices, on the other hand, some little progress has made been in reading glyphs of the second group. The name-glyphs of the principal gods, the signs for the cardinal points and associated colors, and perhaps a very few others may be mentioned in this connection.[1]

Of the unknown glyphs in both the inscriptions and the codices, a part at least have to do with numerical calculations of some kind, a fact which relegates such glyphs to the first group. The author believes that as the reading of the Maya glyphs progresses, more and more characters will be assigned to the first group and fewer and fewer to the second. In the end, however, there will be left what we may perhaps call a "textual residue," that is, those glyphs which explain the nature of the events that are to be associated with the corresponding chronological parts. It is here, if anywhere, that fragments of Maya history will be found recorded, and precisely here is the richest field for future research, since the successful interpretation of this "textual residue" will alone disclose the true meaning of the Maya writings.

Three principal theories have been advanced for the interpretation of Maya writing:

1. That the glyphs are phonetic, each representing some sound, and entirely dissociated from the representation of any thought or idea.

2. That the glyphs are ideographic, each representing in itself some complete thought or idea.

3. That the glyphs are both phonetic and ideographic, that is, a combination of 1 and 2.

It is apparent at the outset that the first of these theories can not be accepted in its entirety; for although there are undeniable traces

---

[1] There can be no doubt that Förstemann has identified the sign for the planet Venus and possibly a few others. (See Förstemann,1906: p. 116.)

of phoneticism among the Maya glyphs, all attempts to reduce them to a phonetic system or alphabet, which will interpret the writing, have signally failed. The first and most noteworthy of these so-called "Maya alphabets," because of its genuine antiquity, is that given by Bishop Landa in his invaluable *Relacion de las cosas de Yucatan*, frequently cited in Chapter I. Writing in the year 1565, within 25 years of the Spanish Conquest, Landa was able to obtain characters for 27 sounds, as follows: Three *a's*, two *b's*, *c*, *t*, *e*, *h*, *i*, *ca*, *k*, two *l's*, *m*, *n*, two *o's*, *pp*, *p*, *cu*, *ku*, two *x's*, two *v's*, *z*. This alphabet, which was first published in 1864 by Abbé Brasseur de Bourbourg (see Landa, 1864), was at once heralded by Americanists as the long-awaited key which would unlock the secrets of the Maya writing. Unfortunately these confident expectations have not been realized, and all attempts to read the glyphs by means of this alphabet or of any of the numerous others[1] which have appeared since, have completely broken down.

This failure to establish the exclusive phonetic character of the Maya glyphs has resulted in the general acceptance of the second theory, that the signs are ideographic. Doctor Brinton (1894 b: p. 14), however, has pointed out two facts deducible from the Landa alphabet which render impossible not only the complete acceptance of this second theory but also the absolute rejection of the first: (1) That a native writer was able to give a written character for an unfamiliar sound, a sound, moreover, which was without meaning to him, as, for example, that of a Spanish letter; and (2) that the characters he employed for this purpose were also used in the native writings. These facts Doctor Brinton regards as proof that some sort of phonetic writing was not unknown, and, indeed, both the inscriptions and the codices establish the truth of this contention. For example, the sign in *a*, figure 13, has the phonetic value *kin*, and the sign in *b* the phonetic value *yax*. In the latter glyph, however, only the upper part (reproduced in *c*) is to be regarded as the essential element. It is strongly indicative of phoneticism therefore to find the sound *yaxkin*, a combination of these two, expressed by the sign found in *d*. Similarly, the character representing the phonetic value *kin* is found also as an element in the glyphs for the words *likin*

---

[1] Brasseur de Bourbourg, the "discoverer" of Landa's manuscript, added several signs of his own invention to the original Landa alphabet. See his introduction to the Codex Troano published by the French Government. Leon de Rosny published an alphabet of 29 letters with numerous variants. Later Dr. F. Le Plongeon defined 23 letters with variants and made elaborate interpretations of the texts with this "alphabet" as his key. Another alphabet was that proposed by Dr. Hilborne T. Cresson, which included syllables as well as letters, and with which its originator also essayed to read the texts. Scarce worthy of mention are the alphabet and volume of interlinear translations from both the inscriptions and the codices published by F. A. de la Rochefoucauld. This is very fantastic and utterly without value unless, as Doctor Brinton says, it be taken "as a warning against the intellectual aberrations to which students of these ancient mysteries seem peculiarly prone." The late Dr. Cyrus Thomas, of the Bureau of American Ethnology, was the last of those who endeavored to interpret the Maya texts by means of alphabets; though he was perhaps the best of them all, much of his work in this particular respect will not stand.

and *chikin* (see *e* and *f*, respectively, fig. 13), each of which has *kin* as
its last syllable. Again, the phonetic value *tun* is expressed by the
glyph in *g*, and the sound *ca* (*c* hard) by the sign *h*. The sound *katun*
is represented by the character in *i*, a combination of these two.
Sometimes the glyph for this same sound takes the form of *j*, the fish
element in *k* replacing the comblike element *h*. Far from destroying the phonetic character of this composite glyph, however, this
variant *k* in reality strengthens it, since in Maya the word for fish is
cay (*c* hard) and consequently the variant reads *caytun*, a close phonetic approximation of *katun*. The remaining element of this glyph
(*l*) has the value *cauac*, the first syllable of which is also expressed by
either *h* or *k*, figure 13. Its use in *i* and *j* probably may be regarded
as but a further emphasis of the phonetic character of the glyph.

It must be remembered, however, that all of the above glyphs have
meanings quite independent of their phonetic values, that primarily

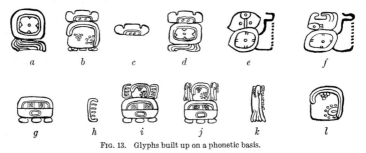

FIG. 13.   Glyphs built up on a phonetic basis.

their function was to convey ideas, and that only secondarily were
they used in their phonetic senses.

If neither the phonetic nor the ideographic character of the glyphs
can be wholly admitted, what then is the true nature of the Maya
writing? The theory now most generally accepted is, that while
chiefly ideographic, the glyphs are sometimes phonetic, and that
although the idea of a glyphic alphabet must finally be abandoned,
the phonetic use of syllables as illustrated above must as surely be
recognized.

This kind of writing Doctor Brinton has called *ikonomatic*, more
familiarly known to us under the name of rebus, or puzzle writing.
In such writing the characters do not indicate the ideas of the objects
which they portray, but only the sounds of their names, and are
used purely in a phonetic sense, like the letters of the alphabet.
For example, the rebus in figure 14 reads as follows: "I believe Aunt
Rose can well bear all for you." The picture of the eye recalls not
the idea "eye" but the sound of the word denoting this object, which
is also the sound of the word for the first person singular of the per-

sonal pronoun I.   Again, the picture of a bee does not represent the idea of that insect, but stands for the sound of its name, which used with a leaf indicates the sound "beeleaf," or in other words, "believe." [1]

It has long been known that the Aztec employed ikonomatic characters in their writing to express the names of persons and places, though this practice does not seem to have been extended by them to the representation of abstract words.   The Aztec codices contain many glyphs which are to be interpreted ikonomatically, that is, like our own rebus writing.   For example in figure 15, *a*, is shown the Aztec hieroglyph for the town of Toltitlan, a name which means "near the place of the rushes."   The word *tollin* means "place of the rushes," but only its first syllable *tol* appears in the word Toltitlan. This syllable is represented in *a* by several rushes.   The word *tetlan*

Fig. 14.   A rebus.   Aztec, and probably Maya, personal and place names were written in a corresponding manner.

means "near something" and its second syllable *tlan* is found also in the word *tlantli*, meaning "teeth."   In *a* therefore, the addition of the teeth to the rushes gives the word Toltitlan.   Another example of this kind of writing is given in figure 15, *b*, where the hieroglyph for the town of Acatzinco is shown.   This word means "the little reed grass," the diminutive being represented by the syllable *tzinco*. The reed grass (*acatl*) is shown by the pointed leaves or spears which emerge from the lower part of a human figure.   This part of the body was called by the Aztecs *tzinco*, and as used here expresses merely the sound *tzinco* in the diminutive *acatzinco*, "the little reed grass," the letter *l* of *acatl* being lost in composition.

The presence of undoubted phonetic elements in these Aztec glyphs expressing personal names and place names would seem to indicate that some similar usage probably prevailed among the Maya.

---

[1] Thus the whole rebus in figure 14 reads: "Eye bee leaf ant rose can well bear awl four ewe."   These words may be replaced by their homophones as follows: "I believe Aunt Rose can well bear all for you."

Rebus writing depends on the principle of homophones; that is, words or characters which sound alike but have different meanings.

While admitting this restricted use of phonetic composition by the Maya, Professor Seler refuses to recognize its further extension:

> Certainly there existed in the Maya writing compound hieroglyphs giving the name of a deity, person, or a locality, whose elements united on the phonetic principle. But as yet it is not proved that they wrote texts. And without doubt the greater part of the Maya hieroglyphics were conventional symbols built up on the ideographic principle.

Doctor Förstemann also regards the use of phonetic elements as restricted to little more than the above when he says, "Finally the graphic system of the Maya . . . never even achieved the expression of a phrase or even a verb."

On the other hand, Mr. Bowditch (1910: p. 255) considers the use of phonetic composition extended considerably beyond these limits:

FIG. 15. Aztec place names: *a*, The sign for the town Toltitlan; *b*, the sign for the town Acatzinco.

> As far as I am aware, the use of this kind of writing [rebus] was confined, among the Aztecs, to the names of persons and places, while the Mayas, if they used the rebus form at all, used it also for expressing common nouns and possibly abstract ideas. The Mayas surely used picture writing and the ideographic system, but I feel confident that a large part of their hieroglyphs will be found to be made up of rebus forms and that the true line of research will be found to lie in this direction.

Doctor Brinton (1894 b: p. 13) held an opinion between these two, perhaps inclining slightly toward the former: "The intermediate position which I have defended, is that while chiefly ideographic, they [the Maya glyphs] are occasionally phonetic, in the same manner as are confessedly the Aztec picture-writings."

These quotations from the most eminent authorities on the subject well illustrate their points of agreement and divergence. All admit the existence of phonetic elements in the glyphs, but disagree as to their extent. And here, indeed, is the crux of the whole phonetic question. Just how extensively do phonetic elements enter into the composition of the Maya glyphs? Without attempting to dispose of this point definitely one way or the other, the author may say that he believes that as the decipherment of Maya writing progresses, more and more phonetic elements will be identified, though the idea conveyed by a glyph will always be found to overshadow its phonetic value.

The various theories above described have not been presented for the reader's extended consideration, but only in order to acquaint him with the probable nature of the Maya glyphs. Success in deciphering, as we shall see, has not come through any of the above mentioned lines of research, which will not be pursued further in this work.

In taking up the question of the meaning of Maya writing, it must be admitted at the outset that in so far as they have been deciphered both the inscriptions and the codices have been found to deal primarily, if indeed not exclusively, with the counting of time in some form or other. Doctor Förstemann, the first successful interpreter of the codices, has shown that these writings have for their principal theme the passage of time in its varying relations to the Maya calendar, ritual, and astronomy. They deal in great part with the sacred year of 260 days, known to the Aztec also under the name of the *tonalamatl*, in connection with which various ceremonies, offerings, sacrifices, and domestic occupations are set forth. Doctor Förstemann believed that this 260-day period was employed by the priests in casting horoscopes and foretelling the future of individuals, classes, and tribes, as well as in predicting coming political events and natural phenomena; or in other words, that in so far as the 260-day period was concerned, the codices are nothing more nor less than books of prophecy and divination.

The prophetic character of some of these native books at least is clearly indicated in a passage from Bishop Landa's *Relacion* (p. 286). In describing a festival held in the month **Uo**, the Bishop relates that "the most learned priest opened a book, in which he examined the omens of the year, which he announced to all those who were present." Other early Spanish writers state that these books contain the ancient prophecies and indicate the times appointed for their fulfillment.

Doctor Thomas regarded the codices as religious calendars, or rituals for the guidance of the priests in the celebration of feasts, ceremonies, and other duties, seemingly a natural inference from the character of the scenes portrayed in connection with these 260-day periods.

Another very important function of the codices is the presentation of astronomical phenomena and calculations. The latter had for their immediate object in each case the determination of the lowest number which would exactly contain all the numbers of a certain group. These lowest numbers are in fact nothing more nor less than the least common multiple of changing combinations of numbers, each one of which represents the revolution of some heavenly body. In addition to these calculations deities are assigned to the several periods, and a host of mythological allusions are introduced, the significance of most of which is now lost.

The most striking proof of the astronomical character of the codices is to be seen in pages 46–50 of the Dresden Manuscript. Here, to begin with, a period of 2,920 days is represented, which exactly contains five Venus years of 584 [1] days each (one on each page) as well as eight solar years of 365 days each. Each of the Venus years is divided into four parts, respectively, 236, 90, 250, and 8 days. The

---

[1] The period of the synodical revolution of Venus as computed to-day is 583.920 days.

first and third of these constitute the periods when Venus was the morning and the evening star, respectively, and the second and fourth, the periods of invisibility after each of these manifestations. This Venus-solar period of 2,920 days was taken as the basis from which the number 37,960 was formed. This contains 13 Venus-solar periods, 65 Venus-years, 104 solar years, and 146 *tonalamatls*, or sacred years of 260 days each. Finally, the last number (37,960) with all the subdivisions above given was thrice repeated, so that these five pages of the manuscript record the passage of 113,880 days, or 312 solar years.

Again, on pages 51–58 of the same manuscript, 405 revolutions of the moon are set down; and so accurate are the calculations involved that although they cover a period of nearly 33 years the total number of days recorded (11,959) is only 89/100 of a day less than the true time computed by the best modern method [1]—certainly a remarkable achievement for the aboriginal mind. It is probable that the revolutions of the planets Jupiter, Mars, Mercury, and Saturn are similarly recorded in the same manuscript.

Toward the end of the Dresden Codex the numbers become greater and greater until, in the so-called "serpent numbers," a grand total of nearly twelve and a half million days (about thirty-four thousand years) is recorded again and again. In these well-nigh inconceivable periods all the smaller units may be regarded as coming at last to a more or less exact close. What matter a few score years one way or the other in this virtual eternity? Finally, on the last page of the manuscript, is depicted the Destruction of the World (see pl. 3), for which these highest numbers have paved the way. Here we see the rain serpent, stretching across the sky, belching forth torrents of water. Great streams of water gush from the sun and moon. The old goddess, she of the tiger claws and forbidding aspect, the malevolent patroness of floods and cloudbursts, overturns the bowl of the heavenly waters. The crossbones, dread emblem of death, decorate her skirt, and a writhing snake crowns her head. Below with downward-pointed spears, symbolic of the universal destruction, the black god stalks abroad, a screeching bird raging on his fearsome head. Here, indeed, is portrayed with graphic touch the final all-engulfing cataclysm.

According to the early writers, in addition to the astronomic, prophetic, and ritualistic material above described, the codices contained records of historical events. It is doubtful whether this is

---

[1] According to modern calculations, the period of the lunar revolution is 29.530588, or approximately 29½ days. For 405 revolutions the accumulated error would be .03×405= 12.15 days. This error the Maya obviated by using 29.5 in some calculations and 29.6 in others, the latter offsetting the former. Thus the first 17 revolutions of the sequence are divided into three groups; the first 6 revolutions being computed at 29.5, each giving a total of 177 days; and the second 6 revolutions also being computed at 29.5 each, giving a total of another 177 days. The third group of 5 revolutions, however, was computed at 29.6 each, giving a total of 148 days. The total number of days in the first 17 revolutions was thus computed to be 177+177+147= 502, which is very close to the time computed by modern calculations, 502.02.

PLATE 3

PAGE 74 OF THE DRESDEN CODEX, SHOWING THE END
OF THE WORLD (ACCORDING TO FÖRSTEMANN)

true of any of the three codices now extant, though there are grounds for believing that the Codex Peresianus may be in part at least of an historical nature.

Much less progress has been made toward discovering the meaning of the inscriptions. Doctor Brinton (1894 b: p. 32) states:

My own conviction is that they [the inscriptions and codices] will prove to be much more astronomical than even the latter [Doctor Förstemann] believes; that they are primarily and essentially records of the motions of the heavenly bodies; and that both figures and characters are to be interpreted as referring in the first instance to the sun and moon, the planets, and those constellations which are most prominent in the nightly sky in the latitude of Yucatan.

Mr. Bowditch (1910: p. 199) has also brought forward very cogent points tending to show that in part at least the inscriptions treat of the intercalation of days necessary to bring the dated monuments, based on a 365-day year, into harmony with the true solar year of 365.2421 days.[1]

While admitting that the inscriptions may, and probably do, contain such astronomical matter as Doctor Brinton and Mr. Bowditch have suggested, the writer believes nevertheless that fundamentally they are historical; that the monuments upon which they are presented were erected and inscribed on or about the dates they severally record; and finally, that the great majority of these dates are those of contemporaneous events, and as such pertain to the subject-matter of history.

The reasons which have led him to this conclusion follow:

First. The monuments at most of the southern Maya sites show a certain periodicity in their sequence. This is most pronounced at Quirigua, where all of the large monuments fall into an orderly series, in which each monument is dated exactly 1,800 days later than the one immediately preceding it in the sequence. This is also true at Copan, where, in spite of the fact that there are many gaps in the sequence, enough monuments conforming to the plan remain to prove its former existence. The same may be said also of Naranjo, Seibal, and Piedras Negras, and in fact of almost all the other large cities which afford sufficient material for a chronological arrangement.

This interval of 1,800 days quite obviously was not determined by the recurrence of any natural phenomenon. It has no parallel in nature, but is, on the contrary, a highly artificial unit. Consequently, monuments the erection of which was regulated by the successive returns of this period could not depend in the least for the fact of their existence on any astronomical phenomenon other than that of the rising and setting of eighteen hundred successive suns, an arbitrary period.

The Maya of Yucatan had a similar method of marking time, though their unit of enumeration was 7,200 days, or four times the

---

[1] This is the tropical year or the time from one equinox to its return.

length of the one used for the same purpose in the older cities. The following quotations from early Spanish chroniclers explain this practice and indicate that the inscriptions presented on these time-markers were of an historical nature:

> There were discovered in the plaza of that city [Mayapan] seven or eight stones each ten feet in length, round at the end, and well worked. These had some writings in the characters which they use, but were so worn by water that they could not be read. Moreover, they think them to be in memory of the foundation and destruction of that city. There are other similar ones, although higher, at Zilan, one of the coast towns. The natives when asked what these things were, replied that they were accustomed to erect one of these stones every twenty years, which is the number they use for counting their ages.[1]

The other is even more explicit:

> Their lustras having reached five in number, which made twenty years, which they call a katun, they place a graven stone on another of the same kind laid in lime and sand in the walls of their temples and the houses of the priests, as one still sees to-day in the edifices in question, and in some ancient walls of our own convent at Merida, about which there are some cells. In a city named Tixhualatun, which signifies "place where one graven stone is placed upon another," they say are their archives, where everybody had recourse for events of all kinds, as we do to Simancas.[2]

It seems almost necessary to conclude from such a parallel that the inscriptions of the southern cities will also be found to treat of historical matters.

Second. When the monuments of the southern cities are arranged according to their art development, that is, in stylistic sequence, they are found to be arranged in their chronological order as well. This important discovery, due largely to the researches of Dr. H. J. Spinden, has enabled us to determine the relative ages of various monuments quite independent of their respective dates. From a stylistic consideration alone it has been possible not only to show that the monuments date from different periods, but also to establish the sequence of these periods and that of the monuments in them. Finally, it has demonstrated beyond all doubt that the great majority of the dates on Maya monuments refer to the time of their erection, so that the inscriptions which they present are historical in that they are the contemporaneous records of different epochs.

Third. The dates on the monuments are such as to constitute a strong antecedent probability of their historical character. Like the records of most ancient peoples, the Maya monuments, judging from their dates, were at first scattered and few. Later, as new cities were founded and the nation waxed stronger and stronger, the number of monuments increased, until at the flood tide of Maya prosperity they were, comparatively speaking, common. Finally, as decline set in, fewer and fewer monuments were erected, and eventually effort in this field ceased altogether. The increasing number of

---

[1] Landa, 1864: p. 52. [2] Cogolludo, 1688: I, lib. IV, v, p. 186.

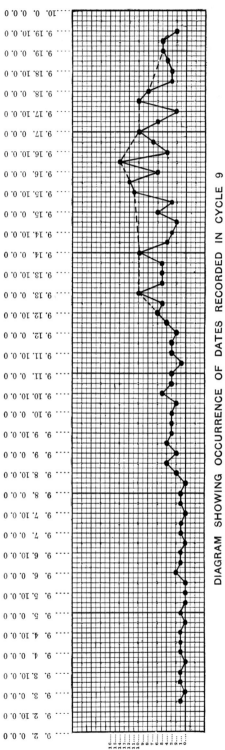

PLATE 4

DIAGRAM SHOWING OCCURRENCE OF DATES RECORDED IN CYCLE 9

the monuments by ten-year periods is shown in plate 4, where the passage of time (i. e., the successive ten-year periods) is represented from left to right, and the number of dates in each ten-year period from bottom to top. Although other dated monuments will be found from time to time, which will necessarily change the details given in this diagram, such additional evidence in all probability will never controvert the following general conclusions, embodied in what has just been stated, which are deducible from it:

1. At first there was a long period of slow growth represented by few monuments, which, however, increased in number toward the end.

2. This was followed without interruption by a period of increased activity, the period from which the great majority of the monuments date.

3. Finally this period came to rather an abrupt end, indicated by the sudden cessation in the erection of dated monuments.

The consideration of these indisputable facts tends to establish the historical rather than the astronomical character of the monuments. For had the erection of the monuments depended on the successive recurrences of some astronomical phenomenon, there would be corresponding intervals between the dates of such monuments[1] the length of which would indicate the identity of the determining phenomenon; and they would hardly have presented the same logical increase due to the natural growth of a nation, which the accompanying diagram clearly sets forth.

Fourth. Although no historical codices[2] are known to have survived, history was undoubtedly recorded in these ancient Maya books. The statements of the early Spanish writers are very explicit on this point, as the following quotations from their works will show. Bishop Landa (here, as always, one of the most reliable authorities) says: "And the sciences which they [the priests] taught were the count of the years, months and days, the feasts and ceremonies, the administration of their sacraments, days, and fatal times, their methods of divination and prophecy, and foretelling events, and the remedies for the sick, and *their antiquities*" [p. 44]. And again, "they [the priests] attended the service of the temples and to the teaching of their sciences *and how to write them in their books.*" And again, [p. 316], "This people also used certain characters or letters with which *they wrote in their books their ancient matters* and sciences."

Father Lizana says (see Landa, 1864: p. 352): "The *history and authorities we can cite* are certain ancient characters, scarcely understood by many and explained by some old Indians, sons of the priests

---

[1] For example, if the revolution of Venus had been the governing phenomenon, each monument would be distant from some other by 584 days; if that of Mars, 780 days; if that of Mercury, 115 or 116 days, etc. Furthermore, the sequence, once commenced, would naturally have been more or less uninterrupted. It is hardly necessary to repeat that the intervals which have been found, namely, 7200 and 1800, rest on no known astronomical phenomena but are the direct result of the Maya vigesimal system of numeration.

[2] It is possible that the Codex Peresianus may treat of historical matter, as already explained.

of their gods, who alone knew how to read and expound them and who were believed in and revered as much as the gods themselves."

Father Ponce (tome LVIII, p. 392) who visited Yucatan as early as 1588, is equally clear: "The natives of Yucatan are among all the inhabitants of New Spain especially deserving of praise for three things. First that before the Spaniards came they made use of characters and letters with which *they wrote out their histories*, their ceremonies, the order of sacrifices to their idols and their calendars in books made of the bark of a certain tree."

Doctor Aguilar, who wrote but little later (1596), gives more details as to the kind of events which were recorded. "On these [the fiber books] they painted in color the reckoning of their years, wars, pestilences, hurricanes, inundations, famines and other events."

Finally, as late as 1697, some of these historical codices were in the possession of the last great independent Maya ruler, one Canek. Says Villagutierre (1701: lib. VI, cap. IV) in this connection: "Because their king [Canek] had read it in his *analtehes* [fiber-books or codices] they had knowledge of the provinces of Yucatan, and of the fact that their ancestors had formerly come from them; *analtehes* or histories being one and the same thing."

It is clear from the foregoing extracts, that the Maya of Yucatan recorded their history up to the time of the Spanish Conquest, in their hieroglyphic books, or codices. That fact is beyond dispute. It must be remembered also in this connection, that the Maya of Yucatan were the direct inheritors of that older Maya civilization in the south, which had produced the hieroglyphic monuments. For this latter reason the writer believes that the practice of recording history in the hieroglyphic writing had its origin, along with many another custom, in the southern area, and consequently that the inscriptions on the monuments of the southern cities are probably, in part at least, of an historical nature.

Whatever may be the meaning of the undeciphered glyphs, enough has been said in this chapter about those of known meaning to indicate the extreme importance of the element of time in Maya writing. The very great preponderance of astronomical, calendary, and numerical signs in both the codices and the inscriptions has determined, so far as the beginner is concerned, the best way to approach the study of the glyphs. First, it is essential to understand thoroughly the Maya system of counting time, in other words, their calendar and chronology. Second, in order to make use of this knowledge, as did the Maya, it is necessary to familiarize ourselves with their arithmetic and its signs and symbols. Third, and last, after this has been accomplished, we are ready to apply ourselves to the deciphering of the inscriptions and the codices. For this reason the next chapter will be devoted to the discussion of the Maya system of counting time.

Chapter III. HOW THE MAYA RECKONED TIME

Among all peoples and in all ages the most obvious unit for the measurement of time has been the day; and the never-failing reappearance of light after each interval of darkness has been the most constant natural phenomenon with which the mind of man has had to deal. From the earliest times successive returns of the sun have regulated the whole scheme of human existence. When it was light, man worked; when it was dark, he rested. Conformity to the operation of this natural law has been practically universal.

Indeed, as primitive man saw nature, day was the only division of time upon which he could absolutely rely. The waxing and waning of the moon, with its everchanging shape and occasional obscuration by clouds, as well as its periodic disappearances from the heavens all combined to render that luminary of little account in measuring the passage of time. The round of the seasons was even more unsatisfactory. A late spring or an early winter by hastening or retarding the return of a season caused the apparent lengths of succeeding years to vary greatly. Even where a 365-day year had been determined, the fractional loss, amounting to a day every four years, soon brought about a discrepancy between the calendar and the true year. The day, therefore, as the most obvious period in nature, as well as the most reliable, has been used the world over as the fundamental unit for the measurement of longer stretches of time.

TABLE I. THE TWENTY MAYA DAY NAMES

Imix	Chuen
Ik	Eb
Akbal	Ben
Kan	Ix
Chicchan	Men
Cimi	Cib
Manik	Caban
Lamat	Eznab
Muluc	Cauac
Oc	Ahau

In conformity with the universal practice just mentioned the Maya made the day, which they called *kin*, the primary unit of their calendar. There were twenty such units, named as in Table I; these followed each other in the order there shown. When **Ahau**, the last day in the list, had been reached, the count began anew with **Imix**, and thus repeated itself again and again without interruption, throughout time. It is important that the student should fix this

Maya conception of the rotation of days firmly in his mind at the
outset, since all that is to follow depends upon the absolute continuity of this twenty-day sequence in endless repetition.

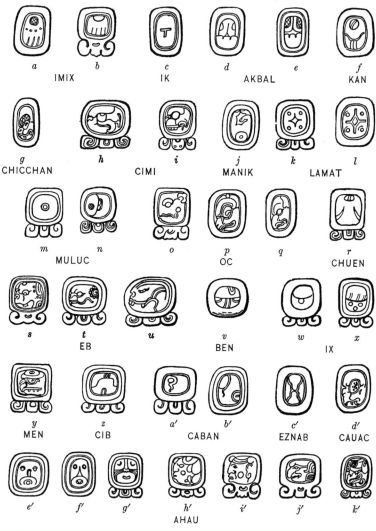

FIG. 16.   The day signs in the inscriptions.

The glyphs for these twenty days are shown in figures 16 and 17.
The forms in figure 16 are from the inscriptions and those in figure
17 from the codices.   In several cases variants are given to facilitate
identification.   A study of the glyphs in these two figures shows on
the whole a fairly close similarity between the forms for the same

day in each.   The sign for the first day, **Imix,** is practically identical in both.   Compare figure 16, *a* and *b*, with figure 17, *a* and *b*.   The usual form for the day **Ik** in the inscriptions (see fig. 16, *c*), however,

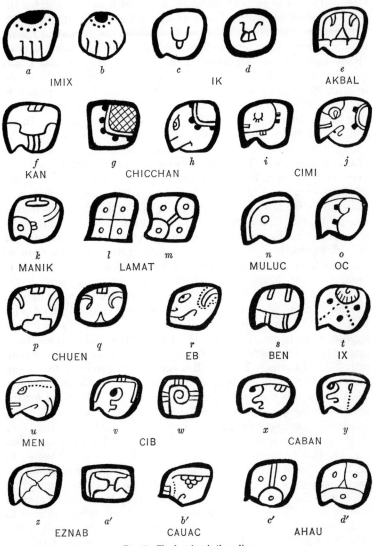

FIG. 17.   The day signs in the codices.

is unlike the glyph for the same day in the codices (fig. 17, *c, d*). The forms for **Akbal** and **Kan** are practically the same in each (see fig. 16, *d, e,* and *f,* and fig. 17, *e* and *f,* respectively).   The day **Chicchan,** figure 16, *g,* occurs rarely in the inscriptions; when present, it takes the form of a grotesque head.   In the codices the common form for this day is very different (fig. 17, g).   The head variant, however (fig. 17, h), shows a slightly closer similarity to the form from the inscriptions.   The forms in both figure 16, h, i, and figure 17, i, j, for the day **Cimi** show little resemblance to each other.   Although figure 17, i, represents the common form in the codices, the variant in j more closely resembles the form in figure 16, h, i.   The day **Manik** is practically the same in both (see figs. 16, j, and 17, k), as is also **Lamat** (figs. 16, k, l, and 17, l, m).   The day **Muluc** occurs rarely in the inscriptions (fig. 16, m, n).   Of these two variants m more closely resembles the form from the codices (fig. 17, n).   The glyph for the day **Oc** (fig. 16, o, p, q) is not often found in the inscriptions.   In the codices, on the other hand, this day is frequently represented as shown in figure 17, o.   This form bears no resemblance to the forms in the inscriptions.   There is, however, a head-variant form found very rarely in the codices that bears a slight resemblance to the forms in the inscriptions.   The day **Chuen** occurs but once in the inscriptions where the form is clear enough to distinguish its characteristic (see fig 16, r).   This form bears a general resemblance to the glyph for this day in the codices (fig. 17, p, q).   The forms for the day **Eb** in both figures 16, s, t, u, and 17, r, are grotesque heads showing but remote resemblance to one another.   The essential element in both, however, is the same, that is, the element occupying the position of the ear.   Although the day **Ben** occurs but rarely in the inscriptions, its form (fig. 16, v) is practically identical with that in the codices (see fig. 17, s).   The day **Ix** in the inscriptions appears as in figure 16, w, x.   The form in the codices is shown in figure 17, t.   The essential element in each seems to be the three prominent dots or circles.   The day **Men** occurs very rarely on the monuments.   The form shown in figure 16, y, is a grotesque head not unlike the sign for this day in the codices (fig. 17, u).   The signs for the day **Cib** in the inscriptions and the codices (figs. 16, z, and 17, v, w), respectively, are very dissimilar.   Indeed, the form for **Cib** (fig. 17, v) in the codices resembles more closely the sign for the day **Caban** (fig. 16, a', b') than it does the form for **Cib** in the inscriptions (see fig. 16, z).   The only element common to both is the line paralleling the upper part of the glyph (*) and the short vertical lines connecting it with the outline at the top.   The glyphs for the day **Caban** in both figures 16, a', b', and 17, x, y, show a satisfactory resemblance to each other.   The forms for the day **Eznab** are also practically identical (see figs. 16, c', and 17, z, a').   The forms for the day **Cauac**, on the other hand, are very dissimilar; compare figures 16, d', and 17, b'.   The only point of resemblance between the two seems to be the element which appears in the eye of the former and at the lower left-hand side of the latter.   The last of the twenty Maya days, and by far the most important, since it is found in both the codices and the inscriptions more frequently than all of the others combined, is **Ahau** (see figs. 16, $e'-k'$, and 17, c', d'). The latter form is the only one found in the codices, and is identical with e', f', figure 16, the usual sign for this day in the inscriptions. The variants in figure 16, $g'-k'$, appear on some of the monuments, and because of the great importance of this day **Ahau** it is necessary to keep all of them in mind.

These examples of the glyphs, which stand for the twenty Maya days, are in each case as typical as possible. The student must remember, however, that many variations occur, which often render the correct identification of a form difficult. As explained in the preceding chapter, such variations are due not only to individual peculiarities of style, careless drawing, and actual error, but also to the physical dissimilarities of materials on which they are portrayed, as the stone of the monuments and the fiber paper of the codices; consequently, such differences may be regarded as unessential. The ability to identify variants differing from those shown in figures 16 and 17 will come only through experience and familiarity with the glyphs themselves. The student should constantly bear in mind, however, that almost every Maya glyph, the signs for the days included, has an *essential element* peculiar to it, and the discovery of such elements will greatly facilitate his study of Maya writing.

Why the named days should have been limited to twenty is difficult to understand, as this number has no parallel period in nature. Some have conjectured that this number was chosen because it represents the number of man's digits, the twenty fingers and toes. Mr. Bowditch has pointed out in this connection that the Maya word for the period composed of these twenty named days is *uinal*, while the word for 'man' is *uinik*. The parallel is interesting and may possibly explain why the number twenty was selected as the basis of the Maya system of numeration, which, as we shall see later, was vigesimal, that is, increasing by twenties or multiples thereof.

THE TONALAMATL, OR 260-DAY PERIOD

Merely calling a day by one of the twenty names given in Table I, however, did not sufficiently describe it according to the Maya notion. For instance, there was no day in the Maya calendar called merely **Imix**, **Ik**, or **Akbal**, or, in fact, by any of the other names given in Table I. Before the name of a day was complete it was necessary to prefix to it a number ranging from 1 to 13, inclusive, as **6 Imix** or **13 Akbal**. Then and only then did a Maya day receive its complete designation and find its proper place in the calendar.

The manner in which these thirteen numbers, 1 to 13, inclusive, were joined to the twenty names of Table I was as follows: Selecting any one of the twenty names [1] as a starting point, **Kan** for example, the number 1 was prefixed to it. See Table II, in which the names of Table I have been repeated with the numbers prefixed to them in a manner to be explained hereafter. The star opposite the name **Kan** indicates the starting point above chosen. The name **Chicchan** immediately following **Kan** in Table II was given the next number in order (2), namely, **2 Chicchan**. The next name, **Cimi**, was given the next number (3), namely, **3 Cimi**, and so on as follows: **4 Manik, 5 Lamat, 6 Muluc, 7 Oc, 8 Chuen, 9 Eb, 10 Ben, 11 Ix, 12 Men, 13 Cib.**

TABLE II. SEQUENCE OF MAYA DAYS

5 Imix	8 Chuen
6 Ik	9 Eb
7 Akbal	10 Ben
*1 Kan	11 Ix
2 Chicchan	12 Men
3 Cimi	13 Cib
4 Manik	1 Caban
5 Lamat	2 Eznab
6 Muluc	3 Cauac
7 Oc	4 Ahau

Instead of giving to the next name in Table II (**Caban**) the number 14, the number 1 was prefixed; for, as previously stated, the numerical coefficients of the days did not rise above the number 13. Following the day **1 Caban**, the sequence continued as before: **2 Eznab, 3 Cauac, 4 Ahau.** After the day **4 Ahau**, the last in Table II, the next number in order, in this case 5, was prefixed to the next name in order—that is, **Imix**, the first name in Table II— and the count continued without interruption: **5 Imix, 6 Ik, 7 Akbal**, or back to the name **Kan** with which it started. There was no break in the sequence, however, even at this point (or at any other, for that matter). The next name in Table II, **Kan**, selected for the starting point, was given the number next in order, i. e., 8, and the day following **7 Akbal** in Table II would be, therefore, **8 Kan**, and the sequence would continue to be formed in the same way: **8 Kan, 9 Chicchan, 10 Cimi, 11 Manik, 12 Lamat, 13 Muluc, 1 Oc, 2 Chuen, 3 Eb**, and so on. So far as the Maya conception of time was concerned, this sequence of days went on without interruption, forever.

While somewhat unusual at first sight, this sequence is in reality exceedingly simple, being governed by three easily remembered rules:

Rule 1. The sequence of the 20 day names repeats itself again and again without interruption.

---

[1] Since the sequence of the twenty day names was continuous, it is obvious that it had no beginning or ending, like the rim of a wheel; consequently any day name may be chosen arbitrarily as the starting point. In the accompanying example **Kan** has been chosen to begin with, though Bishop Landa (p. 236) states with regard to the Maya: "The character or letter with which they commence their count of the days or calendar is called Hun-ymix [i. e. **1 Imix**]". Again, "Here commences the count of the calendar of the Indians, saying in their language Hun Imix (*) [i. e. **1 Imix**]." (Ibid., p. 246.)

$$\begin{array}{r} 20 \\ 13 \\ \hline 60 \\ 20 \\ \hline 260 \end{array}$$

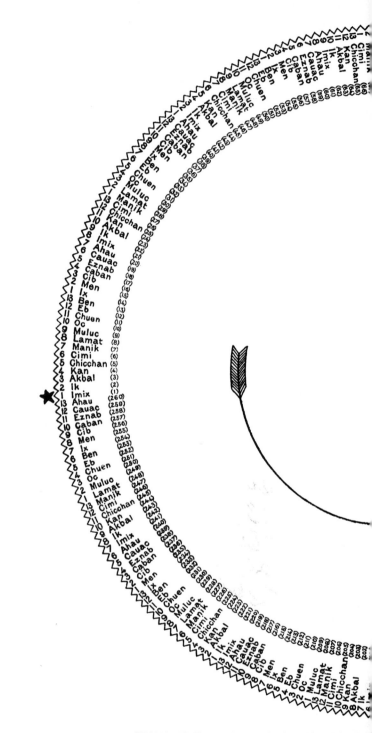

TONALAMATL WHEEL, SHOWING SEQUEN

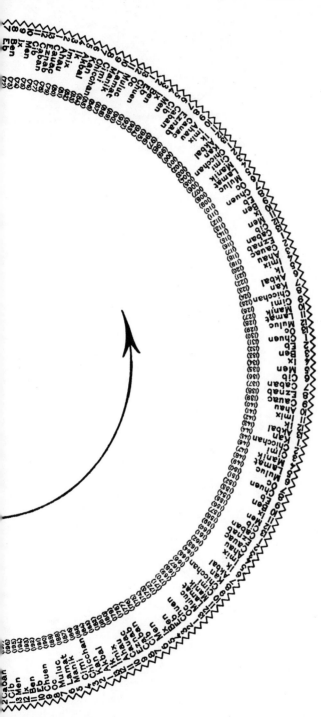

PLATE 5

F THE 260 DIFFERENTLY NAMED DAYS

Rule 2. The sequence of the numerical coefficients 1 to 13, inclusive, repeats itself again and again without interruption, 1 following immediately 13.

Rule 3. The 13 numerical coefficients are attached to the 20 names, so that after a start has been made by prefixing any one of the 13 numbers to any one of the 20 names, the number next in order is given to the name next in order, and the sequence continues indefinitely in this manner.

It is a simple question of arithmetic to determine the number of days which must elapse before a day bearing the same designation as a previous one in the sequence can reappear. Since there are 13 numbers and 20 names, and since each of the 13 numbers must be attached in turn to each one of the 20 names before a given number can return to a given name, we must find the least common multiple of 13 and 20. As these two numbers, contain no common factor, their least common multiple is their product (260), which is the number sought. Therefore, any given day can not reappear in the sequence until after the 259 days immediately following it shall have elapsed. Or, in other words, the 261st day will have the same designation as the 1st, the 262d the same as the 2d, and so on.

This is graphically shown in the wheel figured in plate 5, where the sequence of the days, commencing with **1 Imix**, which is indicated by a star, is represented as extending around the rim of the wheel. After the name of each day, its number in the sequence beginning with the starting point **1 Imix**, is shown in parenthesis. Now, if the star opposite the day **1 Imix** be conceived to be stationary and the wheel to revolve in a sinistral circuit, that is contra-clockwise, the days will pass the star in the order which they occupy in the 260-day sequence. It appears from this diagram also that the day **1 Imix** can not recur until after 260 days shall have passed, and that it always follows the day **13 Ahau**. This must be true since **Ahau** is the name immediately preceding **Imix** in the sequence of the day names and 13 is the number immediately preceding 1. After the day **13 Ahau** (the 260th from the starting point) is reached, the day **1 Imix**, the 261st, recurs and the sequence, having entered into itself again, begins anew as before.

This round of the 260 differently named days was called by the Aztec the *tonalamatl*, or "book of days." The Maya name for this period is unknown [1] and students have accepted the Aztec name for it. The tonalamatl is frequently represented in the Maya codices, there being more than 200 examples in the Codex Tro-Cortesiano alone. It was a very useful period for the calculations of the priests because of the different sets of factors into which it can be resolved,

---

[1] Professor Seler says the Maya of Guatemala called this period the *kin katun*, or "order of the days." He fails to give his authority for this statement, however, and, as will appear later, these terms have entirely different meanings. (See *Bulletin 28*, p. 14.)

namely, 4×65, 5×52, 10×26, 13×20, and 2×130. Tonalamatls divided into 4, 5, and 10 equal parts of 65, 52, and 26 days, respectively, occur repeatedly throughout the codices.

It is all the more curious, therefore, that this period is rarely represented in the inscriptions. The writer recalls but one city (Copan) in which this period is recorded to any considerable extent.

It might almost be inferred from this fact alone that the inscriptions do not treat of prophecy, divinations, or ritualistic and ceremonial matters, since these subjects in the codices are always found in connection with tonalamatls. If true this considerably restricts the field of which the inscriptions may treat.

Fig. 18. Sign for the tonalamatl (according to Goodman).

Mr. Goodman has identified the glyph shown in figure 18 as the sign for the 260-day period, but on wholly insufficient evidence the writer believes. On the other hand, so important a period as the tonalamatl undoubtedly had its own particular glyph, but up to the present time all efforts to identify this sign have proved unsuccessful.

THE HAAB, OR YEAR OF 365 DAYS

Having explained the composition and nature of the tonalamatl, or so-called Sacred Year, let us turn to the consideration of the Solar Year, which was known as *haab* in the Maya language.

The Maya used in their calendar system a 365-day year, though they doubtless knew that the true length of the year exceeds this by 6 hours. Indeed, Bishop Landa very explicitly states that such knowledge was current among them. "They had," he says, "their perfect year, like ours, of 365 days and 6 hours;" and again, "The entire year had 18 of these [20-day periods] and besides 5 days and 6 hours." In spite of Landa's statements, however, it is equally clear that had the Maya attempted to take note of these 6 additional hours by inserting an extra day in their calendar every fourth year, their day sequence would have been disturbed at once. An examination of the tonalamatl, or round of days (see pl. 5), shows also that the interpolation of a single day at any point would have thrown into confusion the whole Maya calendar, not only interfering with the sequence but also destroying its power of reentering itself at the end of 260 days. The explanation of this statement is found in the fact that the Maya calendar had no elastic period corresponding to our month of February, which is increased in length whenever the accumulation of fractional days necessitates the addition of an extra day, in order to keep the calendar year from gaining on the true year.

If the student can be made to realize that all Maya periods, from the lowest to the highest known, are always in a continuous sequence, each returning into itself and beginning anew after completion, he will have grasped the most fundamental principle of Maya chronology—its absolute continuity throughout.

It may be taken for granted, therefore, in the discussion to follow that no interpolation of intercalary days was actually made. It is equally probable, however, that the priests, in whose hands such matters rested, corrected the calendar by additional calculations which showed just how many days the recorded year was ahead of the true year at any given time. Mr. Bowditch (1910: Chap. XI) has cited several cases in which such additional calculations exactly correct the inscriptions on the monument upon which they appear and bring their dates into harmony with the true solar-year.

So far as the calendar is concerned, then, the year consisted of but 365 days. It was divided into 18 periods of 20 days each, designated in Maya *uinal*, and a closing period of 5 days known as the *xma kaba kin*, or "days without name." The sum of these $(18 \times 20 + 5)$ exactly made up the calendar year.

TABLE III. THE DIVISIONS OF THE MAYA YEAR

Pop	Zac
Uo	Ceh
Zip	Mac
Zotz	Kankin
Tzec	Muan
Xul	Pax
Yaxkin	Kayab
Mol	Cumhu
Chen	Uayeb
Yax	

The names of these 19 divisions of the year are given in Table III in the order in which they follow one another; the twentieth day of one month was succeeded by the first day of the next month.

The first day of the Maya year was the first day of the month **Pop**, which, according to the early Spanish authorities, Bishop Landa (1864: p. 276) included, always fell on the 16th of July.[1] **Uayeb**, the last division of the year, contained only 5 days, the last day of **Uayeb** being at the same time the 365th day of the year. Consequently, when this day was completed, the next in order was the Maya New Year's Day, the first day of the month **Pop**, after which the sequence repeated itself as before.

The xma kaba kin, or "days without name," were regarded as especially unlucky and ill-omened. Says Pio Perez (see Landa, 1864: p. 384) in speaking of these closing days of the year: "Some call them *u yail kin* or *u yail haab*, which may be translated, the sorrowful and laborious days or part of the year; for they [the Maya]

---

[1] As Bishop Landa wrote not later than 1579, this is Old Style. The corresponding day in the Gregorian Calendar would be July 27.

believed that in them occurred sudden deaths and pestilences, and that they were diseased by poisonous animals, or devoured by wild beasts, fearing that if they went out to the field to their labors, some tree would pierce them or some other kind of misfortune happen to them." The Aztec held the five closing days of the year in the same superstitious dread. Persons born in this unlucky period were held to be destined by this fact to wretchedness and poverty for life. These days were, moreover, prophetic in character; what occurred during them continued to happen ever afterward. Hence, quarreling was avoided during this period lest it should never cease.

Having learned the number, length, and names of the several periods into which the Maya divided their year, and the sequence in which these followed one another, the next subject which claims attention is the positions of the several days in these periods. In order properly to present this important subject, it is first necessary to consider briefly how we count and number our own units of time, since through an understanding of these practices we shall better comprehend those of the ancient Maya.

It is well known that our methods of counting time are inconsistent with each other. For example, in describing the time of day, that is, in counting hours, minutes, and seconds, we speak in terms of elapsed time. When we say it is 1 o'clock, in reality the first hour after noon, that is, the hour between 12 noon and 1 p. m., has passed and the second hour after noon is about to commence. When we say it is 2 o'clock, in reality the second hour after noon is finished and the third hour about to commence. In other words, we count the time of day by referring to passed periods and not current periods. This is the method used in reckoning astronomical time. During the passage of the first hour after midnight the hours are said to be zero, the time being counted by the number of minutes and seconds elapsed. Thus, half past 12 is written: $0^{hr.} 30^{min.} 0^{sec.}$, and quarter of 1, $0^{hr.} 45^{min.} 0^{sec.}$. Indeed one hour can not be written until the first hour after midnight is completed, or until it is 1 o'clock, namely, $1^{hr.} 0^{min.} 0^{sec.}$.

We use an entirely different method, however, in counting our days, years, and centuries, which are referred to as current periods of time. It is the 1st day of January immediately after midnight December 31. It was the first year of the Eleventh Century immediately after midnight December 31, 1000 A. D. And finally, it was the Twentieth Century immediately after midnight December 31, 1900 A. D. In this category should be included also the days of the week and the months, since the names of these periods also refer to present time. In other words when we speak of our days, months, years, and centuries, we do not have in mind, and do not refer to completed periods of time, but on the contrary to current periods.

It will be seen that in the first method of counting time, in speaking of 1 o'clock, 1 hour, 30 minutes, we use only the cardinal forms of our numbers; but in the second method we say the 1st of January, the Twentieth Century, using the ordinal forms, though even here we permit ourselves one inconsistency. In speaking of our years, which are reckoned by the second method, we say "nineteen hundred and twelve," when, to be consistent, we should say "nineteen hundred and twelfth," using the ordinal "twelfth" instead of the cardinal "twelve."

We may then summarize our methods of counting time as follows: (1) All periods less than the day, as hours, minutes, and seconds, are referred to in terms of past time; and (2) the day and all greater periods are referred to in terms of current time.

The Maya seem to have used only the former of these two methods in counting time; that is, all the different periods recorded in the codices and the inscriptions seemingly refer to elapsed time rather than to current time, to a day passed, rather than to a day present. Strange as this may appear to us, who speak of our calendar as current time, it is probably true nevertheless that the Maya, in so far as their writing is concerned, never designated a present day but always treated of a day gone by. The day recorded is yesterday because to-day can not be considered an entity until, like the hour of astronomical time, it completes itself and becomes a unit, that is, a yesterday.

This is well illustrated by the Maya method of numbering the positions of the days in the months, which, as we shall see, was identical with our own method of counting astronomical time. For example, the first day of the Maya month **Pop** was written **Zero Pop**, (**0 Pop**) for not until one whole day of **Pop** had passed could the day **1 Pop** be written; by that time, however, the first day of the month had passed and the second day commenced. In other words, the second day of **Pop** was written **1 Pop**; the third day, **2 Pop**; the fourth day, **3 Pop**; and so on through the 20 days of the Maya month. This method of numbering the positions of the days in the month led to calling the last day of a month 19 instead of 20. This appears in Table IV, in which the last 6 days of one year and the first 22 of the next year are referred to their corresponding positions in the divisions of the Maya year. It must be remembered in using this Table that the closing period of the Maya year, the xma kaba kin, or **Uayeb**, contained only 5 days, whereas all the other periods (the 18 uinals) had 20 days each.

Curiously enough no glyph for the *haab*, or year, has been identified as yet, in spite of the apparent importance of this period.[1] The

---

[1] This is probably to be accounted for by the fact that in the Maya system of chronology, as we shall see later, the 365-day year was not used in recording time. But that so fundamental a period had therefore no special glyph does not necessarily follow, and the writer believes the sign for the haab will yet be discovered.

glyphs which represent the 18 different uinals and the **xma kaba** kin, however, are shown in figures 19 and 20. The forms in figure 19 are taken from the inscriptions and those in figure 20 from the codices.

TABLE IV. POSITIONS OF DAYS AT THE END OF A YEAR

360th day of the year	19 Cumhu	last day of the month **Cumhu.**
361st day of the year	0 Uayeb	first day of **Uayeb.**
362d day of the year	1 Uayeb	
363d day of the year	2 Uayeb	
364th day of the year	3 Uayeb	
365th day of the year	4 Uayeb	last day of **Uayeb** and of the year.
1st day of next year	0 Pop	first day of the month **Pop**, and of the next
2d day of next year	1 Pop	year.
3d day of next year	2 Pop	
4th day of next year	3 Pop	
5th day of next year	4 Pop	
6th day of next year	5 Pop	
7th day of next year	6 Pop	
8th day of next year	7 Pop	
9th day of next year	8 Pop	
10th day of next year	9 Pop	
11th day of next year	10 Pop	
12th day of next year	11 Pop	
13th day of next year	12 Pop	
14th day of next year	13 Pop	
15th day of next year	14 Pop	
16th day of next year	15 Pop	
17th day of next year	16 Pop	
18th day of next year	17 Pop	
19th day of next year	18 Pop	
20th day of next year	19 Pop	last day of the month **Pop.**
21st day of next year	0 Uo	first day of the month **Uo.**
22d day of next year	1 Uo	
etc.	etc.	

The signs for the first four months, **Pop**, **Uo**, **Zip**, and **Zotz**, show a convincing similarity in both the inscriptions and the codices. The essential elements of **Pop** (figs. 19, *a*, and 20, *a*) are the crossed bands and the *kin* sign. The latter is found in both the forms figured, though only a part of the former appears in figure 20, *a.* **Uo** has two forms in the inscriptions (see fig. 19, *b*, *c*),[1] which are, however, very similar to each other as well as to the corresponding forms in the codices (fig. 20, *b*, *c*). The glyphs for the month **Zip** are identical in both figures 19, *d*, and 20, *d*. The grotesque heads for *Z*otz in figures 19, *e*, *f*,[2] and 20, *e*, are also similar to each other. The essential character-

---

[1] Later researches of the writer (1914) have convinced him that figure 19, *c*, is not a sign for **Uo**, but a very unusual variant of the sign for **Zip**, found only at Copan, and there only on monuments belonging to the final period.

[2] The writer was able to prove during his last trip to the Maya field that figure 19, *f*, is not a sign for the month **Zotz**, as suggested by Mr. Bowditch, but a very unusual form representing **Kankin.** This identification is supported by a number of examples at Piedras Negras.

istic seems to be the prominent upturned and flaring nose. The forms for **Tzec** (figs. 19, *g*, *h*, and 20, *f*) show only a very general similarity, and those for **Xul**, the next month, are even more unlike. The

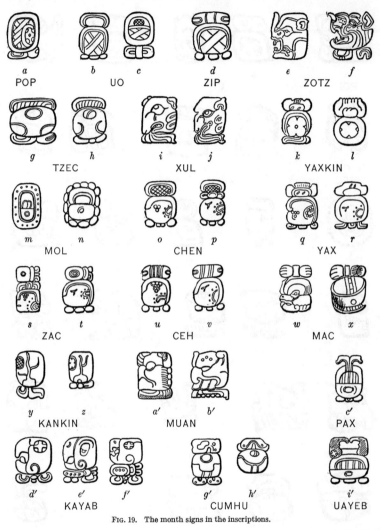

FIG. 19. The month signs in the inscriptions.

only sign for **Xul** in the inscriptions (fig. 19, *i*, *j*) bears very little resemblance to the common form for this month in the codices (fig. 20, *g*), though it is not unlike the variant in *h*, figure 20. The essential characteristic seems to be the familiar ear and the small mouth, shown in the inscription as an oval and in the codices as a hook surrounded with dots.

The sign for the month **Yaxkin** is identical in both figures 19, k, l, and 20, i, j. The sign for the month **Mol** in figures 19, m, n, and 20, k exhibits the same close similarity. The forms for the month **Chen**

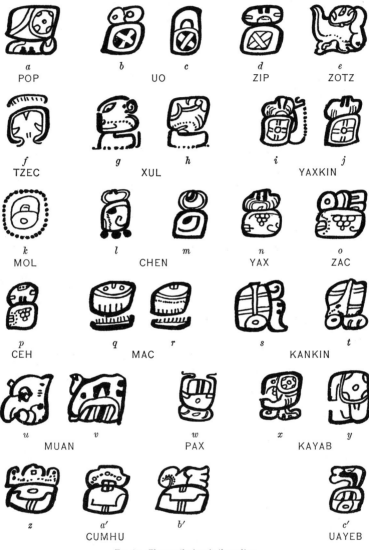

a
POP

b c
UO

d
ZIP

e
ZOTZ

f
TZEC

g h
XUL

i j
YAXKIN

k
MOL

l m
CHEN

n
YAX

o
ZAC

p
CEH

q r
MAC

s t
KANKIN

u v
MUAN

w
PAX

x y
KAYAB

z a' b'
CUMHU

c'
UAYEB

Fig. 20.   The month signs in the codices.

in figures 19, o, p, and 20, l, m, on the other hand, bear only a slight resemblance to each other. The forms for the months **Yax** (figs. 19, q, r, and 20, n), **Zac** (figs. 19, s, t, and 20, o), and **Ceh** (figs. 19, u, v, and

20, p) are again identical in each case.   The signs for the next month,
Mac, however, are entirely dissimilar, the form commonly found in
the inscriptions (fig. 19, w) bearing absolutely no resemblance to that
shown in figure 20, q, r, the only form for this month in the codices.
The very unusual variant (fig. 19, x), from Stela 25 at Piedras Negras
is perhaps a trifle nearer the form found in the codices.   The flattened oval in the main part of the variant is somewhat like the upper
part of the glyph in figure 20, q.   The essential element of the glyph for
the month **Mac**, so far as the inscriptions are concerned, is the element
☺◻☺ (*) found as the superfix in both w and x, figure 19.   The sign
*   for the month **Kankin** (figs. 19, y, z, and 20, s, t) and the signs
for the month **Muan** (figs. 19, a', b', and 20, u, v) show only a general similarity.   The signs for the last three months of the year, **Pax**
(figs. 19, c', and 20, w), **Kayab** (figs. 19, d'–f', and 20, x, y), and **Cumhu**
(figs. 19, g', h', and 20, z, a', b') in the inscriptions and codices,
respectively, are practically identical.   The closing division of the
year, the five days of the xma kaba kin, called **Uayeb**, is represented
by essentially the same glyph in both the inscriptions and the
codices.   Compare figure 19, i', with figure 20, c'.

It will be seen from the foregoing comparison that on the whole the
glyphs for the months in the inscriptions are similar to the corresponding forms in the codices, and that such variations as are found
may readily be accounted for by the fact that the codices and the
inscriptions probably not only emanate from different parts of the
Maya territory but also date from different periods.

The student who wishes to decipher Maya writing is strongly urged
to memorize the signs for the days and months given in figures 16,
17, 19, and 20, since his progress will depend largely on his ability to
recognize these glyphs when he encounters them in the texts.

THE CALENDAR ROUND, OR 18980-DAY PERIOD

Before taking up the study of the Calendar Round let us briefly
summarize the principal points ascertained in the preceding pages
concerning the Maya method of counting time.   In the first place
we learned from the tonalamatl (pl. 5) three things: (1) The number
of differently named days;   (2) the names of these days;   (3) the order
in which they invariably followed one another.   And in the second
place we learned in the discussion of the Maya year, or haab, just
concluded, four other things: (1) The length of the year;   (2) the
number, length, and names of the several periods into which it was
divided;   (3) the order in which these periods invariably followed one
another;   (4) the positions of the days in these periods.

The proper combination of these two, the tonalamatl, or "round of
days," and the haab, or year of uinals, and the xma kaba kin, formed
the Calendar Round, to which the tonalamatl contributed the names

of the days and the haab the positions of these days in the divisions of the year. The Calendar Round was the most important period in Maya chronology, and a comprehension of its nature and of the principles which governed its composition is therefore absolutely essential to the understanding of the Maya system of counting time.

It has been explained (see p. 41) that the complete designation or name of any day in the tonalamatl consisted of two equally essential parts: (1) The name glyph, and (2) the numerical coefficient. Disregarding the latter for the present, let us first see *which* of the twenty names in Table I, that is, the name parts of the days, can stand at the beginning of the Maya year.

In applying any sequence of names or numbers to another there are only three possibilities concerning the names or numbers which can stand at the head of the resulting sequence:

1. When the sums of the units in each of the two sequences contain no common factor, each one of the units in turn will stand at the head of the resulting sequence.

2. When the sum of the units in one of the two sequences is a multiple of the sum of the units in the other, only the first unit can stand at the head of the resulting sequence.

3. When the sums of the units in the two sequences contain a common factor (except in those cases which fall under (2), that is, in which one is a multiple of the other) only certain units can stand at the head of the sequence.

Now, since our two numbers (the 20 names in Table I and the 365 days of the year) contain a common factor, and since neither is a multiple of the other, it is clear that only the last of the three contingencies just mentioned concerns us here; and we may therefore dismiss the first two from further consideration.

The Maya year, then, could begin only with certain of the days in Table I, and the next task is to find out which of these twenty names invariably stood at the beginnings of the years.

When there is a sequence of 20 names in endless repetition, it is evident that the 361st will be the same as the 1st, since $360 = 20 \times 18$. Therefore the 362d will be the same as the 2d, the 363d as the 3d, the 364th as the 4th, and the 365 as the 5th. But the 365th, or 5th, name is the name of the last day of the year, consequently the 1st day of the following year (the 366th from the beginning) will have the 6th name in the sequence. Following out this same idea, it appears that the 361st day of the *second year* will have the same name as that with which it began, that is, the 6th name in the sequence, the 362d day the 7th name, the 363d the 8th, the 364th the 9th, and the 365th, or last day of the *second year*, the 10th name. Therefore the 1st day of the *third year* (the 731st from the beginning) will have the 11th name in the sequence. Similarly it could be shown that the *third year*, beginning with the 11th name, would necessarily end with the 15th name; and the *fourth year*, beginning with the 16th name (the 1096th from the beginning) would necessarily end with the 20th, or last name, in the sequence. It results, therefore, from the foregoing progression that the *fifth year* will have to begin with the 1st name (the 1461st from the beginning), or the same name with which the *first year* also began.

This is capable of mathematical proof, since the 1st day of the *fifth year* has the 1461st name from the beginning of the sequence, for $1461 = 4 \times 365 + 1 = 73 \times 20 + 1$. The *1* in the second term of this equation indicates that the beginning day of the *fifth year* has been reached; and the *1* in the third term indicates that the name-part of this day is the 1st name in the sequence of twenty. In other words, every fifth year began with a day, the name part of which was the same, and consequently only four of the names in Table I could stand at the beginnings of the Maya years.

The four names which successively occupied this, the most important position of the year, were: **Ik, Manik, Eb, and Caban** (see Table V, in which these four names are shown in their relation to the sequence of twenty). Beginning with any one of these, **Ik** for example, the next in order, **Manik**, is 5 days distant, the next, **Eb**, another five days, the next, **Caban**, another 5 days, and the next, **Ik**, the name with which the Table started, another 5 days.

TABLE V. RELATIVE POSITIONS OF DAYS BEGINNING MAYA YEARS

IK	**EB**
Akbal	Ben
Kan	Ix
Chicchan	Men
Cimi	Cib
MANIK	**CABAN**
Lamat	Eznab
Muluc	Cauac
Oc	Ahau
Chuen	Imix

Since one of the four names just given invariably began the Maya year, it follows that in any given year, all of its nineteen divisions, the 18 uinals and the xma kaba kin, also began with the same name, which was the name of the first day of the first uinal. This is necessarily true because these 19 divisions of the year, with the exception of the last, each contained 20 days, and consequently the name of the first day of the first division determined the names of the first days of all the succeeding divisions of that particular year. Furthermore, since the xma kaba kin, the closing division of the year, contained but 5 days, the name of the first day of the following year, as well as the names of the first days of all of its divisions, was shifted forward in the sequence another 5 days, as shown above.

This leads directly to another important conclusion: Since the first days of all the divisions of any given year always had the same name-part, it follows that the second days of all the divisions of that year had the same name, that is, the next succeeding in the sequence of twenty. The third days in each division of that year must have had the same name, the fourth days the same name, and so on, throughout the 20 days of the month. For example, if a year began with the day-name **Ik**, all of the divisions in that year also began with the same name, and the second days of all its divisions had the day-name **Akbal**, the third days the name **Kan**, the fourth days the name **Chicchan**, and so forth. This enables us to formulate the following—

Rule. The 20 day-names always occupy the same positions in all the divisions of any given year.

But since the year and its divisions must begin with one of four names, it is clear that the second positions also must be filled with one of another group of four names, and the third positions with one of another group of four names, and so on, through all the positions of the month. This enables us to formulate a second—

Rule. Only four of the twenty day-names can ever occupy any given position in the divisions of the years.

But since, in the years when **Ik** is the 1st name, **Manik** will be the 6th, **Eb** the 11th, and **Caban** the 16th, and in the years when **Manik** is the 1st, **Eb** will be the 6th, **Caban** the 11th, and **Ik** the 16th, and in the years when **Eb** is the 1st, **Caban** will be the 6th, **Ik** the 11th, and **Manik** the 16th, and in the years when **Caban** is the 1st, **Ik** will be the 6th, **Manik** the 11th, and **Eb** the 16th, it is clear that any one of this group which begins the year may occupy also three other positions in the divisions of the year, these positions being 5 days distant from each other. Consequently, it follows that **Akbal, Lamat, Ben,** and **Eznab** in Table V, the names which occupy the second positions in the divisions of the year, will fill the 7th, 12th, and 17th positions as well. Similarly **Kan, Muluc, Ix,** and **Cauac** will fill the 3d, 8th, 13th, and 18th positions, and so on. This enables us to formulate a third—

Rule. The 20 day-names are divided into five groups of four names each, any name in any group being five days distant from the name next preceding it in the same group, and furthermore, the names of any one group will occupy four different positions in the divisions of successive years, these positions being five days apart in each case. This is expressed in Table VI, in which these groups are shown as well as the positions in the divisions of the years which the names of each group may occupy. A comparison with Table V will demonstrate that this arrangement is inevitable.

TABLE VI. POSITIONS OF DAYS IN DIVISIONS OF MAYA YEAR

Positions held by days	1st, 6th, 11th, 16th	2d, 7th, 12th, 17th	3d, 8th, 13th, 18th	4th, 9th, 14th, 19th	5th, 10th, 15th, 20th
Names of days in each group	Ik Manik Eb Caban	Akbal Lamat Ben Eznab	Kan Muluc Ix Cauac	Chicchan Oc Men Ahau	Cimi Chuen Cib Imix

But we have seen on page 47 and in Table IV that the Maya did not designate the first days of the several divisions of the years according to our system. It was shown there that the first day of **Pop** was not written **1 Pop**, but **0 Pop**, and similarly the second day of **Pop** was written not **2 Pop**, but **1 Pop**, and the last day, not **20 Pop**, but **19 Pop**. Consequently, before we can use the names in Table VI as the Maya used them, we must make this shift, keeping in mind, however, that **Ik, Manik, Eb,** and **Caban** (the only four of the twenty names which could begin the year and which were written **0 Pop, 5 Pop, 10 Pop,** or **15 Pop**) would be written in our notation **1st Pop, 6th Pop, 11th Pop,** and **16th Pop,** respectively. This difference, as has been previously explained, results from the Maya method of counting time by elapsed periods.

Table VII shows the positions of the days in the divisions of the year according to the Maya conception, that is, with the shift in the month coefficient made necessary by this practice of recording their days as elapsed time.

The student will find Table VII very useful in deciphering the texts, since it shows at a glance the only positions which any given day can occupy in the divisions of the year. Therefore when the sign for a day has been recognized in the texts, from Table VII can be ascertained the only four positions which this day can hold in the month, thus reducing the number of possible month coefficients for which search need be made, from twenty to four.

TABLE VII. POSITIONS OF DAYS IN DIVISIONS OF MAYA YEAR
ACCORDING TO MAYA NOTATION

Positions held by days expressed in Maya notation.	0, 5, 10, 15	1, 6, 11, 16	2, 7, 12, 17	3, 8, 13, 18	4, 9, 14, 19
Names of days in each group	Ik Manik Eb Caban	Akbal Lamat Ben Eznab	Kan Muluc Ix Cauac	Chicchan Oc Men Ahau	Cimi Chuen Cib Imix

Now let us summarize the points which we have successively established as resulting from the combination of the tonalamatl and haab, remembering always that as yet we have been dealing only with

the name parts of the days and not their complete designations. Bearing
this in mind, we may state the following facts concerning the 20 day-
names and their positions in the divisions of the year:

1. The Maya year and its several divisions could begin only with
one of these four day-names: **Ik, Manik, Eb,** and **Caban.**

2. Consequently, any particular position in the divisions of the
year could be occupied only by one of four day-names.

3. Consequently, every fifth year any particular day-name returned
to the same position in the divisions of the year.

4. Consequently, any particular day-name could occupy only one
of four positions in the divisions of the year, each of which it held in
successive years, returning to the same position every fifth year.

5. Consequently, the twenty day-names were divided into five
groups of four day-names each, any day-name of any group being
five days distant from the day-name of the same group next preceding it.

6. Finally, in any given year any particular day-name occupied
the same relative position throughout the divisions of that year.

Up to this point, however, as above stated, we have not been dealing with the complete designations of the Maya days, but only their
name parts or name glyphs, the positions of which in the several
divisions of the year we have ascertained.

It now remains to join the tonalamatl, which gives the complete
names of the 260 Maya days, to the haab, which gives the positions
of the days in the divisions of the year, in such a way that any one
of the days whose name-part is **Ik, Manik, Eb,** or **Caban** shall occupy
the first position of the first division of the year; that is, **0 Pop,**
or, as we should write it, the first day of **Pop.** It matters little
which one of these four name parts we choose first, since in four
years each one of them in succession will have appeared in the
position **0 Pop.**

Perhaps the easiest way to visualize the combination of the tonalamatl and the haab is to conceive these two periods as two cogwheels
revolving in contact with each other. Let us imagine that the first
of these, A (fig. 21), has 260 teeth, or cogs, each one of which is
named after one of the 260 days of the tonalamatl and follows the
sequence shown in plate 5. The second wheel, B (fig. 21), is somewhat larger, having 365 cogs. Each of the spaces or sockets between
these represents one of the 365 positions of the days in the divisions
of the year, beginning with **0 Pop** and ending with **4 Uayeb.** See
Table IV for the positions of the days at the end of one year and the
commencement of the next. Finally, let us imagine that these two
wheels are brought into contact with each other in such a way that
the tooth or cog named **2 Ik** in A shall fit into the socket named

0 Pop in B, after which both wheels start to revolve in the directions indicated by the arrows.

The first day of the year whose beginning is shown at the point of contact of the two wheels in figure 21 is **2 Ik 0 Pop,** that is, the day **2 Ik** which occupies the first position in the month **Pop.** The next day in succession will be **3 Akbal 1 Pop,** the next **4 Kan 2 Pop,** the next **5 Chicchan 3 Pop,** the next **6 Cimi 4 Pop,** and so on. As the wheels revolve in the directions indicated, the days of the tonalamatl succes-sively fall into their appropriate positions in the divisions of the year. Since the number of cogs in A is smaller than the number in B, it is clear that the former will have returned to its starting point, **2 Ik** (that is, made one complete revolution), before the latter will have made one complete revolution; and, further, that when the latter (B) has returned to its starting point, **0 Pop,** the corresponding cog in B will not be **2 Ik,**

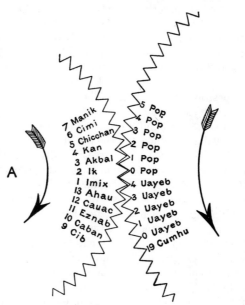

FIG. 21. Diagram showing engagement of tonalamatl wheel of 260 days (A), and haab wheel of 365 positions (B); the combination of the two giving the Calendar Round, or 52-year period.

but another day (**3 Manik**), since by that time the smaller wheel will have progressed 105 cogs, or days, farther, to the cog **3 Manik.**

The question now arises, how many revolutions will each wheel have to make before the day **2 Ik** will return to the position **0 Pop.** The solution of this problem depends on the application of one sequence to another, and the possibilities concerning the numbers or names which stand at the head of the resulting sequence, a subject already discussed on page 52. In the present case the numbers in question, 260 and 365, contain a common factor, therefore our problem falls under the third contingency there presented. Consequently, only certain of the 260 days can occupy the position **0 Pop,** or, in other words, cog **2 Ik** in A will return to the position **0 Pop** in B in fewer than 260 revolutions of A. The actual solution of the problem is a simple question of arithmetic. Since the day **2 Ik** can not return to its original position in A until after 260 days shall have passed, and since the day **0 Pop** can not return to its original position in B until after 365 days shall have passed, it is clear that the day **2 Ik 0 Pop** can not recur until after a number of days shall have passed equal to the least common multiple of these numbers, which is $\frac{260}{5} \times \frac{365}{5} \times 5$, or $52 \times 73 \times 5 = 18,980$ days. But $18,980$ days $= 52 \times 365 = 73 \times 260$; in other words the day **2 Ik 0 Pop** can not recur until after 52 revolutions of B, or 52 years of 365 days each, and 73 revolutions of A, or 73 tonalamatls of 260 days each. The Maya name for this 52-year period is unknown; it has been called the Calendar Round by modern students because it was only after this interval of time had elapsed that any given day could return to the same position in the year. The Aztec name for this period was *xiuhmolpilli* or *toxiuhmolpia*.[1]

The Calendar Round was the real basis of Maya chronology, since its 18,980 dates included all the possible combinations of the 260 days with the 365 positions of the year. Although the Maya developed a much more elaborate system of counting time, wherein any date of the Calendar Round could be fixed with absolute certainty within a period of 374,400 years, this truly remarkable feat was accomplished only by using a sequence of Calendar Rounds, or 52-year periods, in endless repetition from a fixed point of departure.

In the development of their chronological system the Aztec probably never progressed beyond the Calendar Round. At least no greater period of time than the round of 52 years has been found in their texts. The failure of the Aztec to develop some device which would distinguish any given day in one Calendar Round from a day of the same name in another has led to hopeless confusion in regard to various events of their history. Since the same date occurred at intervals of every 52 years, it is often difficult to determine the particular Calendar Round to which any given date with its corresponding event is to be referred; consequently, the true sequence of events in Aztec history still remains uncertain.

Professor Seler says in this connection:[2]

Anyone who has ever taken the trouble to collect the dates in old Mexican history from the various sources must speedily have discovered that the chronology is very much awry, that it is almost hopeless to look for an exact chronology. The date of the fall of Mexico is definitely fixed according to both the Indian and the Christian chronology . . . but in regard to all that precedes this date, even to events tolerably near the time of the Spanish conquest, the statements differ widely.

---

[1] The meanings of these words in Nahuatl, the language spoken by the Aztec, are "year bundle" and "our years will be bound," respectively. These doubtless refer to the fact that at the expiration of this period the Aztec calendar had made one complete round; that is, the years were bound up and commenced anew.

[2] *Bulletin 28*, p. 330.

Such confusion indeed is only to be expected from a system of counting time and recording events which was so loose as to permit the occurrence of the same date twice, or even thrice, within the span of a single life; and when a system so inexact was used to regulate the lapse of any considerable number of years, the possibilities for error and misunderstanding are infinite. Thus it was with Aztec chronology.

On the other hand, by conceiving the Calendar Rounds to be in endless repetition from a fixed point of departure, and measuring time by an accurate system, the Maya were able to secure precision in dating their events which is not surpassed even by our own system of counting time.

The glyph which stood for the Calendar Round has not been determined with any degree of certainty. Mr. Goodman believes the form shown in figure 22, *a*, to be the sign for this period, while Professor Förstemann is equally sure that the form represented by *b* of this figure expressed the same idea. This difference of opinion between two authorities so eminent well illustrates the pre-

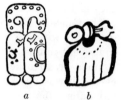

a   b

FIG. 22. Signs for the Calendar Round: *a*, According to Goodman; *b*, according to Förstemann.

vailing doubt as to just what glyph actually represented the 52-year period among the Maya. The sign in figure 22, *a*, as the writer will endeavor to show later, is in all probability the sign for the great cycle.

As will be seen in the discussion of the Long Count, the Maya, although they conceived time to be an endless succession of Calendar Rounds, did not reckon its passage by the lapse of successive Calendar Rounds; consequently, the need for a distinctive glyph which should represent this period was not acute. The contribution of the Calendar Round to Maya chronology was its 18,980 dates, and the glyphs which composed these are found repeatedly in both the codices and the inscriptions (see figs. 16, 17, 19, 20). No signs have been found as yet, however, for either the haab or the tonalamatl, probably because, like the Calendar Round, these periods were not used as units in recording long stretches of time.

It will greatly aid the student in his comprehension of the discussion to follow if he will constantly bear in mind the fact that one Calendar Round followed another without interruption or the interpolation of a single day; and further, that the Calendar Round may be likened to a large cogwheel having 18,980 teeth, each one of which represented one of the dates of this period, and that this wheel revolved forever, each cog passing a fixed point once every 52 years.

THE LONG COUNT

We have seen:

1. How the Maya distinguished 1 day from the 259 others in the tonalamatl;

2. How they distinguished the position of 1 day from the 364 others in the haab, or year; and, finally,

3. How by combining (1) and (2) they distinguished 1 day from the other 18,979 of the Calendar Round.

It remains to explain how the Maya insured absolute accuracy in fixing a day within a period of 374,400 years, as stated above, or how they distinguished 1 day from 136,655,999 others.

The Calendar Round, as we have seen, determined the position of a given day within a period of only 52 years. Consequently, in order to prevent confusion of days of the same name in successive Calendar Rounds or, in other words, to secure absolute accuracy in dating events, it was necessary to use additional data in the description of any date.

In nearly all systems of chronology that presume to deal with really long periods the reckoning of years proceeds from fixed starting points. Thus in Christian chronology the starting point is the Birth of Christ, and our years are reckoned as B. C. or A. D. according as they precede or follow this event. The Greeks reckoned time from the earliest Olympic Festival of which the winner's name was known, that is, the games held in 776 B. C., which were won by a certain Coroebus. The Romans took as their starting point the supposed date of the foundation of Rome, 753 B. C. The Babylonians counted time as beginning with the Era of Nabonassar, 747 B. C. The death of Alexander the Great, in 325 B. C., ushered in the Era of Alexander. With the occupation of Babylon in 311 B. C. by Seleucus Nicator began the so-called Era of Seleucidæ. The conquest of Spain by Augustus Cæsar in 38 B. C. marked the beginning of a chronology which endured for more than fourteen centuries. The Mohammedans selected as their starting point the flight of their prophet Mohammed from Mecca in 622 A. D., and events in this chronology are described as having occurred so many years after the Hegira (The Flight). The Persian Era began with the date 632 A. D., in which year Yezdegird III ascended the throne of Persia.

It will be noted that each of the above-named systems of chronology has for its starting point some actual historic event, the occurrence, if not the date of which, is indubitable. Some chronologies, however, commence with an event of an altogether different character, the date of which from its very nature must always remain hypothetical. In this class should be mentioned such chronologies as reckon time from the Creation of the World. For example, the Era of Constantinople, the chronological system used in the Greek Church, commences with that event, supposed to have occurred in 5509 B. C. The Jews reckoned the same event as having taken place in 3761 B. C. and begin the counting of time from this point. A more familiar chronology, having for its starting point the Creation of the World, is that of Archbishop Usher, in the Old Testament, which assigns this event to the year 4004 B. C.

In common with these other civilized peoples of antiquity the ancient Maya had realized in the development of their chronological system the need for a fixed starting point, from which all subsequent events could be reckoned, and for this purpose they selected one of the dates of their Calendar Round. This was a certain date, **4 Ahau 8 Cumhu**,[1] that is, a day named **4 Ahau**, which occupied the 9th position in the month **Cumhu**, the next to last division of the Maya year (see Table III).

While the nature of the event which took place on this date [2] is unknown, its selection as the point from which time was subsequently reckoned alone indicates that it must have been of exceedingly great importance to the native mind. In attempting to approximate its real character, however, we are not without some assistance from the codices and the inscriptions. For instance, it is clear that all Maya dates which it is possible to regard as contemporaneous [3] refer to a time fully 3,000 years later than the starting point (**4 Ahau 8 Cumhu**) from which each is reckoned. In other words, Maya history is a blank for more than 3,000 years after the initial date of the Maya chronological system, during which time no events were recorded.

This interesting condition strongly suggests that the starting point of Maya chronology was not an actual historical event, as the founding of Rome, the death of Alexander, the birth of Christ, or the flight of Mohammed from Mecca, but that on the contrary it was a purely hypothetical occurrence, as the Creation of the World or the birth of the gods; and further, that the date **4 Ahau 8 Cumhu** was not chosen as the starting point until long after the time it designates. This, or some similar assumption, is necessary to account satisfactorily for the observed facts:

1. That, as stated, after the starting point of Maya chronology there is a silence of more than 3,000 years, unbroken by a single contemporaneous record, and

---

[1] All Initial Series now known, with the exception of two, have the date **4 Ahau 8 Cumhu** as their common point of departure. The two exceptions, the Initial Series on the east side of Stela C at Quirigua and the one on the tablet in the Temple of the Cross at Palenque, proceed from the date **4 Ahau 8 Zotz**— more than 5,000 years in advance of the starting point just named. The writer has no suggestions to offer in explanation of these two dates other than that he believes they refer to some mythological event. For instance, in the belief of the Maya the gods may have been born on the day **4 Ahau 8 Zotz**, and 5,000 years later approximately on **4 Ahau 8 Cumhu** the world, including mankind, may have been created.

[2] Some writers have called the date **4 Ahau 8 Cumhu**, the normal date, probably because it is the standard date from which practically all Maya calculations proceed. The writer has not followed this practice, however.

[3] That is, dates which signified present time when they were recorded.

2. That after this long period had elapsed all the dated monuments[1] had their origin in the comparatively short period of four centuries.

Consequently, it is safe to conclude that no matter what the Maya' may have believed took place on this date **4 Ahau 8 Cumhu**, in reality when this day was present time they had not developed their distinctive civilization or even achieved a social organization.

It is clear from the foregoing that in addition to the Calendar Round, the Maya made use of a fixed starting point in describing their dates. The next question is, Did they record the lapse of more than 3,000 years simply by using so unwieldy a unit as the 52-year period or its multiples? A numerical system based on 52 as its primary unit immediately gives rise to exceedingly awkward numbers for its higher terms; that is, 52, 104, 156, 208, 260, 312, etc. Indeed, the expression of really large numbers in terms of 52 involves the use of comparatively large multipliers and hence of more or less intricate multiplications, since the unit of progression is not decimal or even a multiple thereof. The Maya were far too clever mathematicians to have been satisfied with a numerical system which employed units so inconvenient as 52 or its multiples, and which involved processes so clumsy, and we may therefore dismiss the possibility of its use without further consideration.

In order to keep an accurate account of the large numbers used in recording dates more than 3,000 years distant from the starting point, a numerical system was necessary whose terms could be easily handled, like the units, tens, hundreds, and thousands of our own decimal system. Whether the desire to measure accurately the passage of time actually gave rise to their numerical system, or vice versa, is not known, but the fact remains that the several periods of Maya chronology (except the tonalamatl, haab, and Calendar Round, previously discussed) are the exact terms of a vigesimal system of numeration, with but a single exception. (See Table VIII.)

TABLE VIII. THE MAYA TIME-PERIODS

	1 kin	=	1 day
20 kins	=1 uinal	=	20 days
18 uinals	=1 tun	=	360 days
20 tuns	=1 katun	=	7,200 days
20 katuns	=1 cycle	=	144,000 days
20^2 cycles	=1 great	cycle	=2,880,000 days

Table VIII shows the several periods of Maya chronology by means of which the passage of time was measured. All are the exact terms of a vigesimal system of numeration, except in the 2d place (uinals),

---

[1] This statement does not take account of the Tuxtla Statuette and the Holactun Initial Series, which extend the range of the dated monuments to ten centuries.

[2] For the discussion of the number of cycles in a great cycle, a question concerning which there are two different opinions, see pp. 107 et seq.

in which 18 units instead of 20 make 1 unit of the 3d place, or order next higher (tuns). The break in the regularity of the vigesimal progression in the 3d place was due probably to the desire to bring the unit of this order (the tun) into agreement with the solar year of 365 days, the number 360 being much closer to 365 than 400, the third term of a constant vigesimal progression. We have seen on page 45 that the 18 uinals of the haab were equivalent to 360 days or kins, precisely the number contained in the third term of the above table, the tun. The fact that the haab, or solar year, was composed of 5 days more than the tun, thus causing a discrepancy of 5 days as compared with the third place of the chronological system, may have given to these 5 closing days of the haab—that is, the xma kaba kin—the unlucky character they were reputed to possess.

The periods were numbered from 0 to 19, inclusive, 20 units of any order (except the 2d) always appearing as 1 unit of the order next higher. For example, a number involving the use of 20 kins was written 1 uinal instead.

We are now in possession of all the different factors which the Maya utilized in recording their dates and in counting time:

1. The names of their dates, of which there could be only 18,980 (the number of dates in the Calendar Round).

2. The date, or starting point, **4 Ahau 8 Cumhu**, from which time was reckoned.

3. The counters, that is, the units, used in measuring the passage of time.

It remains to explain how these factors were combined to express the various dates of Maya chronology.

INITIAL SERIES

The usual manner in which dates are written in both the codices and the inscriptions is as follows: First, there is set down a number composed of five periods, that is, a certain number of cycles, katuns, tuns, uinals, and kins, which generally aggregate between 1,300,000 and 1,500,000 days; and this number is followed by one of the 18,980 dates of the Calendar Round. As we shall see in the next chapter, if this large number of days expressed as above be counted forward from the fixed starting point of Maya chronology, **4 Ahau 8 Cumhu**, the date invariably [1] reached will be found to be the date written at the end of the long number. This method of dating has been called the *Initial Series*, because when inscribed on a monument it invariably stands *at the head* of the inscription.

The student will better comprehend this Initial-series method of dating if he will imagine the Calendar Round represented by a large cogwheel A, figure 23, having 18,980 teeth, each one of which is

---

[1] There are only two known exceptions to this statement, namely, the Initial Series on the Temple of the Cross at Palenque and that on the east side of Stela C at Quirigua, already noted.

named after one of the dates of the calendar. Furthermore, let him suppose that the arrow B in the same figure points to the tooth, or cog, named **4 Ahau 8 Cumhu**; and finally that from this as its original position the wheel commences to revolve in the direction indicated by the arrow in A.

It is clear that after one complete revolution of A, 18,980 days will have passed the starting point B, and that after two revolutions 37,960 days will have passed, and after three, 56,940, and so on. Indeed, it is only a question of the number of revolutions of A until as many as 1,500,000, or any number of days in fact, will have passed the starting point B, or, in other words, will have elapsed since the initial date, **4 Ahau 8 Cumhu**. This is actually what happened according to the Maya conception of time.

For example, let us imagine that a certain Initial Series expresses in terms of cycles, katuns, tuns, uinals, and kins, the number 1,461,463, and that the date recorded by this number of days is **7 Akbal 11 Cumhu**.

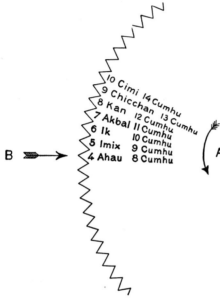

Fig. 23. Diagram showing section of Calendar-round wheel.

Referring to figure 23, it is evident that 77 revolutions of the cogwheel A, that is, 77 Calendar Rounds, will use up 1,461,460 of the 1,461,463 days, since $77 \times 18,980 = 1,461,460$. Consequently, when 77 Calendar Rounds shall have passed we shall still have left 3 days $(1,461,463 - 1,461,460 = 3)$, which must be carried forward into the next Calendar Round. The 1,461,461st day will be **5 Imix 9 Cumhu**, that is, the day following **4 Ahau 8 Cumhu** (see fig. 23); the 1,461,462d day will be **6 Ik 10 Cumhu**, and the 1,461,463d day, the last of the days in our Initial Series, **7 Akbal 11 Cumhu**, the date recorded. Examples of this method of dating (by Initial Series) will be given in Chapter V, where this subject will be considered in greater detail.

THE INTRODUCING GLYPH

In the inscriptions an Initial Series is invariably preceded by the so-called "introducing glyph," the Maya name for which is unknown.

Several examples of this glyph are shown in figure 24.   This sign is composed of four constant elements:

1. The trinal superfix.
2. The pair of comblike lateral appendages.
3. The tun sign (see fig. 29, *a*, *b*).
4. The trinal subfix.

In addition to these four constant elements there is one variable element which is always found between the pair of comblike lateral appendages.   In figure 24, *a*, *b*, *e*, this is a grotesque head; in *c*, a natural head; and in *d*, one of the 20 day-signs, **Ik**.   This element varies greatly throughout the inscriptions, and, judging from its central position in the "introducing glyph" (itself the most prominent character in every inscription in which it occurs), it must have had an exceedingly important meaning.[1]   A variant of the comblike appendages is shown in figure 24, *c*, *e*, in which these elements are

a   *b*   *c*

d   *e*   *f*

FIG. 24.   Initial-series "introducing glyph."

replaced by a pair of fishes.   However, in such cases, all of which occur at Copan, the treatment of the fins and tail of the fish strongly suggests the elements they replace, and it is not improbable, therefore, that the comblike appendages of the "introducing glyph" are nothing more nor less than conventionalized fish fins or tails; in other words, that they are a kind of glyphic synecdoche in which a part (the fin) stands for the whole (the fish).   That the original form of this element was the fish and not its conventionalized fin (*) seems to be indicated by several facts: (1) On Stela D at Copan, where * only full-figure glyphs are presented,[2] the two comblike appendages of the "introducing glyph" appear unmistakably as two fishes.   (2) In some of the earliest stelæ at Copan, as Stelæ 15 and P, while these elements are not fish forms, a head (fish?) appears with the conventionalized comb element in each case.   The writer believes the interpretation of this phenomenon to be, that at the early epoch in which

---

[1] Mr. Bowditch (1910: App. VIII, 310–18) discusses the possible meanings of this element.

[2] For explanation of the term "full-figure glyphs," see p. 67.

Stelæ 15 and P were erected the conventionalization of the element in question had not been entirely accomplished, and that the head was added to indicate the form from which the element was derived. (3) If the fish was the original form of the comblike element in the "introducing glyph," it was also the original form of the same element in the katun glyph. (Compare the comb elements (†) in figures 27, a, b, e, and 24, a, b, d with each other.) If this is true, a natural explanation for the use of the fish in the katun sign lies near at hand. As previously explained on page 28, the comblike element stands for the sound ca (c hard); while kal in Maya means 20. Also the element (**) stands for the sound tun. Therefore catun or katun means 20 tuns. But the Maya word for "fish," cay (c hard) is also a close phonetic approximation of the sound ca or kal. Consequently, the fish sign may have been the original element in the katun glyph, which expressed the concept 20, and which the conventionalization of glyphic forms gradually reduced to the element (††) without destroying, however, its phonetic value.

Without pressing this point further, it seems not unlikely that the comblike elements in the katun glyph, as well as in the "introducing glyph," may well have been derived from the fish sign.

Turning to the codices, it must be admitted that in spite of the fact that many Initial Series are found therein, the "introducing glyph" has not as yet been positively identified. It is possible, however, that the sign shown in figure 24, f, may be a form of the "introducing glyph"; at least it precedes an Initial Series in four places in the Dresden Codex (see pl. 32). It is composed of the trinal superfix and a conventionalized fish (?).

Mr. Goodman calls this glyph (fig. 24, a–e) the sign for the great cycle or unit of the 6th place (see Table VIII). He bases this identification on the fact that in the codices units of the 6th place stand immediately above [1] units of the 5th place (cycles), and consequently since this glyph stands immediately above the units of the 5th place in the inscriptions it must stand for the units of the 6th place. While admitting that the analogy here is close, the writer nevertheless is inclined to reject Mr. Goodman's identification on the following grounds: (1) This glyph *never* occurs with a numerical coefficient, while units of all the other orders—that is, cycles, katuns, tuns, uinals, and kins *are never* without them. (2) Units of the 6th order in the codices invariably have a numerical coefficient, as do all the other orders. (3) In the only three places in the inscriptions [2] in which six periods are seemingly recorded, though not as Initial Series, the 6th period has a numerical coefficient just as have the other five, and,

---

[1] See the discussion of Serpent numbers in Chapter VI.

[2] These three inscriptions are found on Stela N, west side, at Copan, the tablet of the Temple of the Inscriptions at Palenque, and Stela 10 at Tikal. For the discussion of these inscriptions, see pp. 114–127.

moreover, the glyph in the 6th position is unlike the forms in figure 24. (4) Five periods, not six, in every Initial Series express the distance from the starting point, **4 Ahau 8 Cumhu**, to the date recorded at the end of the long numbers.

It is probable that when the meaning of the "introducing glyph" has been determined it will be found to be quite apart from the numerical side of the Initial Series, at least in so far as the distance of the terminal date from the starting point, **4 Ahau 8 Cumhu**, is concerned.

While an Initial Series in the inscriptions, as has been previously explained, is invariably preceded by an "introducing glyph," the opposite does not always obtain. Some of the very earliest monuments at Copan, notably Stelæ 15, 7, and P, have "introducing glyphs" inscribed on two or three of their four sides, although but one Initial Series is recorded on each of these monuments. Examples of this use of the "introducing glyph," that is, other than as standing at the head of an Initial Series, are confined to a few of the earliest monuments at Copan, and are so rare that the beginner will do well to disregard them altogether and to follow this general rule: That in the inscriptions a glyph of the form shown in figure 24, *a–e*, will invariably be followed by an Initial Series.

Having reached the conclusion that the introducing glyph was not a sign for the period of the 6th order, let us next examine the signs for the remaining orders or periods of the chronological system (cycles, katuns, tuns, uinals, and kins), constantly bearing in mind that these five periods alone express the long numbers of an Initial Series.[1]

Each of the above periods has two entirely different glyphs which may express it. These have been called (1) The normal form; (2) The head variant. In the inscriptions examples of both these classes occur side by side in the same Initial Series, seemingly according to no fixed rule, some periods being expressed by their normal forms and others by their head variants. In the codices, on the other hand, no head-variant period glyphs have yet been identified, and although the normal forms of the period glyphs have been found, they do not occur as units in Initial Series.

As head variants also should be classified the so-called "full-figure glyphs," in which the periods given in Table VIII are represented by full figures instead of by heads. In these forms, however, only the heads of the figures are essential, since they alone present the determining characteristics, by means of which in each case identification is possible. Moreover, the head part of any full-figure variant is characterized by precisely the same essential elements as the corre-

---

[1] The discussion of glyphs which may represent the great cycle or period of the 6th order will be presented on pp. 114–127 in connection with the discussion of numbers having six or more orders of units.

sponding head variant for the same period, or in other words, the addition of the body parts in full-figure glyphs in no way influences or changes their meanings. For this reason head-variant and full-figure forms have been treated together. These full-figure glyphs are exceedingly rare, having been found only in five Initial Series throughout the Maya area: (1) On Stela D at Copan; (2) on Zoömorph B at Quirigua; (3) on east side Stela D at Quirigua; (4) on west side Stela D at Quirigua; (5) on Hieroglyphic Stairway at Copan. A few full-figure glyphs have been found also on an oblong altar at Copan, though not as parts of an Initial Series, and on Stela 15 as a period glyph of an Initial Series.

THE CYCLE GLYPH

The Maya name for the period of the 5th order in Table VIII is unknown. It has been called "the cycle," however, by Maya stu-

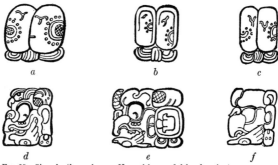

FIG. 25. Signs for the cycle: a–c, Normal forms; d–f, head variants.

dents, and in default of its true designation, this name has been generally adopted. The normal form of the cycle glyph is shown in figure 25, *a*, *b*, *c*. It is composed of an element which appears twice over a knotted support. The repeated element occurs also in the signs for the months **Chen, Yax, Zac,** and **Ceh** (see figs. 19, *o–v*, 20, *l–p*). This has been called the *Cauac* element because it is similar to the sign for the day **Cauac** in the codices (fig. 17, *b′*), though on rather inadequate grounds the writer is inclined to believe. The head variant of the cycle glyph is shown in figure 25, *d–f*. The essential characteristic of this grotesque head with its long beak is the hand element (*) , which forms the lower jaw, though in a *very few instances* even * this is absent. In the full-figure forms this same head is joined to the body of a bird (see fig. 26). The bird intended is clearly a parrot, the feet, claws, and beak being portrayed in a very realistic manner. No glyph for the cycle has yet been found in the codices.

THE KATUN GLYPH

The period of the 4th place or order was called by the Maya the *katun;* that is to say, 20 tuns, since it contained 20 units of the 3d

order (see Table VIII). The normal form of the katun glyph is
shown in figure 27, *a–d*. It is composed of the normal form of the tun
sign (fig. 29, *a, b*) surmounted by the pair of comb-
like appendages, which we have elsewhere seen meant
20, and which were probably derived from the representation of a fish. The whole glyph thus graphically portrays the concept 20 tuns, which according
to Table VIII is equal to 1 katun. The normal
form of the katun glyph in the codices (fig. 27, *c, d*)
is identical with the normal form in the inscriptions
(fig. 27, *a, b*). Several head variants are found. The
most easily recognized, though not the most common, is shown in figure 27, *e*, in which the superfix
is the same as in the normal form; that is, the ele-

FIG. 26. Full-figure variant of cycle sign.

ment (†), which probably signifies 20 in this connection. To
be logical, therefore, the head element should be the same
as the head variant of the tun glyph, but this is not the case (see fig.
29, *e–h*). When this superfix is present, the identification of the head
variant of the katun glyph is an easy matter, but when it is absent

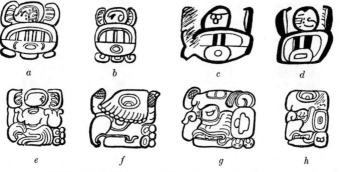

FIG. 27. Signs for the katun: *a–d*, Normal forms; *e–h*, head variants.

it is difficult to fix on any essential characteristic. The general
shape of the head is like the head variant of the cycle glyph. Perhaps
the oval (**) in the top of the head in figure 27, *f–h*, and
the small curling fang (††) represented as protruding from
the back part of the mouth are as constant as any of the other
elements. The head of the full-figure variant in figure 28 presents
the same lack of essential characteristics as the head variant, though
in this form the small curling fang is also found. Again, the body
attached to this head is that of a bird which has been identified as
an eagle.

THE TUN GLYPH

The period of the 3d place or order was called by the Maya the *tun*, which means "stone," possibly because a stone was set up every 360 days or each tun or some multiple thereof. Com-

pare so-called hotun or katun stones described on page 34. The normal sign for the tun in the inscriptions (see fig. 29, *a*, *b*) is identical with the form found in the codices (see fig. 29, *c*). The head variant, which bears a general resemblance to the head variant for

FIG. 28. Full-figure variant of katun sign.

the cycle and katun, has several forms. The one most readily recognized, because it has the normal sign for its superfix, is shown in figure 29, *d*, *e*. The determining characteristic of the head variant of the tun glyph, however, is the fleshless lower jaw (‡), as shown in figure 29 *f*, *g*, though even this is lacking in some few cases. The form shown in figure 29, *h*, is found at Palenque, where it

FIG. 29.   Signs for the tun: *a–d*, Normal forms; *e–h*, head variants.

seems to represent the tun period in several places. The head of the full-figure form (fig. 30) has the same fleshless lower jaw for its essential characteristic as the head-variant forms in figure 29. The body joined to this head is again that of a bird the identity of which has not yet been determined.

THE UINAL GLYPH

The period occupying the 2d place was called by the Maya *uinal* or *u*. This latter word means also " the moon " in Maya, and the fact that the moon is visible

FIG. 30. Full-figure variant of tun sign.

for just about 20 days in each lunation may account for the application of its name to the 20-day period.

The normal form of the uinal glyph in the inscriptions (see fig. 31, *a*, *b*) is practically identical with the form in the codices (see fig. 31, *c*).

Sometimes the subfixial element (‡‡) is omitted in the inscrip-
tions, as in figure 31, *a*. The head variant of the uinal glyph (fig.
31, *d–f*) is the most constant of all of the head forms for the various
periods. Its determining characteristic is the large curl emerging from
the back part of the mouth. The sharp-pointed teeth in the upper
jaw are also a fairly constant feature. In very rare cases both of these
elements are wanting. In
such cases the glyph seems
to be without determining
characteristics. The ani-
mal represented in the full-
figure variants of the uinal
is that of a frog (fig. 32,)
the head of which presents
precisely the same char-
acteristics as the head variants of the uinal, just described. That the head
variant of the uinal-period
glyph was originally de-

FIG. 31. Signs for the uinal: *a–c*, Normal forms; *d–f*, head
variants.

rived from the representation of a frog can hardly be denied in the
face of such striking confirmatory evidence as that afforded by the
full-figure form of the uinal in figure 33. Here the spotted body,
flattened head, prominent mouth, and bulging eyes of the frog are so

FIG. 32. Full-figure variant of uinal sign
on Zoömorph B, Quirigua.

realistically portrayed that there is no
doubt as to the identity of the figure intended. Mr. Bowditch (1910: p. 257) has
pointed out in this connection an interesting phonetic coincidence, which can
hardly be other than intentional. The
Maya word for frog is *uo*, which is a fairly close phonetic approximation of *u*, the Maya word for "moon" or "month." Consequently,
the Maya may have selected the figure of the frog on phonetic grounds
to represent their 20-day period. If this point could be
established it would indicate an unmistakable use of the
rebus form of writing employed by the Aztec. That is,
the figure of a frog in the uinal-period glyph would not
recall the object which it pictures, but the sound of that
object's name, *uo*, approximating the sound of *u*, which
in turn expressed the intended idea, namely, the 20-day
period. Mr. Bowditch has suggested also that the grotesque birds which stand for the cycle, katun, and tun periods in
these full-figure forms may also have been chosen because of the
phonetic similarity of their names to the names of these periods.

FIG. 33. Full-
figure variant
of uinal sign
on Stela D, Co-
pan.

THE KIN GLYPH

The period of the 1st, or lowest, order was called by the Maya *kin*, which meant the "sun" and by association the "day." The kin, as has been explained, was the primary unit used by the Maya in counting time. The normal form of this period glyph in the inscriptions is shown in figure 34, *a*, which is practically identical with the form in the codices (fig. 34, *b*). In addition to the normal form of the kin sign, however, there are several other forms representing this period which can not be classified either as head variants or full-figure variants, as in figure 34, *c*, for example, which bears no resemblance whatever to the normal form of the kin sign. It is difficult to understand

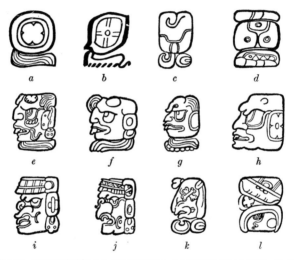

FIG. 34.   Signs for the kin: *a*, *b*, Normal forms; *c*, *d*, miscellaneous; *e–k*, head variants.

how two characters as dissimilar as those shown in *a* and *c*, figure 34, could ever be used to express the same idea, particularly since there seems to be no element common to both. Indeed, so dissimilar are they that one is almost forced to believe that they were derived from two entirely distinct glyphs. Still another and very unusual sign for the kin is shown in figure 34, *d;* indeed, the writer recalls but two places where it occurs: Stela 1 at Piedras Negras, and Stela C (north side) at Quirigua. It is composed of the normal form of the sign for the day **Ahau** (fig. 16, *e'*) inverted and a subfixial element which varies in each of the two cases. These variants (fig. 34, *c*, *d*) are found only in the inscriptions. The head variants of the kin period differ from each other as much as the various normal forms above given. The form shown in figure 34, *e*, may be readily recognized by its subfixial element (*) and the element (†), both of which appear in the normal form, figure 34, *a*.   In some cases, as in figure 34, *f–h*, this variant also has the square irid and the crooked, snag-like teeth projecting from the front of the mouth. Again, any one of these features, or even all, may be lacking.   Another and usually more grotesque type of head (fig. 34, *i*, *j*) has as its essential element the banded head-dress.   A very unusual head variant is that shown in figure 34, *k*, the essential characteristic of which seems to be the crossbones in the eye.   Mr. Bow-ditch has included also in his list of kin signs the form shown in figure 34, *l*, from an inscription at Tikal.   While this glyph in fact does stand between two dates which are separated by one day from each other, that is, **6 Eb 0 Pop** and **7 Ben 1 Pop**, the

FIG. 35.   Full-figure variant of kin sign.

writer believes, nevertheless, that only the element (‡)—an essential part of the normal form for the kin—here represents the period one day, and that the larger characters above and below have other meanings.   In the full-figure variants of the kin sign the figure portrayed is that of a human being (fig. 35), the head of which is similar to the one in figure 34, *i*, *j*, having the same banded head-dress.[1]

This concludes the presentation of the various forms which stand for the several periods of Table VIII.   After an exhaustive study of these as found in Maya texts the writer has reached the following generalizations concerning them:

1. *Prevalence.* The periods in Initial Series are expressed far more frequently by head variants than by normal forms.   The preponderance of the former over the latter in all Initial Series known is in the proportion of about 80 per cent of the total[2] against 12 per cent, the periods in the remaining 8 per cent being expressed by these two forms used side by side.   In other words, four-fifths of all the Initial Series known have their periods expressed by head-variant glyphs.

2. *Antiquity.* Head-variant period glyphs seem to have been used very much earlier than the normal forms.   Indeed, the first use of the former preceded the first use of the latter by about 300 years, while in Initial Series normal-form period glyphs do not occur until nearly 100 years later, or about 400 years after the first use of head variants for the same purpose.

3. *Variation.* Throughout the range of time covered by the Initial Series the normal forms for any given time-period differ but little from one another, all following very closely one fixed type.   Although

---

[1] The figure on Zoömorph B at Quirigua, however, has a normal human head without grotesque characteristics.

[2] The full-figure glyphs are included with the head variants in this proportion.

nearly 200 years apart in point of time, the early form of the tun sign in figure 36, *a*, closely resembles the late form shown in *b* of the same figure, as to its essentials. Or again, although 375 years apart, the early form of the katun sign in figure 36, *c*, is practically identical with the form in figure 36, *d*. Instances of this kind could be multiplied indefinitely, but the foregoing are sufficient to demonstrate that in so far as the normal-form period glyphs are concerned but little variation occurred from first to last. Similarly, it may be said, the head variants for any given period, while differing greatly in appearance at

different epochs, retained, nevertheless, the same essential characteristic throughout. For example, although the uinal sign in figure 36, *e*, precedes the one in figure 36, *f*, by some 800 years, the same essential element —the large mouth curl —appears in both.

a   *b*   *c*   *d*

e   *f*   *g*   *h*

Fig. 36.   Period glyphs, from widely separated sites and of different epochs, showing persistence of essential elements.

Again, although 300 years separate the cycle signs shown in *g* and *h*, figure 36, the essential characteristic of the early form (fig. 36, *g*), the hand, is still retained as the essential part of the late form (*h*).

4. *Derivation.* We have seen that the full-figure glyphs probably show the original life-forms from which the head variants were developed. And since from (2), above, it seems probable that the head variants are older than the so-called normal forms, we may reasonably infer that the full-figure glyphs represent the life-forms whose names the Maya originally applied to their periods, and further that the first signs for those periods were the heads of these life-forms. This develops a contradiction in our nomenclature, for if the forms which we have called head variants are the older signs for the periods and are by far the most prevalent, they should have been called the normal forms and not variants, and vice versa. However, the use of the term "normal forms" is so general that it would be unwise at this time to attempt to introduce any change in nomenclature.

SECONDARY SERIES

The Initial Series method of recording dates, although absolutely accurate,[1] was nevertheless somewhat lengthy, since in order to express a single date by means of it eight distinct glyphs were required, namely: (1) The Introducing glyph; (2) the Cycle glyph;

---

[1] Any system of counting time which describes a date in such a manner that it can not recur, satisfying all the necessary conditions, for 374,400 years, must be regarded as absolutely accurate in so far as the range of human life on this planet is concerned.

(3) the Katun glyph; (4) the Tun glyph; (5) the Uinal glyph; (6) the Kin glyph; (7) the Day glyph; (8) the Month glyph. Moreover, its use in any inscription which contained more than one date would have resulted in needless repetition. For example, if all the dates on any given monument were expressed by Initial Series, every one would show the long distance (more than 3,000 years) which separated it from the common starting point of Maya chronology. It would be just like writing the legal holidays of the current year in this way: February 22d, 1913, A. D., May 30th, 1913, A. D., July 4th, 1913, A. D., December 25th, 1913, A. D.; or in other words, repeating in each case the designation of time elapsed from the starting point of Christian chronology.

The Maya obviated this needless repetition by recording but one Initial Series date on a monument;[1] and from this date as a new point of departure they proceeded to reckon the number of days to the next date recorded; from this date the numbers of days to the next; and so on throughout that inscription. By this device the position of any date in the Long Count (its Initial Series) could be calculated, since it could be referred back to a date, the Initial Series of which was expressed. For example, the terminal day of the Initial Series given on page 64 is **7 Akbal 11 Cumhu,** and its position in the Long Count is fixed by the statement in cycles, katuns, tuns, etc., that 1,461,463 days separate it from the starting point, **4 Ahau 8 Cumhu.** Now let us suppose we have the date **10 Cimi 14 Cumhu,** which is recorded as being 3 days later than the day **7 Akbal 11 Cumhu,**[2] the Initial Series of which is known to be 1,461,463. It is clear that the Initial Series corresponding to the date **10 Cimi 14 Cumhu,** although not actually expressed, will also be known since it must equal 1,461,463 (Initial Series of **7 Akbal 11 Cumhu**) + 3 (distance from **7 Akbal 11 Cumhu** to **10 Cimi 14 Cumhu**), or 1,461,466. Therefore it matters not whether we count three days forward from **7 Akbal 11 Cumhu,** or whether we count 1,461,466 days forward from the starting point of Maya chronology, **4 Ahau 8 Cumhu** since in each case the date reached will be the same, namely, **10 Cimi 14 Cumhu.** The former method, however, was used more frequently than all of the other methods of recording dates combined, since it insured all the accuracy of an Initial Series without repeating for each date so great a number of days.

Thus having one date on a monument the Initial Series of which was expressed, it was possible by referring subsequent dates to it, or to other dates which in turn had been referred to it, to fix accurately

---

[1] There are a very few monuments which have two Initial Series instead of one. So far as the writer knows, only six monuments in the entire Maya area present this feature, namely, Stelæ F, D, E, and A at Quirigua, Stela 17 at Tikal, and Stela 11 at Yaxchilan.

[2] Refer to p. 64 and figure 23. It will be noted that the third tooth (i. e. day) after the one named **7 Akbal 11 Cumhu** is **10 Cimi 14 Cumhu.**

the positions of any number of dates in the Long Count without the use of their corresponding Initial Series. Dates thus recorded are known as "secondary dates," and the periods which express their distances from other dates of known position in the Long Count, as "distance numbers." A secondary date with its corresponding distance number has been designated a Secondary Series. In the example above given the distance number 3 kins and the date **10 Cimi 14 Cumhu** would constitute a Secondary Series.

Here, then, in addition to the Initial Series is a second method, the Secondary Series, by means of which the Maya recorded their dates. The earliest use of a Secondary Series with which the writer is familiar (that on Stela 36 at Piedras Negras) does not occur until some 280 years after the first Initial Series. It seems to have been a later development, probably owing its origin to the desire to express more than one date on a single monument. Usually Secondary Series are to be counted from the dates next preceding them in the inscriptions in which they are found, though occasionally they are counted from other dates which may not even be expressed, and which can be ascertained only by counting backward the distance number from its corresponding terminal date. The accuracy of a Secondary series date depends entirely on the fact that it has been counted from an Initial Series, or at least from another Secondary series date, which in turn has been derived from an Initial Series. If either of these contingencies applies to any Secondary series date, it is as accurate a method of fixing a day in the Long Count as though its corresponding Initial Series were expressed in full. If, on the other hand, a Secondary series date can not be referred ultimately to an Initial Series or to a date the Initial Series of which is known though it may not be expressed, such a Secondary series date becomes only one of the 18,980 dates of the Calendar Round, and will recur at intervals of every 52 years. In other words, its position in the Long Count will be unknown.

Calendar-round Dates

Dates of the character just described may be called Calendar-round dates, since they are accurate only within the Calendar Round, or range of 52 years. While accurate enough for the purpose of distinguishing dates in the course of a single lifetime, this method breaks down when used to express dates covering a long period. Witness the chaotic condition of Aztec chronology. The Maya seem to have realized the limitations of this method of dating and did not employ it extensively. It was used chiefly at Yaxchilan on the Usamacintla River, and for this reason the chronology of that city is very much awry, and it is difficult to assign its various dates to their proper positions in the Long Count.

PERIOD-ENDING DATES

The Maya made use of still another method of dating, which, although not so exact as the Initial Series or the Secondary Series, is, on the other hand, far more accurate than Calendar round dating. In this method a date was described as being at the end of some particular period in the Long Count; that is, closing a certain cycle, katun, or tun.[1] It is clear also that in this method only the name **Ahau** out of the 20 given in Table I can be recorded, since it alone can stand at the end of periods higher than the kin. This is true, since:

1. The higher periods, as the uinal, tun, katun, and cycle are exactly divisible by 20 in every case (see Table VIII), and—

2. They are all counted from a day, **Ahau**, that is, **4 Ahau 8 Cumhu.** Consequently, all the periods of the Long Count, except the kin or primary unit, end with days the name parts of which are the sign **Ahau.**

This method of recording dates always involves the use of at least two factors, and usually three:

1. A particular period of the Long Count, as Cycle 9, or Katun 14, etc.

2. The date which ends the particular period recorded, as **8 Ahau 13 Ceh,** or **6 Ahau 13 Muan,** the closing dates respectively of Cycle 9 and Katun 14 of Cycle 9; and

3. A glyph or element which means "ending" or "is ended," or which indicates at least that the period to which it is attached has come to its close.

The first two of these factors are absolutely essential to this method of dating, while the third, the so-called "ending sign," is usually, though not invariably, present. The order in which these factors are usually found is first the date composed of the day glyph and month glyph, next the "ending sign," and last the glyph of the period whose closing day has just been recorded. Very rarely the period glyph and its ending sign precede the date.

The ending glyph has three distinct variants: (1) the element shown as the prefix or superfix in figure 37, *a–h, t,* all of which are forms of the same variant; (2) the flattened grotesque head appearing either as the prefix or superfix in *i, r, u, v* of the same figure; and (3) the hand, which appears as the main element in the forms shown in figure 37, *j–q*. The two first of these never stand by themselves but always modify some other sign. The first (fig. 37, *a–h, t*) is always attached to the sign of the period whose end is recorded either as a

---

[1] This method of dating does not seem to have been used with either uinal or kin period endings, probably because of the comparative frequency with which any given date might occur at the end of either of these two periods.

superfix (see fig. 37, *a*, whereby the end of Cycle 10 is indicated [1]), or as a prefix (see *t*, whereby the end of Katun 14 is recorded). The second form is seen as a prefix in *u*, whereby the end of Katun 12 is recorded, and in *i*, whereby the end of Katun 11 is shown. This latter sign is found also as a superfix in *r*.

The hand-ending sign rarely appears as modifying period glyphs, although a few examples of such use have been found (see fig. 37,

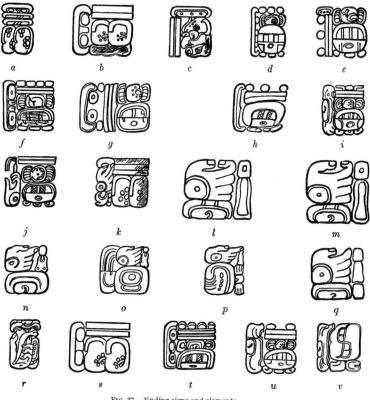

FIG. 37.   Ending signs and elements.

j, *k*). This ending sign usually appears as the main element in a separate glyph, which precedes the sign of the period whose end is recorded (see fig. 37, *l*–*q*). In these cases the subordinate elements differ somewhat, although the element (*) appears as the suffix in *l*, *m*, *n*, *q*, and the element (†) as a postfix therein, also in *o* and *p*. In a few cases the hand is combined with the other ending signs, sometimes with one and sometimes with the other.

---

[1] In Chapter IV it will be shown that two bars stand for the number 10. It will be necessary to anticipate the discussion of Maya numerals there presented to the extent of stating that a bar represented 5 and a dot or ball, 1. The varying combinations of these two elements gave the values up to 20.

The use of the hand as expressing the meaning "ending" is quite natural. The Aztec, we have seen, called their 52-year period the *xiuhmolpilli*, or "year bundle." This implies the concomitant idea of "tying up." As a period closed, metaphorically speaking, it was "tied up" or "bundled up." The Maya use of the hand to express the idea "ending" may be a graphic representation of the member by means of which this "tying up" was effected, the clasped hand indicating the closed period.

This method of describing a date may be called "dating by period endings." It was far less accurate than Initial-series or Secondary-series dating, since a date described as occurring at the end of a certain katun could recur after an interval of about 18,000 years in round numbers, as against 374,400 years in the other 2 methods. For all practical purposes, however, 18,000 years was as accurate as 374,400 years, since it far exceeds the range of time covered by the written records of mankind the world over.

Period-ending dates were not used much, and, as has been stated above, they are found only in connection with the larger periods— most frequently with the katun, next with the cycle, and but very rarely with the tun. Mr. Bowditch (1910: pp. 176 et seq.) has reviewed fully the use of ending signs, and students are referred to his work for further information on this subject.

U KAHLAY KATUNOB

In addition to the foregoing methods of measuring time and recording dates, the Maya of Yucatan used still another, which, however, was probably derived directly from the application of Period-ending dating to the Long Count, and consequently introduces no new elements. This has been designated the Sequence of the Katuns, because in this method the katun, or 7,200-day period, was the unit used for measuring the passage of time. The Maya themselves called the Sequence of the Katuns *u tzolan katun,* "the series of the katuns"; or *u kahlay uxocen katunob,* "the record of the count of the katuns"; or even more simply, *u kahlay katunob,* "the record of the katuns." These names accurately describe this system, which is simply the record of the successive katuns, comprising in the aggregate the range of Maya chronology.

Each katun of the u kahlay katunob was named after the designation of its ending day, a practice derived no doubt from Period-ending dating, and the sequence of these ending days represented passed time, each ending day standing for the katun of which it was the close. The katun, as we have seen on page 77, always ended with some day **Ahau,** consequently this day-name is the only one of the twenty which appears in the u kahlay katunob. In this method the katuns were distinguished from one another, *not* by the positions which they occupied in the cycle, as Katun 14, for example, but by the different days **Ahau** with which they ended, as Katun **2 Ahau,** Katun **13 Ahau,** etc. See Table IX.

TABLE IX.—SEQUENCE OF KATUNS IN U KAHLAY KATUNOB

Katun 2 Ahau	Katun 8 Ahau
Katun 13 Ahau	Katun 6 Ahau
Katun 11 Ahau	Katun 4 Ahau
Katun 9 Ahau	Katun 2 Ahau
Katun 7 Ahau	Katun 13 Ahau
Katun 5 Ahau	Katun 11 Ahau
Katun 3 Ahau	Katun 9 Ahau
Katun 1 Ahau	Katun 7 Ahau
Katun 12 Ahau	Katun 5 Ahau
Katun 10 Ahau	Katun 3 Ahau, etc.

The peculiar retrograding sequence of the numerical coefficients in Table IX, decreasing by 2 from katun to katun, as 2, 13, 11, 9, 7, 5, 3, 1, 12, etc., results directly from the number of days which the katun contains. Since the 13 possible numerical coefficients, 1 to 13, inclusive, succeed each other in endless repetition, 1 following immediately after 13, it is clear that in counting forward any given number from any given numerical coefficient, the resulting numerical coefficient will not be affected if we first deduct all the 13s possible from the number to be counted forward. The mathematical demonstration of this fact follows. If we count forward 14 from any given coefficient, the same coefficient will be reached as if we had counted forward but 1. This is true because, (1) there are only 13 numerical coefficients, and (2) these follow each other without interruption, 1 following immediately after 13; hence, when 13 has been reached, the next coefficient is 1, not 14; therefore 13 or any multiple thereof may be counted forward or backward from any one of the 13 numerical coefficients without changing its value. This truth enables us to formulate the following rule for finding numerical coefficients: Deduct all the multiples of 13 possible from the number to be counted forward, and then count forward the remainder from the known coefficient, subtracting 13 if the resulting number is above 13, since 13 is the highest possible number which can be attached to a day sign. If we apply this rule to the sequence of the numerical coefficients in Table IX, we shall find that it accounts for the retrograding sequence there observed. The first katun in Table IX, Katun **2 Ahau,** is named after its ending day, **2 Ahau.** Now let us see whether the application of this rule will give us **13 Ahau** as the ending day of the next katun. The number to be counted forward from **2 Ahau** is 7,200, the number of days in one katun; therefore we must first deduct from 7,200 all the 13s possible. $7,200 \div 13 = 553\frac{11}{13}$. In other words, after we have deducted all the 13's possible, that is,

553 of them, there is a remainder of 11.   This the rule says is to be
added (or counted forward) from the known coefficient (in this case
2) in order to reach the resulting coefficient.   2 + 11 = 13.   Since
this number is not above 13, 13 is not to be deducted from it; therefore the coefficient of the ending day of the second katun is 13, as
shown in Table IX.   Similarly we can prove that the coefficient of
the ending day of the third katun in Table IX will be 11.   Again, we
have 7,200 to count forward from the known coefficient, in this case
13 (the coefficient of the ending day of the second katun).   But we have
seen above that if we deduct all the 13s possible from 7,200 there will
be a remainder of 11; consequently this remainder 11 must be added
to 13, the known coefficient.   13 + 11 = 24; but since this number is
above 13, we must deduct 13 from it in order to find out the resulting
coefficient.   24 − 13 = 11, and 11 is the coefficient of the ending day
of the third katun in Table IX.   By applying the above rule, all of
the coefficients of the ending days of the katuns could be shown to
follow the sequence indicated in Table IX.   And since the ending
days of the katuns determined their names, this same sequence is also
that of the katuns themselves.

The above table enables us to establish a constant by means of
which we can always find the name of the next katun.   Since 7,200
is always the number of days in any katun, after deducting all the
13s possible the remainder will always be 11, which has to be added
to the known coefficient to find the unknown.   But since 13 has to
be deducted from the resulting number when it is above 13, subtracting 2 will always give us exactly the same coefficient as adding
11; consequently we may formulate for determining the numerical
coefficients of the ending days of katuns the following simple rule:
Subtract 2 from the coefficient of the ending day of the preceding
katun in every case.   A glance at Table IX will demonstrate the
truth of this rule.

In the names of the katuns given in Table IX it is noteworthy that
the positions which the ending days occupied in the divisions of the
haab, or 365-day year, are not mentioned.   For example, the first
katun was not called Katun **2 Ahau 8 Zac**, but simply Katun **2 Ahau**,
the month part of the day, that is, its position in the year, was omitted.
This omission of the month parts of the ending days of the katuns in
the u kahlay katunob has rendered this method of dating far less
accurate than any of the others previously described except Calendar-
round Dating.   For example, when a date was recorded as falling
within a certain katun, as Katun **2 Ahau**, it might occur anywhere
within a period of 7,200 days, or nearly 20 years, and yet fulfill the
given conditions.   In other words, no matter how accurately this
Katun **2 Ahau** itself might be fixed in a *long* stretch of time, there
was always the possibility of a maximum error of about 20 years in

such dating, since the statement of the katun did not fix a date any closer than as occurring somewhere within a certain 20-year period. When greater accuracy was desired the particular tun in which the date occurred was also given, as Tun 13 of Katun **2 Ahau**. This fixed a date as falling somewhere within a certain 360 days, which was accurately fixed in a much longer period of time. Very rarely, in the case of an extremely important event, the Calendar-round date was also given as **9 Imix 19 Zip** of Tun 9 of Katun **13 Ahau**. A date thus described satisfying all the given conditions could not recur until after the lapse of at least 7,000 years. The great majority of events, however, recorded by this method are described only as occurring in some particular katun, as Katun **2 Ahau**, for example, no attempt being made to refer them to any particular division (tun) of this period. Such accuracy doubtless was sufficient for recording the events of tribal history, since in no case could an event be more than 20 years out of the way.

Aside from this initial error, the accuracy of this method of dating has been challenged on the ground that since there were only thirteen possible numerical coefficients, any given katun, as Katun **2 Ahau**, for example, in Table IX would recur in the sequence after the lapse of thirteen katuns, or about 256 years, thus paving the way for much confusion. While admitting that every thirteenth katun in the sequence had the same name (see Table IX), the writer believes, nevertheless, that when the sequence of the katuns was carefully kept, and the record of each entered immediately after its completion, so that there could be no chance of confusing it with an earlier katun of the same name in the sequence, accuracy in dating could be secured for as long a period as the sequence remained unbroken. Indeed, the u kahlay katunob [1] from which the synopsis of Maya history given in Chapter I was compiled, accurately fixes the date of events, ignoring the possible initial inaccuracy of 20 years, within a period of more than 1,100 years, a remarkable feat for any primitive chronology.

How early this method of recording dates was developed is uncertain. It has not yet been found (surely) in the inscriptions in either the south or the north; on the other hand, it is so closely connected with the Long Count and Period-ending dating, which occurs repeatedly throughout the inscriptions, that it seems as though the u kahlay katunob must have been developed while this system was still in use.

There should be noted here a possible exception to the above statement, namely, that the u kahlay katunob has not been found in the inscriptions. Mr. Bowditch (1910: pp. 192 et seq.) has pointed out

---

[1] The u kahlay katunob on which the historical summary given in Chapter I is based shows an absolutely uninterrupted sequence of katuns for more than 1,100 years. See Brinton (1882 b: pp. 152-164). It is necessary to note here a correction on p. 153 of that work. Doctor Brinton has omitted a Katun **8 Ahau** from this u kahlay katunob, which is present in the Berendt copy, and he has incorrectly assigned the abandonment of Chichen Itza to the preceding katun, Katun **10 Ahau**, whereas the Berendt copy shows this event took place during the katun omitted, Katun **8 Ahau**.

what seem to be traces of another method of dating. This consists of some day **Ahau** modified by one of the two elements shown in figure 38 (*a–d* and *e–h*, respectively). In such cases the month part is sometimes recorded, though as frequently the day **Ahau** stands by itself. It is to be noted that in the great majority of these cases the days **Ahau** thus modified are the ending days of katuns, which are either expressed or at least indicated in adjacent glyphs. In other words, the day **Ahau** thus modified is usually the ending day of the next even katun after the last date recorded. The writer believes that this modification of certain days **Ahau** by either of the two elements shown in figure 38 may indicate that such days were the katun ending days nearest to the time when the inscriptions presenting them were engraved. The snake variants shown in figure 38,

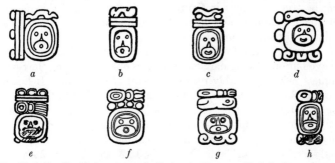

a   b   c   d

e   f   g   h

FIG. 38. "Snake" or "knot" element as used with day sign **Ahau**, possibly indicating presence of the u kahlay katunob in the inscriptions.

a–d, are all from Palenque; the knot variants (*e–h* of the same figure) are found at both Copan and Quirigua.

It may be objected that one katun ending day in each inscription is far different from a sequence of katun ending days as shown in Table IX, and that one katun ending day by itself can not be construed as an u kahlay katunob, or sequence of katuns. The difference here, however, is apparent rather than real, and results from the different character of the monuments and the native chronicles. The u kahlay katunob in Table IX is but a part of a much longer sequence of katuns, which is shown in a number of native chronicles written shortly after the Spanish Conquest, and which record the events of Maya history for more than 1,100 years. They are in fact chronological synopses of Maya history, and from their very nature they have to do with long periods. This is not true of the monuments,[1] which, as we have seen, were probably set up to mark the passage of certain periods, not exceeding a katun in length in any case. Consequently, each monument would have inscribed upon it only one or two

---

[1] There are, of course, a few exceptions to this rule—that is, there are some monuments which indicate an interval of more than 3,000 years between the extreme dates. In such cases, however, this interval is not divided into katuns, nor in fact into any regularly recurring smaller unit, with the single exception mentioned in footnote 1, p. 84.

katun ending days and the events which were connected more or less closely with it.　In other words, the monuments were erected at short intervals [1] and probably recorded events contemporaneous with their erection, while the u kahlay katunob, on the other hand, were historical summaries reaching back to a remote time.　The former were the periodicals of current events, the latter histories of the past.　The former in the great majority of cases had no concern with the lapse of more than one or two katuns, while the latter measured centuries by the repetition of the same unit.　The writer believes that from the very nature of the monuments—markers of current time—no u kahlay katunob will be found on them, but that the presence of the katun ending days above described indicates that the u kahlay katunob had been developed while the other system was still in use.　If the foregoing be true, the signs in figure 38, a–h, would have this meaning: "On this day came to an end the katun in which fall the accompanying dates," or some similar significance.

If we exclude the foregoing as indicating the u kahlay katunob, we have but one aboriginal source, that is one antedating the Spanish Conquest, which probably records a count of this kind.　It has been stated (p. 33) that the Codex Peresianus probably treats in part at least of historical matter.　The basis for this assertion is that in this particular manuscript an u kahlay katunob is seemingly recorded; at least there is a sequence of the ending days of katuns shown, exactly like the one in Table IX, that is, **13 Ahau, 11 Ahau, 9 Ahau**, etc.

At the time of the Spanish Conquest the Long Count seems to have been recorded entirely by the ending days of its katuns, that is, by the u kahlay katunob, and the use of Initial-series dating seems to have been discontinued, and perhaps even forgotten.　Native as well as Spanish authorities state that at the time of the Conquest the Maya measured time by the passage of the katuns, and no mention is made of any system of dating which resembles in the least the Initial Series so prevalent in the southern and older cities.　While the Spanish authorities do not mention the u kahlay katunob as do the native writers, they state very clearly that this was the system used in counting time.　Says Bishop Landa (1864: p. 312) in this connection: "The Indians not only had a count by years and days . . . but they had a certain method of counting time and their affairs by ages, which they made from twenty to twenty years . . . these they call katunes." Cogolludo (1688: lib. iv, cap. v, p. 186) makes a similar statement: "They count their eras and ages, which they put in their books from twenty to twenty years . . . [these] they call katun." Indeed, there can be but little doubt that the u kahlay katunob had entirely replaced the Initial Series in recording the Long Count centuries before the Spanish Conquest; and if the latter method of dating were known

---

[1] On one monument, the tablet from the Temple of the Inscriptions at Palenque, there seems to be recorded a kind of u kahlay katunob; at least, there is a sequence of ten consecutive katuns.

at all, the knowledge of it came only from half-forgotten records the understanding of which was gradually passing from the minds of men.

It is clear from the foregoing that an important change in recording the passage of time took place sometime between the epoch of the great southern cities and the much later period when the northern cities flourished. In the former, time was reckoned and dates were recorded by Initial Series; in the latter, in so far as we can judge from post-Conquest sources, the u kahlay katunob and Calendar-round dating were the only systems used. As to when this change took place, we are not entirely in the dark. It is certain that the use of the Initial Series extended to Yucatan, since monuments presenting this method of dating have been found at a few of the northern cities, namely, at Chichen Itza, Holactun, and Tuluum. On the other hand, it is equally certain that Initial Series could not have been used very extensively in the north, since they have been discovered in only these three cities in Yucatan up to the present time. Moreover, the latest, that is, the most recent of these three, was probably contemporaneous with the rise of the Triple Alliance, a fairly early event of Northern Maya history. Taking these two points into consideration, the limited use of Initial Series in the north and the early dates recorded in the few Initial Series known, it seems likely that Initial-series dating did not long survive the transplanting of the Maya civilization in Yucatan.

Why this change came about is uncertain. It could hardly have been due to the desire for greater accuracy, since the u kahlay katunob was far less exact than Initial-series dating; not only could dates satisfying all given conditions recur much more frequently in the u kahlay katunob, but, as generally used, this method fixed a date merely as occurring somewhere within a period of about 20 years.

The writer believes the change under consideration arose from a very different cause; that it was in fact the result of a tendency toward greater brevity, which was present in the glyphic writing from the very earliest times, and which is to be noted on some of the earliest monuments that have survived the ravages of the passing centuries. At first, when but a single date was recorded on a monument, an Initial Series was used. Later, however, when the need or desire had arisen to inscribe more than one date on the same monument, additional dates were *not* expressed as Initial Series, each of which, as we have seen, involves the use of 8 glyphs, but as a Secondary Series, which for the record of short periods necessitated the use of fewer glyphs than were employed in Initial Series. It would seem almost as though Secondary Series had been invented to avoid the use of Initial Series when more than one date had to be recorded on the same monument. But this tendency toward brevity in dating did not cease with the invention of Secondary Series. Somewhat later, dating by period-endings was introduced, obviating the necessity for the use of even one Initial Series on every monument, in order that one date might be fixed in the Long Count to which the others (Secondary Series) could be referred. For all practical purposes, as we have seen, Period-ending dating was as accurate as Initial-series dating for fixing dates in the Long Count, and its substitution for Initial-series dating resulted in a further saving of glyphs and a corresponding economy of space. Still later, probably after the Maya had colonized Yucatan, the u kahlay katunob, which was a direct application of Period-ending dating to the Long Count, came into general use. At this time a rich history lay behinⁿd the Maya people, and to have recorded all of its events by their corresponding Initial Series would have been far too cumbersome a practice. The u kahlay katunob offered a convenient and facile method by means of which long stretches of time could be recorded and events approximately dated; that is, within 20 years. This, together with the fact that the practice of setting up dated period-markers seems to have languished in the north, thus eliminating the greatest medium of all for the presentation of Initial Series, probably gave rise to the change from the one method of recording time to the other.

This concludes the discussion of the five methods by means of which the Maya reckoned time and recorded dates: (1) Initial-series dating; (2) Secondary-series dating; (3) Calendar-round dating; (4) Period-ending dating; (5) Katun-ending dating, or the u kahlay katunob. While apparently differing considerably from one another, in reality all are expressions of the same fundamental idea, the combination of the numbers 13 and 20 (that is, 260) with the solar year conceived as containing 365 days, and all were recorded by the same vigesimal system of numeration; that is:

1. All used precisely the same dates, the 18,980 dates of the Calendar Round;

2. All may be reduced to the same fundamental unit, the day; and

3. All used the same time counters, those shown in Table VIII.

In conclusion, the student is strongly urged constantly to bear in mind two vital characteristics of Maya chronology:

1. The absolute continuity of all sequences which had to do with the counting of time: The 13 numerical coefficients of the day names, the 20 day names, the 260 days of the tonalamatl, the 365 positions of the haab, the 18,980 dates of the Calendar Round, and the kins, uinals, tuns, katuns, and cycles of the vigesimal system of numeration. When the conclusion of any one of these sequences had been reached, the sequence began anew without the interruption or omission of a single unit and continued repeating itself for all time.

2. All Maya periods expressed not current time, but passed time, as in the case of our hours, minutes, and seconds.

On these two facts rests the whole Maya conception of time.

CHAPTER IV

MAYA ARITHMETIC

The present chapter will be devoted to the consideration of Maya arithmetic in its relation to the calendar. It will be shown how the Maya expressed their numbers and how they used their several time periods. In short, their arithmetical processes will be explained, and the calculations resulting from their application to the calendar will be set forth.

The Maya had two different ways of writing their numerals,[1] namely: (1) With normal forms, and (2) with head variants; that is, each of the numerals up to and including 19 had two distinct characters which stood for it, just as in the case of the time periods and more rarely, the days and months. The normal forms of the numerals may be compared to our Roman figures, since they are built up by the combination of certain elements which had a fixed numerical value, like the letters I, V, X, L, C, D, and M, which in Roman notation stand for the values 1, 5, 10, 50, 100, 500, and 1,000, respectively. The head-variant numerals, on the other hand, more closely resemble our Arabic figures, since there was a special head form for each number up to and including 13, just as there are special characters for the first nine figures and zero in Arabic notation. Moreover, this parallel between our Arabic figures and the Maya head-variant numerals extends to the formation of the higher numbers. Thus, the Maya formed the head-variant numerals for 14, 15, 16, 17, 18, and 19 by applying the essential characteristic of the head variant for 10 to the head variants for 4, 5, 6, 7, 8, and 9, respectively, just as the sign for 10—that is, one in the tens place and zero in the units place—is used in connection with the signs for the first nine figures in Arabic notation to form the numbers 11 to 19, inclusive. Both of these notations occur in the inscriptions, but with very few exceptions [2] no head-variant numerals have yet been found in the codices.

BAR AND DOT NUMERALS

The Maya "Roman numerals"—that is, the normal-form numerals, up to and including 19—were expressed by varying combinations of two elements, the dot (●), which represented the numeral, or numerical value, 1, and the bar, or line (▬), which represented the numeral, or numerical value, 5. By various combinations of these two

---

[1] The word "numeral," as used here, has been restricted to the first twenty numbers, 0 to 19, inclusive.

[2] See p. 96, footnote 1.

elements alone the Maya expressed all the numerals from 1 to 19, inclusive. The normal forms of the numerals in the codices are shown in figure 39, in which one dot stands for 1, two dots for 2, three dots for 3, four dots for 4, one bar for 5, one bar and one dot for 6, one bar and two dots for 7, one bar and three dots for 8, one bar and four dots for 9, two bars for 10, and so on up to three bars and four dots for 19. The normal forms of the numerals in the inscriptions (see fig. 40) are identical with those in the codices, excepting that they are more elaborate, the dots and bars both taking on various decorations. Some of the former contain a concentric circle (*) or cross-hatching (**); some appear as crescents (†) or curls (††), more rarely as (‡) or (‡‡). The bars show even a greater variety of treatment (see fig. 41). All these decorations, however, in no way affect the numerical value of the bar and the dot, which remain 5 and 1, respectively, throughout the Maya writing. Such embellishments as those just described are found only in the inscriptions, and their use was proba-

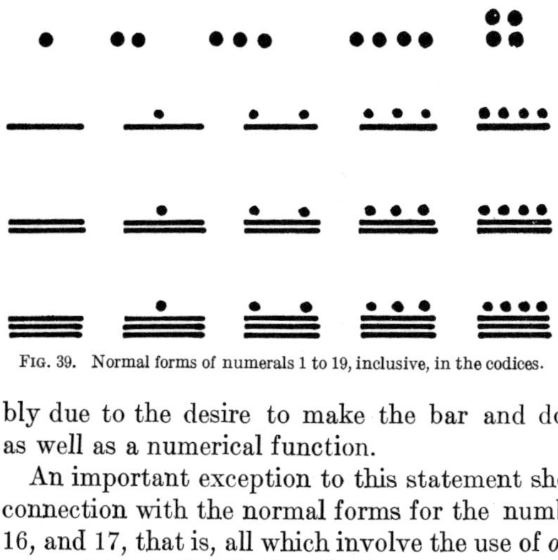

FIG. 39. Normal forms of numerals 1 to 19, inclusive, in the codices.

bly due to the desire to make the bar and dot serve a decorative as well as a numerical function.

An important exception to this statement should be noted here in connection with the normal forms for the numbers 1, 2, 6, 7, 11, 12, 16, and 17, that is, all which involve the use of *one* or *two* dots in their composition.[1] In the inscriptions, as we have seen in Chapter II, every glyph was a balanced picture, exactly fitting its allotted space, even at the cost of occasionally losing some of its elements. To have expressed the numbers 1, 2, 6, 7, 11, 12, 16, and 17 as in the codices, with just the proper number of bars and dots in each case, would have left unsightly gaps in the outlines of the glyph blocks (see fig. 42, *a–h*, where these numbers are shown as the coefficients of the katun sign). In *a, c, e,* and *g* of the same figure (the numbers 1, 6, 11, and 16, respectively) the single dot does not fill the space on the left-hand [2] side of the bar, or bars, as the case may be, and consequently

---

[1] In one case, on the west side of Stela E at Quirigua, the number 14 is also shown with an ornamental element (*). This is very unusual and, so far as the writer knows, is the only example of its kind. The four dots in the numbers 4, 9, 14, and 19 never appear thus separated in any other text known.

[2] In the examples given the numerical coefficients are attached as prefixes to the katun sign. Frequently, however, they occur as superfixes. In such cases, however, the above observations apply equally well.

the left-hand edge of the glyph block in each case is ragged.   Similarly in *b*, *d*, *f*, and *h*, the numbers 2, 7, 12, and 17, respectively, the
two dots at the left of the bar or bars are too far apart to fill in the

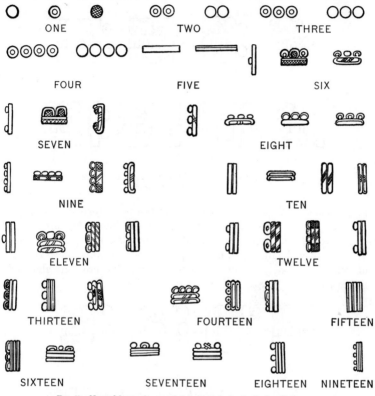

FIG. 40.   Normal forms of numerals 1 to 19, inclusive, in the inscriptions.

left-hand edge of the glyph blocks neatly, and consequently in these
cases also the left edge is ragged.   The Maya were quick to note this
discordant note in glyph design, and in the great majority of the

FIG. 41.   Examples of bar and dot numeral 5, showing the ornamentation which the bar underwent
without affecting its numerical value.

places where these numbers (1, 2, 6, 7, 11, 12, 16, and 17) had to be
recorded, other elements of a purely ornamental character were
introduced to fill the empty spaces.   In figure 43, *a*, *c*, *e*, *g*, the spaces
on each side of the single dot have been filled with ornamental cres-

cents about the size of the dot, and these give the glyph in each case a final touch of balance and harmony, which is lacking without them. In *b, d, f,* and *h* of the same figure a single crescent stands between the two numerical dots, and this again harmoniously fills in the

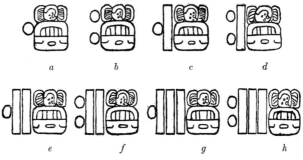

FIG. 42. Examples showing the way in which the numerals 1, 2, 6, 7, 11, 12, 16, and 17 are *not* used with period, day, or month signs.

glyph block. While the crescent (*) is the usual form taken by this purely decorative element, crossed lines (**) are found in places, as in (†); or, again, a pair of dotted elements (††), as in (‡). These variants, however, are of rare occurrence, the common form being the crescent shown in figure 43.

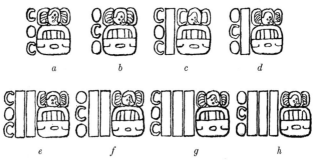

FIG. 43. Examples showing the way in which the numerals 1, 2, 6, 7, 11, 12, 16, and 17 *are* used with period, day, or month signs. Note the filling of the otherwise vacant spaces with ornamental elements.

The use of these purely ornamental elements, to fill the empty spaces in the normal forms of the numerals 1, 2, 6, 7, 11, 12, 16, and 17, is a fruitful source of error to the student of the inscriptions. Slight weathering of an inscription is often sufficient to make ornamental crescents look exactly like numerical dots, and consequently the numerals 1, 2, 3 are frequently mistaken for one another, as are also 6, 7, and 8; 11, 12, and 13; and 16, 17, and 18. The student must exercise the greatest caution at all times in identifying these numerals in the inscriptions, or otherwise he will quickly find himself involved in a tangle from which there seems to be no egress.   Probably more errors in reading the inscriptions have been made through the incorrect identification of these numerals than through any other one cause, and the student is urged to be continually on his guard if he would avoid making this capital blunder.

Although the early Spanish authorities make no mention of the fact that the Maya expressed their numbers by bars and dots, native testimony is not lacking on this point. Doctor Brinton (1882 b: p. 48) gives this extract, accompanied by the drawing shown in figure 44, from a native writer of the eighteenth century who clearly describes this system of writing numbers:

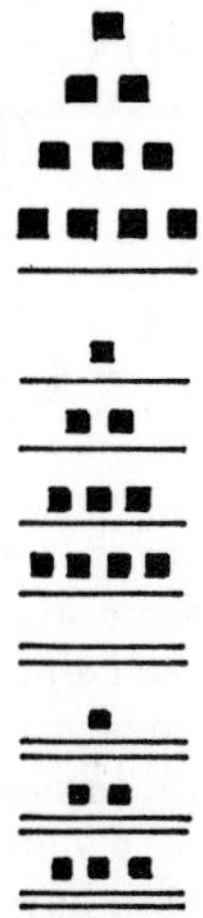

> They [our ancestors] used [for numerals in their calendars] dots and lines [i. e., bars] back of them; one dot for one year, two dots for two years, three dots for three years, four dots for four, and so on; in addition to these they used a line; one line meant five years, two lines meant ten years; if one line and above it one dot, six years; if two dots above the line, seven years; if three dots above, eight years; if four dots above the line, nine; a dot above two lines, eleven; if two dots, twelve; if three dots, thirteen.

Fig. 44. Normal forms of numerals 1 to 13, inclusive, in the Books of Chilan Balam.

This description is so clear, and the values therein assigned to the several combinations of bars and dots have been verified so extensively throughout both the inscriptions and the codices, that we are justified in identifying the bar and dot as the signs for five and one, respectively, wherever they occur, whether they are found by themselves or in varying combinations.

In the codices, as will appear in Chapter VI, the bar and dot numerals were painted in two colors, black and red. These colors were used to distinguish one set of numerals from another, each of which has a different use. In such cases, however, bars of one color are never used with dots of the other color, each number being either all red or all black (see p. 93, footnote 1, for the single exception to this rule).

By the development of a special character to represent the number 5 the Maya had far surpassed the Aztec in the science of mathematics; indeed, the latter seem to have had but one numerical sign, the dot, and they were obliged to resort to the clumsy makeshift of repeating this in order to represent all numbers above 1. It is clearly seen that such a system of notation has very definite limitations, which must have seriously retarded mathematical progress among the Aztec.

In the Maya system of numeration, which was vigesimal, there was no need for a special character to represent the number 20,[1] because

---

[1] Care should be taken to distinguish the number or figure 20 from any period which contained 20 periods of the order next below it; otherwise the uinal, katun, and cycle glyphs could all be construed as signs for 20, since each of these periods contains 20 units of the period next lower.

(1) as we have seen in Table VIII, 20 units of any order (except the 2d, in which only 18 were required) were equal to 1 unit of the order next higher, and consequently 20 could not be attached to any period glyph, since this number of periods (with the above exception) was

FIG. 45. Sign for 20 in the codices.

always recorded as 1 period of the order next higher; and (2) although there were 20 positions in each period except the uinal, as 20 kins in each uinal, 20 tuns in each katun, 20 katuns in each cycle, these positions were numbered not from 1 to 20, but on the contrary from 0 to 19, a system which eliminated the need for a character expressing 20.

In spite of the foregoing fact, however, the number 20 has been found in the codices (see fig. 45). A peculiar condition there, however, accounts satisfactorily for its presence. In the codices the sign for 20 occurs only in connection with tonalamatls, which, as we shall see later, were usually portrayed in such a manner that the numbers of which they were composed could not be presented from bottom to top in the usual way, but had to be written

• FIG. 46. Sign for 0 in the codices.

horizontally from left to right. This destroyed the possibility of numeration by position,[1] according to the Maya point of view, and consequently some sign was necessary which should stand for 20 regardless of its position or relation to others. The sign shown in figure 45 was used for this purpose. It has not yet been found in the inscriptions, perhaps because, as was pointed out in Chapter II, the inscriptions generally do not appear to treat of tonalamatls.

If the Maya numerical system had no vital need for a character to express the number 20, a sign to represent zero was absolutely indis-

---

[1] The Maya numbered by relative position from bottom to top, as will be presently explained.

pensable. Indeed, any numerical system which rises to a second order of units requires a character which will signify, when the need arises, that no units of a certain order are involved; as zero units and zero tens, for example, in writing 100 in our own Arabic notation.

The character zero seems to have played an important part in Maya calculations, and signs for it have been found in both the codices and the inscriptions. The form found in the codices (fig. 46) is lenticu-

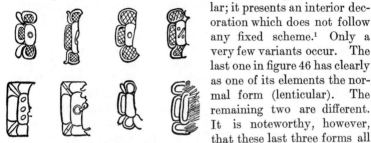

FIG. 47.   Sign for 0 in the inscriptions.

lar; it presents an interior decoration which does not follow any fixed scheme.[1] Only a very few variants occur. The last one in figure 46 has clearly as one of its elements the normal form (lenticular). The remaining two are different. It is noteworthy, however, that these last three forms all stand in the 2d, or uinal, place in the texts in which they occur, though whether this fact has influenced their variation is unknown.

Both normal forms and head variants for zero, as indeed for all the numbers, have been found in the inscriptions. The normal forms for zero are shown in figure 47. They are common and are unmistakable. An interesting origin for this sign has been suggested by Mr. A. P. Maudslay. On pages 75 and 76 of the Codex Tro-Cortesiano[2] the 260 days of a tonalamatl are graphically represented as forming the outline shown in figure 48, a. Half of this (see fig. 48, b) is the sign which stands for zero (compare with fig. 47). The train of association by which half of the graphic representation of a tonalamatl could come to stand for zero is

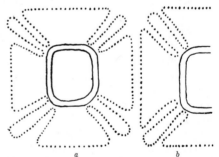

FIG. 48.   Figure showing possible derivation of the sign for 0 in the inscriptions: a, Outline of the days of the tonalamatl as represented graphically in the Codex Tro-Cortesiano; b, half of same outline, which is also sign for 0 shown in fig. 47.

not clear. Perhaps a of figure 48 may have signified that a complete tonalamatl had passed with no additional days. From this the sign may have come to represent the idea of completeness as apart from the tonalamatl, and finally the general idea of completeness applica-

[1] This form of zero is always red and is used with black bar and dot numerals as well as with red in the codices.

[2] It is interesting to note in this connection that the Zapotec made use of the same outline in graphic representations of the tonalamatl. On page 1 of the Zapotec Codex Féjerváry-Mayer an outline formed by the 260 days of the tonalamatl exactly like the one in fig. 48, a, is shown.

ble to any period; for no period could be exactly complete without a fractional remainder unless all the lower periods were wanting; that is, represented by zero. Whether this explains the connection between the outline of the tonalamatl and the zero sign, or whether indeed there be any connection between the two, is of course a matter of conjecture.

There is still one more normal form for zero not included in the examples given above, which must be described. This form (fig. 49), which occurs throughout the inscriptions and in the Dresden Codex,[1] is chiefly interesting because of its highly specialized function. Indeed, it was used for one purpose only, namely, to express the first, or zero, position in each of the 19 divisions of the haab, or year, and for no other. In other words, it denotes the positions **0 Pop**, **0 Uo**, **0 Zip**, etc., which, as we have seen (pp. 47, 48), corresponded

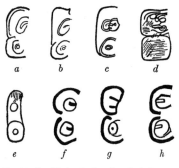

a   b   c   d

e   f   g   h

FIG. 49.   Special sign for 0 used exclusively as a month coefficient.

with our first days of the months. The forms shown in figure 49, *a–e*, are from the inscriptions and those in *f–h* from the Dresden Codex. They are all similar. The general outline of the sign has suggested the name "the spectacle" glyph. Its essential characteristic seems to be the division into two roughly circular parts, one above the other, best seen in the Dresden Codex forms (fig. 49, *f–h*) and a roughly circular infix in each. The lower infix is quite regular in all of the forms, being a circle or ring. The upper infix, however, varies considerably. In figure 49, *a*, *b*, this ring has degenerated into a loop. In *c* and *d* of the same figure it has become elaborated into a head. A simpler form is that in *f* and *g*. Although comparatively rare, this glyph is so unusual in form that it can be readily recognized. Moreover, if the student will bear in mind the two following points concerning its use, he will never fail to identify it in the inscriptions: The "spectacle" sign (1) can be attached only to the glyphs for the 19 divisions of the haab, or year, that is, the 18 uinals and the xma kaba kin; in other words, it is found only with the glyphs shown in figures 19 and 20, the signs for the months in the inscriptions and codices, respectively.

(2) It can occur only in connection with one of the four day-signs, **Ik**, **Manik**, **Eb**, and **Caban** (see figs. 16, *c*, *j*, *s*, *t*, *u*, *a'*, *b'*, and 17, *c*, *d*, *k*, *r*, *x*, *y*, respectively), since these four alone, as appears in Table VII, can occupy the 0 (zero) positions in the several divisions of the haab.

---

[1] This form of zero has been found only in the Dresden Codex. Its absence from the other two codices is doubtless due to the fact that the month glyphs are recorded only a very few times in them—but once in the Codex Tro-Cortesiano and three times in the Codex Peresianus.

Examples of the normal-form numerals as used with the day, month, and period glyphs in both the inscriptions and the codices are shown in figure 50.   Under each is given its meaning in English.[1]

10 Ahau	7 Ahau	4 Ahau	**1 Ik**	**2 Ik**	1 Kan
13 Manik	5 Lamat	2 Cib	12 Caban	5 Caban	5 Eznab
0 Pop	14 Uo	18 Zip	17 Tzec	6 Xul	4 Yaxkin
3 Yaxkin	10 Mol	5 Yax	18 Muan	3 Kayab	8 Cumhu
Cyclu 9	Cycle 9	Katun 8	Katun 3	Tun 5	Tun 1
Uinal 1	Kin 4	Kin 12	Kin 8	Kin 0	Kin 8

FIG. 50.   Examples of the use of bar and dot numerals with period, day, or month signs.   The translation of each glyph appears below it.

The student is advised to familiarize himself with these forms, since on his ability to recognize them will largely depend his progress in reading the inscriptions.   This figure illustrates the use of all the foregoing forms except the sign for 20 in figure 45 and the sign for zero in figure 46.   As these two forms never occur with day, month, or period glyphs, and as they have been found only in the codices, examples showing their use will not be given until Chapter VI is reached, which treats of the codices exclusively.

---

[1] The forms shown attached to these numerals are those of the day and month signs (see figs. 16, 17, and 19, 20, respectively), and of the period glyphs (see figs. 25–35, inclusive).   Reference to these figures will explain the English translation in the case of any form which the student may not remember.

HEAD-VARIANT NUMERALS

Let us next turn to the consideration of the Maya "Arabic notation," that is, the head-variant numerals, which, like all other known head variants, are practically restricted to the inscriptions.[1] It should be noted here before proceeding further that the full-figure numerals found in connection with full-figure period, day, and month glyphs in a few inscriptions, have been classified with the head-variant numerals. As explained on page 67, the body-parts of such glyphs have no function in determining their meanings, and it is only the head-parts which present in each case the determining characteristics of the form intended.

In the "head" notation each of the numerals, 0, 1, 2, 3, 4, 5, 6, 7, 8, 9, 10, 11, 12, 13 [2] is expressed by a distinctive type of head; each type has its own essential characteristic, by means of which it can be distinguished from all of the others. Above 13 and up to but *not including* 20, the head numerals are expressed by the application of the essential characteristic of the head for 10 to the heads for 3 to 9, inclusive. No head forms for the numeral 20 have yet been discovered.

The identification of these head-variant numerals in some cases is not an easy matter, since their determining characteristics are not always presented clearly. Moreover, in the case of a few numerals, notably the heads for 2, 11, and 12, the essential elements have not yet been determined. Head forms for these numerals occur so rarely in the inscriptions that the comparative data are insufficient to enable us to fix on any particular element as the essential one. Another difficulty encountered in the identification of head-variant numerals is the apparent irregularity of the forms in the earlier inscriptions. The essential elements of these early head numerals in some cases seem to differ widely from those of the later forms, and consequently it is sometimes difficult, indeed even impossible, to determine their corresponding numerical values.

[1] The following possible exceptions, however, should be noted: In the Codex Peresianus the normal form of the tun sign sometimes occurs attached to varying heads, as (*). Whether these heads denote numerals is unknown, but the construction of this glyph in such cases (a head attached to the sign of a time period) absolutely parallels the use of head-variant numerals with time-period glyphs in the inscriptions. A much stronger example of the possible use of head numerals with period glyphs in the codices, however, is found in the Dresden Codex. Here the accompanying head (†) is almost surely that for the number 16, the hatchet eye denoting 6 and the fleshless lower jaw 10. Compare (†) with fig. 53, *f–i*, where the head for 16 is shown. The glyph (‡) here shown is the normal form for the kin sign. Compare fig. 34, *b*. The meaning of these two forms would thus seem to be 16 kins. In the passage in which these glyphs occur the glyph next preceding the head for 16 is "8 tuns," the numerical coefficient 8 being expressed by one bar and three dots. It seems reasonably clear here, therefore, that the form in question is a head numeral. However, these cases are so very rare and the context where they occur is so little understood, that they have been excluded in the general consideration of head-variant numerals presented above.

[2] It will appear presently that the number 13 could be expressed in two different ways: (1) by a special head meaning 13, and (2) by the essential characteristic of the head for 10 applied to the head for 3 (i. e., 10+3=13).

The head-variant numerals are shown in figures 51–53.   Taking these up in their numerical order, let us commence with the head signifying 1; see figure 51, *a–e*.   The essential element of this head is

Fig. 51.   Head-variant numerals 1 to 7, inclusive.

its forehead ornament, which, to signify the number 1, must be composed of more than one part (*), in order to distinguish it from the forehead ornament (**), which, as we shall see presently, is the essential element of the head for 8 (fig. 52, *a–f*). Except for their forehead ornaments the heads for 1 and 8 are almost identical, and great care must be exercised in order to avoid mistaking one for the other.

The head for 2 (fig. 51, *f*, *g*) has been found only twice in the inscriptions—on Lintel 2 at Piedras Negras and on the tablet in the Temple of the Initial Series at Holactun. The oval at the top of the head seems to be the only element these two forms have in common, and the writer therefore accepts this element as the essential character-

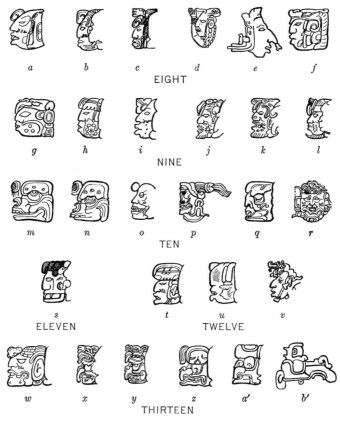

FIG. 52. Head-variant numerals 8 to 13, inclusive.

istic of the head for 2, admitting at the same time that the evidence is insufficient.

The head for 3 is shown in figure 51, *h*, *i*. Its determining characteristic is the fillet, or headdress.

The head for 4 is shown in figure 51, *j–m*. It is to be distinguished by its large prominent eye and square irid (*) (probably eroded in *l*), the snaglike front tooth, and the curling fang protruding from the back part of the mouth (**) (wanting in *l* and *m*).

The head for 5 (fig. 51, *n–s*) is always to be identified by its peculiar headdress(†), which is the normal form of the tun sign. Compare figure 29, *a*, *b*. The same element appears   †
also in the head for 15 (see fig. 53, *b–e*). The head for 5 is one of the most constant of all the head numerals.

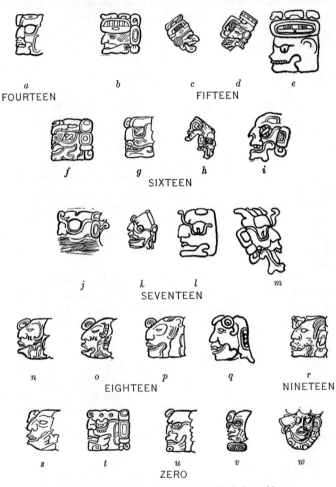

FIG. 53.   Head-variant numerals 14 to 19, inclusive, and 0.

The head for 6 (fig. 51, *t–v*) is similarly unmistakable. It is always characterized by the so-called hatchet eye (††), which appears
also in the head for 16 (fig. 53, *f–i*).   ††

The head for 7 (fig. 51, *w*) is found only once in the inscriptions— on the east side of Stela D at Quirigua. Its essential characteristic, the large ornamental scroll passing under the eye and curling up in front of the forehead (‡), is better seen in the head for 17 ‡ (fig. 53, *j–m*).

The head for 8 is shown in figure 52, *a–f.* It is very similar to the head for 1, as previously explained (compare figs. 51, *a–e* and 52, *a–f*), and is to be distinguished from it only by the character of the forehead ornament, which is composed of but a single element (‡‡). In figure 52, *a*, *b*, this takes the form of a large curl. In *c* of the ‡‡ same figure a flaring element is added above the curl and in *d* and *e* this element replaces the curl. In *f* the tongue or tooth of a grotesque animal head forms the forehead ornament. The heads for 18 (fig. 53, *n–q*) follow the first variants (fig. 51, *a*, *b*), having the large curl, except *q*, which is similar to *d* in having a flaring element instead.

The head for 9 occurs more frequently than all of the others with the exception of the zero head, because the great majority of all Initial Series record dates which fell after the completion of Cycle 9, but before the completion of Cycle 10. Consequently, 9 is the coefficient attached to the cycle glyph in almost all Initial Series.[1] The head for 9 is shown in figure 52, *g–l*. It has for its essential characteristic the dots on the lower cheek or around the mouth (*). Sometimes these occur in a circle or again irregularly. Occa- * sionally, as in *j–l*, the 9 head has a beard, though this is not a constant element as are the dots, which appear also in the head for 19. Compare figure 53, *r*.

The head for 10 (fig. 52, *m–r*) is extremely important since its essential element, the fleshless lower jaw (*), stands for the numerical value 10, in composition with the heads for 3, 4, 5, * 6, 7, 8, and 9, to form the heads for 13, 14, 15, 16, 17, 18, and 19, respectively. The 10 head is clearly the fleshless skull, having the truncated nose and fleshless jaws (see fig. 52, *m–p*). The fleshless lower jaw is shown in profile in all cases but one—Zoömorph B at Quirigua (see *r* of the same figure). Here a full front view of a 10 head is shown in which the fleshless jaw extends clear across the lower part of the head, an interesting confirmation of the fact that this characteristic is the essential element of the head for 10.

The head for 11 (fig. 52, *s*) has been found only once in the inscriptions, namely, on Lintel 2 at Piedras Negras; hence comparative data are lacking for the determination of its essential element. This head has no fleshless lower jaw and consequently would seem, therefore, not to be built up of the heads for 1 and 10.

Similarly, the head for 12 (fig. 52, *t–v*) has no fleshless lower jaw, and consequently can not be composed of the heads for 10 and 2. It is to be noted, however, that all three of the faces are of the same type, even though their essential characteristic has not yet been determined.

---

[1] For the discussion of Initial Series in cycles other than Cycle 9, see pp. 194–207.

The head for 13 is shown in figure 52, *w–b′*.   Only the first of these forms, *w*, however, is built on the 10 + 3 basis.   Here we see the characteristic 3 head with its banded headdress or fillet (compare *h* and *i*, fig. 51), to which has been added the essential element of the 10 head, the fleshless lower jaw, the combination of the two giving the head for 13.   The other form for 13 seems to be a special character, and not a composition of the essential elements of the heads for 3 and 10, as in the preceding example.   This form of the 13 head (fig. 52, *x–b′*) is grotesque.   It seems to be characterized by its long pendulous nose surmounted by a curl (*), its large bulging eye (**), and a curl (†) or fang (††) protruding from the back part of the mouth.   Occurrences of the first type—the composite head—are very rare, there being only two examples of this kind known in all the inscriptions.   The form given in *w* is from the Temple of the Cross at Palenque, and the other is on the Hieroglyphic Stairway at Copan.   The individual type, having the pendulous nose, bulging eye, and mouth curl is by far the more frequent.

The head for 14 (fig. 53, *a*) is found but once—in the inscriptions on the west side of Stela F at Quirigua.   It has the fleshless lower jaw denoting 10, while the rest of the head shows the characteristics of 4—the bulging eye and snaglike tooth (compare fig. 51, *j–m*).   The curl protruding from the back part of the mouth is wanting because the whole lower part of the 4 head has been replaced by the fleshless lower jaw.

The head for 15 (fig. 53, *b–e*) is composed of the essential element of the 5 head (the tun sign; see fig. 51, *n–s*) and the fleshless lower jaw of the head for 10.

The head for 16 (fig. 53, *f–i*) is characterized by the fleshless lower jaw and the hatchet eye of the 6 head.   Compare figures 51, *t–v*, and 52, *m–r*, which together form 16 (10 + 6).

The head for 17 (fig. 53, *j–m*) is composed of the essential element of the 7 head (the scroll projecting above the nose; see fig. 51, *w*) and the fleshless lower jaw of the head for 10.

The head for 18 (fig. 53, *n–q*) has the characteristic forehead ornament of the 8 head (compare fig. 52, *a–f*) and the fleshless lower jaw denoting 10.

Only one example (fig. 53, *r*) of the 19 head has been found in the inscriptions.   This occurs on the Temple of the Cross at Palenque and seems to be formed regularly, both the dots of the 9 head and the fleshless lower jaw of the 10 head appearing.

The head for 0 (zero), figure 53, *s–w*, is always to be distinguished by the hand clasping the lower part of the face (*).   In this sign for zero, the hand probably represents the idea "ending" or "closing," just as it seems to have done in the ending signs used with

Period-ending dates. According to the Maya conception of time, when a period had ended or closed it was at zero, or at least no new period had commenced. Indeed, the normal form for zero in figure 47, the head variant for zero in figure 53, *s–w*, and the form for zero shown in figure 54 are used interchangeably in the same inscription to express the same idea—namely, that no periods thus modified are involved in the calculations and that consequently the end of some higher period is recorded; that is, no fractional parts of it are present.

That the hand in "ending signs" had exactly the same meaning as the hand in the head variants for zero (fig. 53, *s–w*) receives striking corroboration from the rather unusual sign for zero shown in figure 54, to which attention was called above. The essential elements of

Fig. 54. A sign for 0, used also to express the idea "ending" or "end of" in Period-ending dates. (See figs. 47 and 53 *s–w*, for forms used interchangeably in the inscriptions to express the idea of 0 or of completion.)

this sign are [1] (1) the clasped hand, identical with the hand in the head-variant forms for zero, and (2) the large element above it, containing a curling infix. This latter element also occurs though below the clasped hand, in the "ending signs" shown in figure 37, *l*, *m*, *n*, the first two of which accompany the closing date of Katun 14, and the last the closing date of Cycle 13. The resemblance of these three "ending signs" to the last three forms in figure 54 is so close that the conclusion is well-nigh inevitable that they represented one and the same idea. The writer is of the opinion that this meaning of the hand (ending or completion) will be found to explain its use throughout the inscriptions.

In order to familiarize the student with the head-variant numerals, their several essential characteristics have been gathered together in Table X, where they may be readily consulted. Examples covering their use with period, day, and month glyphs are given in figure 55 with the corresponding English translations below.

Head-variant numerals do not occur as frequently as the bar and dot forms, and they seem to have been developed at a much later period. At least, the earliest Initial Series recorded with bar and dot numerals antedates by nearly two hundred years the earliest Initial Series the numbers of which are expressed by head variants. This long priority in the use of the former would doubtless be considerably diminished if it were possible to read the earliest Initial Series which

---

[1] The subfixial element in the first three forms of fig. 54 does not seem to be essential, since it is wanting in the last.

have head-variant numerals; but that the earliest of these latter antedate the earliest bar and dot Initial Series may well be doubted.

TABLE X. CHARACTERISTICS OF HEAD-VARIANT NUMERALS 0 TO 19, INCLUSIVE

Forms	Characteristics
Head for 0......	Clasped hand across lower part of face.
Head for 1......	Forehead ornament composed of *more than one part.*
Head for 2......	Oval in upper part of head. (?)
Head for 3......	Banded headdress or fillet.
Head for 4......	Bulging eye with square irid, snaglike front tooth, curling fang from back of mouth.
Head for 5......	Normal form of tun sign as headdress.
Head for 6......	"Hatchet eye."
Head for 7......	Large scroll passing under eye and curling up in front of forehead.
Head for 8......	Forehead ornament composed of *one part.*
Head for 9......	Dots on lower cheek or around mouth and in some cases beard.
Head for 10......	Fleshless lower jaw and in some cases other death's-head characteristics, truncated nose, etc.
Head for 11......	Undetermined.
Head for 12......	Undetermined; type of head known, however.
Head for 13......	(*a*) Long pendulous nose, bulging eye, and curling fang from back of mouth.
	(*b*) Head for 3 with fleshless lower jaw of head for 10.
Head for 14......	Head for 4 with fleshless lower jaw of head for 10.
Head for 15......	Head for 5 with fleshless lower jaw of head for 10.
Head for 16......	Head for 6 with fleshless lower jaw of head for 10.
Head for 17......	Head for 7 with fleshless lower jaw of head for 10.
Head for 18......	Head for 8 with fleshless lower jaw of head for 10.
Head for 19......	Head for 9 with fleshless lower jaw of head for 10.

Mention should be made here of a numerical form which can not be classified either as a bar and dot numeral or a head variant. This is the thumb (*), which has a numerical value of one. We have seen in the foregoing pages the different characters which stood for the numerals 0 to 19, inclusive. The next point claiming our attention is, how were the higher numbers written, numbers which in the codices are in excess of 12,000,000, and in the inscriptions, in excess of 1,400,000? In short, how were numbers so large expressed by the foregoing twenty (0 to 19, inclusive) characters?

The Maya expressed their higher numbers in two ways, in both of which the numbers rise by successive terms of the same vigesimal system:

1. By using the numbers 0 to 19, inclusive, as multipliers with the several periods of Table VIII (reduced in each case to units of the lowest order) as the multiplicands, and—

2. By using the same numbers[1] in certain relative positions, each of which had a fixed numerical value of its own, like the positions to the right and left of the decimal point in our own numerical notation.

---

[1] As previously explained, the number 20 is used only in the codices and there only in connection with tonalamatls.

The first of these methods is rarely found outside of the inscriptions, while the second is confined exclusively to the codices. Moreover, although the first made use of both normal-form and head-variant

| 1 Ahau | Cycle 1 | 3 Zip | Uinal 4 |

| Tun 5 | 6 Ahau | 7 Ahau | 8 Ahau |

| Katun 8 | Cycle 9 | Katun 9 | 10 Mol |

| 12 Caban | Tun 13 | Tun 13 | 13 Pop |

| Katun 14 | Tun 15 | Kin 16 | Katun 17 |

| 18 Tzec | Katun 19 | Kin 0 | Cycle 1 |

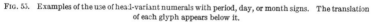

FIG. 55.   Examples of the use of head-variant numerals with period, day, or month signs.   The translation of each glyph appears below it.

numerals, the second could be expressed by normal forms only, that is, bar and dot numerals. This enables us to draw a comparison between these two forms of Maya numerals:

Head-variant numerals never occur independently, but are always prefixed to some period, day, or month sign. Bar and dot numerals, on the other hand, frequently stand by themselves in the codices unattached to other signs. In such cases, however, some sign was to be supplied mentally with the bar and dot numeral.

FIRST METHOD OF NUMERATION

In the first of the above methods the numbers 0 to 19, inclusive, were expressed by multiplying the kin sign by the numerals [1] 0 to 19

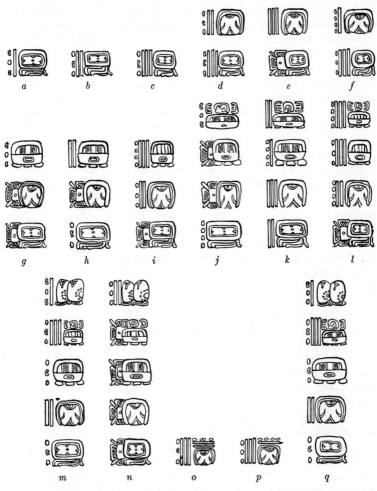

FIG. 56. Examples of the first method of numeration, used almost exclusively in the inscriptions.

in turn.   Thus, for example, 6 days was written as shown in figure 56, *a*, 12 days as shown in *b*, and 17 days as shown in *c* of the same

---

[1] Whether the Maya used their numerical system in the inscriptions and codices for counting anything besides time is not known. As used in the texts, the numbers occur only in connection with calendric matters, at least in so far as they have been deciphered. It is true many numbers are found in both the inscriptions and codices which are attached to signs of unknown meaning, and it is possible that these may have nothing to do with the calendar. An enumeration of cities or towns, or of tribute rolls, for example, may be recorded in some of these places. Both of these subjects are treated of in the Aztec manuscripts and may well be present in Maya texts.

figure. In other words, up to and including 19 the numbers were expressed by prefixing the sign for the number desired to the kin sign, that is, the sign for 1 day.[1]

The numbers 20 to 359, inclusive, were expressed by multiplying both the kin and uinal signs by the numerical forms 0 to 19, and adding together the resulting products. For example, the number 257 was written as shown in figure 56, *d*. We have seen in Table VIII that 1 uinal = 20 kins, consequently 12 uinals (the 12 being indicated by 2 bars and 2 dots) = 240 kins. However, as this number falls short of 257 by 17 kins, it is necessary to express these by 17 kins, which are written immediately below the 12 uinals. The sum of these two products = 257. Again, the number 300 is written as in figure 56, *e*. The 15 uinals (three bars attached to the uinal sign) = 15 × 20 = 300 kins, exactly the number expressed. However, since no kins are required to complete the number, it is necessary to show that none were involved, and consequently 0 kins, or "no kins" is written immediately below the 15 uinals, and 300 + 0 = 300. One more example will suffice to show how the numbers 20 to 359 were expressed. In figure 56, *f*, the number 198 is shown. The 9 uinals = 9 × 20 = 180 kins. But this number falls short of 198 by 18, which is therefore expressed by 18 kins written immediately below the 9 uinals; and the sum of these two products is 198, the number to be recorded.

The numbers 360 to 7,199, inclusive, are indicated by multiplying the kin, uinal, and tun signs by the numerals 0 to 19, and adding together the resulting products. For example, the number 360 is shown in figure 56, *g*. We have seen in Table VIII that 1 tun = 18 uinals; but 18 uinals = 360 kins (18 × 20 = 360); therefore 1 tun also = 360 kins. However, in order to show that no uinals and kins are involved in forming this number, it is necessary to record this fact, which was done by writing 0 uinals immediately below the 1 tun, and 0 kins immediately below the 0 uinals. The sum of these three products equals 360 (360 + 0 + 0 = 360). Again, the number 3,602 is shown in figure 56, *h*. The 10 tuns = 10 × 360 = 3,600 kins. This falls short of 3,602 by only 2 units of the first order (2 kins), therefore no uinals are involved in forming this number, a fact which is shown by the use of 0 uinals between the 10 tuns and 2 kins. The sum of these three products = 3,602 (3,600 + 0 + 2). Again, in figure 56, *i*, the number 7,100 is recorded. The 19 tuns = 19 × 360 = 6,840 kins, which falls short of 7,100 kins by 7,100 − 6,840 = 260 kins. But 260 kins = 13 uinals with no kins

---

[1] The numerals and periods given in fig. 56 are expressed by their normal forms in every case, since these may be more readily recognized than the corresponding head variants, and consequently entail less work for the student. It should be borne in mind, however, that any bar and dot numeral or any period in fig. 56 could be expressed equally well by its corresponding head form without affecting in the least the values of the resulting numbers.

remaining. Consequently, the sum of these products equals 7,100 (6,840 + 260 + 0).

The numbers 7,200 to 143,999 were expressed by multiplying the kin, uinal, tun, and katun signs by the numerals 0 to 19, inclusive, and adding together the resulting products. For example, figure 56, j, shows the number 7,204. We have seen in Table VIII that 1 katun = 20 tuns, and we have seen that 20 tuns = 7,200 kins (20 × 360); therefore 1 katun = 7,200 kins. This number falls short of the number recorded by exactly 4 kins, or in other words, no tuns or uinals are involved in its composition, a fact shown by the 0 tuns and 0 uinals between the 1 katun and the 4 kins. The sum of these four products = 7,204 (7,200 + 0 + 0 + 4). The number 75,550 is shown in figure 56, k. The 10 katuns = 72,000; the 9 tuns, 3,240; the 15 uinals, 300; and the 10 kins, 10. The sum of these four products = 75,550 (72,000 + 3,240 + 300 + 10). Again, the number 143,567 is shown in figure 56, l. The 19 katuns = 136,800; the 18 tuns, 6,480; the 14 uinals, 280; and the 7 kins, 7. The sum of these four products = 143,567 (136,800 + 6,480 + 280 + 7).

The numbers 144,000 to 1,872,000 (the highest number, according to some authorities, which has been found[1] in the inscriptions) were expressed by multiplying the kin, uinal, tun, katun, and cycle signs by the numerals 0 to 19, inclusive, and adding together the resulting products. For example, the number 987,322 is shown in figure 56, m. We have seen in Table VIII that 1 cycle = 20 katuns, but 20 katuns = 144,000 kins; therefore 6 cycles = 864,000 kins; and 17 katuns = 122,400 kins; and 2 tuns, 720 kins; and 10 uinals, 200 kins; and the 2 kins, 2 kins. The sum of these five products equals the number recorded, 987,322 (864,000 + 122,400 + 720 + 200 + 2). The highest number in the inscriptions upon which all are agreed is 1,872,000, as shown in figure 56, n. It equals 13 cycles (13 × 144,000), and consequently all the periods below—the katun, tun, uinal, and kin—are indicated as being used 0 times.

<hr>

NUMBER OF CYCLES IN A GREAT CYCLE

This brings us to the consideration of an extremely important point concerning which Maya students entertain two widely different opinions; and although its presentation will entail a somewhat lengthy digression from the subject under consideration it is so pertinent to the general question of the higher numbers and their formation, that the writer has thought best to discuss it at this point.

In a vigesimal system of numeration the unit of increase is 20, and so far as the codices are concerned, as we shall presently see, this

<hr>

[1] There may be three other numbers in the inscriptions which are considerably higher (see pp. 114–127).

number was in fact the only unit of progression used, except in the 2d order, in which 18 instead of 20 units were required to make 1 unit of the 3d order. In other words, in the codices the Maya carried out their vigesimal system to *six places* without a break other than the one in the 2d place, just noted. See Table VIII.

In the inscriptions, however, there is some ground for believing that only 13 units of the 5th order (cycles), not 20, were required to make 1 unit of the 6th order, or ·1 great cycle. Both Mr. Bowditch (1910: App. IX, 319–321) and Mr. Goodman (1897: p. 25) incline to this opinion, and the former, in Appendix IX of his book, presents the evidence at some length for and against this hypothesis.

This hypothesis rests mainly on the two following points:

1. That the cycles in the inscriptions are numbered from 1 to 13, inclusive, and not from 0 to 19, inclusive, as in the case of all the other periods except the uinal, which is numbered from 0 to 17, inclusive.

2. That the only two Initial Series which are not counted from the date **4 Ahau 8 Cumhu,** the starting point of Maya chronology, are counted from a date **4 Ahau 8 Zotz,** which is exactly 13 cycles in advance of the former date.

Let us examine the passages in the inscriptions upon which these points rest. In three places [1] in the inscriptions the date **4 Ahau 8 Cumhu** is declared to have occurred at the end of a Cycle 13; that is, in these three places this date is accompanied by an "ending sign" and a Cycle 13. In another place in the inscriptions, although the starting point **4 Ahau 8 Cumhu** is not itself expressed, the second cycle thereafter is declared to have been a Cycle 2, not a Cycle 15, as it would have been had the cycles been numbered from 0 to 19, inclusive, like all the other periods.[2] In still another place the ninth cycle after the starting point (that is, the end of a Cycle 13) is not a Cycle 2 in the *following* great cycle, as would be the case if the cycles were numbered from 0 to 19, inclusive, but a Cycle 9, as if the cycles were numbered from 1 to 13. Again, the end of the tenth cycle after the starting point is recorded in several places, but not as Cycle 3 of the following great cycle, as if the cycles were numbered from 0 to 19, inclusive, but as Cycle 10, as would be the case if the cycles were numbered from 1 to 13. The above examples leave little doubt that the cycles were numbered from 1 to 13, inclusive, and not from 0 to 19, as in the case of the other periods. Thus, there can be no question concerning the truth of the first of the two above points on which this hypothesis rests.

---

[1] These are: (1) The tablet from the Temple of the Cross at Palenque; (2) Altar 1 at Piedras Negras; and (3) The east side of Stela C at Quirigua.

[2] This case occurs on the tablet from the Temple of the Foliated Cross at Palenque.

But because this is true it does not necessarily follow that 13 cycles made 1 great cycle. Before deciding this point let us examine the two Initial Series mentioned above, as *not* proceeding from the date **4 Ahau 8 Cumhu**, but from a date **4 Ahau 8 Zotz**, exactly 13 cycles in advance of the former date.

These are in the Temple of the Cross at Palenque and on the east side of Stela C at Quirigua. In these two cases, if the long numbers expressed in terms of cycles, katuns, tuns, uinals, and kins are reduced to kins, and counted forward from the date **4 Ahau 8 Cumhu**, the starting point of Maya chronology, in neither case will the recorded terminal day of the Initial Series be reached; hence these two Initial Series could not have had the day **4 Ahau 8 Cumhu** as their starting point. It may be noted here that these two Initial Series are the only ones throughout the inscriptions known at the present time which are not counted from the date **4 Ahau 8 Cumhu**.[1] However, by counting *backward* each of these long numbers from their respective terminal days, **8 Ahau 18 Tzec**, in the case of the Palenque Initial Series, and **4 Ahau 8 Cumhu**, in the case of the Quirigua Initial Series, it will be found that both of them proceed from the same starting point, a date **4 Ahau 8 Zotz**, exactly 13 cycles in advance of the starting point of Maya chronology. Or, in other words, the starting point of all Maya Initial Series save two, was exactly 13 cycles later than the starting point of these two. Because of this fact and the fact that the cycles were numbered from 1 to 13, inclusive, as shown above, Mr. Bowditch and Mr. Goodman have reached the conclusion that in the inscriptions only 13 cycles were required to make 1 great cycle.

It remains to present the points against this hypothesis, which seem to indicate that the great cycle in the inscriptions contained the same number of cycles (20) as in the codices:

1. In the codices where six orders (great cycles) are recorded it takes 20 of the 5th order (cycles) to make 1 of the 6th order. This absolute uniformity in a strict vigesimal progression in the codices, so similar in other respects to the inscriptions, gives presumptive support at least to the hypothesis that the 6th order in the inscriptions was formed in the same way.

2. The numerical system in both the codices and inscriptions is identical even to the slight irregularity in the second place, where only 18 instead of 20 units were required to make 1 of the third place. It would seem probable, therefore, that had there been any irregularity in the 5th place in the inscriptions (for such the use of 13 in a vigesimal system must be called), it would have been found also in the codices.

---

[1] It seems probable that the number on the north side of Stela C at Copan was not counted from the date **4 Ahau 8 Cumhu**. The writer has not been able to satisfy himself, however, that this number is an Initial Series.

3. Moreover, in the inscriptions themselves the cycle glyph occurs at least twice (see fig. 57, *a*, *b*) with a coefficient greater than 13, which would seem to imply that more than 13 cycles could be recorded, and consequently that it required more than 13 to make 1 of the period next higher. The writer knows of no place in the inscriptions where 20 kins, 18 uinals, 20 tuns, or 20 katuns are recorded, each of these being expressed as 1 uinal, 1 tun, 1 katun, and 1 cycle, respectively.[1] Therefore, if 13 cycles had made 1 great cycle, 14 cycles would not have been recorded, as in figure 57, *a*, but as 1 great cycle and 1 cycle; and 17 cycles would not have been recorded, as in *b* of the same figure, but as 1 great cycle and 4 cycles. The fact that they were not recorded in this latter manner would seem to indicate, therefore, that more than 13 cycles were required to make a great cycle, or unit of the 6th place, in the inscriptions as well as in the codices.

a   *b*

FIG. 57. Signs for the cycle showing coefficients above 13: *a*, From the Temple of the Inscriptions, Palenque; *b*, from Stela N, Copan.

The above points are simply positive evidence in support of this hypothesis, however, and in no way attempt to explain or otherwise account for the undoubtedly contradictory points given in the discussion of (1) on pages 108–109. Furthermore, not until these contradictions have been cleared away can it be established that the great cycle in the inscriptions was of the same length as the great cycle in the codices. The writer believes the following explanation will satisfactorily dispose of these contradictions and make possible at the same time the acceptance of the theory that the great cycle in the inscriptions and in the codices was of equal length, being composed in each case of 20 cycles.

Assuming for the moment that there were 13 cycles in a great cycle, it is clear that if this were the case 13 cycles could never be recorded in the inscriptions, for the reason that, being equal to 1 great cycle, they would have to be recorded in terms of a great cycle. This is true because no period in the inscriptions is ever expressed, so far as now known, as the full number of the periods of which it was composed. For example, 1 uinal never appears as 20 kins; 1 tun is never written as its equivalent, 18 uinals; 1 katun is never recorded as 20 tuns, etc. Consequently, if a great cycle composed of 13 cycles had come to its end with the end of a Cycle 13, which fell on a day **4 Ahau 8 Cumhu,** such a Cycle 13 could never have been expressed, since in its place would have been recorded the end of the great cycle which fell on the same day. In other words, if there had been 13 cycles in a great cycle, the cycles would have been numbered from 0 to 12, inclusive, and the last, Cycle 13, would have been recorded instead as completing some great cycle. It is necessary to

---

[1] Mr. Bowditch (1910: pp. 41–42) notes a seeming exception to this, not in the inscription, however, but in the Dresden Codex, in which, in a series of numbers on pp. 71–73, the number 390 is written 19 uinals and 10 kins, instead of 1 tun, 1 uinal, and 10 kins,

admit this point or repudiate the numeration of all the other periods in the inscriptions.   The writer believes, therefore, that, when the starting point of Maya chronology is declared to be a date **4 Ahau 8 Cumhu,** which an "ending sign" and a Cycle 13 further declare fell at the close of a Cycle 13, this does not indicate that there were 13 cycles in a great cycle, but that it is to be interpreted as a Period-ending date, pure and simple.   Indeed, where this date is found in the inscriptions it occurs with a Cycle 13, and an "ending sign" which is practically identical with other undoubted "ending signs." Moreover, if we interpret these places as indicating that there were only 13 cycles in a great cycle, we have equal grounds for saying that the great cycle contained only 10 cycles.   For example, on Zoömorph G at Quirigua the date **7 Ahau 18 Zip** is accompanied by an "ending sign" and Cycle 10, which on this basis of interpretation would signify that a great cycle had only 10 cycles.   Similarly, it could be shown by such an interpretation that in some cases a cycle had 14 katuns, that is, where the end of a Katun 14 was recorded, or 17 katuns, where the end of a Katun 17 was recorded.   All such places, including the date **4 Ahau 8 Cumhu,** which closed a Cycle 13 at the starting point of Maya chronology, are only Period-ending dates, the writer believes, and have no reference to the number of periods which any higher period contains whatsoever.   They record merely the end of a particular period in the Long Count as the end of a certain Cycle 13, or a certain Cycle 10, or a certain Katun 14, or a certain Katun 17, as the case may be, and contain no reference to the beginning or the end of the period next higher.

There can be no doubt, however, as stated above, that the cycles were numbered from 1 to 13, inclusive, and then began again with 1. This sequence strikingly recalls that of the numerical coefficients of the days, and in the parallel which this latter sequence affords, the writer believes, lies the true explanation of the misconception concerning the length of the great cycle in the inscriptions.

TABLE XI. SEQUENCE OF TWENTY CONSECUTIVE DATES IN THE MONTH POP

1 Ik	0 Pop	11 Eb	10 Pop
2 Akbal	1 Pop	12 Ben	11 Pop
3 Kan	2 Pop	13 Ix	12 Pop
4 Chicchan	3 Pop	1 Men	13 Pop
5 Cimi	4 Pop	2 Cib	14 Pop
6 Manik	5 Pop	3 Caban	15 Pop
7 Lamat	6 Pop	4 Eznab	16 Pop
8 Muluc	7 Pop	5 Cauac	17 Pop
9 Oc	8 Pop	6 Ahau	18 Pop
10 Chuen	9 Pop	7 Imix	19 Pop

The numerical coefficients of the days, as we have seen, were numbered from 1 to 13, inclusive, and then began again with 1.   See

Table XI, in which the 20 days of the month **Pop** are enumerated. Now it is evident from this table that, although the coefficients of the days themselves do not rise above 13, the numbers showing the positions of these days in the month continue up through 19. In other words, two different sets of numerals were used in describing the Maya days: (1) The numerals 1 to 13, inclusive, the coefficients of the days, and an integral part of their names; and (2) The numerals 0 to 19, inclusive, showing the positions of these days in the divisions of the year—the uinals, and the xma kaba kin. It is clear from the foregoing, moreover, that the number of possible day coefficients (13) has nothing whatever to do in determining the number of days in the period next higher. That is, although the coefficients of the days are numbered from 1 to 13, inclusive, it does not necessarily follow that the next higher period (the uinal) contained only 13 days. Similarly, the writer believes that while the cycles were undoubtedly numbered—that is, named—from 1 to 13, inclusive, like the coefficients of the days, it took 20 of them to make a great cycle, just as it took 20 kins to make a uinal. The two cases appear to be parallel. Confusion seems to have arisen through mistaking the *name* of the period for its *position* in the period next higher—two entirely different things, as we have seen.

A somewhat similar case is that of the katuns in the u kahlay katunob in Table IX. Assuming that a cycle commenced with the first katun there given, the name of this katun is Katun **2 Ahau,** although it occupied the *first* position in the cycle. Again, the name of the second katun in the sequence is Katun **13 Ahau**, although it occupied the second position in the cycle. In other words, the katuns of the u kahlay katunob were named quite independently of their position in the period next higher (the cycle), and their names do not indicate the corresponding positions of the katun in the period next higher.

Applying the foregoing explanation to those passages in the inscriptions which show that the enumeration of the cycles was from 1 to 13, inclusive, we may interpret them as follows: When we find the date **4 Ahau 8 Cumhu** in the inscriptions, accompanied by an "ending sign" and a Cycle 13, that "Cycle 13," even granting that it stands at the end of some great cycle, does not signify that there were only 13 cycles in the great cycle of which it was a part. On the contrary, it records only the end of a particular Cycle 13, being a Period-ending date pure and simple. Such passages no more fix the length of the great cycle as containing 13 cycles than does the coefficient 13 of the day name **13 Ix** in Table XI limit the number of days in a uinal to 13, or, again, the 13 of the katun name **13 Ahau** in Table IX limit the number of katuns in a cycle to 13. This explanation not only accounts for the use of the 14 cycles or 17 cycles, as shown in figure 57, *a*, *b*, but also satisfactorily provides for the enumeration of the cycles from 1 to 13, inclusive.

If the date "**4 Ahau 8 Cumhu** ending Cycle 13" be regarded as a Period-ending date, not as indicating that the number of cycles in a great cycle was restricted to 13, the next question is—Did a great cycle also come to an end on the date **4 Ahau 8 Cumhu**—the starting point of Maya chronology and the closing date of a Cycle 13 ? That it did the writer is firmly convinced, although final proof of the point can not be presented until numerical series containing more than 5 terms shall have been considered. (See pp. 114–127 for this discussion.) The following points, however, which may be introduced here, tend to prove this condition:

1. In the natural course of affairs the Maya would have commenced their chronology with the beginning of some great cycle, and to have done this in the Maya system of counting time—that is, by elapsed periods—it was necessary to reckon from the end of the preceding great cycle as the starting point.

2. Moreover, it would seem as though the natural cycle with which to commence counting time would be a *Cycle 1*, and if this were done time would have to be counted from a *Cycle 13*, since a Cycle 1 could follow only a Cycle 13.

On these two probabilities, together with the discussion on pages 114–127, the writer is inclined to believe that the Maya commenced their chronology with the beginning of a great cycle, whose first cycle was named Cycle 1, which was reckoned from the close of a great cycle whose ending cycle was a Cycle 13 and whose ending day fell on the date **4 Ahau 8 Cumhu.**

The second point (see p. 108) on which rests the hypothesis of "13 cycles to a great cycle" in the inscriptions admits of no such plausible explanation as the first point. Indeed, it will probably never be known why in two inscriptions the Maya reckoned time from a starting point different from that used in all the others, one, moreover, which was 13 cycles in advance of the other, or more than 5,000 years earlier than the beginning of their chronology, and more than 8,000 years earlier than the beginning of their historic period. That this remoter starting point, **4 Ahau 8 Zotz**, from which proceed so far as known only two inscriptions throughout the whole Maya area, stood at the *end* of a great cycle the writer does not believe, in view of the evidence presented on pages 114–127. On the contrary, the material given there tends to show that although the cycle which ended on the day **4 Ahau 8 Zotz** was also named Cycle 13,[1] it was the 8th division of the grand cycle which ended on the day **4 Ahau 8 Cumhu,**

---

[1] That it was a Cycle 13 is shown from the fact that it was just 13 cycles in advance of Cycle 13 ending on the date **4 Ahau 8 Cumhu.**

the starting point of Maya chronology, and not the closing division of the preceding grand cycle. However, without attempting to settle this question at this time, the writer inclines to the belief, on the basis of the evidence at hand, that the great cycle in the inscriptions was of the same length as in the codices, where it is known to have contained 20 cycles.

Let us return to the discussion interrupted on page 107, where the first method of expressing the higher numbers was being explained. We saw there how the higher numbers up to and including 1,872,000 were written, and the digression just concluded had for its purpose ascertaining how the numbers above this were expressed; that is, whether 13 or 20 units of the 5th order were equal to 1 unit of the 6th order. It was explained also that this number, 1,872,000, was perhaps the highest which has been found in the inscriptions. Three possible exceptions, however, to this statement should be noted here: (1) On the east side of Stela N at Copan six periods are recorded (see fig. 58); (2) on the west panel from the Temple of the Inscriptions at Palenque six and probably *seven* periods occur (see fig. 59); and (3) on Stela 10 at Tikal eight and perhaps *nine* periods are found (see fig. 60). If in any of these cases all of the periods belong to one and the same numerical series, the resulting numbers would be far higher than 1,872,000. Indeed, such numbers would exceed by many millions all others throughout the range of Maya writings, in either the codices or the inscriptions.

Before presenting these three numbers, however, a distinction should be drawn between them. The first and second (figs. 58, 59) are clearly not Initial Series. Probably they are Secondary Series, although this point can not be established with certainty, since they can not be connected with any known date the position of which is definitely fixed. The third number (fig. 60), on the other hand, is an Initial Series, and the eight or nine periods of which it is composed may fix the initial date of Maya chronology (**4 Ahau 8 Cumhu**) in a much grander chronological scheme, as will appear presently.

The first of these three numbers (see fig. 58), if all its six periods belong to the same series, equals 42,908,400. Although the order of the several periods is just the reverse of that in the numbers in figure 56, this difference is unessential, as will shortly be explained, and in no way affects the value of the number recorded. Commencing at the bottom of figure 58 with the highest period involved and reading up, A6,[1] the 14 great cycles = 40,320,000 kins (see Table VIII, in which 1 great cycle = 2,880,000, and consequently 14 = 14 × 2,880,000 =

---

[1] See p. 156 and fig. 66 for method of designating the individual glyphs in a text.

40,320,000); A5, the 17 cycles = 2,448,000 kins (17 × 144,000); A4, the 19 katuns = 136,800 kins (19 × 7,200); A3, the 10 tuns = 3,600 kins (10 × 360); A2, the 0 uinals, 0 kins; and the 0 kins, 0 kins.   The sum

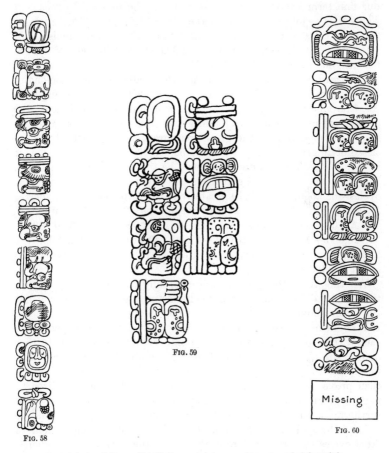

Fig. 59

Fig. 58

Missing

Fig. 60

FIG. 58.   Part of the inscription on Stela N, Copan, showing a number composed of six periods.
FIG. 59.   Part of the inscription in the Temple of the Inscriptions, Palenque, showing a number composed
    of seven periods.
FIG. 60.   Part of the inscription on Stela 10, Tikal (probably an Initial Series), showing a number composed
    of eight periods.

of these products = 40,320,000 + 2,448,000 + 136,800 + 3,600 + 0 + 0 = 42,908,400.

The second of these three numbers (see fig. 59), if all of its seven terms belong to one and the same number, equals 455,393,401. Commencing at the bottom as in figure 58, the first term A4, has the co-efficient 7. Since this is the term following the sixth, or great cycle, we may call it the great-great cycle. But we have seen that the great cycle = 2,880,000; therefore the great-great cycle = twenty times this number, or 57,600,000. Our text shows, however, that seven of these great-great cycles are used in the number in question, therefore our first term = 403,200,000. The rest may be reduced by means of Table VIII as follows: B3, 18 great cycles = 51,840,000; A3, 2 cycles = 288,000; B2, 9 katuns = 64,800; A2, 1 tun = 360; B1, 12 uinals = 240; B1, 1 kin = 1. The sum of these (403,200,000 + 51,840,000 + 288,000 + 64,800 + 360 + 240 + 1) = 455,393,401.

The third of these numbers (see fig. 60), if all of its terms belong to one and the same number, equals 1,841,639,800. Commencing with A2, this has a coefficient of 1. Since it immediately follows the great-great cycle, which we found above consisted of 57,600,000, we may assume that it is the great-great-great cycle, and that it consisted of 20 great-great cycles, or 1,152,000,000. Since its coefficient is only 1, this large number itself will be the first term in our series. The rest may readily be reduced as follows: A3, 11 great-great cycles = 633,600,000; A4, 19 great cycles = 54,720,000; A5, 9 cycles = 1,296,000; A6, 3 katuns = 21,600; A7, 6 tuns = 2,160; A8, 2 uinals = 40; A9, 0 kins = 0.[1] The sum of these (1,152,000,000 + 633,600,000 + 54,720,000 + 1,296,000 + 21,600 + 2,160 + 40 + 0) = 1,841,639,800, the highest number found anywhere in the Maya writings, equivalent to about 5,000,000 years.

Whether these three numbers are actually recorded in the inscriptions under discussion depends solely on the question whether or not the terms above the cycle in each belong to one and the same series. If it could be determined with certainty that these higher periods in each text were all parts of the same number, there would be no further doubt as to the accuracy of the figures given above; and more important still, the 17 cycles of the first number (see A5, fig. 58) would then prove conclusively that more than 13 cycles were required to make a great cycle in the inscriptions as well as in the codices. And furthermore, the 14 great cycles in A6, figure 58, the 18 in B3, figure 59, and the 19 in A4, figure 60, would also prove that more than 13 great cycles were required to make one of the period next higher— that is, the great-great cycle. It is needless to say that this point has not been universally admitted. Mr. Goodman (1897: p. 132) has suggested in the case of the Copan inscription (fig. 58) that only the lowest four periods—the 19 katuns, the 10 tuns, the 0 uinals, and the 0 kins—A2, A3, and A4,[2] here form the number; and that if this number is counted backward from the Initial Series of the inscription, it will reach a Katun 17 of the preceding cycle. Finally, Mr. Goodman

---

[1] The kins are missing from this number (see A9, fig. 60). At the maximum, however, they could increase this large number only by 19. They have been used here as at 0.

[2] As will be explained presently, the kin sign is frequently omitted and its coefficient attached to the uinal glyph. See p. 127.

believes this Katun 17 is declared in the glyph following the 19 katuns (A5), which the writer identifies as 17 cycles, and consequently according to the Goodman interpretation the whole passage is a Period-ending date. Mr. Bowditch (1910: p. 321) also offers the same interpretation as a possible reading of this passage. Even granting the truth of the above, this interpretation still leaves unexplained the lowest glyph of the number, which has a coefficient of 14 (A6).

The strongest proof that this passage will not bear the construction placed on it by Mr. Goodman is afforded by the very glyph upon which his reading depends for its verification, namely, the glyph which he interprets Katun 17. This glyph (A5) bears no resemblance to the katun sign standing immediately above it, but on the contrary has for its lower jaw the clasping hand (*), which, as we have seen, is the determining characteristic of the cycle head. Indeed, this * element is so clearly portrayed in the glyph in question that its identification as a head variant for the cycle follows almost of necessity. A comparison of this glyph with the head variant of the cycle given in figure 25, *d–f*, shows that the two forms are practically identical. This correction deprives Mr. Goodman's reading of its chief support, and at the same time increases the probability that all the 6 terms here recorded belong to one and the same number. That is, since the first five are the kin, uinal, tun, katun, and cycle, respectively, it is probable that the sixth and last, which follows immediately the fifth, without a break or interruption of any kind, belongs to the same series also, in which event this glyph would be most likely to represent the units of the sixth order, or the so-called great cycles.

The passages in the Palenque and Tikal texts (figs. 59 and 60, respectively) have never been satisfactorily explained. In default of calendric checks, as the known distance between two dates, for example, which may be applied to these three numbers to test their accuracy, the writer knows of no better check than to study the characteristics of this possible great-cycle glyph in all three, and of the possible great-great-cycle glyph in the last two.

Passing over the kins, the normal form of the uinal glyph appears in figures 58, A2, and 59, B1 (see fig. 31, *a, b*), and the head variant in figure 60, A8. (See fig. 31, *d–f*.) Below the uinal sign in A3, figure 58, and A2, figure 59, and above A7, in figure 60 the tuns are recorded as head variants, in all three of which the fleshless lower jaw, the determining characteristic of the tun head, appears. Compare these three head variants with the head variant for the tun in figure 29, *d–g*. In the Copan inscription (fig. 58) the katun glyph, A4, appears as a head variant, the essential elements of which seem to be the oval in the top part of the head and the curling fang protruding from the back part of the mouth. Compare this head with the head variant for the katun in figure 27, *e–h.* In the Palenque and Tikal texts (see figs. 59, B2, and 60, A6, respectively), on the other hand, the katun is expressed by its normal form, which is identical with the normal form shown in figure 27, *a*, *b*.   In figures 58, A5, and 59, A3, the cycle is expressed by its head variant, and the determining characteristic, the clasped hand, appears in both.   Compare the cycle signs in figures 58, A5, and 59, A3, with the head variant for the cycle shown in figure 25, *d–f*.   The cycle glyph in the Tikal text (fig. 60, A5) is clearly the normal form.   (See fig. 25, *a–c*.)   The glyph following the cycle sign in these three texts (standing above the cycle sign in figure 60 at A4) probably stands for the period of the sixth order, the so-called great cycle.   These three glyphs are redrawn in figure 61, *a–c*, respectively.   In the Copan inscription this glyph (fig. 61, *a*) is a head variant, while in the Palenque and Tikal texts (*a* and *b* of the same figure, respectively) it is a normal form.

a   *b*   *c*   *d*   *e*

FIG. 61. Signs for the great cycle (*a–c*), and the great-great cycle (*d*, *e*): *a*, Stela N, Copan; *b*, *d*, Temple
of the Inscriptions, Palenque; *c*, *e*, Stela 10, Tikal.

Inasmuch as these three inscriptions are the only ones in which numerical series composed of 6 or more consecutive terms are recorded, it is unfortunate that the sixth term in all three should not have been expressed by the same form, since this would have facilitated their comparison.   Notwithstanding this handicap, however, the writer believes it will be possible to show clearly that the head variant in figure 61, *a*, and the normal forms in *b* and *c* are only variants of one and the same sign, and that all three stand for one and the same thing, namely, the great cycle, or unit of the sixth order.

In the first place, it will be noted that each of the three glyphs just mentioned is composed in part of the cycle sign.   For example, in figure 61, *a*, the head variant has the same clasped hand as the head-variant cycle sign in the same text (see fig. 58, A5), which, as we have seen elsewhere, is the determining characteristic of the head variant for the cycle.   In figure 61, *b*, *c*, the normal forms there presented contain the entire normal form for the cycle sign; compare figure 25, *a*, *c*.   Indeed, except for its superfix, the glyphs in figure 61, *b*, *c*, are normal forms of the cycle sign; and the glyph in *a* of the same figure, except for its superfixial element, is similarly the head variant for the cycle.   It would seem, therefore, that the determining characteristics of these three glyphs must be their superfixial elements.   In the normal form in figure 61, *b*, the superfix is very clear.   Just inside the outline and parallel to it there is a line of smaller circles, and in the middle there are two infixes like shepherds' crooks facing away from the center (*). In c of the last-mentioned figure the superfix is of the same size and shape, and although it is partially destroyed the left-hand "shepherd's crook" can still be distinguished. A faint dot treatment around the edge can also still be traced. Although the superfix of the head variant in a is somewhat weathered, enough remains to show that it was similar to, if indeed not identical with, the superfixes of the normal forms in b and c. The line of circles defining the left side of this superfix, as well as traces of the lower ends of the two "shepherd's crook" infixes, appears very clearly in the lower part of the superfix. Moreover, in general shape and proportions this element is so similar to the corresponding elements in figure 61, b, c, that, taken together with the similarity of the other details pointed out above, it seems more than likely that all three of these superfixes are one and the same element. The points which have led the writer to identify glyphs a, b, and c in figure 61 as forms for the great cycle, or period of the sixth order, may be summarized as follows:

1. All three of these glyphs, head-variant as well as normal forms, are made up of the corresponding forms of the cycle sign plus another element, a superfix, which is probably the determining characteristic in each case.

2. All three of these superfixes are probably identical, thus showing that the three glyphs in which they occur are probably variants of the same sign.

3. All three of these glyphs occur in numerical series, the preceding term of which in each case is a cycle sign, thus showing that by position they are the logical "next" term (the sixth) of the series.

Let us next examine the two texts in which great-great-cycle glyphs may occur. (See figs. 59, 60.) The two glyphs which may possibly be identified as the sign for this period are shown in figure 61, d, e.

A comparison of these two forms shows that both are composed of the same elements: (1) The cycle sign; (2) a superfix in which the hand is the principal element.

The superfix in figure 61, d, consists of a hand and a tassel-like postfix, not unlike the upper half of the ending signs in figure 37, l–q. However, in the present case, if we accept the hypothesis that d of figure 61 is the sign for the great-great cycle, we are obliged to see in its superfix alone the essential *element* of the great-great-cycle sign, since the *rest* of this glyph (the lower part) is quite clearly the normal form for the cycle.

The superfix in figure 61, e, consists of the same two elements as the above, with the slight difference that the hand in e holds a rod. Indeed, the similarity of the two forms is so close that in default of any evidence to the contrary the writer believes they may be accepted as signs for one and the same period, namely, the great-great cycle.

The points on which this conclusion is based may be summarized as follows:

1. Both glyphs are made up of the same elements—(a) The normal form of the cycle sign; (b) a superfix composed of a hand with a tassel-like postfix.

2. Both glyphs occur in numerical series the next term but one of which is the cycle, showing that by position they are the logical next term but one, the seventh or great-great cycle, of the series.

3. Both of these glyphs stand next to glyphs which have been identified as great-cycle signs, that is, the sixth terms of the series in which they occur.

By this same line of reasoning it seems probable that A2 in figure 60 is the sign for the great-great-great cycle, although this fact can not be definitely established because of the lack of comparative evidence.

This possible sign for the great-great-great cycle, or period of the 8th order, is composed of two parts, just like the signs for the great cycle and the great-great cycle already described. These are: (1) The cycle sign; (2) a superfix composed of a hand and a semicircular postfix, quite distinct from the superfixes of the great cycle and great-great cycle signs.

However, since there is no other inscription known which presents a number composed of eight terms, we must lay aside this line of investigation and turn to another for further light on this point.

An examination of figure 60 shows that the glyphs which we have identified as the signs for the higher periods (A2, A3, A4, and A5,) contain one element common to all—the sign for the cycle, or period of 144,000 days. Indeed, A5 is composed of this sign alone with its usual coefficient of 9. Moreover, the next glyphs (A6, A7, A8, and A9 [1]) are the signs for the katun, tun, uinal, and kin, respectively, and, together with A5, form a regular descending series of 5 terms, all of which are of known value.

The next question is, How is this glyph in the sixth place formed? We have seen that in the only three texts in which more than five periods are recorded this sign for the sixth period is composed of the same elements in each: (1) The cycle sign; (2) a superfix containing two "shepherd's crook" infixes and surrounded by dots.

Further, we have seen that in two cases in the inscriptions the cycle sign has a coefficient greater than 13, thus showing that in all probability 20, not 13, cycles made 1 great cycle.

Therefore, since the great-cycle signs in figure 61, a–c, are composed of the cycle sign plus a superfix (*), this superfix must have the value of 20 in order to make the whole glyph have the value of

---

[1] Glyph A9 is missing but undoubtedly was the kin sign and coefficient.

20 cycles, or 1 great cycle (that is, $20 \times 144,000 = 2,880,000$). In other words, it may be accepted (1) that the glyphs in figure 61, a–c, are signs for the great cycle, or period of the sixth place; and (2) that the great cycle was composed of 20 cycles shown graphically by two elements, one being the cycle sign itself and the other a superfix having the value of 20.

It has been shown that the last six glyphs in figure 60 (A4, A5, A6, A7, A8, and A9) all belong to the same series. Let us next examine the seventh glyph or term from the bottom (A3) and see how it is formed. We have seen that in the only two texts in which more than six periods are recorded the signs for the seventh period (see fig. 61, d, e) are composed of the same elements in each: (1) The cycle sign; (2) a superfix having the hand as its principal element. We have seen, further, that in the only three places in which great cycles are recorded in the Maya writing (fig. 61, a–c) the coefficient in every case is greater than 13, thus showing that in all probability 20, not 13, great cycles made 1 great-great cycle.

Therefore, since the great-great cycle signs in figure 61, d, e, are composed of the cycle sign plus a superfix (*), this superfix must have the value of 400 (20×20) in order to make the whole glyph have the value of 20 great cycles, or 1 great-great cycle ($20 \times 2,880,000 = 57,600,000$). In other words, it seems highly probable (1) that the glyphs in figure 61, d, e, are signs for the great-great cycle or period of the seventh place, and (2) that the great-great cycle was composed of 20 great cycles, shown graphically by two elements, one being the cycle sign itself and the other a hand having the value of 400.

It has been shown that the first seven glyphs (A3, A4, A5, A6, A7, A8, and A9) probably all belong to the same series. Let us next examine the eighth term (A2) and see how it is formed.

As stated above, comparative evidence can help us no further, since the text under discussion is the only one which presents a number composed of more than seven terms. Nevertheless, the writer believes it will be possible to show by the morphology of this, the only glyph which occupies the position of an eighth term, that it is 20 times the glyph in the seventh position, and consequently that the vigesimal system was perfect to the highest known unit found in the Maya writing.

We have seen (1) that the sixth term was composed of the fifth term plus a superfix which increased the fifth 20 times, and (2) that the seventh term was composed of the fifth term plus a superfix which increased the fifth 400 times, or the sixth 20 times.

Now let us examine the only known example of a sign for the eighth term (A2, fig. 60). This glyph is composed of (1) the cycle sign; (2) a superfix of two elements, (a) the hand, and (b) a semicircular element in which dots appear.

But this same hand in the superfix of the great-great cycle increased the cycle sign 400 times (20×20; see A3, fig. 60). Therefore we must assume the same condition obtains here. And finally, since the eighth term $= 20 \times 20 \times 20 \times$ cycle, we must recognize in the second ⟨glyph⟩ element of the superfix (*) a sign which means 20.

* A close study of this element shows that it has two important points of resemblance to the superfix of the great-cycle glyph (see A4, fig. 60), which was shown to have the value 20: (1) Both elements have the same outline, roughly semicircular; (2) both elements have the same chain of dots around their edges.

Compare this element in A2, figure 60, with the superfixes in figure 61, *a*, *b*, bearing in mind that there is more than 275 years' difference in time between the carving of A2, figure 60, and *a*, figure 61, and more than 200 years between the former and figure 61, *b*. The writer believes both are variants of the same element, and consequently A2, figure 60, is probably composed of elements which signify 20×400 (20×20) $\times$ the cycle, which equals one great-great-great cycle, or term of the eighth place.

Thus on the basis of the glyphs themselves it seems possible to show that all belong to one and the same numerical series, which progresses according to the terms of a vigesimal system of numeration.

The several points supporting this conclusion may be summarized as follows:

1. The eight periods [1] in figure 60 are consecutive, their sequence being uninterrupted throughout. Consequently it seems probable that all belong to one and the same number.

2. It has been shown that the highest three period glyphs are composed of elements which multiply the cycle sign by 20, 400, and 8,000, respectively, which has to be the case if they are the sixth, seventh, and eighth terms, respectively, of the Maya vigesimal system of numeration.

3. The highest three glyphs have numerical coefficients, just like the five lower ones; this tends to show that all eight are terms of the same numerical series.

4. In the two texts which alone can furnish comparative data for this sixth term, the sixth-period glyph in each is identical with A4, figure 60, thus showing the existence of a sixth period in the inscriptions and a generally [2] accepted sign for it.

5. In the only other text which can furnish comparative data for the seventh term, the period glyph in its seventh place is identical

---

[1] The lowest period, the kin, is missing. See A9, fig. 60.

[2] The use of the word "generally" seems reasonable here; these three texts come from widely separated centers—Copan in the extreme southeast, Palenque in the extreme west, and Tikal in the central part of the area.

with A3, figure 60; thus showing the existence of a seventh period in the inscriptions and a generally accepted sign for it.

6. The one term higher than the cycle in the Copan text, the two terms higher in the Palenque text, and the three terms higher in this text, are all built on the same basic element, the cycle, thus showing that in each case the higher term or terms is a continuation of the same number, not a Period-ending date, as suggested by Mr. Goodman for the Copan text.

7. The other two texts, showing series composed of more than five terms, have all their period glyphs in an unbroken sequence in each, like the text under discussion, thus showing that in each of these other two texts all the terms present probably belong to one and the same number.

8. Finally, the two occurrences of the cycle sign with a coefficient above 13, and the three occurrences of the great-cycle sign with a coefficient above 13, indicate that 20, not 13, was the unit of progression in the higher numbers in the inscriptions just as it was in the codices.

Before closing the discussion of this unique inscription, there is one other important point in connection with it which must be considered, because of its possible bearing on the meaning of the Initial-series introducing glyph.

The first five glyphs on the east side of Stela 10 at Tikal are not illustrated in figure 60. The sixth glyph is A1 in figure 60, and the remaining glyphs in this figure carry the text to the bottom of this side of the monument. The first of these five unfigured glyphs is very clearly an Initial-series introducing glyph. Of this there can be no doubt. The second resembles the day **8 Manik**, though it is somewhat effaced. The remaining three are unknown. The next glyph, A1, figure 60, is very clearly another Initial-series introducing glyph, having all of the five elements common to that sign. Compare A1 with the forms for the Initial series introducing glyph in figure 24. This certainly would seem to indicate that an Initial Series is. to follow. Moreover, the fourth glyph of the eight-term number following in A2–A9, inclusive (that is, A5), records "Cycle 9," the cycle in which practically all Initial-series dates fall. Indeed, if A2, A3, and A4 were omitted and A5, A6, A7, A8, and A9 were recorded immediately after A1, the record would be that of a regular Initial-series number (9. 3. 6. 2. 0). Can this be a matter of chance? If not, what effect can A2, A3, and A4 have on the Initial-series date in A1, A5–A9?

The writer believes that the only possible effect they could have would be to fix Cycle 9 of Maya chronology in a far more comprehensive and elaborate chronological conception, a conception which indeed staggers the imagination, dealing as it does with more than five million years.

If these eight terms all belong to one and the same numerical series, a fact the writer believes he has established in the foregoing pages, it means that Cycle 9, the first historic period of the Maya civilization, was Cycle 9 of Great Cycle 19 of Great-great Cycle 11 of Great-great-great Cycle 1. In other words, the starting point of Maya chronology, which we have seen was the date **4 Ahau 8 Cumhu**, 9 cycles before the close of a Cycle 9, was in reality 1. 11. 19. 0. 0. 0. 0. 0. **4 Ahau 8 Cumhu**, or simply a fixed point in a far vaster chronological conception.

Furthermore, it proves, as contended by the writer on page 113, that a great cycle came to an end on this date, **4 Ahau 8 Cumhu**. This is true because on the above date (1. 11. 19. 0. 0. 0. 0. 0. **4 Ahau 8 Cumhu**) all the five periods lower than the great cycle are at 0. It proves, furthermore, as the writer also contended, that the date **4 Ahau 8 Zotz**, 13 cycles in advance of the date **4 Ahau 8 Cumhu**, did not end a great cycle—

$$\begin{array}{ll} 1.\ 11.\ 19.\quad 0.\ 0.\ 0.\ 0.\ 0. & \textbf{4 Ahau 8 Cumhu} \\ \qquad\quad 13.\ 0.\ 0.\ 0.\ 0. & \\ 1.\ 11.\ 18.\quad 7.\ 0.\ 0.\ 0.\ 0. & \textbf{4 Ahau 8 Zotz} \end{array}$$

but, on the contrary, was a Cycle 7 of Great Cycle 18, the end of which (19. 0. 0. 0. 0. 0. **4 Ahau 8 Cumhu**) was the starting point of Maya chronology.

It seems to the writer that the above construction is the only one that can be put on this text if we admit that the eight periods in A2–A9, figure 60, all belong to one and the same numerical series.

Furthermore, it would show that the great cycle in which fell the first historic period of the Maya civilization (Cycle 9) was itself the closing great cycle of a great-great cycle, namely, Great-great Cycle 11:

$$\begin{array}{l} 1.\ 11.\ 19.\ 0.\ 0.\ 0.\ 0.\ 0. \\ \quad\ 1.\ 0.\ 0.\ 0.\ 0.\ 0. \\ \quad\ 1.\ 12.\quad 0.\ 0.\ 0.\ 0.\ 0. \end{array}$$

That is to say, that when Great Cycle 19 had completed itself, Great-great Cycle 12 would be ushered in.

We have seen on pages 108–113 that the names of the cycles followed one another in this sequence: Cycle 1, Cycle 2, Cycle 3, etc., to Cycle 13, which was followed by Cycle 1, and the sequence repeated itself. We saw, however, that these names probably had nothing to do with the positions of the cycles in the great cycle; that on the contrary these numbers were names and not positions in a higher term.

Now we have seen that Maya chronology began with a Cycle 1; that is, it was counted from the end of a Cycle 13. Therefore, the closing cycle of Great Cycle 19 of Great-great Cycle 11 of Great-great-great Cycle 1 was a Cycle 13, that is to say, 1. 11. 19. 0. 0. 0. 0. 0. **4 Ahau 13 Cumhu** concluded a great cycle, the closing cycle of which was named Cycle 13. This large number, composed of *one* great-great-great cycle, *eleven* great-great cycles, and *nineteen* great cycles, contains exactly 12,780 cycles, as below:

1 great-great-great cycle	$= 1 \times 20 \times 20 \times 20$ cycles $=$	8,000 cycles
11 great-great cycles	$= 11 \times 20 \times 20$ cycles	$=$ 4,400 cycles
19 great cycles	$= 19 \times 20$ cycles	$=$ 380 cycles
		12,780 cycles

But the closing cycle of this number was named Cycle 13, and by deducting all the multiples of 13 possible (983) we can find the name of the first cycle of Great-great-great Cycle 1, the highest Maya time period of which we have any knowledge: $983 \times 13 = 12,779$. And deducting this from the number of cycles involved (12,780), we have—

$$12,780$$
$$12,779$$
$$\overline{1}$$

This counted backward from Cycle 1, brings us again to a Cycle 13 as the name of the first cycle in the Maya conception of time. In other words, the Maya conceived time to have commenced, in so far as we can judge from the single record available, with a Cycle 13, not with the beginning of a Cycle 1, as they did their chronology.

We have still to explain A1, figure 60. This glyph is quite clearly a form of the Initial-series introducing glyph, as already explained, in which the five components of that glyph are present in usual form: (1) Trinal superfix; (2) pair of comb-like lateral appendages; (3) the tun sign; (4) the trinal subfix; (5) the variable central element, here represented by a grotesque head.

Of these, the first only claims our attention here. The trinal superfix in A1 (fig. 60), as its name signifies, is composed of three parts, but, unlike other forms of this element, the middle part seems to be nothing more nor less than a numerical dot or 1. The question at once arises, can the two flanking parts be merely ornamental and the whole element stand for the number 1? The introducing glyph at the beginning of this text (not figured here), so far as it can be made out, has a trinal superfix of exactly the same character—a dot with an ornamental scroll on each side. What can be the explanation of this element, and indeed of the whole glyph? Is it one great-great-great-great cycle—a period twenty times as great as the one recorded in A2, or is it not a term of the series in glyphs A2–A9?

The writer believes that whatever it may be, it is at least *not* a member of this series, and in support of his belief he suggests that if it were, why should it alone be retained in recording *all* Initial-series dates, whereas the other three—the great-great-great cycle, the great-great cycle, and the great-cycle signs—have disappeared.

The following explanation, the writer believes, satisfactorily accounts for all of these points, though it is advanced here only by way of suggestion as a possible solution of the meaning of the Initial-series introducing glyph. It is suggested that in A1 we may have a sign representing "eternity," "this world," "time"; that is to say, a sign denoting the duration of the present world-epoch, the epoch of which the Maya civilization occupied only a small part. The middle dot of the upper element, being 1, denotes that this world-epoch is the first, or present, one, and the whole glyph itself might mean "the present world." The appropriateness of such a glyph ushering in every Initial-series date is apparent. It signified time in general, while the succeeding 7 glyphs denoted what particular day of time was designated in the inscription.

But why, even admitting the correctness of this interpretation of A1, should the great-great-great cycle, the great-great cycle, and the great cycle of their chronological scheme be omitted, and Initial-series dates always open with this glyph, which signifies time in general, followed by the current cycle? The answer to this question, the writer believes, is that the cycle was the greatest period with which the Maya could have had actual experience. It will be shown in Chapter V that there are a few Cycle-8 dates actually recorded, as well as a half a dozen Cycle-10 dates. That is, the cycle, which changed its coefficient every 400 years, was a period which they could *not* regard as never changing within the range of human experience. On the other hand, it was the shortest period of which they were uncertain, since the great cycle could change its coefficient only every 8,000 years—practically eternity so far as the Maya were concerned. Therefore it could be omitted as well as the two higher periods in a date without giving rise to confusion as to which great cycle was the current one. The cycle, on the contrary, had to be given, as its coefficient changed every 400 years, and the Maya are known to have recorded dates in at least three cycles—Nos. 8, 9, and 10. Hence, it was Great Cycle 19 for 8,000 years, Great-great Cycle 11 for 160,000, and Great-great-great Cycle 1 for 3,200,000 years, whereas it was Cycle 9 for only 400 years. This, not the fact that the Maya never had a period higher than the cycle, the writer believes was the reason why the three higher periods were omitted from Initial-series dates—they were unnecessary so far as accuracy was concerned, since there could never be any doubt concerning them.

It is not necessary to press this point further, though it is believed the foregoing conception of time had actually been worked out by the Maya. The archaic date recorded by Stela 10 at Tikal (9. 3. 6. 2. 0) makes this monument one of the very oldest in the Maya territory; indeed, there is only one other stela which has an earlier Initial Series, Stela 3 at Tikal. In the archaic period from which this monument dates the middle dot of the trinal superfix in the Initial-series introducing glyph may still have retained its numerical value, 1, but in later times this middle dot lost its numerical characteristics and frequently appears as a scroll itself.

The early date of Stela 10 makes it not unlikely that this process of glyph elaboration may not have set in at the time it was erected, and consequently that we have in this simplified trinal element the genesis of the later elaborated form; and, finally, that A1, figure 60, may have meant "the present world-epoch" or something similar.

In concluding the presentation of these three numbers the writer may express the opinion that a careful study of the period glyphs in figures 58–60 will lead to the following conclusions: (1) That the six periods recorded in the first, the seven in the second, and the eight or nine in the third, all belong to the same series in each case; and (2) that throughout the six terms of the first, the seven of the second, and the eight of the third, the series in each case conforms strictly to the vigesimal system of numeration given in Table VIII.

As mentioned on page 116 (footnote 2), in this method of recording the higher numbers the kin sign may sometimes be omitted without affecting the numerical value of the series wherein the omission occurs. In such cases the coefficient of the kin sign is usually prefixed to the uinal sign, the coefficient of the uinal itself standing above the uinal sign. In figure 58, for example, the uinal and the kin coefficients are both 0. In this case, however, the 0 on the left of the uinal sign is to be understood as belonging to the kin sign, which is omitted, while the 0 above the uinal sign is the uinal's own coefficient 0. Again in figure 59, the kin sign is omitted and the kin coefficient 1 is prefixed to the uinal sign, while the uinal's own coefficient 12 stands above the uinal sign. Similarly, the 12 uinals and 17 kins recorded in figure 56, *d*, might as well have been written as in *o* of the same figure, that is, with the kin sign omitted and its coefficient 17 prefixed to the uinal sign, while the uinal's own coefficient 12 appears above. Or again, the 9 uinals and 18 kins recorded in *f* also might have been written as in *p*, that is, with the kin sign omitted and the kin coefficient 18 prefixed to the uinal sign while the uinal's own coefficient 9 appears above.

In all the above examples the coefficients of the omitted kin signs are on the *left* of the uinal signs, while the uinal coefficients are *above* the uinal signs. Sometimes, however, these positions are reversed, and the uinal coefficient stands *on the left* of the uinal sign, while the kin coefficient stands *above*. This interchange in certain cases probably resulted from the needs of glyphic balance and symmetry. For example, in figure 62, *a*, had the kin coefficient 19 been placed on the left of the uinal sign, the uinal coefficient 4 would have been insufficient to fill the space above the period glyph, and consequently the corner of the glyph block would have appeared ragged. The use of the 19 *above* and the 4 to the left, on the other hand, properly fills this space, making a symmetrical glyph. Such cases, however, are unusual, and the customary position of the kin coefficient, when the kin sign is omitted, is on the left of the uinal sign, not above it. This practice, namely, omitting the kin sign in numerical series,

a   *b*   *c*

Fig. 62.   Glyphs showing misplacement of the kin coefficient (*a*) or elimination of a period glyph (*b*, *c*):
a, Stela E, Quirigua; *b*, Altar U, Copan; *c*, Stela J, Copan.

seems to have prevailed extensively in connection with both Initial Series and Secondary Series; indeed, in the latter it is the rule to which there are but few exceptions.

The omission of the kin sign, while by far the most common, is not the only example of glyph omission found in numerical series in the inscriptions. Sometimes, though very rarely, numbers occur in which periods other than the kin are wanting. A case in point is figure 62, *b*. Here a tun sign appears with the coefficient 13 above and 3 to the left. Since there are only two coefficients (13 and 3) and three time periods (tun, uinal, and kin), it is clear that the signs of both the lower periods have been omitted as well as the coefficient of one of them. In *c* of the last-mentioned figure a somewhat different practice was followed. Here, although three time periods are recorded—tuns, uinals and kins— one period (the uinal) and its coefficient have been omitted, and there is nothing between the 0 kins and 10 tuns. Such cases are exceedingly rare, however, and may be disregarded by the beginner.

We have seen that the order of the periods in the numbers in figure 56 was just the reverse of that in the numbers shown in figures 58 and 59; that in one place the kins stand at the top and in the other at the bottom; and finally, that this difference was not a vital one, since it had no effect on the values of the numbers. This is true, because in the first method of expressing the higher numbers, it matters not which end of the number comes first, the highest or the lowest period, so long as its several periods always stand in the same relation to each other.   For example, in figure 56, q, 6 cycles, 17 katuns, 2 tuns, 10 uinals, and 0 kins represent exactly the same number as 0 kins, 10 uinals, 2 tuns, 17 katuns, and 6 cycles; that is, with the lowest term first.

It was explained on page 23 that the order in which the glyphs are to be read is from top to bottom and from left to right.   Applying this rule to the inscriptions, the student will find that all Initial Series are descending series; that in reading from top to bottom and left to right, the cycles will be encountered first, the katuns next, the tuns next, the uinals, and the kins last.   Moreover, it will be found also that the great majority of Secondary Series are ascending series, that is, in reading from top to bottom and left to right, the kins will be encountered first, the uinals next, the tuns next, the katuns next, and the cycles last.   The reason why Initial Series always should be presented as descending series, and Secondary Series usually as ascending series is unknown; though as stated above, the order in either case might have been reversed without affecting in any way the numerical value of either series.

This concludes the discussion of the first method of expressing the higher numbers, the only method which has been found in the inscriptions.

SECOND METHOD OF NUMERATION

The other method by means of which the Maya expressed their higher numbers (the second method given on p. 103) may be called "numeration by position," since in this method the numerical value of the symbols depended solely on position, just as in our own decimal system, in which the value of a figure depends on its distance from the decimal point, whole numbers being written to the left and fractions to the right.   The ratio of increase, as the word "decimal" implies, is 10 throughout, and the numerical values of the consecutive positions increase as they recede from the decimal point in each direction, according to the terms of a geometrical progression.   For example, in the number 8888.0, the second 8 from the decimal point, counting from right to left, has a value ten times greater than the first 8, since it stands for 8 tens (80); the third 8 from the decimal point similarly has a value ten times greater than the second 8, since it stands for 8 hundreds (800); finally, the fourth 8 has a value ten times greater than the third 8, since it stands for 8 thousands (8,000).   Hence, although the figures used are the same in each case, each has a different numerical value, depending solely upon its position with reference to the decimal point.

In the second method of writing their numbers the Maya had devised a somewhat similar notation.   Their ratio of increase was 20 in all positions except the third.   The value of these positions increased with their distance from the bottom, according to the terms of the vigesimal system shown in Table VIII. This second method, or "numeration by position," as it may be called, was a distinct advance over the first, since it required for its expression only the signs for the numerals 0 to 19, inclusive, and did not involve the use of any period glyphs, as did the first method. To its greater brevity, no doubt, may be ascribed its use in the codices, where numerical calculations running into numbers of 5 and 6 terms form a large part of the subject matter. It should be remembered that in numeration by position only the normal forms of the numbers—bar and dot numerals—are used. This probably results from the fact that head-variant numerals never occur independently, but are always prefixed to some other glyph, as period, day, or month signs (see p. 104). Since no period glyphs are used in numeration by position, only normal-form numerals, that is, bar and dot numerals, can appear.

The numbers from 1 to 19, inclusive, are expressed in this method, as shown in figure 39, and the number 0 as shown in figure 46. As all of these numbers are below 20, they are expressed as units of the first place or order, and consequently each should be regarded as having been multiplied by 1, the numerical value of the first or lowest position.

The number 20 was expressed in two different ways: (1) By the sign shown in figure 45; and (2) by the numeral 0 in the bottom place and the numeral 1 in the next place above it, as in figure 63, a. The first of these had only a very restricted use in connection with the tonalamatl, wherein numeration by position was impossible, and therefore a special character for 20 (see fig. 45) was necessary. See Chapter VI.

The numbers from 21 to 359, inclusive, involved the use of two places—the kin place and the uinal place—which, according to Table VIII, we saw had numerical values of 1 and 20, respectively. For example, the number 37 was expressed as shown in figure 63, b. The 17 in the kin place has a value of 17 (17×1) and the 1 in the uinal, or second, place a value of 20 (1 (the numeral) $\times 20$ (the fixed numerical value of the second place)). The sum of these two products equals 37. Again, 300 was written as in figure 63, c. The 0 in the kin place has the value 0 (0×1), and the 15 in the second place has the value of 300 (15×20), and the sum of these products equals 300.

To express the numbers 360 to 7,199, inclusive, three places or terms were necessary—kins, uinals, and tuns—of which the last had a numerical value of 360. (See Table VIII.) For example, the number 360 is shown in figure 63, d. The 0 in the lowest place indicates that 0 kins are involved, the 0 in the second place indicates that 0 uinals or 20's are involved, while the 1 in the third place shows that there is 1 tun, or 360, kins recorded (1 (the numeral) $\times 360$ (the fixed numerical value of the third position)); the sum of these three products equals 360. Again, the number 7,113 is expressed as shown in figure 63, e.

The 13 in the lowest place equals 13 (13 × 1); the 13 in the second place, 260 (13 × 20); and the 19 in the third place, 6,840 (19 × 360). The sum of these three products equals 7,113 (13 + 260 + 6,840).

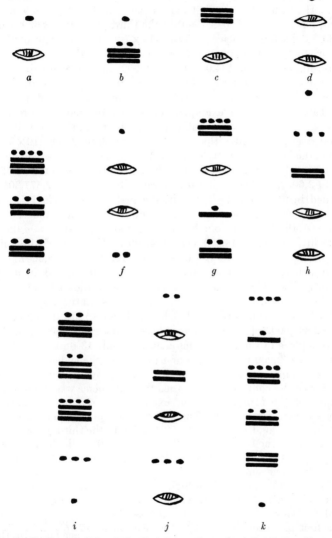

FIG. 63. Examples of the second method of numeration, used exclusively in the codices.

The numbers from 7,200 to 143,999, inclusive, involved the use of four places or terms—kins, uinals, tuns, and katuns—the last of which (the fourth place) had a numerical value of 7,200. (See Table VIII.) For example, the number 7,202 is recorded in figure 63, f.

The 2 in the first place equals 2 (2×1); the 0 in the second place, 0 (0×20); the 0 in the third place, 0 (0×360); and the 1 in the fourth place, 7,200 ($1 \times 7,200$). The sum of these four products equals 7,202 ($2 + 0 + 0 + 7,200$). Again, the number 100,932 is recorded in figure 63, g. Here the 12 in the first place equals 12 (12×1); the 6 in the second place, 120 (6×20); the 0 in the third place, 0 (0×360); and the 14 in the fourth place, 100,800 ($14 \times 7,200$). The sum of these four products equals 100,932 ($12 + 120 + 0 + 100,800$).

The numbers from 144,000 to 2,879,999, inclusive, involved the use of five places or terms—kins, uinals, tuns, katuns, and cycles. The last of these (the fifth place) had a numerical value of 144,000. (See Table VIII.) For example, the number 169,200 is recorded in figure 63, h. The 0 in the first place equals 0 (0×1); the 0 in the second place, 0 (0×20); the 10 in the third place, 3,600 (10×360); the 3 in the fourth place, 21,600 ($3 \times 7,200$); and the 1 in the fifth place, 144,000 ($1 \times 144,000$). The sum of these five products equals 169,200 ($0 + 0 + 3,600 + 21,600 + 144,000$). Again, the number 2,577,301 is recorded in figure 63, i. The 1 in the first place equals 1 (1×1); the 3 in the second place, 60 (3×20); the 19 in the third place, 6,840 (19×360); the 17 in the fourth place, 122,400 ($17 \times 7,200$); and the 17 in the fifth place, 2,448,000 ($17 \times 144,000$). The sum of these five products equals 2,577,301 ($1 + 60 + 6,480 + 122,400 + 2,448,000$).

The writing of numbers above 2,880,000 up to and including 12,489,781 (the highest number found in the codices) involves the use of six places, or terms—kins, uinals, tuns, katuns, cycles, and great cycles—the last of which (the sixth place) has the numerical value 2,880,000. It will be remembered that some have held that the sixth place in the inscriptions contained only 13 units of the fifth place, or 1,872,000 units of the first place. In the codices, however, there are numerous calendric checks which prove conclusively that in so far as the codices are concerned the sixth place was composed of 20 units of the fifth place. For example, the number 5,832,060 is expressed as in figure 63, j. The 0 in the first place equals 0 (0×1); the 3 in the second place, 60 (3×20); the 0 in the third place, 0 (0×360); the 10 in the fourth place, 72,000 ($10 \times 7,200$); the 0 in the fifth place, 0 ($0 \times 144,000$); and the 2 in the sixth place, 5,760,000 ($2 \times 2,880,000$). The sum of these six terms equals 5,832,060 ($0 + 60 + 0 + 72,000 + 0 + 5,760,000$). The highest number in the codices, as explained above, is 12,489,781, which is recorded on page 61 of the Dresden Codex. This number is expressed as in figure 63, k. The 1 in the first place equals 1 (1×1); the 15 in the second place, 300 (15×20); the 13 in the third place, 4,680 (13×360); the 14 in the fourth place, 100,800 ($14 \times 7,200$); the 6 in the fifth place, 864,000 ($6 \times 144,000$); and the 4 in the sixth place, 11,520,000 ($4 \times 2,880,000$). The sum of these six products equals 12,489,781 ($1 + 300 + 4,680 + 100,800 + 864,000 + 11,520,000$).

It is clear that in numeration by position the order of the units could not be reversed as in the first method without seriously affecting their numerical values. This must be true, since in the second method the numerical values of the numerals depend entirely on their position—that is, on their distance above the bottom or first term. In the first method, the multiplicands—the period glyphs, each of which had a fixed numerical value—are always expressed [1] with their corresponding multipliers—the numerals 0 to 19, inclusive; in other words, the period glyphs themselves show whether the series is an ascending or a descending one. But in the second method the multiplicands are not expressed. Consequently, since there is nothing about a column of bar and dot numerals which in itself indicates whether the series is an ascending or a descending one, and since in numeration by position a fixed starting point is absolutely essential, in their second method the Maya were obliged not only to fix arbitrarily the direction of reading, as from bottom to top, but also to confine themselves exclusively to the presentation of one kind of series only—that is, ascending series. Only by means of these two arbitrary rules was confusion obviated in numeration by position.

However dissimilar these two methods of representing the numbers may appear at first sight, fundamentally they are the same, since both have as their basis the same vigesimal system of numeration. Indeed, it can not be too strongly emphasized that throughout the range of the Maya writings, codices, inscriptions, or Books of Chilam Balam [2] the several methods of counting time and recording events found in each are all derived from the same source, and all are expressions of the same numerical system.

That the student may better grasp the points of difference between the two methods they are here contrasted:

TABLE XII. COMPARISON OF THE TWO METHODS OF NUMERATION

FIRST METHOD	SECOND METHOD
1. Use confined almost exclusively to the inscriptions.	1. Use confined exclusively to the codices.
2. Numerals represented by both normal forms and head variants.	2. Numerals represented by normal forms exclusively.
3. Numbers expressed by using the numerals 0 to 19, inclusive, as multipliers with the period glyphs as multiplicands.	3. Numbers expressed by using the numerals 0 to 19, inclusive, as multipliers in certain positions the fixed numerical values of which served as multiplicands.
4. Numbers presented as ascending or descending series.	4. Numbers presented as ascending series exclusively.
5. Direction of reading either from bottom to top, or vice versa.	5. Direction of reading from bottom to top exclusively.

[1] A few exceptions to this have been noted on pp. 127, 128.

[2] The Books of Chilan Balam have been included here as they are also expressions of the native Maya mind.

We have seen in the foregoing pages (1) how the Maya wrote their 20 numerals, and (2) how these numerals were used to express the higher numbers. The next question which concerns us is, How did they use these numbers in their calculations; or in other words, how was their arithmetic applied to their calendar? It may be said at the very outset in answer to this question, that in so far as known, *numbers appear to have had but one use throughout the Maya texts, namely, to express the time elapsing between dates.*[1] In the codices and the inscriptions alike all the numbers whose use is understood have been found to deal exclusively with the counting of time.

This highly specialized use of the numbers in Maya texts has determined the first step to be taken in the process of deciphering them. Since the primary unit of the calendar was the day, all numbers should be reduced to terms of this unit, or in other words, to units of the first order, or place.[2] Hence, we may accept the following as the *first step* in ascertaining the meaning of any number:

First Step in Solving Maya Numbers

Reduce all the units of the higher orders to units of its first, or lowest, order, and then add the resulting quantities together.

The application of this rule to any Maya number, no matter of how many terms, will always give the actual number of primary units which it contains, and in this form it can be more conveniently utilized in connection with the calendar than if it were left as recorded, that is, in terms of its higher orders.

The reduction of units of the higher orders to units of the first order has been explained on pages 105–133, but in order to provide the student with this same information in a more condensed and accessible form, it is presented in the following tables, of which Table XIII is to be used for reducing numbers to their primary units in the inscriptions, and Table XIV for the same purpose in the codices.

---

[1] This excludes, of course, the use of the numerals 1 to 13, inclusive, in the day names, and in the numeration of the cycles; also the numerals 0 to 19, inclusive, when used to denote the positions of the days in the divisions of the year, and the position of any period in the division next higher.

[2] Various methods and tables have been devised to avoid the necessity of reducing the higher terms of Maya numbers to units of the first order. Of the former, that suggested by Mr. Bowditch (1910: pp. 302–309) is probably the most serviceable. Of the tables Mr. Goodman's Archæic Annual Calendar and Archæic Chronological Calendar (1897) are by far the best. By using either of the above the necessity of reducing the higher terms to units of the first order is obviated. On the other hand, the processes by means of which this is achieved in each case are far more complicated and less easy of comprehension than those of the method followed in this book, a method which from its simplicity might be termed perhaps the logical way, since it reduces all quantities to a primary unit, which is the same as the primary unit of the Maya calendar. This method was first devised by Prof. Ernst Förstemann, and has the advantage of being the most readily understood by the beginner, sufficient reason for its use in this book.

TABLE XIII. VALUES OF HIGHER PERIODS IN TERMS OF LOWEST, IN INSCRIPTIONS		TABLE XIV. VALUES OF HIGHER PERIODS IN TERMS OF LOWEST, IN CODICES	
1 great cycle= [1] 2,880,000		1 unit of the 6th place=2,880,000	
1 cycle	144,000	1 unit of the 5th place	144,000
1 katun	7,200	1 unit of the 4th place	7,200
1 tun	360	1 unit of the 3d place	600
1 uinal	20	1 unit of the 2d place	20
1 kin	1	1 unit of the 1st place	1

It should be remembered, in using these tables, that each of the signs for the periods therein given has its own particular numerical value, and that this value in each case is a multiplicand which is to be multiplied by the numeral attached to it, (not shown in Table XIII). For example, a 3 attached to the katun sign reduces to 21,600 units of the first order (3 × 7,200). Again, 5 attached to the uinal sign reduces to 100 units of the first order (5 × 20). In using Table XIV, however, it should be remembered that the position of a numeral multiplier determines at the same time that multiplier's multiplicand. Thus a 5 in the third place indicates that the 5's multiplicand is 360, the numerical value of the third place, and such a term reduces to 1,800 units of the first place (5 × 360 = 1,800). Again, a 10 in the fourth place indicates that the 10's multiplicand is 7,200, the numerical value corresponding to the fourth place, and such a term reduces to 72,000 units of the first place.

Having reduced all the terms of a number to units of the 1st order, the next step in finding out its meaning is to discover the date from which it is counted. This operation gives rise to the *second step*.

SECOND STEP IN SOLVING MAYA NUMBERS

Find the date from which the number is counted.

This is not always an easy matter, since the dates from which Maya numbers are counted are frequently not expressed in the texts; consequently, it is clear that no single rule can be formulated which will cover all cases. There are, however, two general rules which will be found to apply to the great majority of numbers in the texts:

Rule 1. When the starting point or date is expressed, usually, though not invariably, it precedes [2] the number counted from it.

It should be noted, however, in connection with this rule, that the starting date hardly ever immediately precedes the number from which it is counted, but that several glyphs nearly always stand

---

[1] This number is formed on the basis of 20 cycles to a great cycle (20×144,000=2,880,000). The writer assumes that he has established the fact that 20 cycles were required to make 1 great cycle, in the inscriptions as well as in the codices.

[2] This is true in spite of the fact that in the codices the starting points frequently appear to follow—that is, they stand below—the numbers which are counted from them. In reality such cases are perfectly regular and conform to this rule, because there the order is not from top to bottom but from bottom to top, and, therefore, when read in this direction the dates come first.

between.[1] Certain exceptions to the above rule are by no means rare, and the student must be continually on the lookout for such reversals of the regular order. These exceptions are cases in which the starting date (1) follows the number counted from it, and (2) stands elsewhere in the text, entirely disassociated from, and unattached to, the number counted from it.

The second of the above-mentioned general rules, covering the majority of cases, follows:

Rule 2. When the starting point or date is not expressed, if the number is an Inital Series the date from which it should be counted will be found to be **4 Ahau 8 Cumhu**.[2]

This rule is particularly useful in deciphering numbers in the inscriptions. For example, when the student finds a number which he can identify as an Initial Series,[3] he may assume at once that such a number in all probability is counted from the date **4 Ahau 8 Cumhu**, and proceed on this assumption. The exceptions to this rule, that is, cases in which the starting point is not expressed and the number is not an Initial Series, are not numerous. No rule can be given covering all such cases, and the starting points of such numbers can be determined only by means of the calculations given under the third and fourth steps, below.

Having determined the starting point or date from which a given number is to be counted (if this is possible), the next step is to find out which way the count runs; that is, whether it is *forward* from the starting point to some *later date*, or whether it is *backward* from the starting point to some *earlier date*. This process may be called the *third step*.

Third Step in Solving Maya Numbers

Ascertain whether the number is to be counted forward or backward from its starting point.

It may be said at the very outset in this connection that the overwhelming majority of Maya numbers are counted *forward* from their starting points and not backward. In other words, they proceed from *earlier to later dates* and not vice versa. Indeed, the preponderance of the former is so great, and the exceptions are so rare, that the student should always proceed on the postulate that the count is forward until proved definitely to be otherwise.

---

[1] These intervening glyphs the writer believes, as stated in Chapter II, are those which tell the real story of the inscriptions.

[2] Only two exceptions to this rule have been noted throughout the Maya territory: (1) The Initial Series on the east side of Stela C at Quirigua, and (2) the tablet from the Temple of the Cross at Palenque. It has been explained that both of these Initial Series are counted from the date **4 Ahau 8 Zotz.**

[3] In the inscriptions an Initial Series may always be identified by the so-called introducing glyph (see fig. 24) which invariably precedes it.

In the codices, moreover, when the count is backward, or contrary to the general practice, the fact is clearly indicated [1] by a special character. This character, although attached only to the lowest term [2] of the number which is to be counted backward, is to be interpreted as applying to all the other terms as well, its effect extending to the number as a whole. This "backward sign" (shown in fig. 64) is a circle drawn in red around the lowest term of the number which it affects, and is surmounted by a knot of the same color. An example covering the use of this sign is given in figure 64. Although the "backward sign" in this figure surrounds only the numeral in the first place, 0, it is to be interpreted, as we have seen, as applying to the 2 in the second place and the 6 in the third place. This number, expressed as 6 tuns, 2 uinals, and 0 kins, reduces to 2,200 units of the first place, and in this form may be more readily handled (first step). Since the starting point usually precedes the number counted from it and since in figure 64 the number is expressed by the second method, its starting point will be found standing below it. This follows from the fact that in numeration by position the order is from bottom to top. Therefore the starting point from which the 2,200 recorded in figure 64 is counted will be found to be below it, that is, the date **4 Ahau 8 Cumhu** [3] (second step). Finally, the red circle and knot surrounding the lowest (0) term of this 2,200 indicates that this number is to be counted *backward* from its starting point, not forward (third step).

Fig. 64. Figure showing the use of the "minus" or "backward" sign in the codices.

On the other hand, in the inscriptions no special character seems to have been used with a number to indicate that it was to be counted backward; at least no such sign has yet been discovered. In the inscriptions, therefore, with the single exception [4] mentioned below, the student can only apply the general rule given on page 136, that in the great majority of cases the count is forward. This rule will be found to apply to at least nine out of every ten numbers. The exception above noted, that is, where the practice is so uniform as to render possible the formulation of an unfailing rule, has to do with Initial Series. This rule, to which there are no known exceptions, may be stated as follows:

Rule 1. In Initial Series the count is *always forward*, and, in general throughout the inscriptions. The very few cases in which the count *is* backward, are confined chiefly to Secondary Series, and it is in

---

[1] Professor Förstemann has pointed out a few cases in the Dresden Codex in which, although the count is backward, the special character indicating the fact is wanting (fig. 64). (See *Bulletin 28*, p. 401.)

[2] There are a few cases in which the "backward sign" includes also the numeral in the second position.

[3] In the text wherein this number is found the date **4 Ahau 8 Cumhu** stands below the lowest term.

[4] It should be noted here that in the *u kahlay katunob* also, from the Books of Chilan Balam, the count is always forward.

dealing with this kind of series that the student will find the greatest number of exceptions to the general rule.

Having determined the direction of the count, whether it is forward or backward, the next (*fourth*) step may be given.

FOURTH STEP IN SOLVING MAYA NUMBERS

To count the number from its starting point.

We have come now to a step that involves the consideration of actual arithmetical processes, which it is thought can be set forth much more clearly by the use of specific examples than by the statement of general rules. Hence, we will formulate our rules after the processes which they govern have been fully explained.

In counting any number, as 31,741, or 4.8.3.1 as it would be expressed in Maya notation,[1] from any date, as **4 Ahau 8 Cumhu**, there are four unknown elements which have to be determined before we can write the date which the count reaches. These are:

1. The day coefficient, which must be one of the numerals 1 to 13, inclusive.

2. The day name, which must be one of the twenty given in Table I.

3. The position of the day in some division of the year, which must be one of the numerals 0 to 19, inclusive.

4. The name of the division of the year, which must be one of the nineteen given in Table III.

These four unknown elements all have to be determined from (1) the starting date, and (2) the number which is to be counted from it.

If the student will constantly bear in mind that all Maya sequences, whether the day coefficients, day signs, positions in the divisions of the year, or what not, are absolutely continuous, repeating themselves without any break or interruption whatsoever, he will better understand the calculations which follow.

It was explained in the text (see pp. 41–44) and also shown graphically in the tonalamatl wheel (pl. 5) that after the day coefficients had reached the number 13 they returned to 1, following each other indefinitely in this order without interruption. It is clear, therefore, that the highest multiple of 13 which the given number contains may be subtracted from it without affecting in any way the value of the day coefficient of the date which the number will reach when counted from the starting point. This is true, because no matter what the day coefficient of the starting point may be, any multiple of 13 will always bring the count back to the same day coefficient.

---

[1] For transcribing the Maya numerical notation into the characters of our own Arabic notation Maya students have adopted the practice of writing the various terms from left to right in a *descending* series, as the units of our decimal system are written. For example, 4 katuns, 8 tuns, 3 uinals, and 1 kin are written 4.8.3.1; and 9 cycles, 16 katuns, 1 tun, 0 uinal, and 0 kins are written 9.16.1.0.0. According to this method, the highest term in each number is written on the left, the next lower on its right, the next lower on the right of that, and so on down through the units of the first, or lowest, order. This notation is very convenient for transcribing the Maya numbers and will be followed hereafter.

Taking up the number, 31,741, which we have chosen for our first example, let us deduct from it the highest multiple of 13 which it contains. This will be found by dividing the number by 13, and multiplying the *whole-number part* of the resulting quotient by 13: $31,741 \div 13 = 2,441\frac{8}{13}$. Multiplying 2,441 by 13, we have 31,733, which is the highest multiple of 13 that 31,741 contains; consequently it may be deducted from 31,741 without affecting the value of the resulting day coefficient: $31,741 - 31,733 = 8$. In the example under consideration, therefore, 8 is the number which, if counted from the day coefficient of the starting point, will give the day coefficient of the resulting date. In other words, after dividing by 13 the only part of the resulting quotient which is used in determining the new day coefficient is the *numerator* of the fractional part.[1] Hence the following rule for determining the first unknown on page 138 (the day coefficient):

Rule 1. To find the new day coefficient divide the given number by 13, and count forward the numerator of the fractional part of the resulting quotient from the starting point if the count is forward, and backward if the count is backward, deducting 13 in either case from the resulting number if it should exceed 13.

Applying this rule to 31,741, we have seen above that its division by 13 gives as the fractional part of the quotient $\frac{8}{13}$. Assuming that the count is forward from the starting point, **4 Ahau 8 Cumhu**, if 8 (the numerator of the fractional part of the quotient) be counted forward from 4, the day coefficient of the starting point (**4 Ahau 8 Cumhu**), the day coefficient of the resulting date will be 12 (4+8). Since this number is below 13, the last sentence of the above rule has no application in this case. In counting forward 31,741 from the date **4 Ahau 8 Cumhu**, therefore, the day coefficient of the resulting date will be 12; thus we have determined our first unknown. Let us next find the second unknown, the day sign to which this 12 is prefixed.

It was explained on page 37 that the twenty day signs given in Table I succeed one another in endless rotation, the first following immediately the twentieth no matter which one of the twenty was chosen as the first. Consequently, it is clear that the highest multiple of 20 which the given number contains may be deducted from it without affecting in any way the name of the day sign of the date which the number will reach when counted from the starting point. This is true because, no matter what the day sign of the starting point may be, any multiple of 20 will always bring the count back to the same day sign.

---

[1] The reason for rejecting all parts of the quotient except the numerator of the fractional part is that this part alone shows the actual number of units which have to be counted either forward or backward, as the count may be, in order to reach the number which exactly uses up or finishes the dividend—the last unit of the number which has to be counted.

Returning to the number 31,741, let us deduct from it the highest multiple of 20 which it contains, found by dividing the number by 20 and multiplying the whole number part of the resulting quotient by 20; $31,741 \div 20 = 1,587\frac{1}{20}$. Multiplying 1,587 by 20, we have 31,740, which is the highest multiple of 20 that 31,741 contains, and which may be deducted from 31,741 without affecting the resulting day sign; $31,741 - 31,740 = 1$. Therefore in the present example 1 is the number which, if counted forward from the day sign of the starting point in the sequence of the 20 day signs given in Table I, will reach the day sign of the resulting date. In other words, after dividing by 20 the only part of the resulting quotient which is used in determining the new day sign is the numerator of the fractional part. Thus we may formulate the rule for determining the second unknown on page 138 (the day sign):

Rule 2. To find the new day sign, divide the given number by 20, and count forward the numerator of the fractional part of the resulting quotient from the starting point in the sequence of the twenty day signs given in Table I, if the count is forward, and backward if the count is backward, and the sign reached will be the new day sign.

Applying this rule to 31,741, we have seen above that its division by 20 gives us as the fractional part of the quotient, $\frac{1}{20}$. Since the count was forward from the starting point, if 1 (the numerator of the fractional part of the quotient) be counted forward in the sequence of the 20 day signs in Table I from the day sign of the starting point, **Ahau** (**4 Ahau 8 Cumhu**), the day sign reached will be the day sign of the resulting date. Counting forward 1 from **Ahau** in Table I, the day sign **Imix** is reached, and **Imix,** therefore, will be the new day sign. Thus our second unknown is determined.

By combining the above two values, the 12 for the first unknown and **Imix** for the second, we can now say that in counting forward 31,741 from the date **4 Ahau 8 Cumhu**, the day reached will be **12 Imix**. It remains to find what position this particular day occupied in the 365-day year, or haab, and thus to determine the third and fourth unknowns on page 138. Both of these may be found at one time by the same operation.

It was explained on pages 44–51 that the Maya year, at least in so far as the calendar was concerned, contained only 365 days, divided into 18 uinals of 20 days each, and the *xma kaba kin* of 5 days; and further, that when the last position in the last division of the year (**4 Uayeb**) was reached, it was followed without interruption by the first position of the first division of the next year (**0 Pop**); and, finally, that this sequence was continued indefinitely. Consequently it is clear that the highest multiple of 365 which the given number contains may be subtracted from it without affecting in any way the position in the year of the day which the number will reach when counted from the starting point. This is true, because no matter what position in the year the day of the starting point may occupy, any multiple of 365 will bring the count back again to the same position in the year.

Returning again to the number 31,741, let us deduct from it the highest multiple of 365 which it contains. This will be found by dividing the number by 365 and multiplying the whole number part of the resulting quotient by 365: $31,741 \times 365 = 86\frac{351}{365}$. Multiplying 86 by 365, we have 31,390, which is the highest multiple that 31,741 contains. Hence it may be deducted from 31,741 without affecting the position in the year of the resulting day; $31,741 - 31,390 = 351$. Therefore, in the present example, 351 is the number which, if counted forward from the year position of the starting date in the sequence of the 365 positions in the year, given in Table XV, will reach the position in the year of the day of the resulting date. This enables us to formulate the rule for determining the third and fourth unknowns on page 138 (the position in the year of the day of the resulting date):

Rule 3. To find the position in the year of the new day, divide the given number by 365 and count forward the numerator of the fractional part of the resulting quotient from the year position of the starting point in the sequence of the 365 positions of the year shown in Table XV, if the count is forward; and backward if the count is backward, and the position reached will be the position in the year which the day of the resulting date will occupy.

TABLE XV. THE 365 POSITIONS IN THE MAYA YEAR

Month	Pop	Uo	Zip	Zotz	Tzec	Xul	Yaxkin	Mol	Chen	Yax	Zac	Ceh	Mac	Kankin	Muan	Pax	Kayab	Cumhu	Uayeb
Position	0	0	0	0	0	0	0	0	0	0	0	0	0	0	0	0	0	0	0
Do	1	1	1	1	1	1	1	1	1	1	1	1	1	1	1	1	1	1	1
Do	2	2	2	2	2	2	2	2	2	2	2	2	2	2	2	2	2	2	2
Do	3	3	3	3	3	3	3	3	3	3	3	3	3	3	3	3	3	3	3
Do	4	4	4	4	4	4	4	4	4	4	4	4	4	4	4	4	4	4	4
Do	5	5	5	5	5	5	5	5	5	5	5	5	5	5	5	5	5	5	....
Do	6	6	6	6	6	6	6	6	6	6	6	6	6	6	6	6	6	6	....
Do	7	7	7	7	7	7	7	7	7	7	7	7	7	7	7	7	7	7	....
Do	8	8	8	8	8	8	8	8	8	8	8	8	8	8	8	8	8	8	....
Do	9	9	9	9	9	9	9	9	9	9	9	9	9	9	9	9	9	9	....
Do	10	10	10	10	10	10	10	10	10	10	10	10	10	10	10	10	10	10	....
Do	11	11	11	11	11	11	11	11	11	11	11	11	11	11	11	11	11	11	....
Do	12	12	12	12	12	12	12	12	12	12	12	12	12	12	12	12	12	12	....
Do	13	13	13	13	13	13	13	13	13	13	13	13	13	13	13	13	13	13	....
Do	14	14	14	14	14	14	14	14	14	14	14	14	14	14	14	14	14	14	....
Do	15	15	15	15	15	15	15	15	15	15	15	15	15	15	15	15	15	15	....
Do	16	16	16	16	16	16	16	16	16	16	16	16	16	16	16	16	16	16	....
Do	17	17	17	17	17	17	17	17	17	17	17	17	17	17	17	17	17	17	....
Do	18	18	18	18	18	18	18	18	18	18	18	18	18	18	18	18	18	18	....
Do	19	19	19	19	19	19	19	19	19	19	19	19	19	19	19	19	19	19	....

Applying this rule to the number 31,741, we have seen above that its division by 365 gives 351 as the numerator of the fractional part of its quotient. Assuming that the count is forward from the starting point, it will be necessary, therefore, to count 351 forward in Table XV from the position **8 Cumhu,** the position of the day of the starting point, **4 Ahau 8 Cumhu.**

A glance at the month of **Cumhu** in Table XV shows that after the position **8 Cumhu** there are 11 positions in that month; adding to these the 5 in **Uayeb,** the last division of the year, there will be in all 16 more positions before the first of the next year. Subtracting these from 351, the total number to be counted forward, there remains the number 335 (351–16), which must be counted forward in Table XV from the beginning of the year. Since each of the months has 20 positions, it is clear that 16 months will be used before the month is reached in which will fall the 335th position from the beginning of the year. In other words, 320 positions of our 335 will exactly use up all the positions of the first 16 months, namely, **Pop, Uo, Zip, Zotz, Tzec, Xul, Yaxkin, Mol, Chen, Yax, Zac, Ceh, Mac, Kankin, Muan, Pax,** and will bring us to the beginning of the 17th month (**Kayab**) with still 15 more positions to count forward. If the student will refer to this month in Table XV he will see that 15 positions counted forward in this month will reach the position **14 Kayab,** which is also the position reached by counting forward 31,741 positions from the starting position **8 Cumhu.**

Having determined values for all of the unknowns on page 138, we can now say that if the number 31,741 be counted forward from the date **4 Ahau 8 Cumhu,** the date **12 Imix 14 Kayab** will be reached. To this latter date, i. e., the date reached by any count, the name "terminal date" has been given. The rules indicating the processes by means of which this terminal date is reached apply also to examples where the count is *backward,* not forward, from the starting point. In such cases, as the rules say, the only difference is that the numerators of the fractional parts of the quotients resulting from the different divisions are to be counted backward from the starting points, instead of forward as in the example above given.

Before proceeding to apply the rules by means of which our fourth step or process (see p. 138) may be carried out, a modification may sometimes be introduced which will considerably decrease the size of the number to be counted without affecting the values of the several parts of its resulting terminal date.

We have seen on pages 51–60 that in Maya chronology there were possible only 18,980 different dates—that is, combinations of the 260 days and the 365 positions of the year—and further, that any given day of the 260 could return to any given position of the 365 only after the lapse of 18,980 days, or 52 years.

Since the foregoing is true, it follows, that this number 18,980 or any multiple thereof, may be deducted from the number which is to be counted without affecting in any way the terminal date which the number will reach when counted from the starting point. It is obvious that this modification applies only to numbers which are above 18,980, all others being divided by 13, 20, and 365 directly, as indicated in rules 1, 2, and 3, respectively. This enables us to formulate another rule, which should be applied to the number to be counted before proceeding with rules 1, 2, and 3 above, if that number is above 18,980.

Rule. If the number to be counted is above 18,980, first deduct from it the highest multiple of 18,980 which it contains.

This rule should be applied whenever possible, since it reduces the size of the number to be handled, and consequently involves fewer calculations.

In Table XVI are given 80 Calendar Rounds, that is, 80 multiples of 18,980, in terms of both the Maya notation and our own. These will be found sufficient to cover most numbers.

Applying the above rule to the number 31,741, which was selected for our first example, it is seen by Table XVI that 1 Calendar Round, or 18,980 days, may be deducted from it; $31,741 - 18,980 = 12,761$. In other words, we can count the number 12,761 forward (or backward had the count been backward in our example) from the starting point **4 Ahau 8 Cumhu**, and reach exactly the same terminal date as though we had counted forward 31,741, as in the first case.

Mathematical proof of this point follows:

$$12,761 \div 13 = 981\tfrac{8}{13} \quad 12,761 \div 20 = 638\tfrac{1}{20} \quad 12,761 \div 365 = 34\tfrac{351}{365}$$

The numerators of the fractions in these three quotients are 8, 1, and 351; these are identical with the numerators of the fractions in the quotients obtained by dividing 31,741 by the same divisors, those indicated in rules 1, 2, and 3, respectively. Consequently, if these three numerators be counted forward from the corresponding parts of the starting point, **4 Ahau 8 Cumhu**, the resulting terms together will form the corresponding parts of the same terminal date, **12 Imix 14 Kayab.**

Similarly it could be shown that 50,721 or 69,701 counted forward or backward from any starting point would both reach this same terminal date, since subtracting 2 Calendar Rounds, 37,960 (see Table XVI), from the first, and 3 Calendar Rounds, 56,940 (see Table XVI), from the second, there would remain in each case 12,761. The student will find his calculations greatly facilitated if he will apply this rule whenever possible. To familiarize the student with the working of these rules, it is thought best to give several additional examples involving their use.

TABLE XVI. 80 CALENDAR ROUNDS EXPRESSED IN ARABIC AND MAYA NOTATION

Calendar Rounds	Days	Cycles, etc.	Calendar Rounds	Days	Cycles, etc.
1	18,980	2.12.13.0	41	778,180	5. 8. 1.11.0
2	37,960	5. 5. 8.0	42	797,160	5.10.14. 6.0
3	56,940	7.18. 3.0	43	816,140	5.13. 7. 1.0
4	75,920	10.10.16.0	44	835,120	5.15.19.14.0
5	94,900	13. 3.11.0	45	854,100	5.18.12. 9.0
6	113,880	15.16. 6.0	46	873,080	6. 1. 5. 4.0
7	132,860	18. 9. 1.0	47	892,060	6. 3.17.17.0
8	151,840	1. 1. 1.14.0	48	911,040	6. 6.10.12.0
9	170,820	1. 3.14. 9.0	49	930,020	6. 9. 3. 7.0
10	189,800	1. 6. 7. 4.0	50	949,000	6.11.16. 2.0
11	208,780	1. 8.19.17.0	51	967,980	6.14. 8.15.0
12	227,760	1.11.12.12.0	52	986,960	6.17. 1.10.0
13	246,740	1.14. 5. 7.0	53	1,005,940	6.19.14. 5.0
14	265,720	1.16.18. 2.0	54	1,024,920	7. 2. 7. 0.0
15	284,700	1.19.10.15.0	55	1,043,900	7. 4.19.13.0
16	303,680	2. 2. 3.10.0	56	1,062,880	7. 7.12. 8.0
17	322,660	2. 4.16. 5.0	57	1,081,860	7.10. 5. 3.0
18	341,640	2. 7. 9. 0.0	58	1,100,840	7.12.17.16.0
19	360,620	2.10. 1.13.0	59	1,119,820	7.15.10.11.0
20	379,600	2.12.14. 8.0	60	1,138,800	7.18. 3. 6.0
21	398,580	2.15. 7. 3.0	61	1,157,780	8. 0.16. 1.0
22	417,560	2.17.19.16.0	62	1,176,760	8. 3. 8.14.0
23	436,540	3. 0.12.11.0	63	1,195,740	8. 6. 1. 9.0
24	455,520	3. 3. 5. 6.0	64	1,214,720	8. 8.14. 4.0
25	474,500	3. 5.18. 1.0	65	1,233,700	8.11. 6.17.0
26	493,480	3. 8.10.14.0	66	1,252,680	8.13.19.12.0
27	512,460	3.11. 3. 9.0	67	1,271,660	8.16.12. 7.0
28	531,440	3.13.16. 4.0	68	1,290,640	8.19. 5. 2.0
29	550,420	3.16. 8.17.0	69	1,309,620	9. 1.17.15.0
30	569,400	3.19. 1.12.0	70	1,328,600	9. 4.10.10.0
31	588,380	4. 1.14. 7.0	71	1,347,580	9. 7. 3. 5.0
32	607,360	4. 4. 7. 2.0	72	1,366,560	9. 9.16. 0.0
33	626,340	4. 6.19.15.0	73	1,385,540	9.12. 8.13.0
34	645,320	4. 9.12.10.0	74	1,404,520	9.15. 1. 8.0
35	664,300	4.12. 5. 5.0	75	1,423,500	9.17.14. 3.0
36	683,280	4.14.18. 0.0	76	1,442,480	10. 0. 6.16.0
37	702,260	4.17.10.13.0	77	1,461,460	10. 2.19.11.0
38	721,240	5. 0. 3. 8.0	78	1,480,440	10. 5.12. 6.0
39	740,220	5. 2.16. 3.0	79	1,499,420	10. 8. 5. 1.0
40	759,200	5. 5. 8.16.0	80	1,518,400	10.10.17.14.0

Let us count forward the number 5,799 from the starting point **2 Kan 7 Tzec**. It is apparent at the outset that, since this number is less than 18,980, or 1 Calendar Round, the preliminary rule given on page 143 does not apply in this case. Therefore we may proceed with the first rule given on page 139, by means of which the new day coefficient may be determined. Dividing the given number by 13 we have: $5,799 \div 13 = 446\frac{1}{13}$. Counting forward the numerator of the fractional part of the resulting quotient (1) from the day coefficient of the starting point (**2**), we reach **3** as the day coefficient of the terminal date.

The second rule given on page 140 tells how to find the day sign of the terminal date. Dividing the given number by 20, we have: $5,799 \div 20 = 289\frac{19}{20}$. Counting forward the numerator of the fractional part of the resulting quotient (**19**) from the day sign of the starting point, **Kan**, in the sequence of the twenty-day signs given in Table I, the day sign **Akbal** will be reached, which will be the day sign of the terminal date. Therefore the day of the terminal date will be **3 Akbal**.

The third rule, given on page 141, tells how to find the position which the day of the terminal date occupied in the 365-day year. Dividing the given number by 365, we have: $5,799 \div 365 = 15\frac{324}{365}$. Counting forward the numerator of the fractional part of the resulting quotient, 324, from the year position of the starting date, **7 Tzec**, in the sequence of the 365 year positions given in Table XV, the position **6 Zip** will be reached as the position in the year of the day of the terminal date. The count by means of which the position **6 Zip** is determined is given in detail. After the year position of the starting point, **7 Tzec**, it requires 12 more positions (Nos. 8–19, inclusive) before the close of that month (see Table XV) will be reached. And after the close of **Tzec**, 13 uinals and the xma kaba kin must pass before the end of the year; $13 \times 20 + 5 = 265$, and $265 + 12 = 277$. This latter number subtracted from 324, the total number of positions to be counted forward, will give the number of positions which remain to be counted in the next year following: $324 - 277 = 47$. Counting forward 47 in the new year, we find that it will use up the months **Pop** and **Uo** $(20 + 20 = 40)$ and extend 7 positions into the month **Zip**, or to **6 Zip**. Therefore, gathering together the values determined for the several parts of the terminal date, we may say that in counting forward 5,799 from the starting point **2 Kan 7 Tzec**, the terminal date reached will be **3 Akbal 6 Zip**.

For the next example let us select a much higher number, say 322,920, which we will assume is to be counted forward from the starting point **13 Ik 0 Zip**. Since this number is above 18,980, we may apply our preliminary rule (p. 143) and deduct all the Calendar

Rounds possible. By turning to Table XVI we see that 17 Calendar Rounds, or 322,660, may be deducted from our number: 322,920 − 322,660 = 260. In other words, we can use 260 exactly as though it were 322,920. Dividing by 13, we have 260 ÷ 13 = 20. Since there is no fraction in the quotient, the numerator of the fraction will be 0, and counting 0 forward from the day coefficient of the starting point, **13**, we have **13** as the day coefficient of the terminal date (rule 1, p. 139). Dividing by 20 we have 260 ÷ 20 = 13. Since there is no fraction in the quotient, the numerator of the fraction will be 0, and counting forward 0 from the day sign of the starting point, **Ik** in Table I, the day sign **Ik** will remain the day sign of the terminal date (rule 2, p. 140). Combining the two values just determined, we see that the day of the terminal date will be **13 Ik**, or a day of the same name as the day of the starting point. This follows also from the fact that there are only 260 differently named days (see pp. 41–44) and any given day will have to recur, therefore, after the lapse of 260 days.[1] Dividing by 365 we have: $260 \div 365 = \frac{260}{365}$. Counting forward the numerator of the fraction, 260, from the year position of the starting point, **0 Zip**, in Table XV, the position in the year of the day of the terminal date will be found to be **0 Pax**. Since 260 days equal just 13 uinals, we have only to count forward from **0 Zip** 13 uinals in order to reach the year position; that is, **0 Zotz** is 1 uinal; to **0 Tzec** 2 uinals, to **0 Xul** 3 uinals, and so on in Table XV to **0 Pax**, which will complete the last of the 13 uinals (rule 3, p. 141).

Combining the above values, we find that in counting forward 322,920 (or 260) from the starting point **13 Ik 0 Zip**, the terminal date reached is **13 Ik 0 Pax**.

In order to illustrate the method of procedure when the count is *backward*, let us assume an example of this kind. Suppose we count backward the number 9,663 from the starting point **3 Imix 4 Uayeb**. Since this number is below 18,980, no Calendar Round can be deducted from it. Dividing the given number by 13, we have: 9,663 ÷ 13 = $743\frac{4}{13}$. Counting the numerator of the fractional part of this quotient, 4, *backward* from the day coefficient of the starting point, **3**, we reach 12 as the day coefficient of the terminal date, that is, **2, 1, 13, 12** (rule 1, p. 139). Dividing the given number by 20, we have: 9,663 ÷ 20 = $483\frac{3}{20}$. Counting the numerator of the fractional part of this quotient, 3, *backward* from the day sign of the starting point, **Imix**, in Table I, we reach **Eznab** as the day sign of the terminal date (**Ahau, Cauac, Eznab**); consequently the day reached in the count will be **12 Eznab**. Dividing the given number by 365, we have

---

[1] The student can prove this point for himself by turning to the tonalamatl wheel in pl. 5; after selecting any particular day, as **1 Ik** for example, proceed to count 260 days from this day as a starting point, in either direction around the wheel. No matter in which direction he has counted, whether beginning with **13 Imix** or **2 Akbal**, the 260th day will be **1 Ik** again.

$9,663 \div 365 = 26\frac{173}{365}$. Counting *backward* the numerator of the fractional part of this quotient, 173, from the year position of the starting point, **4 Uayeb**, the year position of the terminal date will be found to be **11 Yax**. Before position **4 Uayeb** (see Table XV) there are 4 positions in that division of the year (**3, 2, 1, 0**). Counting these *backward* to the end of the month **Cumhu** (see Table XV), we have left 169 positions $(173 - 4 = 169)$; this equals 8 uinals and 9 days extra. Therefore, beginning with the end of **Cumhu**, we may count *backward* 8 whole uinals, namely: **Cumhu, Kayab, Pax, Muan, Kankin, Mac, Ceh**, and **Zac**, which will bring us to the end of **Yax** (since we are counting backward). As we have left still 9 days out of our original 173, these must be counted backward from position **0 Zac**, that is, beginning with position **19 Yax: 19, 18, 17, 16, 15, 14, 13, 12, 11**; so **11 Yax** is the position in the year of the day of the terminal date. Assembling the above values, we find that in counting the number 9,663 *backward* from the starting point, **2 Imix 4 Uayeb**, the terminal date is **12 Eznab 11 Yax**. Whether the count be forward or backward, the method is the same, the only difference being in the direction of the counting.

This concludes the discussion of the actual arithmetical processes involved in counting forward or backward any given number from any given date; however, before explaining the fifth and final step in deciphering the Maya numbers, it is first necessary to show how this method of counting was applied to the Long Count.

The numbers used above in connection with dates merely express the difference in time between starting points and terminal dates, without assigning either set of dates to their proper positions in Maya chronology; that is, in the Long Count. Consequently, since any Maya date recurred at successive intervals of 52 years, by the time their historic period had been reached, more than 3,000 years after the starting point of their chronology, the Maya had upward of 70 distinct dates of exactly the same name to distinguish from one another.

It was stated on page 61 that the 0, or starting point of Maya chronology, was the date **4 Ahau 8 Cumhu**, from which all subsequent dates were reckoned; and further, on page 63, that by recording the number of cycles, katuns, tuns, uinals, and kins which had elapsed in each case between this date and any subsequent dates in the Long Count, subsequent dates of the same name could be readily distinguished from one another and assigned at the same time to their proper positions in Maya chronology. This method of fixing a date in the Long Count has been designated Initial-series dating.

The generally accepted method of writing Initial Series is as follows:
$$9.0.0.0.0. \quad \textbf{8 Ahau 13 Ceh}$$
The particular Initial-Series written here is to be interpreted thus: "Counting forward 9 cycles, 0 katuns, 0 tuns, 0 uinals, and 0 kins

from **4 Ahau 8 Cumhu,** the starting point of Maya chronology (always unexpressed in Initial Series), the terminal date reached will be **8 Ahau 13 Ceh.**" [1]   Or again:

9.14.13.4.17.   **12 Caban 5 Kayab**

This Inital Series reads thus: "Counting forward 9 cycles, 14 katuns, 13 tuns, 4 uinals, and 17 kins from **4 Ahau 8 Cumhu,** the starting point of Maya chronology (unexpressed), the terminal date reached will be **12 Caban 5 Kayab.**"

The time which separates any date from **4 Ahau 8 Cumhu** may be called that date's Initial-series value.   For example, in the first of the above cases the number 9.0.0.0.0 is the Initial-series value of the date **8 Ahau 13 Ceh,** and in the second the number 9.14.13.4.17 is the Initial-series value of the date **12 Caban 5 Kayab.**   It is clear from the foregoing that although the date **8 Ahau 13 Ceh,** for example, had recurred upward of 70 times since the beginning of their chronology, the Maya were able to distinguish any particular **8 Ahau 13 Ceh** from all the others merely by recording its distance from the starting point; in other words, giving thereto its particular Initial-series value, as 9.0.0.0.0. in the present case.   Similarly, any particular **12 Caban 5 Kayab,** by the addition of its corresponding Initial-series value, as 9.14.13.4.17 in the case above cited, was absolutely fixed in the Long Count—that is, in a period of 374,400 years.

Returning now to the question of how the counting of numbers was applied to the Long Count, it is evident that *every date in Maya chronology, starting points as well as terminal dates, had its own particular Initial-series value,* though in many cases these values are not recorded.   However, in most of the cases in which the Initial-series values of dates are not recorded, they may be calculated by means of their distances from other dates, whose Initial-series values are known.   This adding and subtracting of numbers to and from Initial Series [2] constitutes the application of the above-described arithmetical processes to the Long Count.   Several examples of this use are given below.

Let us assume for the first case that the number 2.5.6.1 is to be counted forward from the Initial Series 9.0.0.0.0 **8 Ahau 13 Ceh.**   By multiplying the values of the katuns, tuns, uinals, and kins given in Table XIII by their corresponding coefficients, in this case 2, 5, 6, and 1, respectively, and adding the resulting products together, we find that 2.5.6.1 reduces to 16,321 units of the first order.

Counting this forward from **8 Ahau 13 Ceh** as indicated by the rules on pages 138–143, the terminal date **1 Imix 9 Yaxkin** will be reached.

---

[1] The student may prove this for himself by reducing 9.0.0.0.0 to days (1,296,000), and counting forward this number from the date **4 Ahau 8 Cumhu,** as described in the rules on pages 138–143.   The terminal date reached will be **8 Ahau 13 Ceh,** as given above.

[2] Numbers may also be added to or subtracted from Period-ending dates, since the positions of such dates are also fixed in the Long Count, and consequently may be used as bases of reference for dates whose positions in the Long Count are not recorded.

Moreover, since the Initial-series value of the starting point **8 Ahau 13 Ceh** was 9.0.0.0.0, the Initial-series value of **1 Imix 9 Yaxkin**, the terminal date, may be calculated by adding its distance from **8 Ahau 13 Ceh** to the Initial-series value of that date:

9.0.0.0.0 (Initial-series value of starting point) **8 Ahau 13 Ceh**
2.5.6.1 (distance from **8 Ahau 13 Ceh** to **1 Imix 9 Yaxkin**)
9.2.5.6.1 (Initial-series value of terminal date) **1 Imix 9 Yaxkin**

That is, by calculation we have determined the Initial-series value of the particular **1 Imix 9 Yaxkin**, which was distant 2.5.6.1 from 9.0.0.0.0 **8 Ahau 13 Ceh**, to be 9.2.5.6.1, notwithstanding that this fact was not recorded.

The student may prove the accuracy of this calculation by treating 9.2.5.6.1 **1 Imix 9 Yaxkin** as a new Initial Series and counting forward 9.2.5.6.1 from **4 Ahau 8 Cumhu**, the starting point of all Initial Series known except two. If our calculations are correct, the former date will be reached just as if we had counted forward only 2.5.6.1 from 9.0.0.0.0 **8 Ahau 13 Ceh.**

In the above example the distance number 2.5.6.1 and the date **1 Imix 9 Yaxkin** to which it reaches, together are called a Secondary Series. This method of dating already described (see pp. 74–76 et seq.) seems to have been used to avoid the repetition of the Initial-series values for all the dates in an inscription.   For example, in the accompanying text—

9.12. 2. 0.16   **5 Cib 14 Yaxkin**
12. 9.15
[9.12.14.10.11] [1]   **9 Chuen 9 Kankin**
5
[9.12.14.10.16]   **1 Cib 14 Kankin**
1. 0. 2. 5
[9.13.14.13. 1]   **5 Imix 19 Zac**

---

[1] In adding two Maya numbers, for example 9.12.2.0.16 and 12.9.5, care should be taken first to arrange like units under like, as:

9.12. 2. 0.16
12. 9. 5

9.12.14.10. 1

Next, beginning at the right, the kins or units of the 1st place are added together, and after all the 20s (here 1) have been deducted from this sum, place the remainder (here 1) in the kin place. Next add the uinals, or units of the 2d place, adding to them 1 for each 20 which was carried forward from the 1st place. After all the 18s possible have been deducted from this sum (here 0) place the remainder (here 10) in the uinal place. Next add the tuns, or units of the 3d place, adding to them 1 for each 18 which was carried forward from the 2d place, and after deducting all the 20s possible (here 0) place the remainder (here 14) in the tun place. Proceed in this manner until the highest units present have been added and written below.

Subtraction is just the reverse of the preceding. Using the same numbers:

9.12. 2.0.16
12.9. 5

9.11. 9.9.11

5 kins from 16=11; 9 uinals from 18 uinals (1 tun has to be borrowed)=9; 12 tuns from 21 tuns (1 katun has to be borrowed, which, added to the 1 tun left in the minuend, makes 21 tuns)=9 tuns; 0 katuns from 11 katuns (1 katun having been borrowed)=11 katuns; and 0 cycles from 9 cycles=9 cycles.

the only parts actually recorded are the Initial Series 9.12.2.0.16 **5 Cib 14 Yaxkin,** and the Secondary Series 12.9.15 leading to **9 Chuen 9 Kankin;** the Secondary Series 5 leading to **1 Cib 14 Kankin;** and the Secondary Series 1.0.2.5 leading to **5 Imix 19 Zac.** The Initial-series values: 9.12.14.10.11; 9.12.14.10.16; and 9.13.14.13.1, belonging to the three dates of the Secondary Series, respectively, do not appear in the text at all (a fact indicated by the brackets), but are found only by calculation. Moreover, the student should note that in a succession of interdependent series like the ones just given the terminal date reached by one number, as **9 Chuen 9 Kankin,** becomes the starting point for the next number, 5. Again, the terminal date reached by counting 5 from **9 Chuen 9 Kankin,** that is, **1 Cib 14 Kankin,** becomes the starting point from which the next number, 1.0.2.5, is counted. In other words, these terms are only relative, since the terminal date of one number will be the starting point of the next.

Let us assume for the next example that the number 3.2 is to be counted forward from the Initial Series 9.12.3.14.0 **5 Ahau 8 Uo.** Reducing 3 uinals and 2 kins to kins, we have 62 units of the first order. Counting forward 62 from **5 Ahau 8 Uo,** as indicated by the rules on pages 138–143, it is found that the terminal date will be **2 Ik 10 Tzec.** Since the Initial-series value of the starting point **5 Ahau 8 Uo** is known, namely, 9.12.3.14.0, the Initial Series corresponding to the terminal date may be calculated from it as before:

9.12.3.14.0   (Initial-series value of the starting point) **5 Ahau 8 Uo**
        3.2   (distance from **5 Ahau 8 Uo** forward to **2 Ik 10 Tzec**)
[9.12.3.17.2] (Initial-series value of the terminal date) **2 Ik 10 Tzec**

The bracketed 9.12.3.17.2 in the Initial-series value corresponding to the date **2 Ik 10 Tzec** does not appear in the record but was reached by calculation. The student may prove the accuracy of this result by treating 9.12.3.17.2 **2 Ik 10 Tzec** as a new Initial Series, and counting forward 9.12.3.17.2 from **4 Ahau 8 Cumhu** (the starting point of Maya chronology, unexpressed in Initial Series). If our calculations are correct, the same date, **2 Ik 10 Tzec,** will be reached, as though we had counted only 3.2 forward from the Initial Series 9.12.3.14.0 **5 Ahau 8 Uo.**

One more example presenting a "backward count" will suffice to illustrate this method. Let us count the number 14.13.4.17 *backward* from the Initial Series 9.14.13.4.17 **12 Caban 5 Kayab.** Reducing 14.13.4.17 to units of the 1st order, we have 105,577. Counting this number *backward* from **12 Caban 5 Kayab,** as indicated in the rules on pages 138–143, we find that the terminal date will be **8 Ahau 13 Ceh.** Moreover, since the Initial-series value of the starting point **12 Caban 5 Kayab** is known, namely, 9.14.13.4.17, the Initial-series value of the terminal date may be calculated by *subtracting* the distance number 14.13.4.17 from the Initial Series of the starting point:

    9.14.13.4.17 (Initial-series value of the starting point) **12 Caban 5 Kayab**

    14.13.4.17 (distance from **12 Caban 5 Kayab** backward to **8 Ahau 13 Ceh**)

  [9. 0. 0.0. 0] (Initial-series value of the terminal date) **8 Ahau 13 Ceh**

The bracketed parts are not expressed. We have seen elsewhere that the Initial Series 9.0.0.0.0 has for its terminal date **8 Ahau 13 Ceh**; therefore our calculation proves itself.

The foregoing examples make it sufficiently clear that the distance numbers of Secondary Series may be used to determine the Initial-series values of Secondary-series dates, either by their addition to or subtraction from known Initial-series dates.

We have come now to the final step in the consideration of Maya numbers, namely, the identification of the terminal dates determined by the calculations given under the fourth step, pages 138–143. This step may be summed up as follows:

Fifth Step in Solving Maya Numbers

Find the terminal date to which the number leads.

As explained under the fourth step (pp. 138–143), the terminal date may be found by calculation. The above direction, however, refers to the actual finding of the terminal dates in the texts; that is, where to look for them. It may be said at the outset in this connection that terminal dates in the great majority of cases follow immediately the numbers which lead to them. Indeed, the connection between distance numbers and their corresponding terminal dates is far closer than between distance numbers and their corresponding starting points. This probably results from the fact that the closing dates of Maya periods were of far more importance than their opening dates. Time was measured by elapsed periods and recorded in terms of the ending days of such periods. The great emphasis on the closing date of a period in comparison with its opening date probably caused the suppression and omission of the date **4 Ahau 8 Cumhu**, the starting point of Maya chronology, in all Initial Series. To the same cause also may probably be attributed the great uniformity in the positions of almost all terminal dates, i. e., immediately after the numbers leading to them.

We may formulate, therefore, the following general rule, which the student will do well to apply in every case, since exceptions to it are very rare:

Rule. The terminal date reached by a number or series almost invariably follows immediately the last term of the number or series leading to it.

This applies equally to all terminal dates, whether in Initial Series, Secondary Series, Calendar-round dating or Period-ending dating, though in the case of Initial Series a peculiar division or partition of the terminal date is to be noted.

Throughout the inscriptions, excepting in the case of Initial Series, the month parts of the dates almost invariably follow immediately the days whose positions in the year they designate, without any other glyphs standing between; as, for example, **8 Ahau 13 Ceh, 12 Caban 5 Kayab,** etc. In Initial Series, on the other hand, the day parts of the dates, as **8 Ahau** and **12 Caban,** in the above examples, are almost invariably separated from their corresponding month parts, **13 Ceh** or **5 Kayab,** by several intervening glyphs. The positions of the day parts in Initial-series terminal dates are quite regular according to the terms of the above rule; that is, they follow immediately the lowest period of the number which in each case shows their distance from the unexpressed starting point, **4 Ahau 8 Cumhu.** The positions of the corresponding month parts are, on the other hand, irregular. These, instead of standing immediately after the days whose positions in the year they designate, follow at the close of some six or seven intervening glyphs. These intervening glyphs have been called the Supplementary Series, though the count which they record has not as yet been deciphered.[1] The month glyph in the great majority of cases follows immediately the closing [2] glyph of the Supplementary Series. The form of this latter sign is always unmistakable (see fig. 65), and it is further characterized by its numerical coefficient, which can never be anything but 9 or 10.[3] See examples of this sign in the figure just mentioned, where both normal forms *a, c, e, g,* and *h* and head variants *b, d,* and *f* are included.

The student will find this glyph exceedingly helpful in locating the month parts of Initial-series terminal dates in the inscriptions. For example, let us suppose in deciphering the Initial Series 9.16.5.0.0 **8 Ahau 8 Zotz** that the number 9.16.5.0.0 has been counted forward

---

[1] The Supplementary Series present perhaps the most promising field for future study and investigation in the Maya texts. They clearly have to do with a numerical count of some kind, which of itself should greatly facilitate progress in their interpretation. Mr. Goodman (1897: p. 118) has suggested that in some way the Supplementary Series record the dates of the Initial Series they accompany according to some other and unknown method, though he offers no proof in support of this hypothesis. Mr. Bowditch (1910: p. 244) believes they probably relate to time, because the glyphs of which they are composed have numbers attached to them. He has suggested the name Supplementary Series by which they are known, implying in the designation that these Series in some way supplement or complete the meaning of the Initial Series with which they are so closely connected. The writer believes that they treat of some lunar count. It seems almost certain that the moon glyph occurs repeatedly in the Supplementary Series (see fig. 65).

[2] The word "closing" as used here means only that in reading from left to right and from top to bottom—that is, in the normal order—the sign shown in fig. 65 is always the last one in the Supplementary Series, usually standing immediately before the month glyph of the Initial-series terminal date. It does not signify, however, that the Supplementary Series were to be read in this direction, and, indeed, there are strong indications that they followed the reverse order, from right to left and bottom to top.

[3] In a few cases the sign shown in fig. 65 occurs elsewhere in the Supplementary Series than as its "closing" glyph. In such cases its coefficient is not restricted to the number 9 or 10.

from **4 Ahau 8 Cumhu** (the unexpressed starting point), and has been found by calculation to reach the terminal date **8 Ahau 8 Zotz**; and further, let us suppose that on inspecting the text the day part of this date (**8 Ahau**) has been found to be recorded immediately after the 0 kins of the number 9.16.5.0.0. Now, if the student will follow the next six or seven glyphs until he finds one like any of the forms in figure 65, the glyph immediately following the latter sign will be in all probability the month part, **8 Zotz** in the above example, of an Initial-series' terminal date. In other words, although the meaning of the glyph shown in the last-mentioned figure is unknown, it is important for the student to recognize its form, since it is almost invariably the "indicator" of the month sign in Initial Series.

In all other cases in the inscriptions, including also the exceptions

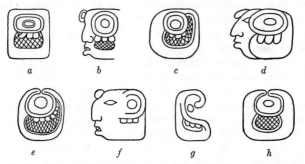

FIG. 65.   Sign for the "month indicator": *a, c, e, g, h,* Normal forms; *b, d, f,* head variants.

to the above rule, that is, where the month parts of Initial-series terminal dates do not immediately follow the closing glyph of the Supplementary Series, the month signs follow immediately the day signs whose positions in the year they severally designate.

In the codices the month signs when recorded [1] usually follow immediately the days signs to which they belong. The most notable exception [2] to this general rule occurs in connection with the Venus-solar periods represented on pages 46–50 of the Dresden Codex, where one set of day signs is used with three different sets of month signs to form three different sets of dates. For example, in one place the day **2 Ahau** stands above three different month signs—**3 Cumhu, 3 Zotz,** and **13 Yax**—with each of which it is used to form a

---

[1] In the codices frequently the month parts of dates are omitted and starting points and terminal dates alike are expressed as days only; thus, **2 Ahau, 5 Imix, 7 Kan,** etc. This is nearly always the case in tonalamatls and in certain series of numbers in the Dresden Codex.

[2] Only a very few month signs seem to be recorded in the Codex Tro-Cortesiano and the Codex Peresianus. The Tro-Cortesiano has only one (p. 73b), in which the date **13 Ahau 13 Cumhu** is recorded thus (*). Compare the month form in this date with fig. 20, *z–b'*. Mr. Gates (1910: p. 21) finds three month signs in the Codex Peresianus, on pp. 4, 7, and 18 at 4c7, 7c2, and 18b4, respectively. The first of these is **16 Zac** (**). Compare this form with fig. 20, *o*. The second is **1 Yaxkin** (†). Compare this form with fig. 20, *i–j*. The third is **12 Cumhu** (††); see fig. 20, *z–b'*.

different date—**2 Ahau 3 Cumhu, 2 Ahau 3 Zotz,** and **2 Ahau 13 Yax.** In these pages the month signs, with a few exceptions, do not follow immediately the days to which they belong, but on the contrary they are separated from them by several intervening glyphs. This abbreviation in the record of these dates was doubtless prompted by the desire or necessity for economizing space. In the above example, instead of repeating the **2 Ahau** with each of the two lower month signs, **3 Zotz** and **13 Yax,** by writing it once above the upper month sign, **3 Cumhu,** the scribe intended that it should be used in turn with each one of the three month signs standing below it, to form three different dates, saving by this abbreviation the space of two glyphs, that is, double the space occupied by **2 Ahau.**

With the exception of the Initial-series dates in the inscriptions and the Venus-Solar dates on pages 46–50 of the Dresden Codex, we may say that the regular position of the month glyphs in Maya writing was immediately following the day glyphs whose positions in the year they severally designated.

In closing the presentation of this last step in the process of deciphering numbers in the texts, the great value of the terminal date as a final check for all the calculations involved under steps 1–4 (pp. 134–151) should be pointed out. If after having worked out the terminal date of a given number according to these rules the terminal date thus found should differ from that actually recorded under step 5, we must accept one of the following alternatives:

1. There is an error in our own calculations; or
2. There is an error in the original text; or
3. The case in point lies without the operation of our rules.

It is always safe for the beginner to proceed on the assumption that the first of the above alternatives is the cause of the error; in other words, that his own calculations are at fault. If the terminal date as calculated does not agree with the terminal date as recorded, the student should repeat his calculations several times, checking up each operation in order to eliminate the possibility of a purely arithmetical error, as a mistake in multiplication. After all attempts to reach the recorded terminal date by counting the given number from the starting point have failed, the process should be reversed and the attempt made to reach the starting point by counting backward the given number from its recorded terminal date. Sometimes this reverse process will work out correctly, showing that there must be some arithmetical error in our original calculations which we have failed to detect. However, when both processes have failed several times to connect the starting point with the recorded terminal date by use of the given number, there remains the possibility that either the starting point or the terminal date, or perhaps both, do not belong to the given number. The rules for determining this fact have been given under step 2, page 135, and step 4, page 138.   If after applying these to the case in point it seems certain that the starting point and terminal date used in the calculations both belong to the given number, we have to fall back on the second of the above alternatives, that is, that there is an error in the original text.

Although very unusual, particularly in the inscriptions, errors in the original texts are by no means entirely unknown.   These seem to be restricted chiefly to errors in numerals, as the record of 7 for 8, or 7 for 12 or 17, that is, the omission or insertion of one or more bars or dots.   In a very few instances there seem to be errors in the month glyph.   Such errors usually are obvious, as will be pointed out in connection with the texts in which they are found (see Chapters V and VI).

If both of the above alternatives are found not to apply, that is, if both our calculations and the original texts are free from error, we are obliged to accept the third alternative as the source of trouble, namely, that the case in point lies without the operation of our rules.   In such cases it is obviously impossible to go further in the present state of our knowledge.   Special conditions presented by glyphs whose meanings are unknown may govern such cases.   At all events, the failure of the rules under 1–4 to reach the terminal dates recorded as under 5 introduces a new phase of glyph study— the meaning of unknown forms with which the beginner has no concern.   Consequently, when a text falls without the operation of the rules given in this chapter—a very rare contingency—the beginner should turn his attention elsewhere.

Chapter V

THE INSCRIPTIONS

The present chapter will be devoted to the interpretation of texts drawn from monuments, a process which consists briefly in the application to the inscriptions [1] of the material presented in Chapters III and IV.

Before proceeding with this discussion it will first be necessary to explain the method followed in designating particular glyphs in a

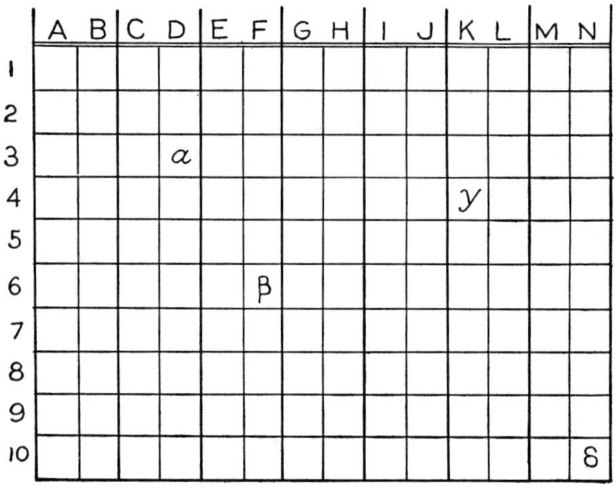

Fig. 66. Diagram showing the method of designating particular glyphs in a text.

text. We have seen (p. 23) that the Maya glyphs were presented in parallel columns, which are to be read two columns at a time, the order of the individual glyph-blocks [2] in each pair of columns being from left to right and from top to bottom. For convenience in referring to particular glyphs in the texts, the vertical columns of glyph-blocks are lettered from left to right, thus, A, B, C, D, etc., and the horizontal rows numbered from top to bottom, thus, 1, 2, 3, 4, etc. For example, in figure 66 the glyph-blocks in columns A and B are read together from left to right and top to bottom, thus, A1 B1, A2 B2, A3 B3, etc. When glyph-block B10 is reached the next in order

---

[1] As used throughout this work, the word "inscriptions" is applied only to texts from the monuments.

[2] The term glyph-block has been used instead of glyph in this connection because in many inscriptions several different glyphs are included in one glyph-block. In such cases, however, the glyphs within the glyph-block follow precisely the same order as the glyph-blocks themselves follow in the pairs of columns, that is, from left to right and top to bottom.

PLATE 6

A. ZOÖMORPH P, QUIRIGUA

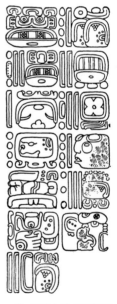

C. STELA I, QUIRIGUA

B. STELA 22, NARANJO

D. STELA 24, NARANJO

GLYPHS REPRESENTING INITIAL SERIES, SHOWING USE OF BAR
AND DOT NUMERALS AND NORMAL-FORM PERIOD GLYPHS

is C1, which is followed by D1, C2 D2, C3 D3, etc. Again, when D10 is reached the next in order is E1, which is followed by F1, E2 F2, E3 F3, etc. In this way the order of reading proceeds from left to right and from top to bottom, in pairs of columns, that is, G H, I J, K L, and M N throughout the inscription, and usually closes with the glyph-block in the lower right-hand corner, as N10 in figure 66. By this simple system of coordinates any particular glyph in a text may be readily referred to when the need arises. Thus, for example, in figure 66 glyph α is referred to as D3; glyph β as F6; glyph γ as K4; glyph δ as N10. In a few texts the glyph-blocks are so irregularly placed that it is impracticable to designate them by the above coordinates. In such cases the order of the glyph-blocks will be indicated by numerals, 1, 2, 3, etc. In two Copan texts, Altar S (fig. 81) and Stela J (pl. 15), made from the drawings of Mr. Maudslay, his numeration of the glyphs has been followed. This numeration appears in these two figures.

Texts Recording Initial Series

Because of the fundamental importance of Initial Series in the Maya system of chronology, the first class of texts represented will illustrate this method of dating. Moreover, since the normal forms for the numerals and the period glyphs will be more easily recognized by the beginner than the corresponding head variants, the first Initial Series given will be found to have all the numerals and period glyphs expressed by normal forms.[1]

In plate 6 is figured the drawing of the Initial Series [2] from Zoömorph P at Quirigua, a monument which is said to be the finest piece of aboriginal sculpture in the western hemisphere. Our text opens with one large glyph, which occupies the space of four glyph-blocks, A1–B2.[3] Analysis of this form shows that it possesses all the elements mentioned on page 65 as belonging to the so-called Initial-series introducing glyph, without which Initial Series never seem to have been recorded in the inscriptions. These elements are: (1) the trinal

---

[1] Initial Series which have all their period glyphs expressed by normal forms are comparatively rare; consequently the four examples presented in pl. 6, although they are the best of their kind, leave something to be desired in other ways. In pl. 6, A, for example, the month sign was partially effaced though it is restored in the accompanying reproduction; in B of the same plate the closing glyph of the Supplementary Series (the month-sign indicator) is wanting, although the month sign itself is very clear. Again, in D the details of the day glyph and month glyph are partially effaced (restored in the reproduction), and in C, although the entire text is very clear, the month sign of the terminal date irregularly follows immediately the day sign. However, in spite of these slight irregularities, it has seemed best to present these particular texts as the first examples of Initial Series, because their period glyphs are expressed by normal forms exclusively, which, as pointed out above, are more easily recognized on account of their greater differentiation than the corresponding head variants.

[2] In most of the examples presented in this chapter the full inscription is not shown, only that part of the text illustrating the particular point in question being given. For this reason reference will be made in each case to the publication in which the entire inscription has been reproduced. The full text on Zoömorph P at Quirigua will be found in Maudslay, 1889–1902: II, pls. 53, 54, 55, 56, 57, 59, 63, 64.

[3] All glyphs expressed in this way are to be understood as inclusive. Thus A1–B2 signifies 4 glyphs, namely, A1, B1, A2, B2.

superfix, (2) the pair of comblike lateral appendages, (3) the normal form of the tun sign, (4) the trinal subfix, and (5) the variable central element. As stated above, all these appear in the large glyph A1–B2. Moreover, a comparison of A1–B2 with the introducing glyphs given in figure 24 shows that these forms are variants of one and the same sign. Consequently, in A1–B2 we have recorded an Initial-series introducing glyph. The use of this sign is so highly specialized that, on the basis of its occurrence alone in a text, the student is perfectly justified in assuming that an Initial Series will immediately follow.[1] Exceptions to this rule are so very rare (see p. 67) that the beginner will do well to disregard them altogether.

The next glyph after the introducing glyph in an Initial Series is the cycle sign, the highest period ever found in this kind of count[2]. The cycle sign in the present example appears in A3 with the coefficient 9 (1 bar and 4 dots). Although the period glyph is partially effaced in the original enough remains to trace its resemblance to the normal form of the cycle sign shown in figure 25, *a-c.* The outline of the repeated **Cauac** sign appears in both places. We have then, in this glyph, the record of 9 cycles[3]. The glyph following the cycle sign in an Initial Series is always the katun sign, and this should appear in B3, the glyph next in order. This glyph is quite clearly the normal form of the katun sign, as a comparison of it with figure 27, *a, b,* the normal form for the katun, will show. It has the normal-form numeral 18 (3 bars and 3 dots) prefixed to it, and this whole glyph therefore signifies 18 katuns. The next glyph should record the tuns, and a comparison of the glyph in A4 with the normal form of the tun sign in figure 29, *a, b,* shows this to be the case. The numeral 5 (1 bar prefixed to the tun sign) shows that this period is to be used 5 times; that is, multiplied by 5. The next glyph (B4) should be the uinal sign, and a comparison of B4 with figure 31, *a-c,* the normal form of the uinal sign, shows the identity of these two glyphs. The coefficient of the uinal sign contains as its most conspicuous element the clasped hand, which suggests that we may have 0 uinals recorded in B4. A comparison of this coefficient with the sign for zero in figure 54 proves this to be the case. The next glyph (A5) should be the kin sign, the lowest period involved in recording Initial Series. A comparison of A5 with the normal form of the kin sign in figure 34, *a,* shows that these two forms are identical. The coefficient of A5 is, moreover, exactly like the coefficient of B4, which, we have seen, meant zero, hence glyph A5 stands for 0 kins. Summarizing the above, we may say that glyphs A3–A5 record an Initial-series number consisting of 6 cycles, 18 katuns, 5 tuns, 0 uinals, and 0 kins, which we may write thus: 9.18.5.0.0 (see p. 138, footnote 1).

---

[1] The introducing glyph, so far as the writer knows, always stands at the beginning of an inscription, or in the second glyph-block, that is, at the top. Hence an Initial Series can never precede it.

[2] The Initial Series on Stela 10 at Tikal is the only exception known. See pp. 123–127.

[3] As will appear in the following examples, nearly all Initial Series have 9 as their cycle coefficient.

Now let us turn to Chapter IV and apply the several steps there given, by means of which Maya numbers may be solved. The first step on page 134 was to reduce the given number, in this case 9.18.5.0.0, to units of the first order; this may be done by multiplying the recorded coefficients by the numerical values of the periods to which they are respectively attached. These values are given in Table XIII, and the sum of the products arising from their multi-ͺlication by the coefficients recorded in the Initial Series in plate 6, A are given below:

$$
\begin{aligned}
A3 &= 9 \times 144,000 = 1,296,000 \\
B3 &= 18 \times 7,200 = 129,600 \\
A4 &= 5 \times 360 = 1,800 \\
B4 &= 0 \times 20 = 0 \\
A5 &= 0 \times 1 = 0 \\
\hline
& \qquad\qquad\quad 1,427,400
\end{aligned}
$$

Therefore 1,427,400 will be the number used in the following calculations.

The second step (see step 2, p. 135) is to determine the starting point from which this number is counted. According to rule 2, page 136, if the number is an Initial Series the starting point, although never recorded, is practically always the date **4 Ahau 8 Cumhu.** Exceptions to this rule are so very rare that they may be disregarded by the beginner, and it may be taken for granted, therefore, in the present case, that our number 1,427,400 is to be counted from the date **4 Ahau 8 Cumhu.**

The third step (see step 3, p. 136) is to determine the direction of the count, whether forward or backward. In this connection it was stated that the general practice is to count forward, and that the student should always proceed upon this assumption. However, in the present case there is no room for uncertainty, since the direction of the count in an Initial Series is governed by an invariable rule. In Initial Series, according to the rule on page 137, the count is always *forward*, consequently 1,427,400 is to be counted *forward* from **4 Ahau 8 Cumhu.**

The fourth step (see step 4, p. 138) is to count the given number from its starting point; and the rules governing this process will be found on pages 139–143. Since our given number (1,427,400) is greater than 18,980, or 1 Calendar Round, the preliminary rule on page 143 applies in the present case, and we may therefore subtract from 1,427,400 all the Calendar Rounds possible before proceeding to count it from the starting point. By referring to Table XVI, it appears that 1,427,400 contains 75 complete Calendar Rounds, or 1,423,500; hence, the latter number may be subtracted from 1,427,400 without affecting the value of the resulting terminal date: 1,427,400 − 1,423,500 = 3,900. In other words, in counting forward 3,900 from **4 Ahau 8 Cumhu**, the same terminal date will be reached as though we had counted forward 1,427,400.[1]

In order to find the coefficient of the day of the terminal date, it is necessary, by rule 1, page 139, to divide the given number or its equivalent by 13; 3,900 ÷ 13 = 300. Now since there is no fractional part in the resulting quotient, the numerator of an assumed fractional part will be 0; counting forward 0 from the coefficient of the day of the starting point, 4 (that is, **4 Ahau 8 Cumhu**), we reach 4 as the coefficient of the day of the terminal date.

In order to find the day sign of the terminal date, it is necessary, under rule 2, page 140, to divide the given number or its equivalent by 20; 3,900 ÷ 20 = 195. Since there is no fractional part in the resulting quotient, the numerator of an assumed fractional part will be 0; counting forward 0 in Table I, from **Ahau**, the day sign of the starting point (**4 Ahau 8 Cumhu**), we reach **Ahau** as the day sign of the terminal date. In other words, in counting forward either 3,900 or 1,427,400 from **4 Ahau 8 Cumhu**, the day reached will be **4 Ahau**. It remains to show what position in the year this day **4 Ahau** distant 1,427,400 from the date **4 Ahau 8 Cumhu**, occupied.

In order to find the position in the year which the day of the terminal date occupied, it is necessary, under rule 3, page 141, to divide the given number or its equivalent by 365; $3,900 ÷ 365 = 10\frac{250}{365}$. Since the numerator of the fractional part of the resulting quotient is 250, to reach the year position of the day of the terminal date desired it is necessary to count 250 forward from **8 Cumhu**, the year position of the day of the starting point **4 Ahau 8 Cumhu**. It appears from Table XV, in which the 365 positions of the year are given, that after position **8 Cumhu** there are only 16 positions in the year—11 more in **Cumhu** and 5 in **Uayeb**. These must be subtracted, therefore, from 250 in order to bring the count to the end of the year; 250 − 16 = 234, so 234 is the number of positions we must count forward in the new year. It is clear that the first 11 uinals in the year will use up exactly 220 of our 234 positions (11 × 20 = 220), and that 14 positions will be left, which must be counted in the next uinal, the 12th. But the 12th uinal of the year is **Ceh** (see Table XV); counting forward 14 positions in **Ceh**, we reach **13 Ceh**, which is, therefore, the month glyph of our terminal date. In other words, counting 250 forward from **8 Cumhu**, position **13 Ceh** is reached. Assembling the above values, we find that by calculation we have determined the terminal date of the Initial Series in plate 6, *A*, to be **4 Ahau 13 Ceh**.

---

[1] In the present case therefore so far as these calculations are concerned, 3,900 is the equivalent of 1,427,400.

At this point there are several checks which the student may apply
to his result in order to test the accuracy of his calculations; for
instance, in the present example if 115, the difference between 365
and 250 (115 + 250 = 365) is counted forward from position **13 Ceh**, position **8 Cumhu** will be reached if our calculations were correct. This
is true because there are only 365 positions in the year, and having
reached **13 Ceh** in counting forward 250 from **8 Cumhu**, counting the
remaining 115 days forward from day reached by 250, that is, **13 Ceh**,
we should reach our starting point (**8 Cumhu**) again. Another good
check in the present case would be to count *backward* 250 from
13 Ceh; if our calculations have been correct, the starting point
8 Cumhu will be reached. Still another check, which may be applied
is the following: From Table VII it is clear that the day sign **Ahau**
can occupy only positions 3, 8, 13, or 18 in the divisions of the year;[1]
hence, if in the above case the coefficient of **Ceh** had been any other
number but one of these four, our calculations would have been
incorrect.

We come now to the final step (see step 5, p. 151), the actual finding
of the glyphs in our text which represent the two parts of the terminal date—the day and its corresponding position in the year. If
we have made no arithmetical errors in calculations and if the text
itself presents no irregular and unusual features, the terminal date
recorded should agree with the terminal date obtained by calculation.

It was explained on page 152 that the two parts of an Initial-
series terminal date are usually separated from each other by several
intervening glyphs, and further that, although the day part follows
immediately the last period glyph of the number (the kin glyph),
the month part is not recorded until after the close of the Supplementary Series, usually a matter of six or seven glyphs. Returning to
our text (pl. 6, *A*), we find that the kins are recorded in A5, therefore
the day part of the terminal date should appear in B5. The glyph
in B5 quite clearly records the day **4 Ahau** by means of 4 dots prefixed
to the sign shown in figure 16, *e'–g'*, which is the form for the day
name **Ahau**, thereby agreeing with the value of the day part of the
terminal date as determined by calculation. So far then we have read
our text correctly. Following along the next six or seven glyphs,
A6–C1a, which record the Supplementary Series,[2] we reach in C1a
a sign similar to the forms shown in figure 65. This glyph, which
always has a coefficient of 9 or 10, was designated on page 152 the
month-sign "indicator," since it usually immediately precedes the
month sign in Initial-series terminal dates. In C1a it has the coefficient 9 (4 dots and 1 bar) and is followed in C1b by the month part

---

[1] It should be remembered in this connection, as explained on pp. 47, 55, that the positions in the divisions of the year which the Maya called 3, 8, 13, and 18 correspond in our method of naming the positions
of the days in the months to the 4th, 9th, 14th, and 19th positions, respectively.

[2] As stated in footnote 1, p. 152, the meaning of the Supplementary Series has not yet been worked out.

of the terminal date, **13 Ceh.** The bar and dot numeral 13 appears very clearly above the month sign, which, though partially effaced, yet bears sufficient resemblance to the sign for **Ceh** in figure 19, *u, v,* to enable us to identify it as such.

Our complete Initial Series, therefore, reads: 9.18.5.0.0 **4 Ahau 13 Ceh,** and since the terminal date recorded in B5, C1b agrees with the terminal date determined by calculation, we may conclude that this text is without error and, furthermore, that it records a date, **4 Ahau 13 Ceh,** which was distant 9.18.5.0.0 from the starting point of Maya chronology. The writer interprets this text as signifying that 9.18.5.0.0 **4 Ahau 13 Ceh** was the date on which Zoömorph P at Quirigua was formally consecrated or dedicated as a time-marker, or in other words, that Zoömorph P was the monument set up to mark the hotun, or 5-tun period, which came to a close on the date 9.18.5.0.0 **4 Ahau 13 Ceh** of Maya chronology.[1]

In plate 6, *B,* is figured a drawing of the Initial Series on Stela 22 at Naranjo.[2] The text opens in A1 with the Initial-series introducing glyph, which is followed in B1–B3 by the Initial-series number 9.12.15.13.7. The five period glyphs are all expressed by their corresponding normal forms, and the student will have no difficulty in identifying them and reading the number, as above recorded.

By means of Table XIII this number may be reduced to units of the 1st order, in which form it may be more conveniently used. This reduction, which forms the first step in the process of solving Maya numbers (see step 1, p. 134), follows:

$$
\begin{aligned}
B1 &= 9 \times 144,000 = 1,296,000 \\
A2 &= 12 \times 7,200 = 86,400 \\
B2 &= 15 \times 360 = 5,400 \\
A3 &= 13 \times 20 = 260 \\
B3 &= 7 \times 1 = 7 \\
\hline
& 1,388,067
\end{aligned}
$$

And 1,388,067 will be the number used in the following calculations.

The next step is to find the starting point from which 1,388,067 is counted (see step 2, p. 135). Since this number is an Initial Series, in all probability its starting point will be the date **4 Ahau 8 Cumhu**; at least it is perfectly safe to proceed on that assumption.

The next step is to find the direction of the count (see step 3, p. 136); since our number is an Initial Series, the count can only be forward (see rule 2, p. 137).[3]

---

[1] The reasons which have led the writer to this conclusion are given at some length on pp. 33–36.

[2] For the full text of this inscription see Maler, 1908 b: pl. 36.

[3] Since nothing but Initial-series texts will be presented in the plates and figures immediately following, a fact which the student will readily detect by the presence of the introducing glyph at the head of each text, it is unnecessary to repeat for each new text step 2 (p. 135) and step 3 (p. 136), which explain how to determine the starting point of the count and the direction of the count, respectively; and the student may assume that the starting point of the several Initial Series hereinafter figured will always be the date **4 Ahau 8 Cumhu** and that the direction of the count will always be forward.

Having determined the number to be counted, the starting point from which the count commences, and the direction of the count, we may now proceed with the actual process of counting (see step 4, p. 138).

Since 1,388,067 is greater than 18,980 (1 Calendar Round), we may deduct from the former number all the Calendar Rounds possible (see preliminary rule, page 143). According to Table XVI it appears that 1,388,067 contains 73 Calendar Rounds, or 1,385,540; after deducting this from the given number we have left 2,527 (1,388,067 − 1,385,540), a far more convenient number to handle than 1,388,067.

Applying rule 1 (p. 139) to 2,527, we have: $2{,}527 \div 13 = 194\frac{5}{13}$, and counting forward 5, the numerator of the fractional part of the quotient, from 4, the day coefficient of the starting point, **4 Ahau 8 Cumhu**, we reach 9 as the day coefficient of the terminal date.

Applying rule 2 (p. 140) to 2,527, we have: $2{,}527 \div 20 = 126\frac{7}{20}$; and counting forward 7, the numerator of the fractional part of the quotient, from **Ahau**, the day sign of our starting point, **4 Ahau 8 Cumhu**, in Table I, we reach **Manik** as the day sign of the terminal date. Therefore, the day of the terminal date will be **9 Manik.**

Applying rule 3 (p. 141) to 2,527, we have: $2{,}527 \div 365 = 6\frac{337}{365}$; and counting forward 337, the numerator of the fractional part of the quotient, from **8 Cumhu**, the year position of the starting point, **4 Ahau 8 Cumhu**, in Table XV, we reach **0 Kayab** as the year position of the terminal date. The calculations by means of which **0 Kayab** is reached are as follows: After **8 Cumhu** there are 16 positions in the year, which we must subtract from 337; 337 − 16 = 321, which is to be counted forward in the new year. This number contains just 1 more than 16 uinals, that is, $321 = (16 \times 20) + 1$; hence it will reach through the first 16 uinals in Table XV and to the first position in the 17th uinal, **0 Kayab**. Combining this with the day obtained above, we have for our terminal date determined by calculation, **9 Manik 0 Kayab.**

The next and last step (see step 5, p. 151) is to find the above date in the text. In Initial Series (see p. 152) the two parts of the terminal date are generally separated, the day part usually following immediately the last period glyph and the month part the closing glyph of the Supplementary Series. In plate 6, B, the last period glyph, as we have seen, is recorded in B3; therefore the day should appear in A4. Comparing the glyph in A4 with the sign for **Manik** in figure 16, j, the two forms are seen to be identical. Moreover, A4 has the bar and dot coefficient 9 attached to it, that is, 4 dots and 1 bar; consequently it is clear that in A4 we have recorded the day **9 Manik**, the same day as reached by calculation. For some unknown reason, at Naranjo the month glyphs of the Initial-series terminal dates do not regularly follow the closing glyphs of the Supplementary Series;

indeed, in the text here under discussion, so far as we can judge from the badly effaced glyphs, no Supplementary Series seems to have been recorded. However, reversing our operation, we know by calculation that the month part should be **0 Kayab**, and by referring to figure 49 we find the only form which can be used to express the 0 position with the month signs—the so-called "spectacles" glyph—which must be recorded somewhere in this text to express the idea 0 with the month sign **Kayab**. Further, by referring to figure 19, d'–f', we may fix in our minds the sign for the month **Kayab**, which should also appear in the text with one of the forms shown in figure 49.

Returning to our text once more and following along the glyphs after the day in A4, we pass over B4, A5, and B5 without finding a glyph resembling one of the forms in figure 49 joined to figure 19, d'–f'; that is, **0 Kayab**. However, in A6 such a glyph is reached, and the student will have no difficulty in identifying the month sign with d'–f' in the above figure. Consequently, we have recorded in A4, A6 the same terminal date, **9 Manik 0 Kayab**, as determined by calculation, and may conclude, therefore, that our text records without error the date 9.12.15.13.7 **9 Manik 0 Kayab**[1] of Maya chronology.

The next text presented (pl. 6, C) shows the Initial Series from Stela I at Quirigua.[2] Again, as in plate 6, A, the introducing glyph occupies the space of four glyph-blocks, namely, A1–B2. Immediately after this, in A3–A4, is recorded the Initial-series number 9.18.10.0.0, all the period glyphs and coefficients of which are expressed by normal forms. The student's attention is called to the form for 0 used with the uinal and kin signs in A4a and A4b, respectively, which differs from the form for 0 recorded with the uinal and kin signs in plate 6, A, B4, and A5, respectively. In the latter text the 0 uinals and 0 kins were expressed by the hand- and curl form for zero shown in figure 54; in the present text, however, the 0 uinals and 0 kins are expressed by the form for 0 shown in figure 47, a new feature.

Reducing the above number to units of the 1st order by means of Table XIII, we have:

$$
\begin{aligned}
A3 &= 9 \times 144,000 = 1,296,000 \\
B3a &= 18 \times 7,200 = 129,600 \\
B3b &= 10 \times 360 = 3,600 \\
A4a &= 0 \times 20 = 0 \\
A4b &= 0 \times 1 = 0 \\
\hline
& 1,429,200
\end{aligned}
$$

---

[1] As will appear later, in connection with the discussion of the Secondary Series, the Initial-series date of a monument does not always correspond with the ending date of the period whose close the monument marks. In other words, the Initial-series date is not always the date contemporaneous with the formal dedication of the monument as a time-marker. This point will appear much more clearly when the function of Secondary Series has been explained.

[2] For the full text of this inscription see Hewett, 1911: pl. xxxv C.

Deducting from this number all the Calendar Rounds possible, 75 (see Table XVI), it may be reduced to 5,700 without affecting its value in the present connection.

Applying rules 1 and 2 (pp. 139 and 140, respectively) to this number, the day reached will be found to be **10 Ahau**; and by applying rule 3 (p. 141), the position of this day in the year will be found to be **8 Zac**. Therefore, by calculation we have determined that the terminal date reached by this Initial Series is **10 Ahau 8 Zac**. It remains to find this date in the text. The regular position for the day in Initial-series terminal dates is immediately following the last period glyph, which, as we have seen above, was in A4b. Therefore the day glyph should be B4a. An inspection of this latter glyph will show that it records the day **10 Ahau**, both the day sign and the coefficient being unusually clear, and practically unmistakable. Compare B4a with figure 16, *e'–g'*, the sign for the day name **Ahau**. Consequently the day recorded agrees with the day determined by calculation. The month glyph in this text, as mentioned on page 157, footnote 1, occurs out of its regular position, following immediately the day of the terminal date.

As mentioned on page 153, when the month glyph in Initial-series terminal dates is *not* to be found in its usual position, it will be found in the regular position for the month glyphs in all other kinds of dates in the inscriptions, namely, immediately following the day glyph to which it belongs. In the present text we found that the day, **10 Ahau**, was recorded in B4a; hence, since the month glyph was not recorded in its regular position, it must be in B4b, immediately following the day glyph. By comparing the glyph in B4b with the month signs in figure 19, it will be found exactly like the month sign for **Zac** (*s–t*), and we may therefore conclude that this is our month glyph and that it is **Zac**. The coefficient of B4b is quite clearly 8 and the month part therefore reads, **8 Zac**. Combining this with the day recorded in B4a, we have the date **10 Ahau 8 Zac**, which corresponds with the terminal date determined by calculation. The whole text therefore reads 9.18.10.0.0 **10 Ahau 8 Zac**.

It will be noted that this date 9.18.10.0.0 **10 Ahau 8 Zac** is just 5.0.0 (5 tuns) later than the date recorded by the Initial Series on Zoömorph P at Quirigua (see pl. 6, *A*). As explained in Chapter II (pp. 33–34), the interval between succeeding monuments at Quirigua is in every case 1,800 days, or 5 tuns. Therefore, it would seem probable that at Quirigua at least this period was the unit used for marking the lapse of time. As each 5-tun period was completed, its close was marked by the erection of a monument, on which was recorded its ending date. Thus the writer believes Zoömorph P marked the close of the 5-tun period ending 9.18.5.0.0 **4 Ahau 13 Ceh**, and Stela I, the 5-tun period next following, that ending 9.18.10.0.0

10 Ahau 8 Zac. In other words, Zoömorph P and Stela I were two successive time-markers, or "period stones," in the chronological record at Quirigua. For this 5-tun period so conspicuously recorded in the inscriptions from the older Maya cities the writer would suggest the name *hotun*, *ho* meaning 5 in Maya and *tun* being the name of the 360-day period. This word has an etymological parallel in the Maya word for the 20-tun period, *katun*, which we have seen may have been named directly from its numerical value, *kal* being the word for 20 in Maya and *kaltun* contracted to katun, thus meaning 20 tuns. Although no glyph for the *hotun* has as yet been identified,[1] the writer is inclined to believe that the sign in figure 67, *a*, *b*, which is frequently encountered in the texts, will be found to represent this time period. The bar at the top in both *a* and *b*, figure 67, surely signifies 5; therefore the glyph itself must mean "1 tun." This form recalls the very unusual variant of the tun from Palenque (see fig. 29, *h*). Both have the wing and the (*) element.

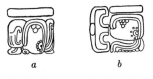

a   *b*

FIG. 67. Signs representing the hotun, or 5-tun, period.

The next Initial Series presented (see pl. 6, *D*) is from Stela 24 at Naranjo.[2] The text opens with the introducing glyph, which is in the same relative position as the introducing glyph in the other Naranjo text (pl. 6, *B*) at A1. Then follows regularly in B1–B3 the number 9.12.10.5.12, the numbers and period glyphs of which are all expressed by normal forms. By this time the student should have no difficulty in recognizing these and in determining the number as given above. Reducing this according to rule 1, page 134, the following result should be obtained:

$$
\begin{aligned}
B1 &= 9 \times 144,000 = 1,296,000 \\
A2 &= 12 \times 7,200 = 86,400 \\
B2 &= 10 \times 360 = 3,600 \\
A3 &= 5 \times 20 = 100 \\
B3 &= 12 \times 1 = 12 \\
&\overline{1,386,112}
\end{aligned}
$$

Deducting[3] from this number all the Calendar Rounds possible, 73 (see preliminary rule, p. 143, and Table XVI), we may reduce it to 572 without affecting its value in so far as the present calculations are concerned (1,386,112 − 1,385,540). First applying rule 1, page

---

[1] So far as the writer knows, the existence of a period containing 5 tuns has not been suggested heretofore. The very general practice of closing inscriptions with the end of some particular 5-tun period in the Long Count, as 9.18.5.0.0, or 9.18.10.0.0, or 9.18.15.0.0, or 9.19.0.0.0, for example, seems to indicate that this period was the unit used for measuring time in Maya chronological records, at least in the southern cities. Consequently, it seems likely that there was a special glyph to express this unit.

[2] For the full text of this inscription see Maler, 1908 b: pl. 39.

[3] The student should note that from this point steps 2 (p. 139) and 3 (p. 140) have been omitted in discussing each text (see p. 162, footnote 3).

PLATE 7

A. STELA B, COPAN   *B.* STELA A, COPAN

GLYPHS REPRESENTING INITIAL SERIES, SHOWING USE OF BAR
AND DOT NUMERALS AND HEAD-VARIANT PERIOD GLYPHS

139, and next rule 2, page 140, to this number (572), the student will find the day reached to be **4 Eb**. And applying rule 3, page 141, he will find that the year position reached will be **10 Yax;** [1] hence, the terminal date as determined by calculation will be **4 Eb 10 Yax.**

Turning again to the text (pl. 6, *D*), the next step (see step 5, p. 151) is to find the glyphs representing the above terminal date. In this connection it should be remembered that the day part of an Initial-series terminal date usually follows immediately the last period glyph of the number. The glyph in A4, therefore, should record the day reached. Comparing this form with the several day signs in figure 16, it appears that A4 more closely resembles the sign for **Eb** (fig. 16, *s–u*) than any of the others, hence the student may accept **Eb** as the day sign recorded in A4. The 4 dots prefixed to this sign show that the day **4 Eb** is here indicated. The month sign, as stated on page 152, usually follows the last glyph of the Supplementary Series; passing over B4, A5, B5, and A6, we reach the latter glyph in B6. Compare the left half of B6 with the forms given in figure 65. The coefficient 9 or 10 is expressed by a considerably effaced head numeral. Immediately following the month-sign "indicator" is the month sign itself in A7. The student will have little difficulty in tracing its resemblance to the month **Yax** in figure 19, *q*, *r*, although in A7 the **Yax** element itself appears as the prefix instead of as the superfix, as in *q* and *r*, just cited. This difference, however, is immaterial. The month coefficient is quite clearly 10,[2] and the whole terminal date recorded will read **4 Eb 10 Yax**, which corresponds exactly with the terminal date determined by calculation. We may accept this text, therefore, as recording the Initial-series date 9.12.10.5.12 **4 Eb 10 Yax** of Maya chronology.

In the foregoing examples nothing but normal-form period glyphs have been presented, in order that the first exercises in deciphering the inscriptions may be as easy as possible. By this time, however, the student should be sufficiently familiar with the normal forms of the period glyphs to be able to recognize them when they are present in the text, and the next Initial Series figured will have its period glyphs expressed by head variants.

In *A*, plate 7, is figured the Initial Series from Stela B at Copan.[3] The introducing glyph appears at the head of the inscription in A1

---

[1] In each of the above cases—and, indeed, in all the examples following—the student should perform the various calculations by which the results are reached, in order to familiarize himself with the workings of the Maya chronological system.

[2] The student may apply a check at this point to his identification of the day sign in A4 as being that for the day **Eb**. Since the month coefficient in A7 is surely 10 (2 bars), it is clear from Table VII that the only days which can occupy this position in any division of the year are **Ik, Manik, Eb,** and **Caban.** Now, by comparing the sign in A4 with the signs for **Ik, Manik,** and **Caban,** *c, j,* and *a', b',* respectively, of fig. 16, it is very evident that A4 bears no resemblance to any of them; hence, since **Eb** is the only one left which can occupy a position 10, the day sign in A4 must be **Eb,** a fact supported by the comparison of A4 with fig. 16, *s–u,* above.

[3] The full text of this inscription will be found in Maudslay, 1889–1901: I, pls. 35–37.

and is followed by a head-variant glyph in A2, to which is prefixed a bar and dot coefficient of 9.   By its position, immediately following the introducing glyph, we are justified in assuming that A2 records 9 cycles, and after comparing it with *d–f*, figure 25, where the head variant of the cycle sign is shown, this assumption becomes a certainty.   Both heads have the same clasped hand in the same position, across the lower part of the face, which, as explained on page 68, is the essential element of the cycle head; therefore, A2 records 9 cycles.   The next glyph, A3, should be the katun sign, and a comparison of this form with the head variant for katun in *e–h*, figure 27, shows this to be the case.   The determining characteristic (see p. 69) is probably the oval in the top of the head, which appears in both of these forms for the katun.   The katun coefficient is 15 (3 bars).   The next glyph, A4, should record the tuns, and by comparing this form with the head variant for the tun sign in *e–g*, figure 29, this also is found to be the case.   Both heads show the same essential characteristic—the fleshless lower jaw (see p. 70).   The coefficient is 0 (compare fig. 47).   The uinal head in A5 is equally unmistakable. Note the large curl protruding from the back part of the mouth, which was said (p. 71) to be the essential element of this sign. Compare figure 31, *d–f*, where the head variant for the uinal is given. The coefficient of A5 is like the coefficient of A4 (0), and we have recorded, therefore, 0 uinals.   The closing period glyph of the Initial Series in A6 is the head variant for the kin sign.   Compare this form with figure 34, *e–g*, where the kin head is figured.   The determining characteristic of this head is the subfixial element, which appears also in the normal form for the kin sign (see fig. 34, *a*).   Again, the coefficient of A6 is like the coefficient of A4 and A5, hence we have recorded here 0 kins.

The number recorded by the head-variant period glyphs and normal-form numerals in A2–A6 is therefore 9.15.0.0.0; reducing this by means of Table XIII, we have:

$$A2 = \ 9 \times 144,000 = 1,296,000$$
$$A3 = 15 \times \ \ 7,200 = \ \ \ 108,000$$
$$A4 = \ 0 \times \ \ \ \ \ 360 = \ \ \ \ \ \ \ \ \ \ \ 0$$
$$A5 = \ 0 \times \ \ \ \ \ \ \ 20 = \ \ \ \ \ \ \ \ \ \ \ 0$$
$$A6 = \ 0 \times \ \ \ \ \ \ \ \ \ 1 = \ \ \ \ \ \ \ \ \ \ \ 0$$

$$1,404,000$$

Deducting from this number all the Calendar Rounds possible, 73 (see Table XVI), it may be reduced to 18,460.   Applying to this number rules 1 and 2 (pp. 139 and 140, respectively), the day reached will be found to be **4 Ahau**.   Applying rule 3 (p. 141), the position of **4 Ahau** in the year will be found to be **13 Yax**.   Therefore the terminal date determined by calculation will be **4 Ahau 13 Yax**.

According to step 5 (p. 151), the day reached should follow immediately the last period glyph, which in this case was in A6; hence the day should be recorded in A7. This glyph has a coefficient 4, but the glyph does not resemble either of the forms for **Ahau** shown in B5, plate 6, *A*, or in B4a, *C* of the same plate. However, by comparing this glyph with the second variant for the day sign **Ahau** in figure 16, *h'–i'*, the two forms will be found to be identical, and we may accept A7 as recording the day **4 Ahau**. Immediately following in A8 is the month sign, again out of its usual place as in plate 6, *C*. Comparing it with the month signs in figure 19, it will be found to exactly correspond with the sign for **Yax** in *q–r*. The coefficient is 13. Therefore the terminal date recorded, **4 Ahau 13 Yax**, agrees with the terminal date reached by calculation, and the whole Initial Series reads 9.15.0.0.0 **4 Ahau 13 Yax**. This date marks the close not only of a hotun in the Long Count, but of a katun as well.

In *B*, plate 7, is figured the Initial Series from Stela A at Copan.[1] The introducing glyph appears in A1 B1, and is followed by the Initial-series number in A2–A4. The student will have no difficulty in picking out the clasped hand in A2, the oval in the top of the head in B2, the fleshless lower jaw in A3, the large mouth curl in B3, and the flaring subfix in A4, which are the essential elements of the head variants for the cycle, katun, tun, uinal, and kin, respectively. Compare these glyphs with figures 25, *d–f*, 27, *e–h*, 29, *e–g*, 31, *d–f*, and 34, *e–g*, respectively. The coefficients of these period glyphs are all normal forms and the student will have no difficulty in reading this number as 9.14.19.8.0.[2]

Reducing this by means of Table XIII to units of the 1st order, we have:

$$
\begin{aligned}
A2 &= 9 \times 144,000 = 1,296,000 \\
B2 &= 14 \times 7,200 = 100,800 \\
A3 &= 19 \times 360 = 6,840 \\
B3 &= 8 \times 20 = 160 \\
A4 &= 0 \times 1 = 0 \\
\hline
& \qquad\qquad\qquad 1,403,800
\end{aligned}
$$

Deducting from this all the Calendar Rounds possible, 73 (see Table XVI), and applying rules 1 and 2 (pp. 139 and 140, respectively), to the remainder, the day reached will be **12 Ahau**. And applying rule 3 (p. 141), the month reached will be **18 Cumhu**, giving for the terminal date as reached by calculation **12 Ahau 18 Cumhu**. The day should be recorded in B4, and an examination of this glyph shows that its coefficient is 12, the day coefficient reached by calculation. The glyph itself, however, is unlike the forms for **Ahau** previously encountered in plate 6, *A*, B5 and *C*, B4b, and in plate 7, *A*, A7. Turning

---

[1] The full text of this inscription is given in Maudslay, 1889–1902: I, pls. 27–30.
[2] Note the decoration on the numerical bar.

now to the forms for the day sign **Ahau** in figure 16, it is seen that the form in A4 resembles the third variant j' or k', the grotesque head, and it is clear that the day **12 Ahau** is here recorded. At first sight the student might think that the month glyph follows in A5, but a closer inspection of this form shows that this is not the case. In the first place, since the day sign is **Ahau** the month coefficient must be either 3, 8, 13, or 18, not 7, as recorded (see Table VII), and, in the second place, the glyph itself in A5 bears no resemblance whatsoever to any of the month signs in figure 19. Consequently the month part of the Initial-series terminal date of this text should follow the closing glyph of the Supplementary Series. Following along the glyphs next in order, we reach in A9 a glyph with a coefficient 9, although the sign itself bears no resemblance to the month-glyph "indicators" heretofore encountered (see fig. 65).

The glyph following, however, in A9b is quite clearly **18 Cumhu** (see fig. 19, $g'-h'$), which is the month part of the terminal date as reached by calculation. Therefore, since A9a has the coefficient 9 it is probable that it is a variant of the month-glyph "indicator"; [1] and consequently that the month glyph itself follows, as we have seen, in B9. In other words, the terminal date recorded, **12 Ahau 18 Cumhu**, agrees with the terminal date reached by calculation, and the whole text, so far as it can be deciphered, reads 9.14.19.8.0 **12 Ahau 18 Cumhu**. The student will note that this Initial Series precedes the Initial Series in plate 7, A by exactly 10 uinals, or 200 days. Compare A and B, plate 7.

In plate 8, A, is figured the Initial Series from Stela 6 at Copan.[2] The introducing glyph occupies the space of four glyph-blocks, A1–B2, and there follows in A3–B4a the Initial-series number 9.12.10.0.0. The cycle glyph in A3 is partially effaced; the clasped hand, however, the determining characteristic of the cycle head, may still be distinguished. The katun head in B3 is also unmistakable, as it has the same superfix as in the normal form for the katun. At first sight the student might read the bar and dot coefficient as 14, but the two middle crescents are purely decorative and have no numerical value, and the numeral recorded here is 12 (see pp. 88–91). Although the tun and uinal period glyphs in A4a and A4b,[3] respectively, are effaced, their coefficients may be distinguished as 10 and 0, respectively. In such a case the student is per-

---

[1] So far as known to the writer, this very unusual variant for the closing glyph of the Supplementary Series occurs in but two other inscriptions in the Maya territory, namely, on Stela N at Copan. See pl. 26, Glyph A14, and Inscription 6 of the Hieroglyphic Stairway at Naranjo, Glyph A1 (?). (Maler, 1908 b: pl. 27.)

[2] For the full text of this inscription see Maudslay, 1889–1902: I, pls. 105–107.

[3] In this glyph-block, A4, the order of reading is irregular; instead of passing over to B4a after reading A4a (the 10 tuns), the next glyph to be read is the sign below A4a, A4b, which records 0 uinals, and only after this has been read does B4a follow.

PLATE 8

A. STELA 6, COPAN   *B.* STELA 9, COPAN

GLYPHS REPRESENTING INITIAL SERIES, SHOWING USE OF BAR
AND DOT NUMERALS AND HEAD-VARIANT PERIOD GLYPHS

fectly justified in assuming that the tun and uinal signs originally stood here. In B4a the kin period glyph is expressed by its normal form and the kin coefficient by a head-variant numeral, the clasped hand of which indicates that it stands for 0 (see fig. 53, *s–w*).[1] The number here recorded is 9.12.10.0.0.

Reducing this to units of the 1st order by means of Table XIII, we have:

$$
\begin{aligned}
A3 &= 9 \times 144,000 = 1,296,000 \\
B3 &= 12 \times 7,200 = 86,400 \\
A4a &= 10 \times 360 = 3,600 \\
A4b &= 0 \times 20 = 0 \\
B4a &= 1 \times 0 = 0
\end{aligned}
$$

$$1,386,000$$

Deducting from this number all the Calendar Rounds possible, 73 (see Table XVI), and applying to the remainder rules 1, 2, and 3 (pp. 139–141), respectively, the date reached by the resulting calculations will be **9 Ahau 18 Zotz**. Turning to our text again, the student will have little difficulty in identifying B4b as **9 Ahau**, the day of the above terminal date. The form **Ahau** here recorded is the grotesque head, the third variant *j′* or *k′* in figure 16. Following the next glyphs in order, A5–A6, the closing glyph of the Supplementary Series is reached in B6a. Compare this glyph with the forms in figure 65. The coefficient of B6a is again a head-variant numeral, as in the case of the kin period glyph in B4a, above. The fleshless lower jaw and other skull-like characteristics indicate that the numeral 10 is here recorded. Compare B6a with figure 52, *m–r*. Since B6a is the last glyph of the Supplementary Series, the next glyph B6b should represent the month sign. By comparing the latter form with the month signs in figure 19 the student will readily recognize that the sign for **Zotz** in *e* or *f* is the month sign here recorded. The coefficient 18 stands above. Consequently, B4b and B6b represent the same terminal date, **9 Ahau 18 Zotz**, as reached by calculation. This whole Initial Series reads 9.12.10.0.0 **9 Ahau 18 Zotz**, and according to the writer's view, the monument upon which it occurs (Stela 6 at Copan) was the period stone for the hotun which began with the day 9.12.5.0.1 **4 Imix 4 Xul**[2] and ended with the day 9.12.10.0.0 **9 Ahau 18 Zotz**, here recorded.

In plate 8, *B*, is figured the Initial Series from Stela 9 at Copan.[3] The introducing glyph stands in A1–B2 and is followed by the five period glyphs in A3–A5. The cycle is very clearly recorded in A3, the clasped hand being of a particularly realistic form. Although

---

[1] Texts illustrating the head-variant numerals in full will be presented later.

[2] The preceding hotun ended with the day 9.12.5.0.0 **3 Ahau 3 Xul** and therefore the opening day of the next hotun, 1 day later, will be 9.12.5.0.1 **4 Imix 4 Xul**.

[3] For the full text of this inscription, see Maudslay, 1889–1902: I, pls. 109, 110.

the coefficient is partially effaced, enough remains to show that it was above 5, having had originally more than the one bar which remains, and less than 11, there being space for only one more bar or row of dots. In all the previous Initial Series the cycle coefficient was 9, consequently it is reasonable to assume that 4 dots originally occupied the effaced part of this glyph. If the use of 9 cycles in this number gives a terminal date which agrees with the terminal date recorded, the above assumption becomes a certainty. In B3 six katuns are recorded. Note the ornamental dotted ovals on each side of the dot in the numeral 6. Although the head for the tun in A4 is partially effaced, we are warranted in assuming that this was the period originally recorded here. The coefficient 10 appears clearly. The uinal head in B4 is totally unfamiliar and seems to have the fleshless lower jaw properly belonging to the tun head; from its position, however, the 4th in the number, we are justified in calling this glyph the uinal sign. Its coefficient denotes that 0 uinals are recorded here. Although the period glyph in A5 is also entirely effaced, the coefficient appears clearly as 0, and from position again, 5th in the number, we are justified once more in assuming that 0 kins were originally recorded here. It seems at first glance that the above reading of the number A3–A5 rests on several assumptions:

1. That the cycle coefficient was originally 9.
2. That the effaced glyph in A4 was a tun head.
3. That the irregular head in B4 is a uinal head.
4. That the effaced glyph in A5 was a kin sign.

The last three are really certainties, since the Maya practice in recording Initial Series demanded that the five period glyphs requisite— the cycle, katun, tun, uinal, and kin—should follow each other in this order, and in no other. Hence, although the 3d, 4th, and 5th glyphs are either irregular or effaced, they must have been the tun, uinal, and kin signs, respectively. Indeed, the only important assumption consisted in arbitrarily designating the cycle coefficient 9, when, so far as the appearance of A3 is concerned, it might have been either 6, 7, 8, 9, or 10. The reason for choosing 9 rests on the overwhelming evidence of antecedent probability. Moreover, as stated above, if the terminal date recorded agrees with the terminal date determined by calculation, using the cycle coefficient as 9, our assumption becomes a certainty. Designating the above number as 9.6.10.0.0 then and reducing this by means of Table XIII, we obtain:

$$
\begin{array}{rrlr}
A3 = & 9 \times 144,000 & = & 1,296,000 \\
B3 = & 6 \times 7,200 & = & 43,200 \\
A4 = & 10 \times 360 & = & 3,600 \\
B4 = & 0 \times 30 & = & 0 \\
A5 = & 0 \times 1 & = & 0 \\
\hline
 & & & 1,342,800
\end{array}
$$

Deducting from this number all the Calendar Rounds possible, 70 (see Table XVI), and applying rules 1, 2, and 3 (pp. 139, 140, and 141, respectively) to the remainder, the date determined by the resulting calculations will be **8 Ahau 13 Pax.** Turning to our text again, the student will have little difficulty in recognizing the first part of this date, the day **8 Ahau,** in B5. The numeral 8 appears clearly, and the day sign is the profile-head h' or i', the second variant for **Ahau** in figure 16. The significance of the element standing between the numeral and the day sign is unknown. Following along through A6, B6, A7, B7, the closing glyph of the Supplementary Series is reached in A8. The glyph itself is on the left and the coefficient, here expressed by a head variant, is on the right. The student will have no difficulty in recognizing the glyph and its coefficient by comparing the former with figure 65, and the latter with the head variant for 10 in figure 52, m–r. Note the fleshless lower jaw in the head numeral in both places. The following glyph, B8, is one of the clearest in the entire text. The numeral is 13, and the month sign on comparison with figure 19 unmistakably proves itself to be the sign for **Pax** in c'. Therefore the terminal date recorded in B5, B8, namely, **8 Ahau 13 Pax,** agrees with the terminal date determined by calculation; it follows, further, that the effaced cycle coefficient in A3 must have been 9, the value tentatively ascribed to it in the above calculations. The whole Initial Series reads 9.6.10.0.0 **8 Ahau 13 Pax.**

Some of the peculiarities of the numerals and signs in this text are doubtless due to its very great antiquity, for the monument presenting this inscription, Stela 9, records the next to earliest Initial Series [1] yet deciphered at Copan.[2] Evidences of antiquity appear in the glyphs in several different ways. The bars denoting 5 have square ends and all show considerable ornamentation. This type of bar was an early manifestation and gave way in later times to more rounded forms. The dots also show this greater ornamentation, which is reflected, too, by the signs themselves. The head forms show greater attention to detail, giving the whole glyph a more ornate appearance. All this embellishment gave way in later times to more simplified forms, and we have represented in this text a stage in glyph morphology before conventionalization had worn down the different signs to little more than their essential elements.

In figure 68, A, is figured the Initial Series on the west side of Stela C at Quirigua.[3] The introducing glyph in A1–B2 is followed by the number in A3–A5, which the student will have no difficulty in reading

---

[1] The oldest Initial Series at Copan is recorded on Stela 15, which is 40 years older than Stela 9. For a discussion of this text see pp. 187, 188.

[2] An exception to this statement should be noted in an Initial Series on the Hieroglyphic Stairway, which records the date 9.5.19.3.0 **8 Ahau 3 Zotz.** The above remark applies only to the large monuments, which, the writer believes, were period-markers. Stela 9 is therefore the next to the oldest "period stone" yet discovered at Copan. It is more than likely, however, that there are several older ones as yet undeciphered.

[3] For the full text of this inscription, see Maudslay, 1889–1902: II, pls. 17–19.

except for the head-variant numeral attached to the kin sign in A5. The clasped hand in this glyph, however, suggests that 0 kins are recorded here, and a comparison of this form with figure 53, *s–w*, confirms the suggestion. The number therefore reads 9.1.0.0.0. Re-

FIG. 68. Initial Series showing bar and dot numerals and head-variant period glyphs: *A*, Stela C (west side), Quirigua; *B*, Stela M, Copan.

ducing this number by means of Table XIII to units of the 1st order, we obtain:

$$A3 = 9 \times 144,000 = 1,296,000$$
$$B3 = 1 \times 7,200 = 7,200$$
$$A4 = 0 \times 360 = 0$$
$$B4 = 0 \times 20 = 0$$
$$A5 = 0 \times 1 = 0$$

$$\overline{1,303,200}$$

Deducting from this number all the Calendar Rounds possible, 68 (see Table XVI), and applying rules 1, 2, and 3 (pp. 139, 140, and 141, respectively) to the remainder, we reach for the terminal date **6 Ahau 13 Yaxkin.** Looking for the day part of this date in B5, we find that the form there recorded bears no resemblance to **6 Ahau**, the day determined by calculation. Moreover, comparison of it with the day signs in figure 16 shows that it is unlike all of them; further, there is no bar and dot coefficient. These several points indicate that the day sign is not the glyph in B5, also that the day sign is, therefore, out of its regular position. The next glyph in the text, A6, instead of being one of the Supplementary Series is the day glyph **6 Ahau,** which should have been recorded in B5. The student will readily make the same identification after comparing A6 with figure 16, *e'–g'*. A glance at the remainder of the text will show that no Supplementary Series is recorded, and consequently that the month glyph will be found immediately following the day glyph in B6. The form in B6 has a coefficient 13, one of the four (3, 8, 13, 18) which the month must have, since the day sign is **Ahau** (see Table VII). A comparison of the form in B6 with the month signs in figure 19 shows that the month **Yaxkin** in *k* or *l* is the form here recorded; therefore the terminal date recorded agrees with the terminal date reached by calculation, and the text reads 9.1.0.0.0 **6 Ahau 13 Yaxkin.**[1]

In figure 68, *B*, is shown the Initial Series on Stela M at Copan.[2] The introducing glyph appears in A1 and the Initial-series number in B1a–B2a. The student will note the use of both normal-form and head-variant period glyphs in this text, the cycle, tun, and uinal in B1a, A2a, and A2b, respectively, being expressed by the latter, and the katun and kin in B1b and B2a, respectively, by the former. The number recorded is 9.16.5.0.0, and this reduces to units of the first order, as follows (see Table XIII):

$$
\begin{aligned}
\text{B1a} &= 9 \times 144,000 = 1,296,000 \\
\text{B1b} &= 16 \times 7,200 = 115,200 \\
\text{A2a} &= 5 \times 360 = 1,800 \\
\text{A2b} &= 0 \times 20 = 0 \\
\text{B2a} &= 0 \times 1 = 0 \\
\hline
&\qquad\qquad\quad 1,413,000
\end{aligned}
$$

Deducting from this number all the Calendar Rounds possible, 74 (see Table XVI), and applying rules 1, 2, and 3 (pp. 139, 140, and 141, respectively) to the remainder, the terminal date reached by the resulting calculations will be **8 Ahau 8 Zotz.** Turning to our text, the student will have no difficulty in recognizing in B2b the day **8 Ahau.** The month glyph in this inscription irregularly follows immediately

---

[1] Although this date is considerably older than that on Stela 9 at Copan, its several glyphs present none of the marks of antiquity noted in connection with the preceding example (pl. 8, *B*). For example, the ends of the bars denoting 5 are not square but round, and the head-variant period glyphs do not show the same elaborate and ornate treatment as in the Copan text. This apparent contradiction permits of an easy explanation. Although the Initial Series on the west side of Stela C at Quirigua undoubtedly refers to an earlier date than the Initial Series on the Copan monument, it does not follow that the Quirigua monument is the older of the two. This is true because on the other side of this same stela at Quirigua is recorded another date, 9.17.5.0.0 **6 Ahau 13 Kayab,** more than three hundred years later than the Initial Series 9.1.0.0.0 **6 Ahau 13 Yaxkin** on the west side, and this later date is doubtless the one which referred to present time when this monument was erected. Therefore the Initial Series 9.1.0.0.0 **6 Ahau 13 Yaxkin** does not represent the period which Stela C was erected to mark, but some far earlier date in Maya history.

[2] For the full text of this inscription see Maudslay, 1889–1902: I, pl. 74.

the day glyph. Compare the form in A3a with the month signs in figure 19 and it will be found to be the sign for **Zotz** (see fig. 19, *e–f*). The coefficient is 8 and the whole glyph represents the month part **8 Zotz**, the same as determined by calculation. This whole Initial Series reads 9.16.5.0.0 **8 Ahau 8 Zotz.**

The Maya texts presented up to this point have all been drawings of originals, which are somewhat easier to make out than either photographs of the originals or the originals themselves. However, in order to familiarize the student with photographic reproductions of Maya texts a few will be inserted here illustrating the use of bar and dot numerals with both normal-form and head-variant period glyphs, with which the student should be perfectly familiar by this time.

In plate 9, *A*, is figured a photograph of the Initial Series on the front of Stela 11 at Yaxchilan.[1] The introducing glyph appears in A1 B1; 9 cycles in A2; 16 katuns in B2, 1 tun in A3, 0 uinals in B3, and 0 kins in B4. The student will note the clasped hand in the cycle head, the oval in the top of the katun head, the large mouth curl in the uinal head, and the flaring postfix in the kin head. The tun is expressed by its normal form. The number here recorded is 9.16.1.0.0, and reducing this to units of the first order by means of Table XIII, we have:

$$
\begin{aligned}
A2 &= \ 9 \times 144,000 = 1,296,000 \\
B2 &= 16 \times \ \ \ 7,200 = \ \ \ 115,200 \\
A3 &= \ 1 \times \ \ \ \ \ 360 = \ \ \ \ \ \ \ 360 \\
B3 &= \ 0 \times \ \ \ \ \ \ 20 = \ \ \ \ \ \ \ \ \ \ 0 \\
A4 &= \ 0 \times \ \ \ \ \ \ \ 1 = \ \ \ \ \ \ \ \ \ \ 0 \\
\hline
& \ \ \ \ \ \ \ \ \ \ \ \ \ \ \ \ \ 1,411,560
\end{aligned}
$$

Deducting from this number all the Calendar Rounds possible, 74 (see Table XVI), and applying rules 1, 2, and 3 (pp. 139, 140, and 141, respectively), to the remainder, the terminal date reached by the resulting calculations will be **11 Ahau 8 Tzec**. The day part of this date is very clearly recorded in B4 immediately after the last period glyph, and the student will readily recognize the day **11 Ahau** in this form. Following along the glyphs of the Supplementary Series in C1 D1, C2 D2, the closing glyph is reached in C3b. It is very clear and has a coefficient of 9. The glyph following (D3) should record the month sign. A comparison of this form with the several month signs in figure 19 shows that **Tzec** is the month here recorded. Compare D3 with figure 19, *g–h*. The month coefficient is 8. The terminal date, therefore, recorded in B4 and D3 (**11 Ahau 8 Tzec**) agrees with the terminal date determined by calculation, and this whole text reads 9.16.1.0.0 **11 Ahau 8 Tzec.** The meaning of the element

---

[1] For the full text of this inscription see Maler, 1903: II, No. 2, pls. 74, 75.

PLATE 9

A. STELA 11, YAXCHILAN

B. ALTAR IN FRONT OF STRUCTURE 44, YAXCHILAN

GLYPHS REPRESENTING INITIAL SERIES, SHOWING USE
OF BAR AND DOT NUMERALS AND HEAD-VARIANT
PERIOD GLYPHS

between the tun coefficient and the tun sign in A3, which is repeated again in D3 between the month coefficient and the month sign, is unknown.

In plate 9, *B*, is figured the Initial Series on an altar in front of Structure 44 at Yaxchilan.[1]   The introducing glyph appears in A1 B1 and is followed by the number in A2–A4.   The period glyphs are all expressed as head variants and the coefficients as bar and dot numerals. Excepting the kin coefficient in A4, the number is quite easily read as 9.12.8.14. ?   An inspection of our text shows that the coefficient must be 0, 1, 2, or 3.   Let us work out the terminal dates for all four of these values, commencing with 0, and then see which of the resulting terminal days is the one actually recorded in A4.   Reducing the number 9.12.8.14.0 to units of the first order by means of Table XIII, we have:

$$A2 = \ 9 \times 144,000 = 1,296,000$$
$$B2 = 12 \times \ \ \ 7,200 = \ \ \ \ 86,400$$
$$A3 = \ 8 \times \ \ \ \ \ 360 = \ \ \ \ \ \ 2,880$$
$$B3 = 14 \times \ \ \ \ \ \ \ 20 = \ \ \ \ \ \ \ \ \ 280$$
$$A4 = \ 0 \times \ \ \ \ \ \ \ \ \ 1 = \ \ \ \ \ \ \ \ \ \ \ 0$$

$$\overline{1,385,560}$$

Deducting from this number all the Calendar Rounds possible, 73 (see Table XVI), and applying rules 1, 2, and 3 (pp. 139, 140, and 141, respectively), to the remainder, the terminal day reached will be **11 Ahau 3 Pop**.   Therefore the Initial-series numbers 9.12.8.14.1, 9.12.8.14.2, and 9.12.8.14.3 will lead to the three days immediately following 9.12.8.14.0 **11 Ahau 3 Pop**.   Therefore our four possible terminal dates will be:

$$9.12.8.14.0 \quad \textbf{11 Ahau 3 Pop}$$
$$9.12.8.14.1 \quad \textbf{12 Imix 4 Pop}$$
$$9.12.8.14.2 \quad \textbf{13 Ik \ \ 5 Pop}$$
$$9.12.8.14.3 \quad \textbf{1 Akbal 6 Pop}$$

Now let us look for one of these four terminal dates in the text.   The day reached by an Initial Series is almost invariably recorded immediately after the last period glyph; therefore, if this inscription is regular, the day glyph should be B4.   This glyph probably has the coefficient 12 (2 bars and 2 numerical dots), the oblong element between probably being ornamental only.   This number must be either 11 or 12, since if it were 13 the 3 dots would all be of the same size, which is not the case.   An inspection of the coefficient in B4 eliminates from consideration, therefore, the last two of the above four possible terminal dates, and reduces the possible values for the kin coefficient in A4 to 0 or 1.   Comparing the glyph in B4 with the day signs in figure 16, the form here recorded will be found to be identical with the sign for **Imix** in figure 16, *a*.   This eliminates the first terminal date above and leaves the second, the day part of which

---

[1] For the full text of this inscription see Maler, 1903: II, No. 2, pl. 79, 2.

we have just seen appears in B4.   This further proves that the kin coefficient in A4 is 1.   The final confirmation of this identification will come from the month glyph, which must be **4 Pop** if we have correctly identified the day as **12 Imix**.   If, on the other hand, the day were **11 Ahau**, the month glyph would be **3 Pop**.   Passing over A5 B5, A6 B6, C1 D1, and C2, we reach in D2a the closing glyph of the Supplementary Series, here showing the coefficient 9.   Compare this form with figure 65.   The month glyph, therefore, should appear in D2b.   The coefficient of this glyph is very clearly 4, thus confirming our identification of B4 as **12 Imix**.   (See Table VII.) And finally, the month glyph itself is **Pop**.   Compare D2b with figure 19, *a*.   The whole Initial Series in plate 9, *B*, therefore reads 9.12.8.14.1 **12 Imix 4 Pop.**

In plate 10, is figured the Initial Series from Stela 3 at Tikal.[1] The introducing glyph, though somewhat effaced, may still be recognized in A1.   The Initial-series number follows in B1–B3.   The head-variant period glyphs are too badly weathered to show the determining characteristic in each case, except the uinal head in A3, the mouth curl of which appears clearly, and their identification rests on their relative positions with reference to the introducing glyph. The reliability of this basis of identification for the period glyphs of Initial Series has been thoroughly tested in the texts already presented and is further confirmed in this very inscription by the uinal head.   Even if the large mouth curl of the head in A3 had not proved that the uinal was recorded here, we should have assumed this to be the case because this glyph, A3, is the fourth from the introducing glyph.   The presence of the mouth curl therefore confirms the identification based on position.   The student will have no difficulty in reading the number recorded in B1–B3 as 9.2.13.0.0.

Reducing this number by means of Table XIII to units of the first order, we obtain:

$$
\begin{aligned}
B1 &= 9 \times 144,000 = 1,296,000 \\
A2 &= 2 \times 7,200 = 14,400 \\
B2 &= 13 \times 360 = 4,680 \\
A3 &= 0 \times 20 = 0 \\
B3 &= 0 \times 1 = 0
\end{aligned}
$$

$$1,315,080$$

Deducting all the Calendar Rounds possible from this number, 69 (see Table XVI), and applying rules 1, 2, and 3 (pp. 139, 140, and 141, respectively) to the remainder, the terminal date reached will be **4 Ahau 13 Kayab**.   It remains to find this date in the text.   The glyph in A4, the proper position for the day glyph, is somewhat effaced, though the profile of the human head may yet be traced, thus enabling us to identify this form as the day sign **Ahau**.   Com-

---

[1] For the full text of this inscription see Maler, 1911: v, No. 1, pl. 15.

PLATE 10

GLYPHS REPRESENTING INITIAL SERIES, SHOW-
ING USE OF BAR AND DOT NUMERALS AND
HEAD-VARIANT PERIOD GLYPHS—STELA 3,
TIKAL

PLATE 11

GLYPHS REPRESENTING INITIAL SERIES, SHOWING USE OF BAR
AND DOT NUMERALS AND HEAD-VARIANT PERIOD GLYPHS—STELA
A (EAST SIDE), QUIRIGUA

pare figure 16, *h'*, *i'*. The coefficient of A4 is very clearly 4 dots, that is, 4, and consequently this glyph agrees with the day as determined by calculation, **4 Ahau.** Passing over B4, A5, B5, and A6, we reach in B6 the closing glyph of the Supplementary Series, here recorded with a coefficient of 9. Compare B6 with figure 65. The month glyph follows in A7 with the coefficient 13. Comparing this latter glyph with the month signs in figure 19, it is evident that the month **Kayab** (fig. 19, *d'–f'*) is recorded in A7, which reads, therefore, **13 Kayab.** Hence the whole text records the Initial Series 9.2.13.0.0 **4 Ahau 13 Kayab.**

This Initial Series is extremely important, because it records the earliest contemporaneous [1] date yet found on a monument [2] in the Maya territory.

In plate 11 is figured the Initial Series from the east side of Stela A at Quirigua. [3] The introducing glyph appears in A1–B2 and the Initial-series number in A3–A5. The student will have little difficulty in picking out the clasped hand in A3, the oval in the top of the head in B3, the fleshless lower jaw in A4, the mouth curl in B4, as the essential characteristic of the cycle, katun, tun, and uinal heads, respectively. The kin head in A5 is the banded-headdress variant (compare fig. 34, *i*, *j*), and this completes the number, which is 9.17.5.0.0. Reducing this by means of Table XIII to units of the first order, we have:

$$
\begin{aligned}
\text{A3} &= \ 9 \times 144,000 = 1,296,000 \\
\text{B3} &= 17 \times \ \ \ 7,200 = \ \ \ 122,400 \\
\text{A4} &= \ 5 \times \ \ \ \ \ \ 360 = \ \ \ \ \ \ 1,800 \\
\text{B4} &= \ 0 \times \ \ \ \ \ \ \ 20 = \ \ \ \ \ \ \ \ \ \ \ 0 \\
\text{A5} &= \ 0 \times \ \ \ \ \ \ \ \ 0 = \ \ \ \ \ \ \ \ \ \ \ 0 \\
\hline
& \qquad\qquad\qquad\qquad \ \ 1,420,200
\end{aligned}
$$

Deducting from this number all the Calendar Rounds possible, 73 (see Table XVI), and applying rules 1, 2, and 3 (pp. 139, 140, and 141,

---

[1] As used throughout this book, the expression "the contemporaneous date" designates the time when the monument on which such a date is found was put into formal use, that is, the time of its erection. As will appear later in the discussion of the Secondary Series, many monuments present several dates between the extremes of which elapse long periods. Obviously, only one of the dates thus recorded can represent the time at which the monument was erected. In such inscriptions the final date is almost invariably the one designating contemporaneous time, and the earlier dates refer probably to historical, traditional, or even mythological events in the Maya past. Thus the Initial Series 9.0.19.2.4 **2 Kan 2 Yax** on Lintel 21 at Yaxchilan, 9.1.0.0.0 **6 Ahau 13 Yaxkin** on the west side of Stela C at Quirigua, and 9.4.0.0.0 **13 Ahau 18 Yax** from the Temple of the Inscriptions at Palenque, all refer probably to earlier historical or traditional events in the past of these three cities, but they do not indicate the dates at which they were severally recorded. As Initial Series which refer to purely mythological events may be classed the Initial Series from the Temples of the Sun, Cross, and Foliated Cross at Palenque, and from the east side of Stela C at Quirigua, all of which are concerned with dates centering around or at the beginning of Maya chronology. Stela 3 at Tikal (the text here under discussion), on the other hand, has but one date, which probably refers to the time of its erection, and is therefore contemporaneous.

[2] There are one or two earlier Initial Series which probably record contemporaneous dates; these are not inscribed on large stone monuments but on smaller antiquities, namely, the Tuxtla Statuette and the Leyden Plate. For the discussion of these early contemporaneous Initial Series, see pp. 194–198.

[3] For the full text of this inscription see Maudslay, 1889–1902: II, pls. 4–7.

respectively) to the remainder, the terminal day reached will be found to be **6 Ahau 13 Kayab.**

In B5 the profile variant of the day sign, **Ahau,** is clearly recorded (fig. 16, h', i'), and to it is attached a head-variant numeral. Comparing this with the head-variant numerals in figures 51–53, the student will have little difficulty in identifying it as the head for 6 (see fig. 51, t–v). Note the so-called "hatchet eye" in A5, which is the determining characteristic of the head for 6 (see p. 99). Passing over A6 B6, A7 B7, A8 B8, we reach in A9 the closing glyph of the Supplementary Series, here showing the head-variant coefficient 10 (see fig. 52, m–r). In B9, the next glyph, is recorded the month **13 Kayab** (see fig. 19, d'–f'). The whole Initial Series therefore reads 9.17.5.0.0 **6 Ahau 13 Kayab.**

All the Initial Series heretofore presented have had normal-form numerals with the exception of an incidental head-variant number here and there. By this time the student should have become thoroughly familiar with the use of bar and dot numerals in the inscriptions and should be ready for the presentation of texts showing head-variant numerals, a more difficult group of glyphs to identify.

In plate 12, A, is figured the Initial Series on the tablet from the Temple of the Foliated Cross at Palenque.[1] The introducing glyph appears in A1 B2, and is followed by the Initial-series number in A3–B7. The student will have little difficulty in identifying the heads in B3, B4, B5, B6, and B7 as the head variants for the cycle, katun, tun, uinal, and kin, respectively. The head in A3 prefixed to the cycle glyph in B3 has for its determining characteristic the forehead ornament composed of *more than one part* (here, of two parts). As explained on page 97, this is the essential element of the head for 1. Compare A3 with figure 51, a–e, and the two glyphs will be found to be identical. We may conclude, therefore, that in place of the usual 9 cycles heretofore encountered in Initial Series, we have recorded in A3–B3 1 cycle.[2] The katun coefficient in A4 resembles closely the cycle coefficient except that its forehead ornament is composed of but a single part, a large curl. As explained on page 97, the heads for 1 and 8 are very similar, and are to be distinguished from each other only by their forehead ornaments, the former having a forehead ornament composed of more than one part, as in A3, and the latter a forehead ornament composed of but one part, as here in A4. This head, moreover, is very similar to the head for 8 in figure 52, a–f; indeed, the only difference is that the former has a fleshless lower jaw. This is the essential element of the head for 10 (see p. 100); when applied to the head for any other numeral it increases the value of the resulting head by 10. Therefore we have recorded in

---

[1] For the full text of this inscription see Maudslay, 1889–1902: IV, pls. 80–82.

[2] As explained on p. 179, footnote 1, this Initial Series refers probably to some mythological event rather than to any historical occurrence. The date here recorded precedes the historic period of the Maya civilization by upward of 3,000 years.

PLATE 12

A. TEMPLE OF THE FOLIATED
CROSS, PALENQUE

B. TEMPLE OF THE SUN,
PALENQUE

GLYPHS REPRESENTING INITIAL SERIES, SHOWING USE OF
HEAD-VARIANT NUMERALS AND PERIOD GLYPHS

A4 B4, 18 (8 + 10) katuns. The tun coefficient in A5 has for its determining characteristic the tun headdress, which, as explained on page 99, is the essential element of the head for 5 (see fig. 51, *n–s*). Therefore A5 represents 5, and A5 B5, 5 tuns. The uinal coefficient in A6 has for its essential elements the large bulging eye, square irid, and snaglike front tooth. As stated on page 98, these characterize the head for 4, examples of which are given in figure 51, *j–m*. Consequently, A6 B6 records 4 uinals. The kin coefficient in A7 is quite clearly 0. The student will readily recognize the clasped hand, which is the determining characteristic of the 0 head (see p. 101 and fig. 53, *s–w*). The number recorded in A3–B7 is, therefore, 1.18.5.4.0. Reducing this number to units of the 1st order by means of Table XIII, we obtain:

$$
\begin{aligned}
\text{A3B3} &= 1 \times 144,000 = 144,000 \\
\text{A4B4} &= 18 \times 7,200 = 129,600 \\
\text{A5B5} &= 5 \times 360 = 1,800 \\
\text{A6B6} &= 4 \times 20 = 80 \\
\text{A7B7} &= 0 \times 1 = 0 \\
\hline
& 275,480
\end{aligned}
$$

Deducting from this number all the Calendar Rounds possible, 14 (see Table XVI), and applying rules 1, 2, and 3 (pp. 139, 140, and 141, respectively), the terminal date reached will be **1 Ahau 13 Mac.** Of this date, the day part, **1 Ahau**, is recorded very clearly in A8 B8. Compare the head in A8 with the head in A3, which, we have seen, stood for 1 and also with figure 51, *a–e*, and the head in B8 with figure 16, *h'*, *i'*, the profile head for the day sign **Ahau.** This text is irregular in that the month glyph follows immediately the day glyph, i. e., in A9. The glyph in A9 has a coefficient 13, which agrees with the month coefficient determined by calculation, and a comparison of B9 with the forms for the months in figure 19 shows that the month **Mac** (fig. 19, *w, x*) is here recorded. The whole Initial Series therefore reads 1.18.5.4.0 **1 Ahau 13 Mac.**

In plate 12, *B*, is figured the Initial Series on the tablet from the Temple of the Sun at Palenque.[1] The introducing glyph appears in A1–B2 and is followed by the Initial-series number in A3–B7. The student will have no difficulty in identifying the period glyphs in B3, B4, B5, B6, and B7; and the cycle, katun, and tun coefficients in A3, A4, and A5, respectively, will be found to be exactly like the corresponding coefficients in the preceding Initial Series (pl. 12, *A*, A3, A4, A5), which, as we have seen, record the numbers 1, 18, and 5, respectively. The uinal coefficient in A6, however, presents a new form. Here the determining characteristic is the banded headdress, or fillet, which distinguishes the head for 3, as explained on page 98 (see fig. 51 *h, i*). We have then in A6 B6 record of 3

---

[1] For the full text of this inscription see Maudslay, 1889–1902; IV, pls. 87–89.

uinals. The kin coefficient in A7 is very clearly 6. Note the "hatchet eye," which, as explained on page 99, is the essential element of this head numeral, and also compare it with figure 51, t–v. The number recorded in A3–B7 therefore is 1.18.5.3.6. Reducing this to units of the first order by means of Table XIII, we obtain:

$$
\begin{aligned}
\text{A3B3} &= & 1 \times 144,000 &= 144,000 \\
\text{A4B4} &= 18 \times & 7,200 &= 129,600 \\
\text{A5B5} &= 5 \times & 360 &= 1,800 \\
\text{A6B6} &= 3 \times & 20 &= 60 \\
\text{A7B7} &= 6 \times & 1 &= 6 \\
\hline
& & & 275,466
\end{aligned}
$$

Deducting from this number all the Calendar Rounds possible, 14 (see Table XVI), and applying rules 1, 2, and 3 (pp. 139, 140, and 141), respectively, to the remainder, the terminal date reached will be **13 Cimi 19 Ceh**. If this inscription is regular, the day part of the above date should follow in A8 B8, the former expressing the coefficient and the latter the day sign. Comparing A8 with the head numerals in figures 51–53, it will be found to be like the second variant for 13 in figure 52, x–b', the essential element of which seems to be the pendulous nose surmounted by a curl, the protruding mouth fang, and the large bulging eye. Comparing the glyph in B8 with the day signs in figure 16, it will be seen that the form here recorded is the day sign **Cimi** (fig. 16, h, i). Therefore A8 B8 expresses the day **13 Cimi**. The month glyph is recorded very irregularly in this text, since it occurs neither immediately after the Supplementary Series or the day sign, but the second glyph after the day sign, in B9. A comparison of this form with figure 19, u–v, shows that the month **Ceh** is recorded here. The coefficient is 19. Why the glyph in A9 should stand between the day and its month glyph is unknown; this case constitutes one of the many unsolved problems in the study of the Maya glyphs. This whole Initial Series reads 1.18.5.3.6 **13 Cimi 19 Ceh.**

The student will note that this Initial Series records a date 14 days earlier than the preceding Initial Series (pl. 12, A). That two dates should be recorded which were within 14 days of each other, and yet were more than 3,000 years earlier than practically all other Maya dates, is a puzzling problem. These two Initial Series from the Temple of the Sun and that of the Foliated Cross at Palenque, together with a Secondary-series date from the Temple of the Cross in the same city, have been thoroughly reviewed by Mr. Bowditch (1906). The conclusions he reaches and the explanation he offers to account for the occurrence of three dates so remote as these are very reasonable, and, the writer believes, will be generally accepted by Maya students.

In figure 69, *A*, is shown the Initial Series inscribed on the rises
and treads of the stairway leading to House C in the Palace at
Palenque.[1]   The introducing glyph is recorded in A1, and the Initial-
series number follows in B1–B3.   The student will readily recognize
the period glyphs in B1b, A2b, B2b, A3b, and B3b.   The head
expressing the cycle coefficient in B1a has for its essential element
the dots centering around the corner of the mouth.   As explained on
page 100, this characterizes the head for 9 (see fig. 52, *g–l*, where variants for the 9 head are figured).   In B1, therefore, we have recorded 9

A   B

FIG. 69.   Initial Series showing head-variant numerals and period glyphs: *A*, House C of the Palace
Group at Palenque; *B*, Stela P at Copan.

cycles, the number almost always found in Initial Series as the cycle
coefficient.   The essential element of the katun coefficient in A2a is
the forehead ornament composed of a single part.   This denotes the
head for 8 (see p. 100, and fig. 52, *a–f;* also compare A2a with the heads
denoting 18 in the two preceding examples, pl. 12, *A*, A4, and pl. 12,
B, A4, each of which shows the same forehead ornament).   The tun
coefficient in B2a is exactly like the cycle coefficient just above
it in B1a; that is, 9, having the same dotting of the face near the
corner of the mouth.   The uinal coefficient in A3a is 13.   Compare this head numeral with A8, plate 12, *B*, which also denotes 13,
and also with figure 52, *x–b'*.   The essential elements (see p. 101)

---

[1] For the full text of this inscription, see Maudslay, 1889–1902: IV, pl. 23.

are the large pendulous nose surmounted by a curl, the bulging eye, and the mouth fang, the last mentioned not appearing in this case. Since the kin coefficient in B3a is somewhat effaced, let us call it 0 for the present[1] and proceed to reduce our number 9.8.9.13.0 to units of the first order by means of Table XIII:

$$
\begin{aligned}
B1 &= 9 \times 144,000 = 1,296,000 \\
A2 &= 8 \times 7,200 = 57,600 \\
B2 &= 9 \times 360 = 3,240 \\
A3 &= 13 \times 20 = 260 \\
B3 &= 0 \times 1 = 0 \\
\hline
& \qquad\qquad 1,357,100
\end{aligned}
$$

Deducting from this number all the Calendar Rounds possible, 71 (see Table XVI), and applying rules 1, 2, and 3 (pp. 139, 140, and 141, respectively) to the remainder, we reach as the terminal date **8 Ahau 13 Pop**. Now let us examine the text and see what is the terminal date actually recorded. In A4b the student will have little difficulty in recognizing the profile variant of the day sign **Ahau** (see fig. 16, h', i'). This at once gives us the missing value for the kin coefficient in B3, for the day **Ahau** can never be reached in an Initial Series if the kin coefficient is other than 0. Similarly, the day **Imix** can never be reached in Initial Series if the kin coefficient is other than 1, etc. Every one of the 20 possible kin coefficients, 0 to 19, has a corresponding day to which it will always lead, that is, **Ahau** to **Cauac**, respectively (see Table I). Thus, if the kin coefficient in an Initial-series number were 5, for example, the day sign of the resulting terminal date must be **Chicchan**, since **Chicchan** is the fifth name after **Ahau** in Table I. Thus the day sign in Initial-series terminal dates may be determined by inspection of the kin coefficient as well as by rule 2 (p. 140), though, as the student will see, both are applications of the same principle, that is, deducting all of the 20s possible and counting forward only the remainder. Returning to our text, we can now say without hesitation that our number is 9.8.9.13.0 and that the day sign in A4b is **Ahau**. The day coefficient in A4a is just like the katun coefficient in A2a, having the same determining characteristic, namely, the forehead ornament composed of one part. A comparison of this ornament with the ornament on the head for 8 in A2a will show that the two forms are identical. The bifurcate ornament surmounting the head in A4a is a part of the headdress, and as such should not be confused with the forehead ornament. The failure to recognize this point might cause the student to identify

---

[1] It is clear that if all the period coefficients above the kin have been correctly identified, even though the kin coefficient is unknown, by designating it 0 the date reached will be within 19 days of the date originally recorded. Even though its maximum value (19) had originally been recorded here, it could have carried the count only 19 days further. By using 0 as the kin coefficient, therefore, we can not be more than 19 days from the original date.

A4a as the head for 1, that is, having a forehead ornament composed of more than one part, instead of the head for 8. The month glyph, which follows in B4b, is unfortunately effaced, though its coefficient in B4a is clearly the head for 13. Compare B4a with the uinal coefficient in A3a and with the heads for 13 in figure 52, *x–b′*. As recorded, therefore, the terminal date reads **8 Ahau 13** ?, thus agreeing in every particular so far as it goes with the terminal date reached by calculation, **8 Ahau 13 Pop**. In all probability the effaced sign in B4b originally was the month **Pop**. The whole Initial Series therefore reads 9.8.9.13.0 **8 Ahau 13 Pop**.

In figure 69, *B*, is shown the Initial Series from Stela P at Copan.[1] The introducing glyph appears in A1–B2 and is followed by the Initial-series number in A3–B4. The student will readily identify A3, B3, and A4 as 9 cycles, 9 katuns, and 10 tuns, respectively. Note the beard on the head representing the number 9 in both A3a and B3a. As explained on page 100, this characteristic of the head for 9 is not always present (see fig. 52, *g–i*). The uinal and kin glyphs have been crowded together into one glyph-block, B4, the uinal appearing in B4a and the kin in B4b. Both their coefficients are 0, which is expressed in each case by the form shown in figure 47. The whole number recorded is 9.9.10.0.0; reducing this to units of the first order by means of Table XIII, we obtain:

$$
\begin{aligned}
\text{A3} &= 9 \times 144,000 = 1,296,000 \\
\text{B3} &= 9 \times 7,200 = 64,800 \\
\text{A4} &= 10 \times 360 = 3,600 \\
\text{B4a} &= 0 \times 20 = 0 \\
\text{B4b} &= 0 \times 1 = 0 \\
\hline
& \qquad\qquad\qquad 1,364,400
\end{aligned}
$$

Deducting from this number all of the Calendar Rounds possible, 71 (see Table XVI), and applying rules 1, 2, and 3 (pp. 139, 140, and 141, respectively) to the remainder, the terminal date reached will be **2 Ahau 13 Pop**. In A5a the day **2 Ahau** is very clearly recorded, the day sign being expressed by the profile variant and the 2 by two dots (incorrectly shown as one dot in the accompanying drawing).[2] Passing over A5b, B5, and A6 we reach in B6a the closing glyph of the Supplementary Series, and in the following glyph, B6b, the month part of this terminal date. The coefficient is 13, and comparing the sign itself with the month signs in figure 19, it will be seen that the form in *a* (**Pop**) is the month recorded here. The whole Initial Series therefore reads 9.9.10.0.0 **2 Ahau 13 Pop**.

---

[1] For the full text of this inscription see Maudslay, 1889–1902: I, pls. 88, 89.

[2] While at Copan the writer made a personal examination of this monument and found that Mr. Maudslay's drawing is incorrect as regards the coefficient of the day sign. The original has two numerical dots between two crescents, whereas the Maudslay drawing shows one numerical dot between two distinct pairs of crescents, each pair, however, of different shape.

In figure 70 is illustrated the Initial Series from Zoömorph G at Quirigua.[1] The introducing glyph appears in A1–B2 and is followed in C1–H1 by the Initial-series number. Glyphs C1 D1 record 9

FIG. 70. Initial Series, showing head-variant numerals and period glyphs, from Zoömorph G at Quirigua.

cycles. The dots on the head for 9 in C1 are partially effaced. In C2 is the katun coefficient and in D2 the katun sign. The determining characteristic of the head for 7 appears in C2, namely, the scroll passing under the eye and projecting upward and in front of the forehead. See page 100 and figure 51, *w*. It would seem, then, at first sight that 7 katuns were recorded in C2 D2. That this was not the case, however, a closer examination of C2 will show. Although the lower part of this glyph is somewhat weathered, enough still remains to show that this head originally had a fleshless lower jaw, a character increasing its value by 10. Consequently, instead of having 7 katuns in C2 D2 we have 17 (7 + 10) katuns. Compare C2 with figure 53, *j–m*. In E1 F1, 15 tuns are recorded. The tun headdress in E1 gives the value 5 to the head there depicted (see fig. 51, *n–s*) and the fleshless lower jaw adds 10, making the value of E1 15. Compare figure 53, *b–e*, where examples of the head for 15 are given. Glyphs E2 and F2 represent 0 uinals and G1 H1 0 kins; note the clasped hand in E2 and G1, which denotes the 0 in each case. This whole number therefore reads 9.17.15.0.0. Reducing this to units of the first order by means of Table XIII, we have:

$$C1 \ D1 = \ 9 \times 144,000 = 1,296,000$$
$$C2 \ D2 = 17 \times \ \ \ 7,200 = \ \ 122,400$$
$$E1 \ F1 = 15 \times \ \ \ \ \ \ 360 = \ \ \ \ \ 5,400$$
$$E2 \ F2 = \ 0 \times \ \ \ \ \ \ \ 20 = \ \ \ \ \ \ \ \ \ \ 0$$
$$G1 \ H1 = \ 0 \times \ \ \ \ \ \ \ \ \ 1 = \ \ \ \ \ \ \ \ \ \ 0$$

$$1,423,800$$

Deducting from this number all the Calendar Rounds possible, 75 (see Table XVI), and applying rules 1, 2, and 3 (pp. 139, 140, and 141, respectively), to the remainder, the terminal day reached will be **5 Ahau 3 Muan**. The day is recorded in G2 H2. The day sign in H2 is quite clearly the grotesque head variant for **Ahau** in figure 16, *j'—k'*. The presence of the tun headdress in G2 indicates that the coefficient here recorded must have been either 5 or 15, depending

---

[1] For the full text of this inscription see Maudslay, 1889–1902: II, pls. 41–44.

PLATE 13

OLDEST INITIAL SERIES AT COPAN—STELA 15

on whether or not the lower part of the head originally had a flesh-less lower jaw or not. In this particular case there is no room for doubt, since the numeral in G2 is a day coefficient, and day coefficients as stated in Chapter III, can never rise above 13. Consequently the number 15 can not be recorded in G2, and this form must stand for the number 5.

Passing over I1 J1, I2 J2, K1 L1, K2 L2, we reach in M1 the closing glyph of the Supplementary Series, here shown with a coefficient of 10, the head having a fleshless lower jaw. The month sign follows in N1. The coefficient is 3 and by comparing the sign itself with the month glyphs in figure 19, it will be apparent that the sign for **Muan** in a' or b' is recorded here. The Initial Series of this monument therefore is **9.17.15.0.0 5 Ahau 3 Muan.**

In closing the presentation of Initial-series texts which show both head-variant numerals and period glyphs, the writer has thought best to figure the Initial Series on Stela 15 at Copan, because it is not only the oldest Initial Series at Copan, but also the oldest one known in which head-variant numerals are used [1] (see pl. 13). The introducing glyph appears at A1–B2. There follows in A3 a number too much effaced to read, but which, on the basis of all our previous experience, we are justified in calling 9. Similarly B3 must be the head variant of the cycle sign. The numeral 4 is clearly recorded in A4. Note the square irid, protruding fang, and mouth curl. Compare A4 with figure 51, j–m. Although the glyph in B4 is too much effaced to read, we are justified in assuming that it is the head variant of the katun sign. The glyph in A5 is the numeral 10. Note the fleshless lower jaw and other characteristics of the death's-head. Again we are justified in assuming that B5 must be the head variant of the tun sign. The glyphs A6, B6 clearly record 0 uinals. Note the clasped hand denoting zero in A6, and the curling mouth fang of the uinal period glyph in B6. This latter glyph is the full-figure form of the uinal sign [2] (a frog). Compare B6 with figure 33, which shows the uinal sign on Stela D at Copan. The stela is broken off just below the uinal sign and its coefficient; and therefore the kin coefficient and sign, the day coefficient and sign, and the month coefficient and sign, are missing. Assembling the four periods present, we have 9.4.10.0.?. Calling the missing kin coefficient 0, and reducing this number to units of the first order by means of Table XIII, we have:

$$
\begin{array}{lrcr}
\text{A3 B3} = & 9 \times 144,000 = & 1,296,000 \\
\text{A4 B4} = & 4 \times 7,200 = & 28,800 \\
\text{A5 B5} = & 10 \times 360 = & 3,600 \\
\text{A6 B6} = & 0 \times 20 = & 0 \\
& 0 \times 1 = & 0 \\
\hline
& & 1,328,400
\end{array}
$$

---

[1] For the text of this monument see Spinden, 1913: VI, pl. 23, 2.
[2] For the discussion of full-figure glyphs, see pp. 65–73.

Deducting from this number all the Calendar Rounds possible, 69 (see Table XVI), and applying rules 1, 2, and 3 (pp. 139, 140, and 141, respectively) to the remainder, the terminal date reached will be **12 Ahau 8 Mol.**   This date is reached on the assumption that the missing kin coefficient was zero.   This is a fairly safe assumption, since when the tun coefficient is either 0, 5, 10, or 15 (as here) and the uinal coefficient is 0 (as here), the kin coefficient is almost invariably zero. That is, the close of an even hotun in the Long Count is recorded.

While at Copan in May, 1912, the writer was shown a fragment of a stela which he was told was a part of this monument (Stela 15). This showed the top parts of two consecutive glyphs, the first of which very clearly had a coefficient of 12 and the one following of 8. The glyphs to which these coefficients belonged were missing, but the coincidence of the two numbers 12 (?) 8 (?) was so striking when taken into consideration with the fact that these were the day and month coefficients reached by calculation, that the writer was inclined to accept this fragment as the missing part of Stela 15 which showed the terminal date.   This whole Initial Series therefore reads: 9.4.10.0.0 **12 Ahau 8 Mol.**   It is chiefly interesting because it shows the earliest use of head-variant numerals known.

In the foregoing texts plate 12, *A*, *B*, figure 69, *A*, *B*, and figure 70, the head-variant numerals 0, 1, 3, 4, 5, 6, 8, 9, 10, 13, 14, 15, 17, and 18 have been given, and, excepting the forms for 2, 11, and 12, these include examples of all the head numerals.[1]   No more texts specially illustrating this type of numeral will be presented, but when any of the head numerals not figured above (2, 7, 11, 12, 16, and 19) occur in future texts their presence will be noted.

Before taking up the consideration of unusual or irregular Initial Series the writer has thought best to figure one Initial Series the period glyphs and numerals of which are expressed by full-figure forms.   As mentioned on page 68, such inscriptions are exceedingly rare, and such glyphs, moreover, are essentially the same as head-variant forms, since their determining characteristics are restricted to their head parts, which are exactly like the corresponding head-variant forms.   This fact will greatly aid the student in identifying the full-figure glyphs in the following text.

In plate 14 is figured the Initial Series from Stela D at Copan.[2] The introducing glyph is recorded in A1.   The variable central element in keeping with the other glyphs of the inscription appears here as a full figure, the lower part of which is concealed by the tun-sign.[3]

---

[1] The characteristics of the heads for 7, 14, 16, and 19 will be found in the heads for 17, 4, 6, and 9, respectively.

[2] For the full text of this inscription see Maudslay, 1889–1902: I, pls. 47, 48.

[3] The student will note also in connection with this glyph that the pair of comblike appendages usually found are here replaced by a pair of fishes.   As explained on pp. 65–66, the fish represents probably the original form from which the comblike element was derived in the process of glyph conventionalization. The full original form of this element is therefore in keeping with the other full-figure forms in this text.

PLATE 14

INITIAL SERIES ON STELA D, COPAN, SHOWING FULL-
FIGURE NUMERAL GLYPHS AND PERIOD GLYPHS

The Initial-series number itself appears in B1–B3. The cycle sign is a grotesque bird, designated by Mr. Bowditch a parrot, an identification which the hooked beak and claws strongly suggest. The essential element of the cycle sign, however, the clasped hand, appears only in the head of this bird, where the student will readily find it. Indeed, the head of this full-figure form is nothing more nor less than a head-variant cycle glyph, and as such determines the meaning of the whole figure. Compare this head with figure 25, *d–f*, or with any of the other head-variant cycle forms figured in the preceding texts. This grotesque "cycle bird," perhaps the parrot, is bound to the back of an anthropomorphic figure, which we have every reason to suppose records the cycle coefficient. An examination of this figure will show that it has not only the dots on the lower part of the cheek, but also the beard, both of which are distinctive features of the head for 9. Compare this head with figure 52, *g–l*, or with any other head variants for the numeral 9 already figured. Bearing in mind that the heads only present the determining characteristics of full-figure glyphs, the student will easily identify B1 as recording 9 cycles.

The katun and its coefficient are represented in A2, the former by a grotesque bird, an eagle according to Mr. Bowditch, and the latter by another anthropomorphic figure. The period glyph shows no essential element recognizable as such, and its identification as the katun sign therefore rests on its position, immediately following the cycle sign. The head of the full figure, which represents the katun coefficient, shows the essential element of the head for 5, the tun headdress. It has also the fleshless lower jaw of the head for 10. The combination of these two elements in one head, as we have seen, indicates the numeral 15, and A2 therefore records 15 katuns. Compare the head of this anthropomorphic figure with figure 53, *b–e*.

The tun and its coefficient are represented in B2. The former again appears as a grotesque bird, though in this case of undetermined nature. Its head, however, very clearly shows the essential element of the head-variant tun sign, the fleshless lower jaw. Compare this form with figure 29, *e–g*, and the other head-variant tun signs already illustrated. The head of the anthropomorphic figure, which denotes the tun coefficient, is just like the head of the anthropomorphic figure in the preceding glyph (A2), except that in B2 the head has no fleshless lower jaw.

Since the head in A2 with the fleshless lower jaw and the tun headdress represents the numeral 15, the head in B2 without the former but with the latter represents the numeral 5. Compare the head of the anthropomorphic figure in B2 with figure 51, *n–s*. It is clear, therefore, that 5 tuns are recorded in B2.

The uinal and its coefficient in A3 are equally clear. The period glyph here appears as a frog (Maya, *uo*), which, as we have seen elsewhere, may have been chosen to represent the 20-day period because of the similarity of its name, *uo*, to the name of this period, *u*, or uinal. The head of the anthropomorphic figure which clasps the frog's foreleg is the head variant for 0. Note the clasped hand across the lower part of the face, and compare this form with figure 53, *s–w*. The whole glyph, therefore, stands for 0 uinals.

In B3 are recorded the kin and its coefficient. The period glyph here is represented by an anthropomorphic figure with a grotesque head. Its identity, as representing the kins of this number, is better established from its position in the number than from its appearance, which is somewhat irregular. The kin coefficient is just like the uinal coefficient—an anthropomorphic figure the head of which has the clasped hand as its determining characteristic. Therefore B3 records 0 kins.

The whole number expressed by B1–B3 is 9.15.5.0.0; reducing this by means of Table XIII to units of the first order, we have:

$$
\begin{aligned}
B1 &= 9 \times 144,000 = 1,296,000 \\
A2 &= 15 \times 7,200 = 108,000 \\
B2 &= 5 \times 360 = 1,800 \\
A3 &= 0 \times 20 = 0 \\
B3 &= 0 \times 1 = 0 \\
\hline
& 1,405,800
\end{aligned}
$$

Deducting from this number all the Calendar Rounds possible, 74 (see Table XVI), and applying rules 1, 2, and 3 (pp. 139, 140, and 141 respectively), to the remainder, the terminal date reached will be **10 Ahau 8 Chen.**

The day part of this terminal date is recorded in A4. The day sign **Ahau** is represented as an anthropomorphic figure, crouching within the customary day-sign cartouche. The head of this figure is the familiar profile variant for the day sign **Ahau**, seen in figure 16, *h′*, *i′*. This cartouche is clasped by the left arm of another anthropomorphic figure, the day coefficient, the head of which is the skull, denoting the numeral 10. Note the fleshless lower jaw of this head and compare it with the same element in figure 52, *m–r*. This glyph A4 records, therefore, the day reached by the Initial Series, **10 Ahau.**

The position of the month glyph in this text is most unusual. Passing over B4, the first glyph of the Supplementary Series, the month glyph follows it immediately in A5. The month coefficient appears again as an anthropomorphic figure, the head of which has for its determining characteristic the forehead ornament composed of one part, denoting the numeral 8. Compare this head with the heads for 8, in figure 52, *a–f*. The month sign itself appears as a large grotesque head, the details of which present the essential elements of the month here recorded—**Chen.** Compare with figure 19, *o*, *p*.

PLATE 15

A. THE INSCRIPTION ARRANGED ACCORDING TO A MAT PATTERN

B. KEY TO SEQUENCE OF GLYPHS IN *A*

INITIAL SERIES ON STELA J, COPAN

The superfix of figure 16, *o*, *p*, has been retained unchanged as the superfix in A5b. The element (*) appears just *above* the eye of the grotesque head, and the element (**) on the left-hand side about where the ear lobe should be. The whole glyph *   ** unmistakably records a head variant of the month glyph **Chen**, and this Initial Series therefore reads 9.15.5.0.0 **10 Ahau 8 Chen.**

The student will note that this Initial Series records a date just 5 tuns later than the Initial Series on Stela B at Copan (pl. 7, *A*). According to the writer's opinion, therefore, Stelæ B and D marked two successive hotuns at this city.

We come now to the consideration of Initial Series which are either unusual or irregular in some respect, examples of which it is necessary to give in order to familiarize the student with all kinds of texts. The Initial Series in plate 15, *A*,[1] is figured because of the very unusual order followed by its glyphs. The sequence in which these succeed each other is given in *B* of that plate. The scheme followed seems to have been that of a mat pattern. The introducing glyph appears in position 0 (pl. 15, *B*), and the student will readily recognize it in the same position in *A* of the same plate. The Initial Series number follows in 1, 2, 3, 4, and 5 (pl. 15, *B*). Referring to these corresponding positions in *A*, we find that 9 cycles are recorded in 1, and 13 katuns in 2. At this point the diagonal glyph-band passes under another band, emerging at 3, where the tun sign with a coefficient of 10 is recorded. Here the band turns again and, crossing backward diagonally, shows 0 uinals in 4. At this point the band passes under three diagonals running in the opposite direction, emerging at position 5, the glyph in which are recorded 0 kins.

This number 9.13.10.0.0 reduces by means of Table XIII to units of the first order, as follows:

$$
\begin{aligned}
1 &= \ 9 \times 144,000 = 1,296,000 \\
2 &= 13 \times \ \ 7,200 = \ \ \ 93,600 \\
3 &= 10 \times \ \ \ \ 360 = \ \ \ \ \ 3,600 \\
4 &= \ 0 \times \ \ \ \ \ 20 = \ \ \ \ \ \ \ \ \ \ 0 \\
5 &= \ 0 \times \ \ \ \ \ \ \ 1 = \ \ \ \ \ \ \ \ \ \ 0 \\
\end{aligned}
$$

$$
\overline{1,393,200}
$$

Deducting from this number all the Calendar Rounds possible, 73 (see Table XVI), and applying rules 1, 2, and 3 (pp. 139, 140, and 141, respectively) to the remainder, the terminal date reached will be **7 Ahau 3 Cumhu.** Referring again to plate 15, *B*, for the sequence of the glyphs in this text, it is clear that the day of this terminal date should be recorded in 6, immediately after the kins of the Initial-series number in 6. It will be seen, however, in plate 15, *A*, that

---

[1] For the full text of this inscription, see Maudslay, 1889–1902: I, pls. 66–71.

glyph 6 is effaced, and consequently the day is missing. Passing over 7, 8, 9, 10, and 11, in *A* and *B* of the plate named, we reach in the lower half of 12 the closing glyph of the Supplementary Series here shown with a coefficient of 10. Compare this form with figure 65. The month glyph, therefore, should follow in the upper half of 13.[1] This glyph is very clearly the form for the month **Cumhu** (see fig. 19, *g'*, *h'*), and it seems to have attached to it the bar and dot coefficient 8. A comparison of this with the month coefficient 3, determined above by calculation, shows that the two do not agree, and that the month coefficient as recorded exceeds the month coefficient determined by calculation, by 5, or in Maya notation, 1 bar. Since the Initial-series number is very clearly 9.13.10.0.0, and since this number leads to the terminal date **7 Ahau 3 Cumhu**, it would seem that the ancient scribes had made an error in this text, recording 1 bar and 3 dots instead of 3 dots alone. The writer is inclined to believe, however, that the bar here is only ornamental and has no numerical value whatsoever, having been inserted solely to balance this glyph. If it had been omitted, the month sign would have had to be greatly elongated and its proportions distorted in order to fill completely the space available. According to the writer's interpretation, this Initial Series reads 9.13.10.0.0 **7 Ahau 3 Cumhu**.

The opposite face of the above-mentioned monument presents the same interlacing scheme, though in this case the glyph bands cross at right angles to each other instead of diagonally.

The only other inscription in the whole Maya territory, so far as the writer knows, which at all parallels the curious interlacing pattern of the glyphs on the back of Stela J at Copan, just described, is Stela H at Quirigua, illustrated in figure 71.[2] The drawing of this inscription appears in *a* of this figure and the key to the sequence of the glyphs in *b*. The introducing glyph occupies position 1 and is followed by the Initial Series in 2–6. The student will have little difficulty in identifying 2, 3, and 4 as 9 cycles, 16 katuns, and 0 tuns, respectively. The uinal and kin glyphs in 5 and 6, respectively, are so far effaced that in order to determine the values of their coefficients we shall have to rely to a large extent on other inscriptions here at Quirigua. For example, every monument at Quirigua which presents an Initial Series marks the close of some particular hotun in the Long Count; consequently, all the Initial Series at Quirigua which record these hotun endings have 0 for their uinal and kin coefficients.[3] This abso-

---

[1] The student should remember that in this diagonal the direction of reading is from bottom to top. See pl. 15, *B*, glyphs 7, 8, 9, 10, 11, 12, etc. Consequently the upper half of 13 follows the lower half in this particular glyph.

[2] For the full text of this inscription see Hewett, 1911: pl. xxii *B*.

[3] A few monuments at Quirigua, namely, Stelæ F, D, E, and A, have two Initial Series each. In A both of the Initial Series have 0 for the coefficients of their uinal and kin glyphs, and in F, D, E, the Initial Series which shows the position of the monument in the Long Count, that is, the Initial Series showing the hotun ending which it marks, has 0 for its uinal and kin coefficients.

lute uniformity in regard to the uinal and kin coefficients in all the other Initial Series at Quirigua justifies the assumption that in the text here under discussion 0 uinals and 0 kins were originally recorded in glyphs 5 and 6, respectively. Furthermore, an inspection of the coefficients of these two glyphs in figure 71, *a*, shows that both of them are of the same general size and shape as the tun coefficient in 4, which, as we have seen, is very clearly 0. It is more than probable that the uinal and kin coefficients in this text were originally 0, like the tun coefficient, and that through weathering they have been eroded down to their present shape. In figure 72, *a*, is shown the tun coefficient and beside it in *b*, the uinal or kin coefficient. The dotted parts in *b* are the lines which have disappeared through erosion, if this coefficient was originally 0. It seems more than likely from the foregoing that the uinal and kin coefficients in this number were originally 0, and proceeding on this assumption, we have recorded in glyphs 2–6, figure 71, *a*, the number 9.16.0.0.0.

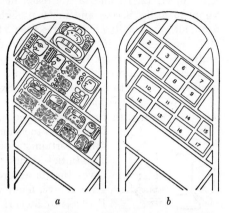

FIG. 71. Initial Series on Stela H, Quirigua: *a*, Mat pattern of glyph sequence; *b*, key to sequence of glyphs in *a*.

Reducing this to units of the first order by means of Table XIII, we have:

$$5 = 9 \times 144,000 = 1,296,000$$
$$6 = 16 \times 7,200 = 115,200$$
$$7 = 0 \times 360 = 0$$
$$8 = 0 \times 20 = 0$$
$$9 = 0 \times 1 = 0$$

$$\overline{1,411,200}$$

Deducting from this number all the Calendar Rounds possible, 74 (see Table XVI), and applying rules 1, 2, and 3 (pp. 139, 140, and 141, respectively) to the remainder, the terminal date **2 Ahau 13 Tzec** will be reached.

In spite of some weathering, the day part of the terminal date appears in glyph 7 immediately after the kin glyph in 6. The coefficient, though somewhat eroded, appears quite clearly as 2 (2 dots separated by an ornamental crescent). The day sign itself is the profile variant for **Ahau** shown in figure 16, *h′, i′*. The agreement of the day recorded with the day determined by calculations based on the assumption that the kin and uinal coefficients are both 0, of itself tends to establish the accuracy of these assumptions. Passing over 8, 9, 10, 11, 12, 13, and 14, we reach in 15 the closing glyph of the Supplementary Series, and in 16 probably the month glyph. This form, although badly eroded, presents no features either in the outline of its coefficient or in the sign itself which would prevent it representing the month part **13 Tzec.** The coefficient is just wide enough for three vertical divisions (2 bars and 3 dots), and the month glyph itself is divided into two parts, a superfix comprising about one-third of the glyph and the main element the remaining two-thirds. Compare this form with the sign for **Tzec** in figure 19, *g*, *h*. Although

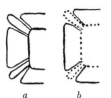

this text is too much weathered to permit absolute certainty with reference to the reading of this Initial Series, the writer nevertheless believes that in all probability it records the date given above, namely, 9.16.0.0.0 **2 Ahau 13 Tzec.** If this is so, Stela H is the earliest hotun-marker at Quirigua.[1]

a   *b*

Fig. 72. The tun, uinal, and kin coefficients on Stela H, Quirigua: *a*, Tun coefficient; *b*, suggested restoration of the uinal and kin coefficients like the tun coefficient.

The student will have noticed from the foregoing texts, and it has also been stated several times, that the cycle coefficient is almost invariably 9. Indeed, the only two exceptions to this rule in the inscriptions already figured are the Initial Series from the Temples of the Foliated Cross and the Sun at Palenque (pl. 12, *A* and *B*, respectively), in which the cycle coefficient in each case was 1. As explained on page 179, footnote 1, these two Initial Series refer probably to mythological events, and the dates which they record were not contemporaneous with the erection of the temples on whose walls they are inscribed; and, finally, Cycle 9 was the first historic period of the Maya civilization, the epoch which witnessed the rise and fall of all the southern cities.

As explained on page 179, footnote 2, however, there are one or two Initial Series which can hardly be considered as referring to mythological events, even though the dates which they record fall in a cycle earlier than Cycle 9. It was stated, further, in the same place that these two Initial Series were not found inscribed on large monuments but on smaller antiquities, one of them being a small nephrite figure which has been designated the Tuxtla Statuette, and the other a nephrite plate, designated the Leyden Plate; and, finally, that the dates recorded on these two antiquities probably designated contemporaneous events in the historic period of the Maya civilization.

---

[1] In 1913 Mr. M. D. Landry, superintendent of the Quirigua district, Guatemala division of the United Fruit Co., found a still earlier monument about half a mile west of the main group. This has been named Stela S. It records the hotun ending prior to the one on Stela H, i. e., 9.15.15.0.0 **9 Ahau 18 Xul.**

These two minor antiquities have several points in common. Both are made of the same material (nephrite) and both have their glyphs incised instead of carved. More important, however, than these similarities is the fact that the Initial Series recorded on each of them has for its cycle coefficient the numeral 8; in other words, both record dates which fell in the cycle immediately preceding that of the historic period, or Cycle 9. Finally, at least one of these two Initial

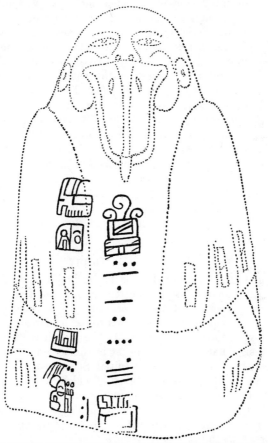

FIG. 73. The Initial Series on the Tuxtla Statuette, the oldest Initial Series known (in the early part of Cycle 8).

Series (that on the Leyden Plate), if indeed not both, records a date so near the opening of the historic period, which we may assume occurred about 9.0.0.0.0 **8 Ahau 13 Ceh** in round numbers, that it may be considered as belonging to the historic period, and hence constitutes the earliest historical inscription from the Maya territory.

The Initial Series on the first of these minor antiquities, the Tuxtla Statuette, is shown in figure 73.[1] The student will note at the outset one very important difference between this Initial Series—if indeed it is one, which some have doubted—and those already presented. No period glyphs appear in the present example, and consequently the Initial-series number is expressed by the second method (p. 129), that is, numeration by position, as in the codices. See the discussion of Initial Series in the codices in Chapter VI (pp. 266–273), and plates 31 and 32. This at once distinguishes the Initial Series on the Tuxtla Statuette from every other Initial Series in the inscriptions now known. The number is preceded by a character which bears some general resemblance to the usual Initial-series introducing glyph. See figure 74. The most striking point of similarity is the trinal superfix, which is present in both signs. The student will have little difficulty in reading the number here recorded as 8 cycles, 6 katuns, 2 tuns, 4 uinals, and 17 kins, that is, 8.6.2.4.17; reducing this to units of the first order by means of Table XIII, we have:

FIG. 74. The introducing glyph (?) of the Initial Series on the Tuxtla Statuette.

$$
\begin{array}{rcr}
8 \times 144,000 = & 1,152,000 \\
6 \times 7,200 = & 43,200 \\
2 \times 360 = & 720 \\
4 \times 20 = & 80 \\
17 \times 1 = & 17 \\
\hline
& 1,196,017
\end{array}
$$

Solving this Initial-series number for its terminal date, it will be found to be **8 Caban 0 Kankin.** Returning once more to our text (see fig. 73), we find the day coefficient above reached, 8, is recorded just below the 17 kins and appears to be attached to some character the details of which are, unfortunately, effaced. The month coefficient 0 and the month sign **Kankin** do not appear in the accompanying text, at least in recognizable form. This Initial Series would seem to be, therefore, 8.6.2.4.17 **8 Caban 0 Kankin,** of which the day sign, month coefficient, and month sign are effaced or unrecognizable. In spite of its unusual form and the absence of the day sign, and the month coefficient and sign the writer is inclined to accept the above date as a contemporaneous Initial Series.[2]

The other Initial Series showing a cycle coefficient 8 is on the Leyden Plate, a drawing of which is reproduced in figure 75, *A.* This Initial Series is far more satisfactory than the one just described, and

---

[1] For the full text of this inscription see Holmes, 1907: pp. 691 et seq., and pls. 34–41.

[2] For a full discussion of the Tuxtla Statuette, including the opinions of several writers as to its inscription, see Holmes, 1907: pp. 691 et seq. The present writer gives therein at some length the reasons which have led him to accept this inscription as genuine and contemporaneous.

its authenticity, generally speaking, is unquestioned. The student will easily identify A1–B2 as an Initial-series introducing glyph, even though the pair of comblike appendages flanking the central element and the tun tripod are both wanting. Compare this form with figure 24. The Initial-series number, expressed by normal-form numerals and head-variant period glyphs, follows in A3–A7. The former are all very clear, and the number may be read from them in spite of certain irregularities in the corresponding period glyphs. For example, the katun head in A4 has the clasped hand, which is the distinguishing characteristic of the cycle head, and as such should have appeared in the head in A3. Neither the tun head in A5 nor the kin head in A7 shows an essential element heretofore found distinguishing these particular period glyphs. Indeed, the only period glyph of the five showing the usual essential element is the uinal head in A6, where the large mouth curl appears very clearly. However, the number recorded here may be read as 8.14.3.1.12 from the sequence of the coefficients—that is, their position with reference to the

A   B

Fig. 75. Drawings of the Initial Series: *A*, On the Leyden Plate. This records a Cycle-8 date and next to the Tuxtla Statuette Initial Series, is the earliest known. *B*, On a lintel from the Temple of the Initial Series, Chichen Itza. This records a Cycle-10 date, and is one of the latest Initial Series known.

introducing glyph—a reading, moreover, which is confirmed by the only known period glyph, the uinal sign, standing in the fourth position after the introducing glyph.

Reducing this number to units of the first order by means of Table XIII, we have:

$$
\begin{aligned}
A3 &= 8 \times 144,000 = 1,152,000 \\
A4 &= 14 \times 7,200 = 100,800 \\
A5 &= 3 \times 360 = 1,080 \\
A6 &= 1 \times 20 = 20 \\
A7 &= 12 \times 1 = 12 \\
\hline
& \qquad\qquad\quad 1,253,912
\end{aligned}
$$

Deducting from this number all the Calendar Rounds possible, 66 (see Table XVI), and applying rules 1, 2, and 3 (pp. 139, 140, and 141, respectively) to the remainder, the terminal date reached will be **1 Eb 0 Yaxkin**. The day part of this date is very clearly recorded in A8, the coefficient 1 being expressed by one dot, and the day sign itself having the hook surrounded by dots, and the prominent teeth, both of which are characteristic of the grotesque head which denotes the day **Eb**. See figure 16, *s–u*.

The month glyph appears in A9a, the lower half of which unmistakably records the month **Yaxkin**. (See fig. 19, *k*, *l*.) Note the *yax* and *kin* elements in each. The only difficulty here seems to be the fact that a bar (5) is attached to this glyph. The writer believes, however, that the unexplained element (*) is the month coefficient in this text, and that it is an archaic form for 0. He would explain the bar as being merely ornamental. The whole Initial Series reads: 8.14.3.1.12 **1 Eb 0 Yaxkin**.

The fact that there are some few irregularities in this text confirms rather than invalidates the antiquity which has been ascribed to it by the writer. Dating from the period when the Maya were just emerging from savagery to the arts and practices of a semicivilized state, it is not at all surprising that this inscription should reflect the crudities and uncertainties of its time. Indeed, it is quite possible that at the very early period from which it probably dates (8.14.3.1.12 **1 Eb 0 Yaxkin**) the period glyphs had not yet become sufficiently conventionalized to show individual peculiarities, and their identity may have been determined solely by their position with reference to the introducing glyph, as seemingly is the case in some of the period glyphs of this text.

The Initial Series on the Leyden Plate precedes the Initial Series on Stela 3 at Tikal, the earliest contemporaneous date from the monuments, by more than 160 years, and with the possible exception of the Tuxtla Statuette above described, probably records the earliest date of Maya history. It should be noted here that Cycle-8 Initial Series are occasionally found in the Dresden Codex, though none are quite so early as the Initial Series from the Tuxtla Statuette.

Passing over the Initial Series whose cycle coefficient is 9, many of which have already been described, we come next to the consideration of Initial Series whose cycle coefficient is 10, a very limited number indeed. As explained in Chapter I, the southern cities did not long survive the opening of Cycle 10, and since Initial-series dating did not prevail extensively in the later cities of the north, Initial Series showing 10 cycles are very unusual.

In figure 75, *B*, is shown the Initial Series from the Temple of the Initial Series at Chichen Itza, the great metropolis of northern Yucatan. This inscription is not found on a stela but on the under side of a lintel over a doorway leading into a small and comparatively insignificant temple. The introducing glyph appears in A1–B2 and is followed by the Initial-series number in A3–A5. The student will have little difficulty in deciphering all of the coefficients except that belonging to the kin in A5, which is a head-variant numeral, and the whole number will be found to read 10.2.9.1.?. The coefficient of the day of the terminal date is very clearly 9 (see B5) and the month part, **7 Zac** (see A6). We may now read this Initial Series as 10.2.9.1.? 9? **7 Zac**; in other words, the kin coefficient and the day sign are still indeterminate. First substituting 0 as the missing value of the kin coefficient, the terminal date reached will be 10.2.9.1.0 **13 Ahau 18 Yax.** But according to Table XV, position **18 Yax** is just 9 days earlier than position **7 Zac**, the month part recorded in A6. Consequently, in order to reach **7 Zac** from 10.2.9.1.0 **13 Ahau 18 Yax,** 9 more days are necessary. Counting these forward from 10.2.9.1.0 **13 Ahau 18 Yax**, the date reached will be 10.2.9.1.9 **9 Muluc 7 Zac,** which is the date recorded on this lintel. Compare the day sign with figure 16, *m*, *n*, and the month sign with figure 19, *s*, *t*.

Two other Initial Series whose cycle coefficient is 10 yet remain to be considered, namely, Stelæ 1 and 2 at Quen Santo.[1] The first of these is shown in figure 76, *A*, but unfortunately only a fragment of this monument has been recovered. In A1–B2 appears a perfectly regular form of the introducing glyph (see fig. 24), and this is followed in A3–B4 by the Initial-series number itself, with the exception of the kin, the glyph representing which has been broken off. The student will readily identify A3 as 10 cycles, noting the clasped hand on the head-variant period glyph, and B3 as 2 katuns. The glyph in A4 has very clearly the coefficient 5, and even though it does not seem to have the fleshless lower jaw of the tun head, from its position alone—after the unmistakable katun sign in B3—we are perfectly justified in assuming that 5 tuns are recorded here. Both the coefficient and the glyph in B4 are unfamiliar. However, as the former

---

[1] For the full text of these inscriptions, see Seler, 1902–1908: II, 253, and 1901 c: I, 23, fig. 7. During his last visit to the Maya territory the writer discovered that Stela 11 at Tikal has a Cycle-10 Initial Series, namely, 10.2.0.0.0. **3 Ahau 3 Ceh.**

must be one of the numerals 0 to 19, inclusive, since it is not one of
the numerals 1 to 19, inclusive, it is clear that it must be a new form
for 0. The sign to which it is attached bears no resemblance to either
the normal form for the uinal or the head variant; but since it occupies the 4th position after the introducing glyph, B4, we are justified
in assuming that 0 uinals are recorded here. Beyond this we can
not proceed with certainty, though the values for the missing parts

A   B

Fig. 76. The Cycle-10 Initial Series from Quen Santo (from drawings): A, Stela 1; B, Stela 2. There is
less than a year's difference in time between the Chichen Itza Initial Series and the Initial Series in B.

suggested below are probably those recorded on the lost fragments
of the monument. As recorded in A3–B4 this number reads
10.2.5.0. ?. Now, if we assume that the missing term is filled with 0,
we shall have recorded the end of an even hotun in the Long Count,
and this monument becomes a regular hotun-marker. That this
monument was a hotun-marker is corroborated by the fact that Stela
2 from Quen Santo very clearly records the close of the hotun next
after 10.2.5.0.0, which the writer believes this monument marks. For

this reason it seems probable that the glyph which stood in A5 recorded 0 kins.

Reducing this number to units of the first order by means of Table XIII, we obtain:

$$
\begin{aligned}
A3 &= 10 \times 144,000 = 1,440,000 \\
B3 &= 2 \times 7,200 = 14,400 \\
A4 &= 5 \times 360 = 1,800 \\
B4 &= 0 \times 20 = 0 \\
A5^1 &= 0 \times 1 = 0 \\
\hline
& \; 1,456,200
\end{aligned}
$$

Deducting from this number all the Calendar Rounds possible, 76 (see Table XVI), and applying rules 1, 2, and 3 (pp. 139, 140, and 141, respectively) to the remainder, the terminal date reached will be **9 Ahau 18 Yax,** and the whole Initial Series originally recorded on this monument was probably 10.2.5.0.0 **9 Ahau 18 Yax.**

In figure 76, *B,* is shown Stela 2 from Quen Santo. The workmanship on this monument is somewhat better than on Stela 1 and, moreover, its Initial Series is complete. The introducing glyph appears in A1–B2 and is followed by the Initial-series number in A3–A5. Again, 10 cycles are very clearly recorded in A3, the clasped hand of the cycle head still appearing in spite of the weathering of this glyph. The katun sign in B3 is almost entirely effaced, though sufficient traces of its coefficient remain to enable us to identify it as 2. Note the position of the uneffaced dot with reference to the horizontal axis of the glyph. Another dot the same distance above the axis would come as near the upper left-hand corner of the glyph-block as the uneffaced dot does to the lower left-hand corner. Moreover, if 3 had been recorded here the uneffaced dot would have been nearer the bottom. It is clear that 1 and 4 are quite out of the question and that 2 remains the only possible value of the numeral here. We are justified in assuming that the effaced period glyph was the katun sign. In A4 10 tuns are very clearly recorded; note the fleshless lower jaw of the tun head. The uinal head with its characteristic mouth curl appears in B4. The coefficient of this latter glyph is identical with the uinal coefficient in the preceding text (see fig. 76, *A*) in B4, which we there identified as a form for 0. Therefore we must make the same identification here, and B4 then becomes 0 uinals. From its position, if not from its appearance, we are justified in designating the glyph in A5 the head for the kin period; since the coefficient attached to this head is the same as the one in the preceding glyph (B4), we may therefore conclude that 0 kins are recorded here. The whole number expressed in A3–A5 is

---

[1] Missing.

therefore 10.2.10.0.0. Reducing this to units of the first order by means of Table XIII, we have:

$$A3 = 10 \times 144,000 = 1,440,000$$
$$B3 = 2 \times 7,200 = 14,400$$
$$A4 = 10 \times 360 = 3,600$$
$$B4 = 0 \times 20 = 0$$
$$A5 = 0 \times 1 = 0$$
$$\overline{1,458,000}$$

Deducting from this number all the Calendar Rounds possible, 76 (see Table XVI), and applying rules 1, 2, and 3 (pp. 139, 140, and 141, respectively) to the remainder, the terminal date reached will be **2 Ahau 13 Chen**. Although the day sign in B5 is effaced, the coefficient 2 appears quite clearly. The month glyph is recorded in A6. The student will have little difficulty in restoring the coefficient as 13, and the month glyph is certainly either **Chen, Yax, Zac,** or **Ceh** (compare fig. 19, *o* and *p*, *q* and *r*, *s* and *t*, and *u* and *v*, respectively). Moreover, since the month coefficient is 13, the day sign in B5 can have been only **Chicchan, Oc, Men,** or **Ahau** (see Table VII); since the kin coefficient in A5 is 0, the effaced day sign must have been **Ahau**. Therefore the Initial Series on Stela 2 at Quen Santo reads 10.2.10.0.0 **2 Ahau 13 Chen** and marked the hotun immediately following the hotun commemorated by Stela 1 at the same site.

The student will note also that the date on Stela 2 at Quen Santo is less than a year later than the date recorded by the Initial Series on the Temple lintel from Chichen Itza (see fig. 75, *B*). And a glance at the map in plate 1 will show, further, that Chichen Itza and Quen Santo are separated from each other by almost the entire length (north and south) of the Maya territory, the former being in the extreme northern part of Yucatan and the latter considerably to the south of the central Maya cities. The presence of two monuments so close together chronologically and yet so far apart geographically is difficult to explain. Moreover, the problem is further complicated by the fact that not one of the many cities lying between has yielded thus far a date as late as either of these.[1] The most logical explanation of this interesting phenomenon seems to be that while the main body of the Maya moved northward into Yucatan after the collapse of the southern cities others retreated southward into the highlands of Guatemala; that while the northern emigrants

---

[1] At Seibal a Period-ending date 10.1.0.0.0 **5 Ahau 3 Kayab** is clearly recorded, but this is some 30 years earlier than either of the Initial Series here under discussion, a significant period just at this particular epoch of Maya history, which we have every reason to believe was filled with stirring events and quickly shifting scenes. Tikal, with the Initial Series 10.2.0.0.0 **3 Ahau 3 Ceh**, and Seibal with the same date (not as an Initial Series, however) are the nearest, though even these fall 10 years short of the Quen Santo and Chichen Itza Initial Series.

were colonizing Yucatan the southern branch was laying the foundation of the civilization which was to flourish later under the name of the Quiche and other allied peoples; and finally, that as Chichen Itza was a later northern city, so Quen Santo was a later southern site, the two being at one period of their existence at least approximately contemporaneous, as these two Initial Series show.

It should be noted in this connection that Cycle-10 Initial Series are occasionally recorded in the Dresden Codex, though the dates in these cases are all later than those recorded on the Chichen Itza lintel and the Quen Santo stelæ. Before closing the presentation of Initial-series texts it is first necessary to discuss two very unusual and highly irregular examples of this method of dating, namely, the Initial Series from the east side of Stela C at Quirigua and the Initial Series from the tablet in the Temple of the Cross at Palenque. The dates recorded in these two texts, so far as known,[1] are the only ones which are not counted from the starting point of Maya chronology, the date **4 Ahau 8 Cumhu.**

In figure 77, *A*, is shown the Initial Series on the east side of Stela C at Quirigua.[2] The introducing glyph appears in A1–B2, and is followed by the Initial-series number in A3–A5. The student will easily read this as 13.0.0.0.0. Reducing this number to units of the first order by means of Table XIII, we have:

$$A3 = 13 \times 144,000 = 1,872,000$$
$$B3 = 0 \times 7,200 = 0$$
$$A4 = 0 \times 360 = 0$$
$$B4 = 0 \times 20 = 0$$
$$A5 = 0 \times 1 = 0$$

$$1,872,000$$

Deducting from this number all the Calendar Rounds possible, 98 [3] (see Table XVI), and applying rules 1, 2, and 3 (pp. 139, 140, and 141), respectively, to the remainder, the terminal date reached should be, under ordinary circumstances, **4 Ahau 3 Kankin.** An inspection of our text, however, will show that the terminal date recorded in B5–A6 is unmistakably **4 Ahau 8 Cumhu,** and not **4 Ahau 3 Kankin.** The month part in A6 is unusually clear, and there can be no doubt

---

[1] Up to the present time no successful interpretation of the inscription on Stela C at Copan has been advanced. The inscription on each side of this monument is headed by an introducing glyph, but in neither case is this followed by an Initial Series. A number consisting of 11.14.5.1.0 is recorded in connection with the date **6 Ahau 18 Kayab,** but as this date does not appear to be fixed in the Long Count, there is no way of ascertaining whether it is earlier or later than the starting point of Maya chronology. Mr. Bowditch (1910: pp. 195–196) offers an interesting explanation of this monument, to which the student is referred for the possible explanation of this text. A personal inspection of this inscription failed to confirm, however, the assumption on which Mr. Bowditch's conclusions rest. For the full text of this inscription, see Maudslay, 1889–1902: I, pls. 39–41.

[2] For the full text of this inscription, see ibid.: II, pls. 16, 17, 19.

[3] Table XVI contains only 80 Calendar Rounds (1,518,400), but by adding 18 Calendar Rounds (341,640) the number to be subtracted, 98 Calendar Rounds (1,860,040), will be reached.

that it is **8 Cumhu**. Compare A6 with figure 19, *g'*, *h'*. If we have made no mistake in calculations, then it is evident that 13.0.0.0.0 counted forward from the starting point of Maya chronology, **4 Ahau 8 Cumhu**, will not reach the terminal date recorded. Further, since the count in Initial Series has never been known to be backward,[1] we are forced to accept one of two conclusions: Either the starting point is not **4 Ahau 8 Cumhu**, or there is some error in the original text.

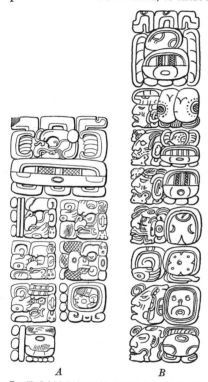

However, there is one way by means of which we can ascertain the date from which the number 13.0.0.0.0 is counted. The terminal date reached by the count is recorded very clearly as **4 Ahau 8 Cumhu**. Now, if we reverse our operation and count the given number, 13.0.0.0.0, *backward* from the known terminal date, **4 Ahau 8 Cumhu**, we reach the starting point from which the count proceeds.

Deducting from this number, as before, all the Calendar Rounds possible, 98 (see p. 203, footnote 3), and applying rules 1, 2, and 3 (pp. 139, 140, 141, respectively) to the remainder, remembering that in each operation the direction of the count is *backward*, not forward, the starting point will be found to be **4 Ahau 8 Zotz**. This is the first Initial Series yet encountered which has not proceeded from the date **4 Ahau 8 Cumhu**, and

FIG. 77. Initial Series which proceed from a date prior to **4 Ahau 8 Cumhu**, the starting point of Maya chronology: *A*, Stela C (east side) at Quirigua; *B*, Temple of the Cross at Palenque.

until the new starting point here indicated can be substantiated it will be well to accept the correctness of this text only with a reservation. The most we can say at present is that if the number recorded in A3–A5, 13.0.0.0.0, be counted forward from **4 Ahau 8 Zotz** as a starting point, the terminal date reached by calculation will agree with the terminal date as recorded in B5–A6, **4 Ahau 8 Cumhu**.

---

[1] Counting 13.0.0.0.0 *backward* from the starting point of Maya chronology, **4 Ahau 8 Cumhu**, gives the date **4 Ahau 8 Zotz**, which is no nearer the terminal date recorded in B5–A6 than the date **4 Ahau 3 Kankin** reached by counting forward.

Let us next examine the Initial Series on the tablet from the Temple of the Cross at Palenque, which is shown in figure 77, B.[1] The introducing glyph appears in A1–B2, and is followed by the Initial-series number in A3–B7. The period glyphs in B3, B4, B5, B6, and B7 are all expressed by their corresponding normal forms, which will be readily recognized. Passing over the cycle coefficient in A3 for the present, it is clear that the katun coefficient in A4 is 19. Note the dots around the mouth, characteristic of the head for 9 (fig. 52, g–l), and the fleshless lower jaw, the essential element of the head for 10 (fig. 52, m–r). The combination of the two gives the head in A4 the value of 19. The tun coefficient in A5 is equally clear as 13. Note the banded headdress, characteristic of the head for 3 (fig. 51, h, i), and the fleshless lower jaw of the 10 head, the combination of the two giving the head for 13 (fig. 52, w).[2] The head for 4 and the hand zero sign appear as the coefficient of the uinal and kin signs in A6 and A7, respectively. The number will read, therefore, ?.19.13.4.0. Let us examine the cycle coefficient in A3 again. The natural assumption, of course, is that it is 9. But the dots characteristic of the head for 9 are not to be found here. As this head has no fleshless lower jaw, it can not be 10 or any number above 13, and as there is no clasped hand associated with it, it can not signify 0, so we are limited to the numbers, 1, 2, 3, 4, 5,[3] 6, 7, 8, 11, 12, and 13, as the numeral here recorded. Comparing this form with these numerals in figures 51 and 52, it is evident that it can not be 1, 3, 4, 5, 6, 7, 8, or 13, and that it must therefore be 2, 11, or 12. Substituting these three values in turn, we have 2.19.13.4.0, 11.19.13.4.0, and 12.19.13.4.0 as the possible numbers recorded in A3–B7, and reducing these numbers to units of the first order and deducting the highest number of Calendar Rounds possible from each, and applying rules 1, 2, and 3 (pp. 139, 140, and 141, respectively) to their remainders, the terminal dates reached will be:

2.19.13.4.0   **5 Ahau 3 Pax**

11.19.13.4.0   **9 Ahau 8 Yax**

12.19.13.4.0   **8 Ahau 13 Pop**

If this text is perfectly regular and our calculations are correct, one of these three terminal dates will be found recorded, and the value of the cycle coefficient in A3 can be determined.

The terminal date of this Initial Series is recorded in A8–B9 and the student will easily read it as **8 Ahau 18 Tzec**. The only difference

---

[1] For the full text of this inscription, see Maudslay, 1889–1902: IV, pls. 73–77.

[2] As noted in Chapter IV, this is one of the only two heads for 13 found in the inscriptions which is composed of the essential element of the 10 head applied to the 3 head, the combination of the two giving 13. Usually the head for 13 is represented by a form peculiar to this number alone and is not built up by the combination of lower numbers as in this case.

[3] Although at first sight the headdress resembles the tun sign, a closer examination shows that it is not this element.

between the day coefficient and the month coefficient is that the latter
has a fleshless lower jaw, increasing its value by 10. Moreover, comparison of the month sign in B9 with *g* and *h*, figure 19, shows unmistakably that the month here recorded is **Tzec**. But the terminal
date as recorded does not agree with any one of the three above
terminal dates as reached by calculation and we are forced to accept
one of the two conclusions which confronted us in the preceding text
(fig. 77, A): Either the starting point of this Initial Series is not the
date **4 Ahau 8 Cumhu**, or there is some error in the original text.[1]

Assuming that the ancient scribes made no mistakes in this inscription, let us count backward from the recorded terminal date, **8 Ahau
18 Tzec**, each of the three numbers 2.19.13.4.0, 11.19.13.4.0, and
12.19.13.4.0, one of which, we have seen, is recorded in A3–B7.

Reducing these numbers to units of the first order by means of
Table XIII, and deducting all the Calendar Rounds possible from
each (see Table XVI), and, finally, applying rules 1, 2, and 3 (pp. 139,
140, and 141, respectively), to the remainders, the starting points will
be found to be:

> **7 Ahau 3 Mol** for   2.19.13.4.0
> **3 Ahau 18 Mac** for 11.19.13.4.0
> **4 Ahau 8 Zotz** for   12.19.13.4.0

Which of these starting points are we to accept as the one from which
this number is counted? The correct answer to this question will
give at the same time the value of the cycle coefficient, which, as
we have seen, must be 2, 11, or 12. Most Maya students have
accepted as the starting point of this Initial-series number the last
of the three dates above given, **4 Ahau 8 Zotz**, which involves also the
identification of the cycle coefficient in A3 as 12. The writer has
reached the same conclusion from the following points:

1. The cycle coefficient in A3, except for its very unusual headdress,
is almost identical with the other two head-variant numerals, whose
values are known to be 12. These three head numerals are shown
side by side in figure 52, *t–v*, *t* being the form in A3 above, inserted
in this figure for the sake of comparison. Although these three heads
show no single element or characteristic that is present in all (see p.
100), each is very similar to the other two and at the same time is
dissimilar from all other head-variant numerals. This fact warrants
the conclusion that the head in A3 represents the numeral 12, and if
this is so the starting point of the Initial Series under discussion is
4 Ahau 8 Zotz.

2. Aside from the fact that 12 seems to be the best reading of the
head in A3, and consequently that the starting point of this number
is **4 Ahau 8 Zotz**, the writer believes that **4 Ahau 8 Zotz** should be

---

[1] Similarly, it could be shown that the use of every other possible value of the cycle coefficient will
not give the terminal date actually recorded.

PLATE 16

INITIAL SERIES AND SECONDARY SERIES ON LINTEL 21, YAXCHILAN

selected, if for no other reason than that another Initial Series has been found which proceeds from this same date, while no other Initial Series known is counted from either **7 Ahau 3 Mol** or **3 Ahau 18 Mac**.

As we have seen in discussing the preceding text, from the east side of Stela C at Quirigua (fig. 77, *A*), the Initial Series there recorded was counted from the same starting point, **4 Ahau 8 Zotz**, as the Initial Series from the Temple of the Cross at Palenque, if we read the latter as 12.19.13.4.0. This coincidence, the writer believes, is sufficient to warrant the identification of the head in A3 (fig. 77, *B*) as the head numeral 12 and the acceptance of this Initial Series as proceeding from the same starting point as the Quirigua text just described, namely, the date **4 Ahau 8 Zotz**. With these two examples the discussion of Initial-series texts will be closed.

Texts Recording Initial Series and Secondary Series

It has been explained (see pp. 74–76) that in addition to Initial-series dating the Maya had another method of expressing their dates, known as Secondary Series, which was used when more than one date had to be recorded on the same monument. It was stated, further, that the accuracy of Secondary-series dating depended solely on the question whether or not the Secondary Series was referred to some date whose position in the Long Count was fixed either by the record of its Initial Series or in some other way. The next class of texts to be presented will be those showing the use of Secondary Series in connection with an Initial Series, by means of which the Initial-series values of the Secondary-series dates, that is, their proper positions in the Long Count, may be worked out even though they are not recorded in the text.

The first example presented will be the inscription on Lintel 21 at Yaxchilan, which is figured in plate 16.[1] As usual, when an Initial Series is recorded, the introducing glyph opens the text and this sign appears in A1, being followed by the Initial-series number itself in B1–B3. This the student will readily decipher as 9.0.19.2.4, recording apparently a very early date in Maya history, within 20 years of 9.0.0.0.0 **8 Ahau 13 Ceh**, the date arbitrarily fixed by the writer as the opening of the first great period.

Reducing this number by means of Table XIII to units of the first order [2] and deducting all the Calendar Rounds possible, 68 (see Table XVI), and applying rules 1, 2, and 3 (pp. 139, 140, and 141, respectively) to the remainder, the terminal date reached will be **2 Kan 2 Yax**. This date the student will find recorded in A4 and A7a, glyph B6b being the month-sign "indicator," or the closing glyph of the

---

[1] For the full text of this inscription see Maler, 1903: II, No. 2, pl. 56.

[2] From this point on this step will be omitted, but the student is urged to perform the calculations necessary in each case to reach the terminal dates recorded.

Supplementary Series, here shown with the coefficient 9. Compare the day sign in A4a with the sign for **Kan** in figure 16, *f*, and the month sign in A7a with the sign for **Yax** in figure 19, *q, r*. We have then recorded in A1–A4[1], and A7a the Initial-series date 9.0.19.2.4 **2 Kan 2 Yax**. At first sight it would appear that this early date indicates the time at or near which this lintel was inscribed, but a closer examination reveals a different condition. Following along through the glyphs of this text, there is reached in C3–C4 still another number in which the normal forms of the katun, tun, and uinal signs clearly appear in connection with bar and dot coefficients. The question at once arises, Has the number recorded here anything to do with the Initial Series, which precedes it at the beginning of this text?

Let us first examine this number before attempting to answer the above question. It is apparent at the outset that it differs from the Initial-series numbers previously encountered in several respects:

1. There is no introducing glyph, a fact which at once eliminates the possibility that it might be an Initial Series.

2. There is no kin period glyph, the uinal sign in C3 having two coefficients instead of one.

3. The order of the period glyphs is reversed, the highest period, here the katun, closing the series instead of commencing it as heretofore.

It has been explained (see p. 129) that in Secondary Series the order of the period glyphs is almost invariably the reverse of that shown by the period glyphs in Initial Series; and further, that the former are usually presented as ascending series, that is, with the lowest units first, and the latter invariably as descending series, with the highest units first. It has been explained also (see p. 128) that in Secondary Series the kin period glyph is usually omitted, the kin coefficient being attached to the left of the uinal sign. Since both of these points (see 2 and 3, above) are characteristic of the number in C3–C4, it is probable that a Secondary Series is recorded here, and that it expresses 5 kins, 16 uinals, 1 tun, and 15 katuns. Reversing this, and writing it according to the notation followed by most Maya students (see p. 138, footnote 1), we have as the number recorded by C3–C4, 15.1.16.5.

Reducing this number to units of the first order by means of Table XIII, we have:

$$
\begin{aligned}
\text{C4} &= 15 \times 7,200 = 108,000 \\
\text{D3} &= 1 \times 360 = 360 \\
\text{C3} &= 16 \times 20 = 320 \\
\text{C3} &= 5 \times 1 = 5 \\
\hline
& 108,685
\end{aligned}
$$

---

[1] Since the introducing glyph always accompanies an Initial Series, it has here been included as a part of it, though, as has been explained elsewhere, its function is unknown.

Since all the Calendar Rounds which this number contains, 5 (see Table XVI) may be deducted from it without affecting its value, we can further reduce it to 13,785 (108,685 − 94,900), and this will be the number used in the following calculations.

It was stated (on p. 135) in describing the direction of the count that numbers are usually counted forward from the dates next preceding them in a text, although this is not invariably true. Applying this rule to the present case, it is probable that the Secondary-series number 15.1.16.5, which we have reduced to 13,785 units of the first order, is counted *forward* from the date **2 Kan 2 Yax**, the one next preceding it in our text, a date, moreover, the Initial-series value of which is known.

Remembering that this date **2 Kan 2 Yax** is our new starting point, and that the count is forward, by applying rules 1, 2, and 3 (pp. 139, 140, and 141, respectively), to 13,785, the new terminal date reached will be **7 Muluc 17 Tzec**; and this date is recorded in C5–D5. Compare C5 with the sign for the day **Muluc** in figure 16, *m*, *n*, and D5 with the sign for the month **Tzec** in figure 19, *g*, *h*. Furthermore, by adding the Secondary-series number 15.1.16.5 to 9.0.19.2.4 (the Initial-series number which fixes the position of the date **2 Kan 2 Yax** in the Long Count), the Initial-series value of the terminal date of the Secondary Series (calculated and identified above as **7 Muluc 17 Tzec**) can also be determined as follows:

9. 0.19. 2.4	**2 Kan 2 Yax**	Initial Series
15. 1.16.5		Secondary-series number
9.16. 1. 0.9	**7 Muluc 17 Tzec**	Initial Series of the Secondary-series terminal date **7 Muluc 17 Tzec**

The student may verify the above calculations by treating 9.16.1.0.9 as a new Initial-series number, and counting it forward from **4 Ahau 8 Cumhu**, the starting point of Maya chronology. The terminal date reached will be found to be the same date as the one recorded in C5–D5, namely, **7 Muluc 17 Tzec**.

What is the meaning then of this text, which records two dates nearly 300 years apart?[1] It must be admitted at the outset that the nature of the events which occurred on these two dates, a matter probably set forth in the glyphs of unknown meaning in the text, is totally unknown. It is possible to gather from other sources, however, some little data concerning their significance. In the first place, 9.16.1.0.9 **7 Muluc 17 Tzec** is almost surely the "contemporaneous date" of this lintel, the date indicating the time at or near which it was formally dedicated or put into use. This point is established almost to a certainty by the fact that all the other dates known at Yaxchilan are very much nearer to 9.16.1.0.9 **7 Muluc 17 Tzec** in point

---

[1] The number 15.1.16.5 is equal to 108,685 days, or 297½ years.

of time than to 9.0.19.2.4 **2 Kan 2 Yax,** the Initial-series date recorded on this lintel. Indeed, while they range from 9 days [1] to 75 years from the former, the one nearest the latter is more than 200 years later. This practically proves that 9.16.1.0.9 **7 Muluc 17 Tzec** indicates the "contemporaneous time" of this lintel and that 9.0.19.2.4 **2 Kan 2 Yax** referred to some earlier event which took place perhaps even before the founding of the city. And finally, since this inscription is on a lintel, we may perhaps go a step further and hazard the conclusion that 9.16.1.0.9 **7 Muluc 17 Tzec** records the date of the erection of the structure of which this lintel is a part.

We may draw from this inscription a conclusion which will be found to hold good in almost all cases, namely, that the last date in a text almost always indicates the "contemporaneous time" of the monument upon which it appears. In the present text, for example, the Secondary-series date **7 Muluc 17 Tzec,** the Initial-series value of which was found to be 9.16.1.0.9, is in all probability its contemporaneous date, or very near thereto. It will be well to remember this important point, since it enables us to assign monuments upon which several different dates are recorded to their proper periods in the Long Count.

The next example illustrating the use of Secondary Series with an Initial Series is the inscription from Stela 1 at Piedras Negras, figured in plate 17.[2] The order of the glyphs in this text is somewhat irregular. It will be noted that there is an uneven number of glyph columns, so that one column will have to be read by itself. The natural assumption would be that A and B, C and D, and E and F are read together, leaving G, the last column, to be read by itself. This is not the case, however, for A, presenting the Initial Series, is read first, and then B C, D E, and F G, in pairs. The introducing glyph of the Initial Series appears in A1 and is followed by the Initial-series number 9.12.2.0.16 in A2–A6. The student should be perfectly familiar by this time with the processes involved in counting this number from its starting point, and should have no difficulty in determing by calculation the terminal date recorded in A7, C2, namely, **5 Cib 14 Yaxkin.**[3] Compare A7 with the sign for **Cib** in figure 16, *z*, and C2 with the sign for **Yaxkin** in figure 19, *k*, *l*. The Initial Series recorded in A1–A7, C2 is 9.12.2.0.16 **5 Cib 14 Yaxkin.**

Passing over the glyphs in B3–E1, the meanings of which are unknown, we reach in D2 E2 a number showing very clearly the tun and uinal signs, the latter having two coefficients instead of one. Moreover, the order of these period glyphs is reversed, the lower standing first in the series. As explained in connection with the pre-

---

[1] It is interesting to note in this connection that the date 9.16.1.0.0 **11 Ahau 8 Tzec,** which is within 9 days of 9.16.1.0.9 **7 Muluc 17 Tzec,** is recorded in four different inscriptions at Yaxchilan, one of which (see pl. 9, *A*) has already been figured.

[2] For the full text of this inscription see Maler, 1901: II, No. 1, pl. 12.

[3] The month-sign indicator appears in B2 with a coefficient 10.

PLATE 17

INITIAL SERIES AND SECONDARY SERIES ON
STELA 1, PIEDRAS NEGRAS

ceding text, these points are both characteristic of Secondary-series numbers, and we may conclude therefore that D2 E2 records a number of this kind. Finally, since the kin coefficient in Secondary Series usually appears on the left of the uinal sign, we may express this number in the commonly accepted notation as follows: 12.9.15. Reducing this to units of the first order, we have:

$$
\begin{aligned}
E2 &= 12 \times 360 = 4,320 \\
D2 &= 9 \times 20 = 180 \\
D2 &= 15 \times 1 = 15 \\
\hline
& 4,515
\end{aligned}
$$

Remembering that Secondary-series numbers are usually counted from the dates next preceding them in the texts, in this case **5 Cib 14 Yaxkin,** and proceeding according to rules 1, 2, and 3 (pp. 139, 140, and 141, respectively), the terminal date of the Secondary Series reached will be **9 Chuen 9 Kankin,** which is recorded in F1 G1, though unfortunately these glyphs are somewhat effaced. Moreover, since the position of **5 Cib 14 Yaxkin** in the Long Count is known, that is, its Initial-series value, it is possible to determine the Initial-series value of this new date, **9 Chuen 9 Kankin:**

$$
\begin{aligned}
&9.12.\ 2.\ 0.16 \quad \textbf{5 Cib \quad 14 Yaxkin} \\
&12.\ 9.15 \\
&9.12.14.10.11 \quad \textbf{9 Chuen 9 Kankin}
\end{aligned}
$$

But the end of this text has not been reached with the date **9 Chuen 9 Kankin** in F1 G1. Passing over F2 G2, the meanings of which are unknown, we reach in F3 an inverted **Ahau** with the coefficient 5 above it. As explained on page 72, this probably signifies 5 kins, the inversion of the glyph changing its meaning from that of a particular day sign, **Ahau,** to a general sign for the kin day period (see fig. 34, *d*). The writer recalls but one other instance in which the inverted **Ahau** stands for the kin sign—on the north side of Stela C at Quirigua.

We have then another Secondary-series number consisting of 5 kins, which is to be counted from some date, and since Secondary-series numbers are usually counted from the date next preceding them in the text, we are justified in assuming that **9 Chuen 9 Kankin** is our new starting point.

Counting 5 forward from this date, according to rules 1, 2, and 3 (pp. 139, 140, and 141, respectively), the terminal date reached will be **1 Cib 14 Kankin,** and this latter date is recorded in G3–G4. Compare G3 with the sign for **Cib** in A7 and in figure 16, *z*, and G4 with the sign for **Kankin** in figure 19, *y*, *z*. Moreover, since the Initial-series value of **9 Chuen 9 Kankin** was calculated above as 9.12.14.10.11, the Initial-series value of this new date, **1 Cib 14 Kankin**, also can be calculated from it:

$$9.12.14.10.11 \quad \textbf{9 Chuen 9 Kankin}$$
$$5$$
$$9.12.14.10.16 \quad \textbf{1 Cib} \quad \textbf{14 Kankin}$$

Passing over G5 as unknown, we reach in G6–G7 another Secondary-series number. The student will have little difficulty in identifying G6 as 2 uinals, 5 kins, and G7 as 1 katun. It will be noted that no tun sign appears in this number, which is a very unusual condition. By far the commoner practice in such cases in which 0 units of some period are involved is to record the period with a coefficient 0. However, this was not done in the present case, and since no tuns are recorded, we may conclude that none were involved, and G6–G7 may be written 1.(0).2.5. Reducing this number to units of the first order, we have:

$$G7 = 1 \times 7,200 = 7,200$$
$$(^1) \quad 0 \times \quad 360 = \quad\quad 0$$
$$G6 = 2 \times \quad 20 = \quad\quad 40$$
$$G6 = 5 \times \quad\quad 1 = \quad\quad\quad 5$$
$$\overline{\quad\quad\quad\quad\quad\quad 7,245}$$

Remembering that the starting point from which this number is counted is the date next preceding it, **1 Cib 14 Kankin,** and applying rules 1, 2, and 3 (pp. 139, 140, and 141, respectively), the terminal date reached will be **5 Imix 19 Zac**; this latter date is recorded in G8–G9. Compare G8 with the sign for **Imix** in figure 16, *a, b,* and G9 with the sign for **Zac** in figure 19, *s, t.* Moreover, since the Initial Series of **1 Cib 14 Kankin** was obtained by calculation from the date next preceding it, the Initial Series of **5 Imix 19 Zac** may be determined in the same way.

$$9.12.\ 14.10.16 \quad \textbf{1 Cib 14 Kankin}$$
$$1.\ \ 0.^1 2.\ 5$$
$$9.13.\ 14.13.\ 1 \quad \textbf{5 Imix 19 Zac}$$

With the above date closes the known part of this text, the remaining glyphs, G10–G12, being of unknown meaning.

Assembling all the glyphs deciphered above, the known part of this text reads as follows:

9.12. 2. 0.16	A1–A7, C2	**5 Cib 14 Yaxkin**
12. 9.15	D2 E2	
9.12. 14.10.11	F1 G1	**9 Chuen 9 Kankin**
5	F3	
9.12. 14.10.16	G3 G4	**1 Cib 14 Kankin**
1. 0.¹ 2. 5	G6 G7	
9.13. 14.13. 1	G8 G9	**5 Imix 19 Zac**

---

¹ Not expressed.

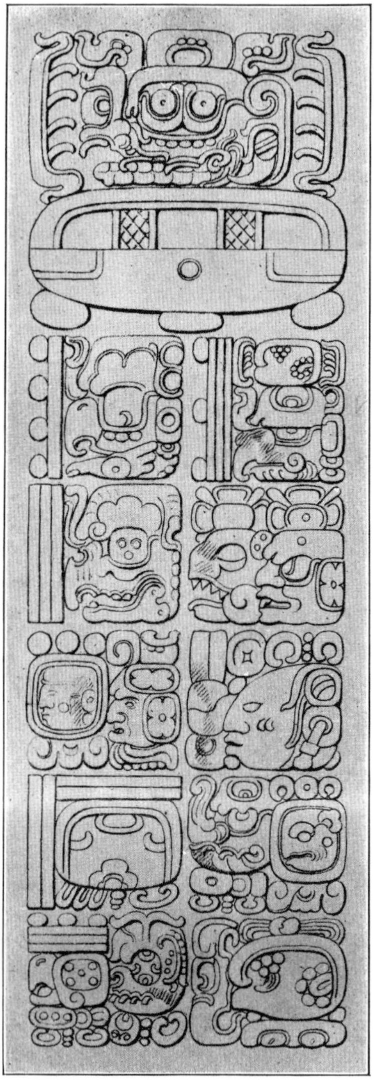

PLATE 18

INITIAL SERIES (*A*) AND SECONDARY SERIES (*B*) ON STELA K, QUIRIGUA

We have recorded here four different dates, of which the last, 9.13.14.13.1 **5 Imix 19 Zac,** probably represents the actual date, or very near thereto, of this monument.[1] The period covered between the first and last of these dates is about 32 years, within the range of a single lifetime or, indeed, of the tenure of some important office by a single individual.   The unknown glyphs again probably set forth the nature of the. events which occurred on the dates recorded.

In the two preceding texts the Secondary Series given are regular in every way.   Not only was the count forward each time, but it also started in every case from the date immediately preceding the number counted.   This regularity, however, is far from universal in Secondary-series texts, and the following examples comprise some of the more common departures from the usual practice.

In plate 18 is figured the Initial Series from Stela K at Quirigua.[2] The text opens on the north side of this monument (see pl. 18, *A*) with the introducing glyph in A1–B2.   This is followed by the Initial-series number 9.18.15.0.0 in A3–B4, which leads to the terminal date **3 Ahau 3 Yax.**   The day part of this date the student will find recorded in its regular position, A5a.   Passing over A5b and B5, the meanings of which are unknown, we reach in A6 a Secondary-series number composed very clearly of 10 uinals and 10 kins (10.10), which reduces to the following number of units of the first order:

$$A6 = 10 \times 20 = 200$$
$$A6 = 10 \times 1 = 10$$
$$\overline{\ 210}$$

The first assumption is that this number is counted forward from the terminal date of the Initial Series, **3 Ahau 3 Yax,** and performing the operations indicated in rules 1, 2, and 3 (pp. 139, 140, and 141, respectively) the terminal date reached will be **5 Oc 8 Uo.**   Now, although the day sign in B6b is clearly **Oc** (see fig. 16, *o–q*), its coefficient is very clearly 1, not 5, and, moreover, the month in A7a is unmistakably **18 Kayab** (see fig. 19, *d'–f'*).   Here then instead of finding the date determined by calculation, **5 Oc 8 Uo,** the date recorded is **1 Oc 18 Kayab,** and consequently there is some departure from the practices heretofore encountered.

Since the association of the number 10.10 is so close with (1) the terminal date of the Initial Series, **3 Ahau 3 Yax,** and (2) the date **1 Oc 18 Kayab** almost immediately following it, it would almost seem as though these two dates must be the starting point and terminal date, respectively, of this number.   If the count is forward, we have just proved that this can not be the case; so let us next count the

---

[1] The writer has recently established the date of this monument as 9.13.15.0.0 **13 Ahau 18 Pax,** or 99 days later than the above date.

[2] For the full text of this inscription, see Maudslay, 1889–1902: II, pls. 47–49.

number backward and see whether we can reach the date recorded in B6b–A7a (**1 Oc 18 Kayab**) in this way.

Counting 210 *backward* from **3 Ahau 3 Yax**, according to rules 1, 2, and 3 (pp. 139, 140, and 141, respectively), the terminal date reached will be **1 Oc 18 Kayab,** as recorded in B6b–A7. In other words, the Secondary Series in this text is counted backward from the Initial Series, and therefore precedes it in point of time. This will appear from the Initial-series value of **1 Oc 18 Kayab,** which may be determined by calculation:

$$9.18.15.\ 0.\ 0 \quad \textbf{3 Ahau 3 Yax}$$
$$10.10$$
$$9.18.14.\ 7.10 \quad \textbf{1 Oc 18 Kayab}$$

This text closes on the south side of the monument in a very unusual manner (see pl. 18, *B*). In B3a appears the month-sign indicator, here recorded as a head variant with a coefficient 10, and following immediately in B3b a Secondary-series number composed of 0 uinals and 0 kins, or, in other words, nothing. It is obvious that in counting this number 0.0, or nothing, either backward or forward from the date next preceding it in the text, **1 Oc 18 Kayab** in B6b–A7a on the north side of the stela, the same date **1 Oc 18 Kayab** will remain. But this date is not repeated in A4, where the terminal date of this Secondary Series, 0.0, seems to be recorded. However, if we count 0.0 from the terminal date of the Initial Series, **3 Ahau 3 Yax**, we reach the date recorded in A4, **3 Ahau 3 Yax,**[1] and this whole text so far as deciphered will read:

$$9.18.15.\ 0.\ 0 \quad \textbf{3 Ahau 3 Yax}$$
$$10.10 \quad \text{backward}$$
$$9.18.14.\ 7.10 \quad \textbf{1 Oc 18 Kayab}$$
$$0.\ 0 \quad \text{forward from Initial Series}$$
$$9.18.15.\ 0.\ 0 \quad \textbf{3 Ahau 3 Yax}$$

The reason for recording a Secondary-series number equal to zero, the writer believes, was because the first Secondary-series date **1 Oc 18 Kayab** precedes the Initial-series date, which in this case marks the time at which this monument was erected. Hence, in order to have the closing date on the monument record the contemporaneous time of the monument, it was necessary to repeat the Initial-series date; this was accomplished by adding to it a Secondary-series date denoting zero. Stela K is the next to the latest hotun-marker at Quirigua following immediately Stela I, the Initial series of which marks the hotun ending 9.18.10.0.0 **10 Ahau 8 Zac** (see pl. 6, *C*).

Mr. Bowditch (1910: p. 208) has advanced a very plausible explanation to account for the presence of the date 9.18.14.7.10 **1 Oc 18 Kayab**

---

[1] Although the details of the day and month signs are somewhat effaced, the coefficient in each case is 3, agreeing with the coefficients in the Initial-series terminal date, and the outline of the month glyph suggests that it is probably **Yax.** See fig. 19, *q, r*.

on this monument. He shows that at the time when Stela K was erected, namely, 9.18.15.0.0 **3 Ahau 3 Yax,** the official calendar had outrun the seasons by just 210 days, or exactly the number of days recorded in A6, plate 18, *A* (north side); and further, that instead of being the day **3 Yax,** which occurred at Quirigua about the beginning of the dry season,[1] in reality the season was 210 days behind, or at **18 Kayab,** about the beginning of the rainy season. This very great discrepancy between calendar and season could not have escaped the notice of the priests, and the 210 days recorded in A6 may well represent the days actually needed on the date 9.18.15.0.0 **3 Ahau 3 Yax** to bring the calendar into harmony with the current season. If this be true, then the date 9.18.14.7.0 **1 Oc 18 Kayab** represented the day indicated by the sun when the calendar showed that the 3d hotun in Katun 18 of Cycle 9 had been completed. Mr. Bowditch suggests the following free interpretation of this passage: "The sun has just set at its northern point[2] and we are counting the day **3 Yax**—210 days from **18 Kayab**—which is the true date in the calendar according to our traditions and records for the sun to set at this point on his course." As stated above, the writer believes this to be the true explanation of the record of 210 days on this monument.

In figures 78 and 79 are illustrated the Initial Series and Secondary Series from Stela J at Quirigua.[3] For lack of space the introducing glyph in this text has been omitted; it occupies the position of six glyph-blocks, however, A1–B3, after which the Initial-series number 9.16.5.0.0 follows in A4–B8. This leads to the terminal date **8 Ahau 8 Zotz,** which is recorded in A9, B9, B13, the glyph in A13 being the month-sign indicator here shown with the coefficient 9. Compare B9 with the second variant for **Ahau** in figure 16 *h'*, *i'*, and B13 with the sign for **Zotz** in figure 19, *e, f.* The Initial-

FIG. 78. The Initial Series on Stela J, Quirigua.

---

[1] Since the Maya New Year's day, **0 Pop,** always fell on the 16th of July, the day **3 Yax** always fell on Jan. 15th, at the commencement of the dry season.

[2] Since **0 Pop** fell on July 16th (Old Style), **18 Kayab** fell on June 19th, which is very near the summer solstice, that is, the seeming northern limit of the sun, and roughly coincident with the beginning of the rainy season at Quirigua.

[3] For the full text of this inscription, see Maudslay, 1889–1902: II, pl. 46.

series part of this text therefore in A1–B9, B13, is perfectly regular and reads as follows: 9.16.5.0.0 **8 Ahau 8 Zotz.** The Secondary Series, however, are unusual and differ in several respects from the ones heretofore presented.

The first Secondary Series inscribed on this monument (see fig. 79, *A*) is at B1–B2. This series the student should readily decipher as 3 kins, 13 uinals, 11 tuns, and 0 katuns, which we may write 0.11.13.3. This number presents one feature, which, so far as the writer knows, is unique in the whole range of Maya texts. The highest order of units actually involved in this number is the tun, but for some unknown reason the ancient scribe saw fit to add the katun sign also, B2, which, how-

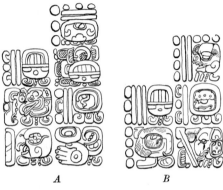

ever, he proceeded to nullify at once by attaching to it the coefficient 0. For in so far as the numerical value is concerned, 11.13.3 and 0.11.13.3 are equal. The next peculiarity is that the date which follows this number in B3–A4 is not its terminal date, as we have every reason to expect, but, on the contrary, its starting point. In other words, in this

A   *B*

FIG. 79. The Secondary Series on Stela J, Quirigua.

Secondary Series the starting point follows instead of precedes the number counted from it. This date is very clearly **12 Caban 5 Kayab**; compare B3 with the sign for **Caban** in figure 16, *a′*, *b′*, and A4 with the sign for **Kayab** in figure 19, *d′–f′*. So far as Stela J is concerned there is no record of the position which this date occupied in the Long Count; that is, there are no data by means of which its Initial Series may be calculated. Elsewhere at Quirigua, however, this date is recorded twice as an Initial Series and in each place it has the same value, 9.14.13.4.17. We may safely conclude, therefore, that the date in A3–B4 is 9.14.13.4.17 **12 Caban 5 Kayab**, and use it in our calculations as such. Reducing 0.11.13.3 to units of the first order, we have:

$$
\begin{aligned}
B2 &= 0 \times 7,200 = 0 \\
A2 &= 11 \times 360 = 3,960 \\
B1 &= 13 \times 20 = 260 \\
B1 &= 3 \times 1 = 3 \\
\hline
& \qquad\qquad\quad 4,223
\end{aligned}
$$

Applying rules 1, 2, and 3 (pp. 139, 140, and 141, respectively) to this number, the terminal date reached will be **10 Ahau 8 Chen,** which is nowhere recorded in the text (see fig. 79, *A*).

The Initial Series corresponding to this date, however, may be calculated from the Initial Series which we have assigned to the date **12 Caban 5 Kayab:**

$$9.14.13.\ 4.17 \quad \textbf{12 Caban 5 Kayab}$$
$$0.11.13.\ 3$$
$$9.15.\ 5.\ 0.\ 0 \quad \textbf{10 Ahau \ 8 Chen}$$

Although the date 9.15.5.0.0 **10 Ahau 8 Chen** is not actually recorded at Quirigua, it is reached on another monument by calculation just as here. It has a peculiar fitness here on Stela J in that it is just one katun earlier than the Initial Series on this monument (see fig. 78), 9.16.5.0.0 **8 Ahau 8 Zotz.**

The other Secondary Series on this monument (see fig. 79, *B*) appears at B1–A2, and records 18 tuns, 3 uinals, and 14 kins, which we may write thus: 18.3.14. As in the preceding case, the date following this number in B2–A3 is its starting point, not its terminal date, a very unusual feature, as has been explained. This date is **6 Cimi 4 Tzec**—compare B2 with the sign for **Cimi** in figure 16, *h*, *i*, and A3 with the sign for **Tzec** in figure 19, *g*, *h*—and as far as Stela J is concerned it is not fixed in the Long Count. However, elsewhere at Quirigua this date is recorded in a Secondary Series, which is referred back to an Initial Series, and from this passage its corresponding Initial Series is found to be 9.15.6.14.6 **6 Cimi 4 Tzec.** Reducing the number recorded in B1–A2, 18.3.14, to units of the first order, we have:

$$A2 = 18 \times 360 = 6,480$$
$$B2 = \ 3 \times \ 20 = \ \ \ 60$$
$$B2 = 14 \times \ \ 1 = \ \ \ \ 14$$
$$\overline{6,554}$$

Applying rules 1, 2, and 3 (pp. 139, 140, and 141, respectively) to the number, the terminal date reached will be **8 Ahau 8 Zotz,** which does not appear in figure 79, *B*. The Initial Series corresponding to this date may be calculated as follows:

$$9.15.\ 6.14.\ 6 \quad \textbf{6 Cimi 4 Tzec}$$
$$18.\ 3.14$$
$$9.16.\ 5.\ 0.\ 0 \quad \textbf{8 Ahau 8 Zotz}$$

But this was the Initial Series recorded on the reverse of this monument, consequently the Secondary-series dates, both of which have pre-

ceded the Initial-series date in point of time, bring this count up to
the contemporaneous time of this monument, which was 9.16.5.0.0
8 Ahau 8 Zotz. In view of the fact that the Secondary Series on
Stela J are both earlier than the Initial Series, the chronological
sequence of the several dates is better preserved by regarding the
Initial Series as being at the close of the inscription instead of at the
beginning, thus:

9.14.13. 4.17	**12 Caban 5 Kayab**	Figure 79, *A*, B3–A4
0.11.13. 3		B1–B2
[9.15. 5. 0. 0]	[**10 Ahau 8 Chen**] [1]	
[1.14. 6] [2]		
9.15. 6.14. 6	**6 Cimi 4 Tzec**	Figure 79, *B*, B2–A3
18. 3.14		B1–A2
9.16. 5. 0. 0	**8 Ahau 8 Zotz**	Figure 78, A1–B9, B13

By the above arrangement all the dates present in the text lead up
to 9.16.5.0.0 **8 Ahau 8 Zotz** as the most important date, because it
alone records the particular hotun-ending which Stela J marks. The
importance of this date over the others is further emphasized by the
fact that it alone appears as an Initial Series.

The text of Stela J illustrates two points in connection with Secondary Series which the student will do well to bear in mind: (1)
The starting points of Secondary-series numbers do not always precede the numbers counted from them, and (2) the terminal dates and
starting points are not always both recorded.

The former point will be illustrated in the following example:

In plate 19, *A*, is figured the Initial Series from the west side of Stela
F at Quirigua.[3] The introducing glyph appears in A1–B2 and is
followed by the Initial-series number in A3–A5. This is expressed
by head variants and reads as follows: 9.14.13.4.17. The terminal
date reached by this number is **12 Caban 5 Kayab,** which is recorded
in B5–A6. The student will readily identify the numerals as above
by comparing them with the forms in figures 51–53, and the day and
month signs by comparing them with figures 16, *a'*, *b'*, and 19, *d'–f'*,
respectively. The Initial Series therefore reads 9.14.13.4.17 **12 Caban
5 Kayab.**[4]

---

[1] Bracketed dates are those which are not actually recorded but which are reached by numbers appearing
in the text.

[2] Although not recorded, the number 1.14.6 is the distance from the date 9.15.5.0.0 reached by the Secondary Series on one side to the starting point of the Secondary Series on the other side, that is, 9.15.6.14.6
6 Cimi 4 Tzec.

[3] For the full text of this inscription see Maudslay, 1889–1902: II, pls. 37, 39, 40. For convenience in
figuring, the lower parts of columns A and B are shown in *B* instead of below the upper part. The
numeration of the glyph-blocks, however, follows the arrangement in the original.

[4] This is one of the two Initial Series which justified the assumptions made in the previous text that
the date **12 Caban 5 Kayab,** which was recorded there, had the Initial-series value 9.14.13.4.17, as here.

PLATE 19

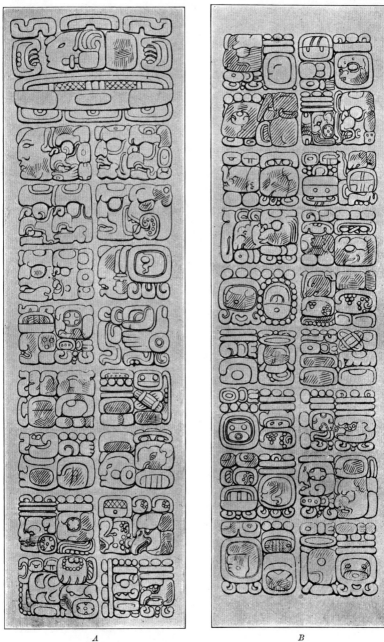

A *B*

INITIAL SERIES (*A*) AND SECONDARY SERIES (*B*) ON STELA F (WEST SIDE), QUIRIGUA

Passing over B6–A10, the meanings of which are unknown, we reach in B10 the Secondary-series number 13.9.9. Reducing this to units of the first order, we have:

$$
\begin{aligned}
\text{B6b} &= 13 \times 360 = 4,680 \\
\text{B6a} &= 9 \times 20 = 180 \\
\text{B6a} &= 9 \times 1 = 9 \\
\hline
& \quad\quad\quad 4,869
\end{aligned}
$$

Assuming that our starting point is the date next preceding this number in the text, that is, the Initial-series terminal date **12 Caban 5 Kayab** in B5–A6, and applying rules 1, 2, and 3 (pp. 139, 140, and 141, respectively), the terminal day reached will be **6 Cimi 4 Tzec**. This date the student will find recorded in plate 19, *B*, B11b–A12a. Compare B11b with the sign for **Cimi** in figure 16, *h*, *i*, and A12a with the sign for **Tzec** in figure 19, *g*, *h*. Moreover, since the Initial-series value of the starting point **12 Caban 5 Kayab** is known, the Initial-series value of the terminal date **6 Cimi 4 Tzec** may be calculated from it:

$$
\begin{aligned}
9.14.13.\ 4.17 &\quad \textbf{12 Caban 5 Kayab} \\
13.\ 9.\ 9 & \\
\hline
9.15.\ 6.14.\ 6 &\quad \textbf{6 Cimi 4 Tzec}\ [1]
\end{aligned}
$$

In A15 is recorded the date **3 Ahau 3 Mol** (compare A15a with fig. 16, *h'*, *i'*, and A15b with fig. 19, *m*, *n*) and in A17 the date **4 Ahau 13 Yax** (compare A17a with fig. 16, *e'–g'* and A17b with fig. 19, *q*, *r*). This latter date, **4 Ahau 13 Yax**, is recorded elsewhere at Quirigua in a Secondary Series attached to an Initial Series, where it has the Initial-series value 9.15.0.0.0. This value we may assume, therefore, belongs to it in the present case, giving us the full date 9.15.0.0.0 **4 Ahau 13 Yax**. For the present let us pass over the first of these two dates, namely, **3 Ahau 3 Mol**, the Initial Series of which as well as the reason for its record here will better appear later.

In B17–A18a is recorded another Secondary-series number composed of 3 kins, 13 uinals, 16 tuns, and 1 katun, which we may write thus: 1.16.13.3. The student will note that the katun coefficient in A18a is expressed by an unusual form, the thumb. As explained on page 103, this has a numerical value of 1. Again, our text presents another irregular feature. Instead of being counted either forward or backward from the date next preceding it in the text; that is, **4 Ahau 13 Yax** in A17, this number is counted from the date following it in the text, like the two Secondary-series numbers in Stela J, just discussed. This starting date recorded in A18b B18a is **12 Caban 5 Kayab**, which, as we have seen, is also the date recorded by the Initial Series in plate 19, *A*, A1–A6. We are perfectly justified in

[1] This is the text in which the Initial-series value 9.15.6.14.6 was found attached to the date **6 Cimi 4 Tzec.**

assuming, therefore, that the **12 Caban 5 Kayab** in A18b–B18a had the same Initial-series value as the **12 Caban 5 Kayab** in plate 19, *A*, B5–A6, namely, 9.14.13.4.17. Reducing the number in B17–A18a, namely, 1.16.13.3, to units of the first order, we have:

$$A18a = \ 1 \times 7,200 = \ 7,200$$
$$B17b = 16 \times \ \ \ 360 = \ 5,760$$
$$B17a = 13 \times \ \ \ \ 20 = \ \ \ \ 260$$
$$B17a = \ 3 \times \ \ \ \ \ \ 1 = \ \ \ \ \ \ \ 3$$
$$\overline{}$$
$$13,223$$

Remembering that this number is to be counted forward from the date **12 Caban 5 Kayab,** and applying rules 1, 2, and 3 (pp. 139, 140, and 141, respectively), the terminal date reached will be **1 Ahau 3 Zip,** which is recorded in A19. Compare the coefficient of the day sign in A19a with the coefficient of the katun sign in A18a, and the day sign itself with the profile variant for **Ahau** in figure 16, *h′*, *i′*. For the month sign, compare A19b with figure 19, *d*. But since the Initial-series value of the starting point is known, we may calculate from it the Initial-series value of the new terminal date:

$$9.14.13.\ 4.17 \quad \textbf{12 Caban 5 Kayab}$$
$$1.16.13.\ 3$$
$$9.16.10.\ 0.\ 0 \quad \textbf{1 Ahau 3 Zip}$$

Passing over to the east side of this monument, the student will find recorded there the continuation of this inscription (see pl. 20).[1] This side, like the other, opens with an introducing glyph A1–B2, which is followed by an Initial Series in A3–A5. Although this number is expressed by head variants, the forms are all familiar, and the student will have little difficulty in reading it as 9.16.10.0.0. The terminal date which this number reaches is recorded in B5–B8; that is, **1**[2] **Ahau 3 Zip,** the "month indicator" appearing as a head variant in A8 with the head-variant coefficient 10. But this date is identical with the date determined by calculation and actually recorded at the close of the inscription on the other side of this monument, and since no later date is recorded elsewhere in this text, we may conclude that 9.16.10.0.0 **1 Ahau 3 Zip** represents the contemporaneous time of Stela F, and hence that it was a regular hotun-marker. Here again, as in the case of Stela J at Quirigua, the importance of the "contemporaneous date" is emphasized not only by the fact that all the other dates lead up to it, but also by the fact that it is expressed as an Initial Series.

---

[1] For the full text of this inscription see Maudslay, 1889–1902: II, pls. 38, 40.

[2] The frontlet seems to be composed of but one element, indicating for this head the value 8 instead of 1. However, as the calculations point to 1, it is probable there was originally another element to the frontlet.

PLATE 20

INITIAL SERIES ON STELA F (EAST SIDE), QUIRIGUA

We have explained all the dates figured except **3 Ahau 3 Mol** in plate 19, *B*, A15, the discussion of which was deferred until after the rest of the inscription had been considered.   It will be remembered in connection with Stela J (figs. 78, 79) that one of the dates reached in the course of the calculations was just 1 katun earlier than the date recorded by the Initial Series on the same monument.   Now, one of the Initial-series values corresponding to the date **3 Ahau 3 Mol** here under discussion is 9.15.10.0.0, exactly 1 katun earlier than the Initial-series date on Stela F.   In other words, if we give to the date **3 Ahau 3 Mol** in A15 the value 9.15.10.0.0, the cases are exactly parallel.   While it is impossible to prove that this particular Initial Series was the one which the ancient scribes had in mind when they recorded this date **3 Ahau 3 Mol**,

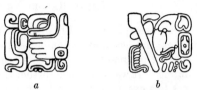

a   *b*

FIG. 80.   Glyphs which may disclose the nature of the events that happened at Quirigua on the dates: *a*, 9. 14. 13. 4. 17 **12 Caban 5 Kayab**; *b*, 9. 15. 6. 14. 6 **6 Cimi 4 Tzec**.

the writer believes that the coincidence and parallel here presented are sufficient to warrant the assumption that this is the case.   The whole text reads as follows:

9.14.13. 4.17	**12 Caban 5 Kayab**	Plate 19, *A*, A1–A6
13. 9. 9		Plate 19, *A*, A10
9.15. 6.14. 6	**6 Cimi 4 Tzec**	Plate 19, *B*, B11b–A12a
[9.15.10. 0. 0]	**3 Ahau 3 Mol**	Plate 19, *B*, A15
[9.15. 0. 0. 0]	**4 Ahau 13 Yax**	Plate 19, *B*, A17
9.14.13. 4.17	**12 Caban 5 Kayab**	Plate 19, *B*, A18b B18a
1.16.13. 3		Plate 19, *B*, B17 A18a
9.16.10. 0. 0	**1 Ahau 3 Zip**	Plate 19, *B*, A19

(repeated as Initial Series on east side of monument)

9.16.10. 0. 0	**1 Ahau 3 Zip**	Plate 20, A1–B5–B8

The student will note the close similarity between this inscription and that on Stela J (figured in figs. 78 and 79), a summary of which appears on page 239.   Both commence with the same date, 9.14.13.4.17 **12 Caban 5 Kayab**; both show the date 9.15.6.14.6 **6 Cimi 4 Tzec**; both have dates which are just 1 katun in advance of the hotuns which they mark; and finally, both are hotun-markers, Stela J preceding Stela F by just 1 hotun.   The date from which both proceed, 9.14.13.4.17 **12 Caban 5 Kayab**, is an important one at Quirigua, being the earliest date there.   It appears on four monuments, namely, Stelæ J, F, and E, and Zoömorph G.   Although the writer has not been able to prove the point, he is of the opinion that the glyph shown in figure 80, *a*, tells the meaning of the event which happened on this date, which is, moreover, the earliest date at Quirigua which it is possible to regard as being contemporaneous.   Hence, it is not improbable that it might refer to the founding of the city or some similar event, though this is of course a matter of speculation.   The fact, however, that 9.14.13.4.17 **12 Caban 5 Kayab** is the earliest date on four different hotun-markers shows that it was of supreme importance in the history of Quirigua.   This concludes the discussion of texts showing the use of Secondary Series with Initial Series.

Texts Recording Period Endings

It was explained in Chapter III (p. 77) that in addition to Initial-series dating and Secondary-series dating, the Maya used still another method in fixing events, which was designated Period-ending dating.   It was explained further that, although Period-ending dating was less exact than the other two methods, it served equally well for all practical purposes, since dates fixed by it could not recur until after a lapse of more than 18,000 years, a considerably longer period than that covered by the recorded history of mankind.   Finally, the student will recall that the katun was said to be the period most commonly used in this method of dating.

The reason for this is near at hand.   Practically all of the great southern cities rose, flourished, and fell within the period called Cycle 9 of Maya chronology.   There could have been no doubt throughout the southern area which particular cycle was meant when the "current cycle" was spoken of.   After the date 9.0.0.0.0 **8 Ahau 13 Chen** had ushered in a new cycle there could be no change in the cycle coefficient until after a lapse of very nearly 400 (394.250 +) years.   Consequently, after Cycle 9 had commenced many succeeding generations of men knew no other, and in time the term "current cycle" came to mean as much on a monument as "Cycle 9."   Indeed, in Period-ending dating the Cycle 9 was taken for granted and scarcely ever recorded.   The same practice obtains very generally to-day in regard to writing the current century, such expressions as July 4, '12, December 25, '13, being frequently seen in place of the full forms July 4, 1912, A. D., December 25, 1913, A. D.; or again, even more briefly, 7/4/12 and 12/25/13 to express the same dates, respectively.   The desire for brevity, as has been explained, probably gave rise to Period-ending dating in the first place, and in this method the cycle was the first period to be eliminated as superfluous for all practical purposes.   No one could have forgotten the number of the current cycle.

When we come to the next lower period, however, the katun, we find a different state of affairs.   The numbers belonging to this period were changing every 20 (exactly, 19.71 +) years; that is, three or four times in the lifetime of many individuals; hence, there was

PLATE 21

A. STELA 2, COPAN

B. TEMPLE OF THE FOLIATED
CROSS, PALENQUE

C. STELA 23, NARANJO

D. STELA 16, TIKAL

E. STELA 4, COPAN

G. STELA 5, TIKAL

F. TEMPLE OF THE INSCRIPTIONS, PALENQUE

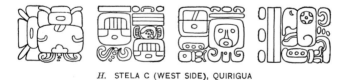

H. STELA C (WEST SIDE), QUIRIGUA

EXAMPLES OF PERIOD-ENDING DATES IN CYCLE 9

plenty of opportunity for confusion about the number of the katun in which a particular event occurred. Consequently, in order to insure accuracy the katun is almost always the unit used in Period-ending dating.

In plate 21 are figured a number of Period-ending dates, the glyphs of which have been ranged in horizontal lines, and are numbered from left to right for convenience in reference. The true positions of these glyphs in the texts from which they have been taken are given in the footnotes in each case. In plate 21, *A*, is figured a Period-ending date from Stela 2 at Copan.[1] The date **12 Ahau 8 Ceh** appears very clearly in glyphs 1 and 2. Compare the month sign with figure 19, *u, v*. There follows in 3 a glyph the upper part of which probably represents the "ending sign" of this date. By comparing this form with the ending signs in figure 37 its resemblance to figure 37, *o*, will be evident. Indeed, figure 37, *o*, has precisely the same lower element as glyph 3. In glyph 4 follows the particular katun, 11, whose end fell on the date recorded in glyphs 1 and 2. The student can readily prove this for himself by reducing the Period-ending date here recorded to its corresponding Initial Series and counting the resulting number forward from the common starting point, **4 Ahau 8 Cumhu**, as follows: Since the cycle glyph is not expressed, we may fill this omission as the Maya themselves filled it, by supplying Cycle 9. Moreover, since the *end* of a katun is recorded here, it is clear that all the lower periods—the tuns, uinals, and kins—will have to appear with the coefficient 0, as they are all brought to their respective ends with the ending of any katun. Therefore we may write the Initial-series number corresponding to the end of Katun 11, as 9.11.0.0.0. Treating this number as an Initial Series, that is, first reducing it to units of the first order, then deducting from it all the Calendar Rounds possible, and finally applying rules 1, 2, and 3 (pp. 139, 140, and 141, respectively) to the remainder, the student will find that the terminal date reached will be the same as the date recorded in glyphs 1 and 2, namely, **12 Ahau 8 Ceh**. In other words, the Katun 11, which ended on the date **12 Ahau 8 Ceh**, was 9.11.0.0.0 **12 Ahau 8 Ceh**, and both indicate exactly the same position in the Long Count. The next example (pl. 21, *B*) is taken from the tablet in the Temple of the Foliated Cross at Palenque.[2] In glyph 1 appears the date **8 Ahau 8 Uo** (compare the month form with fig. 19, *b, c*) and in glyph 3 the "ending" of Katun 13. The ending sign here is the variant shown in figure 37, *a–h*, and it occurs just above the coefficient 13. These two glyphs therefore record the fact that Katun 13 ended with the day **8 Ahau 8 Uo**. The student may again test the accuracy of the record by changing this Period-ending date to its

---

[1] See Maudslay, 1889–1902: I, pl. 102, west side, glyphs A5b–A7a.
[2] See ibid.: IV, pl. 81, glyphs N15 O15.

corresponding Initial-series number, 9.13.0.0.0, and performing the various operations indicated in such cases. The resulting Initial-series terminal date will be the same as the date recorded in glyphs 1 and 2, **8 Ahau 8 Uo.**

In plate 21, *C*, is figured a Period-ending date taken from Stela 23 at Naranjo.[1] The date **6 Ahau 13 Muan** appears very clearly in glyphs 1 and 2 (compare the month form with fig. 19, *a′*, *b′*). Glyph 3 is the ending sign, here showing three common "ending elements," (1) the clasped hand; (2) the element with the curl infix; (3) the tassel-like postfix. Compare this form with the ending signs in figure 37, *l–q*, and with the zero signs in figure 54. In glyph 4 is recorded the particular katun, 14, which came to its end on the date recorded in 1 and 2. The element prefixed to the Katun 14 in glyph 4 is also an ending sign, though it always occurs as a prefix or superfix attached to the sign of the period whose close is recorded. Examples illustrating its use are shown in figure 37, *a–h*, with which the ending element in glyph 4 should be compared. The glyphs 1 to 4 in plate 21, *C*, therefore record that Katun 14 came to an end on the date **6 Ahau 13 Muan.** As we have seen above, this could be shown to correspond with the Initial Series 9.14.0.0.0 **6 Ahau 13 Muan.**

This same date, **6 Ahau 13 Muan** ending Katun 14, is also recorded on Stela 16 at Tikal (see pl. 21, *D*).[2] The date itself appears in glyphs 1 and 2 and is followed in 3 by a sign which is almost exactly like the ending sign in glyph 3 just discussed (see pl. 21, *C*). The subfixes are identical in both cases, and it is possible to distinguish the lines of the hand element in the weathered upper part of the glyph in 3. Compare glyph 3 with the ending signs in figure 37, *l–q*, and with the zero signs in figure 54. As in the preceding example, glyph 4 shows the particular katun whose end is recorded here—Katun 14. The period glyph itself appears as a head variant to which is prefixed the same ending prefix or superfix shown with the period glyph in the preceding example. See also figure 37, *a–h*. As above stated, the Initial Series corresponding to this date is 9.14.0.0.0 **6 Ahau 13 Muan.**

One more example will suffice to illustrate the use of katun Period-ending dates. In plate 21, *E*, is figured a Period-ending date from Stela 4 at Copan.[3] In glyphs 1 and 2 appears the date **4 Ahau 13 Yax** (compare the month in glyph 2 with fig. 19, *q*, *r*), which is followed by the ending sign in 3. This is composed of the hand, a very common "ending" element (see fig. 37, *j*, *k*) with a grotesque head superfix, also another "ending sign" (see *i*, *r*, *u*, *v* of the plate just named). In glyph 4 follows the particular katun (Katun 15) whose

---

[1] See Maler, 1908 b: IV, No. 2, pl. 38, east side, glyphs A17–B18.

[2] See ibid., 1911: V, pl. 26, glyphs A1–A4.

[3] See Maudslay, 1889–1902: I, pl. 104, glyphs A7, B7.

end is here recorded. This date corresponds to the Initial Series
9.15.0.0.0 **4 Ahau 13 Yax.**

Cases where tun endings are recorded are exceedingly rare.
The bare statement that a certain tun, as Tun 10, for example, had
come to its end left much to be desired in the way of accuracy, since
there was a Tun 10 in every katun, and consequently any given tun
recurred after an interval of 20 years; in other words, there were
three or four different Tun 10's to be distinguished from one another
in the average lifetime. Indeed, to keep them apart at all it was
necessary either to add the particular katun in which each fell or to
add the date on which each closed. The former was a step away
from the brevity which probably prompted the use of Period-ending
dating in the first place, and the latter imposed too great a task on
the memory, that is, keeping in mind the 60 or 70 various tun endings which the average lifetime included. For these reasons tun-
ending dates occur but rarely, only when there was little or no doubt
concerning the particular katun in which they fell.

In plate 21, *F*, is figured a tun-ending date from the tablet in the
Temple of the Inscription at Palenque.[1] In glyph 1 appears an ending
sign showing the hand element and the grotesque flattened head (for
the latter see fig. 37, *i*, *r*, *u*, *v*), both common ending signs. The
remaining element, another grotesque head with a flaring postfix, is
an unusual variant of the tun head found only at Palenque (see fig.
29, *h*). The presence of the tun sign with these two ending signs
indicates probably that some tun ending follows. Glyphs 2 and 3
record the date **5 Ahau 18 Tzec**, and glyph 4 records Tun 13. We
have here then the record of a Tun 13, which ended on the date
5 Ahau 18 Tzec. But which of the many Tun 13s in the Long Count
was the one that ended on this particular date? To begin with, we are
perfectly justified in assuming that this particular tun occurred somewhere in Cycle 9, but this assumption does not aid us greatly, since
there were twenty different Tun 13s in Cycle 9, one for each of the
twenty katuns. However, in the full text of the inscription from
which this example is taken, **5 Ahau 3 Chen** is the date next preceding,
and although the fact is not recorded, this latter date closed Katun 8
of Cycle 9. Moreover, shortly after the tun-ending date here under
discussion, the date "**3 Ahau 3 Zotz**, end of Katun 9," is recorded. It
seems likely, therefore, that this particular Tun 13, which ended on
the date **5 Ahau 18 Tzec**, was 9.8.13.0.0 of the Long Count, after
9.8.0.0.0 but before 9.9.0.0.0. Reducing this number to units of the
first order, and applying the several rules given for solving Initial
Series, the terminal date of 9.8.13.0.0 will be found to agree with the
terminal date recorded in glyphs 2 and 3, namely, **5 Ahau 18 Tzec**,

---

[1] See Maudslay, 1889–1902: IV, pl. 60, glyphs M1–N2.

and this tun ending corresponded, therefore, to the Initial Series 9.8.13.0.0 **5 Ahau 18 Tzec.**

Another tun-ending date from Stela 5 at Tikal is figured in plate 21, G.[1] In glyphs 1 and 2 the date **4 Ahau 8 Yaxkin** appears, the month sign being represented as a head variant, which has the essential elements of the sign for **Yaxkin** (see fig. 19, k, l). Following this in glyph 3 is Tun 13, to which is prefixed the same ending-sign variant as the prefixial or superfixial elements in figure 37, i, r, u, v. We have recorded here then "Tun 13 ending on **4 Ahau 8 Yaxkin,**" though there seems to be no mention elsewhere in this inscription of the number of the katun in which this particular tun fell. By referring to Great Cycle 54 of Goodman's Tables (Goodman, 1897), however, it appears that Tun 13 of Katun 15 of Cycle 9 closed with this date **4 Ahau 8 Yaxkin,** and we may assume, therefore, that this is the correct position in the Long Count of the tun-ending date here recorded. This date corresponds to the Initial Series 9.15.13.0.0 **4 Ahau 8 Yaxkin.**

There is a very unusual Period-ending date on the west side of Stela C at Quirigua[2] (see pl. 21, H). In glyphs 1 and 2 appears the number 0 kins, 0 uinals, 5 tuns, and 17 katuns, which we may write 17.5.0.0; and following this in glyphs 3 and 4 is the date **6 Ahau 13 Kayab.** At first sight this would appear to be a Secondary Series, the number 17.5.0.0 being counted forward from some preceding date to reach the date **6 Ahau 13 Kayab** recorded just after it. The next date preceding this on the west side of Stela C at Quirigua is the Initial-series terminal date **6 Ahau 13 Yaxkin,** illustrated together with its corresponding Initial-series number in figure 68, A. However, all attempts to reach the date **6 Ahau 13 Kayab** by counting either forward or backward the number 17.5.0.0 from the date **6 Ahau 13 Yaxkin** will prove unsuccessful, and we must seek another explanation for the four glyphs here under discussion. If this were a Period-ending date it would mean that Tun 5 of Katun 17 came to an end on the date **6 Ahau 13 Kayab.** Let us see whether this is true. Assuming that our cycle coefficient is 9, as we have done in all the other Period-ending dates presented, we may express glyphs 1 and 2 as the following Initial-series number, *provided* they represent a period ending, *not* a Secondary-series number: 9.17.5.0.0. Reducing this number to units of the 1st order, and applying the rules previously given for solving Initial Series, the terminal date reached will be **6 Ahau 13 Kayab,** identical with the date recorded in glyphs 3 and 4. We may conclude, therefore, that this example records the fact that "Tun 5 of Katun 17 ended on the date **6 Ahau 13 Kayab,**" this being identical with the Initial Series 9.17.5.0.0 **6 Ahau 13 Kayab.**

---

[1] Maler, 1911: v, pl. 17, east side, glyphs A4–A5.
[2] See Maudslay, 1889–1902: II, pl. 19, west side, glyphs B10–A12.

PLATE 22

A. CYCLE 13: TEMPLE OF THE CROSS, PALENQUE

B. CYCLE 13: ROUND ALTAR, PIEDRAS NEGRAS

C. CYCLE 2: TEMPLE OF THE FOLIATED CROSS, PALENQUE

D. CYCLE 10: STELA 11, SEIBAL

E. CYCLE 10: STELA 8, COPAN

F. CYCLE 10: ZOÖMORPH G, QUIRIGUA

G. CYCLE 8: TEMPLE OF THE CROSS, PALENQUE

EXAMPLES OF PERIOD-ENDING DATES IN CYCLES OTHER THAN CYCLE 9

The foregoing Period-ending dates have all been in Cycle 9, even though this fact has not been recorded in any of the above examples. We come next to the consideration of Period-ending dates which occurred in cycles other than Cycle 9.

In plate 22, *A*, is figured a Period-ending date from the tablet in the Temple of the Cross at Palenque.[1] In glyphs 1 and 2 appears the date **4 Ahau 8 Cumhu** (compare the month form in glyph 2 with fig. 19, *g'*, *h'*), and in glyph 3 an ending sign (compare glyph 3 with the ending signs in fig. 37, *l–q*, and with the zero signs in fig. 54). There follows in glyph 4, Cycle 13. These four glyphs record the fact, therefore, that Cycle 13 closed on the date **4 Ahau 8 Cumhu**, the starting point of Maya chronology. This same date is again recorded on a round altar at Piedras Negras (see pl. 22, *B*).[2] In glyphs 1 and 2 appears the date **4 Ahau 8 Cumhu**, and in glyph 3a the ending sign, which is identical with the ending sign in the preceding example, both having the clasped hand, the subfix showing a curl infix, and the tassel-like postfix. Compare also figure 37, *l–q*, and figure 54. Glyph 3b clearly records Cycle 13. The dates in plate 22, *A*, *B*, are therefore identical. In both cases the cycle is expressed by its normal form.

In plate 22, *C*, is figured a Period-ending date from the tablet in the Temple of the Foliated Cross at Palenque.[3] In glyph 1 appears an ending sign in which the hand element and tassel-like postfix show clearly. This is followed in glyph 2 by Cycle 2, the clasped hand on the head variant unmistakably indicating the cycle head. Finally, in glyphs 3 and 4 appears the date **2 Ahau 3 Uayeb** (compare the month form with fig. 19, *i'*).[4] The glyphs in plate 22, *C*, record, therefore, the fact that Cycle 2 closed on the date **2 Ahau 3 Uayeb**, a fact which the student may prove for himself by converting this Period-ending date into its corresponding Initial Series and solving the same. Since the end of a cycle is recorded here, it is evident that the katun, tun, uinal, and kin coefficients must all be 0, and our Initial-series number will be, therefore, 2.0.0.0.0. Reducing this to units of the 1st order and proceeding as in the case of Initial Series, the terminal date reached will be **2 Ahau 3 Uayeb**, just as recorded in glyphs 3 and 4. The Initial Series corresponding to this Period-ending date will be 2.0.0.0.0 **2 Ahau 3 Uayeb**.

These three Period-ending dates (pl. 22, *A–C*) are not to be considered as referring to times contemporaneous with the erection of the monuments upon which they are severally inscribed, since they pre-

---

[1] See Maudslay, 1889–1902: IV, pl. 75, glyphs D3–C5.
[2] See Maler, 1901: II, No. 1, pl. 8, glyphs A1–A2.
[3] See Maudslay, op. cit., pl. 81, glyphs C7–D8.
[4] It will be remembered that **Uayeb** was the name for the *xma kaba kin*, the 5 closing days of the year. Dates which fall in this period are exceedingly rare, and in the inscriptions, so far as the writer knows, have been found only at Palenque and Tikal.

cede the opening of Cycle 9, the first historic epoch of the Maya civilization, by periods ranging from 2,700 to 3,500 years. As explained elsewhere, they probably referred to mythological events. There is a date, however, on a tablet in the Temple of the Cross at Palenque which falls in Cycle 8, being fixed therein by an adjoining Period-ending date that may have been historical. This case is figured in plate 22, *G*.[1] In glyphs 4 and 5 appears the date **8 Ahau 13 Ceh** (compare the month form in glyph 5 with fig. 16, *u*, *v*). This is followed in glyph 6 by a sign which shows the same ending element as the forms in figure 37, *i*, *r*, *u*, *v*, and this in turn is followed by Cycle 9 in glyph 7. The date recorded in this case is Cycle 9 ending on the date **8 Ahau 13 Ceh**, which corresponds to the Initial Series 9.0.0.0.0 **8 Ahau 13 Ceh.**

Now, in glyphs 1 and 2 is recorded the date **2 Caban 10 Xul** (compare the day sign with fig. 16, *a'*, *b'*, and the month sign with fig. 19, *i*, *j*), and following this date in glyph 3 is the number 3 kins, 6 uinals, or 6.3. This looks so much like a Secondary Series that we are justified in treating it as such until it proves to be otherwise. As the record stands, it seems probable that if we count this number 6.3 in glyph 3 forward from the date **2 Caban 10 Xul** in glyphs 1 and 2, the terminal date reached will be the date recorded in glyphs 4 and 5; that is, the next date following the number. Reducing 6.3 to units of the first order, we have:

$$\text{Glyph } 6 = 6 \times 20 = 120$$
$$\text{Glyph } 6 = 3 \times 1 = 3$$
$$\overline{123}$$

Counting this number forward from **2 Caban 10 Xul** according to the rules which apply in such cases, the terminal day reached will be **8 Ahau 13 Ceh**, exactly the date which is recorded in glyphs 4 and 5. But this latter date, we have just seen, is declared by the text to have closed Cycle 9, and therefore corresponded with the Initial Series 9.0.0.0.0 **8 Ahau 13 Ceh.** Hence, from this known Initial Series we may calculate the Initial Series of the date **2 Caban 10 Xul** by subtracting from 9.0.0.0.0 the number 6.3, by which the date **2 Caban 10 Xul** precedes the date 9.0.0.0.0 **8 Ahau 13 Ceh:**

$$9.\ 0.\ 0.\ 0.\ 0 \quad \textbf{8 Ahau 13 Ceh}$$
$$6.\ 3$$
$$8.19.19.11.17 \quad \textbf{2 Caban 10 Xul}$$

This latter date fell in Cycle 8, as its Initial Series indicates. It is quite possible, as stated above, that this date may have referred to some actual historic event in the annals of Palenque, or at least of

---

[1] See Maudslay, 1889–1902: IV, pl. 77, glyphs P14–R2. Glyphs Q15–P17 are omitted from pl. 22, *G*, as they appear to be uncalendrical.

the southern Maya, though the monument upon which it is recorded probably dates from an epoch at least 200 years later.

In a few cases Cycle-10 ending dates have been found. Some of these are surely "contemporaneous," that is, the monuments upon which they appear really date from Cycle 10, while others are as surely "prophetic," that is, the monuments upon which they are found antedate Cycle 10. Examples of both kinds follow.

In plate 22, *É*, is figured a Period-ending date from Stela 8 at Copan.[1] Glyphs 1 and 2 declare the date **7 Ahau 18** ?, the month sign in glyph 2 being effaced. In glyph 3 is recorded Cycle 10, the cycle sign being expressed by its corresponding head variant. Note the clasped hand, the essential characteristic of the cycle head. Above this appears the same ending sign as that shown in figure 37, *a–h*, and it would seem probable, therefore, that these three glyphs record the end of Cycle 10. Let us test this by changing the Period-ending date in glyph 3 into its corresponding Initial-series number and then solving this for the resulting terminal date. Since the end of a cycle is here indicated, the katun, tun, uinal, and kin coefficients must be 0 and the Initial-series number will be, therefore, 10.0.0.0.0. Reducing this to units of the first order and applying the rules indicated in such cases, the resulting terminal date will be found to be **7 Ahau 18 Zip.** But this agrees exactly with the date recorded in glyphs 1 and 2 so far as the latter go, and since the two agree so far as they go, we may conclude that glyphs 1–3 in plate 22, *E*, express "Cycle 10 ending on the date **7 Ahau 18 Zip**," Although this is a comparatively late date for Copan, the writer is inclined to believe that it was "contemporaneous" rather than "prophetic."

The same can not be said, however, for the Cycle-10 ending date on Zoömorph G at Quirigua (see pl. 22, *F*). Indeed, this date, as will appear below, is almost surely "prophetic" in character. Glyphs 1 and 2 record the date **7 Ahau 18 Zip** (compare the month form in glyph 2 with fig. 19, *d*) and glyph 3 shows very clearly "the end of Cycle 10." Compare the ending prefix in glyph 4 with the same element in fig. 37, *a–h*. Hence we have recorded here the fact that "Cycle 10 ended on the date **7 Ahau 18 Zip**," a fact proved also by calculation in connection with the preceding example. Does this date represent, therefore, the contemporaneous time of Zoömorph G, the time at which it was erected, or at least dedicated? Before answering this question, let us consider the rest of the text from which this example is taken. The Initial Series on Zoömorph G at Quirigua has already been shown in figure 70, and, according to page 187, it records the date 9.17.15.0.0 **5 Ahau 3 Muan.** On the grounds of antecedent probability, we are justified in assuming at the outset that this date

---

[1] See Maudslay, 1889–1902: I, pl. 109, glyphs C1 D1, A2.

therefore indicates the epoch or position of Zoömorph G in the Long Count, because it alone appears as an Initial Series. In the case of all the other monuments at Quirigua,[1] where there is but one Initial Series in the inscription, that Initial Series marks the position of the monument in the Long Count. It seems likely, therefore, judging from the general practice at Quirigua, that 9.17.15.0.0 **5 Ahau 3 Muan** was the contemporaneous date of Zoömorph G, not 10.0.0.0.0 **7 Ahau 18 Zip**, that is, the Initial Series corresponding to the Period-ending date here under discussion (see pl. 22, *F*).[2]

Other features of this text point to the same conclusion. In addition to the Initial Series on this monument there are upward of a dozen Secondary-series dates, all of which except *one* lead to 9.17.15.0.0 **5 Ahau 3 Muan**. Moreover, this latter date is recorded thrice in the text, a fact which points to the conclusion that it was the contemporaneous date of this monument.

There is still another, perhaps the strongest reason of all, for believing that Zoömorph G dates from 9.17.15.0.0 **5 Ahau 3 Muan** rather than from 10.0.0.0.0 **7 Ahau 18 Zip**. If assigned to the former date, every hotun from 9.15.15.0.0 **9 Ahau 18 Xul** to 9.19.0.0.0 **9 Ahau 18 Mol** has its corresponding marker or period-stone at Quirigua, there being not a single break in the sequence of the fourteen monuments necessary to mark the thirteen hotun endings between these two dates. If, on the other hand, the date 10.0.0.0.0 **7 Ahau 18 Zip** is assigned to this monument, the hotun ending 9.17.15.0.0 **5 Ahau 3 Muan** is left without its corresponding monument at this city, as are also all the hotuns after 9.19.0.0.0 **9 Ahau 18 Mol** up to 10.0.0.0.0 **7 Ahau 18 Zip**, a total of four in all. The perfect sequence of the monuments at Quirigua developed by regarding Zoömorph G as dating from 9.17.15.0.0 **5 Ahau 3 Muan**, and the very fragmentary sequence which arises if it is regarded as dating from 10.0.0.0.0 **7 Ahau 18 Zip**, is of itself practically sufficient to prove that the former is the correct date, and when taken into consideration with the other points above mentioned leaves no room for doubt.

If this is true, as the writer believes, the date "Cycle 10 ending on **7 Ahau 18 Zip**" on Zoömorph G is "prophetic" in character, since it did not occur until nearly 45 years after the erection of the monument upon which it was recorded, at which time the city of Quirigua had probably been abandoned, or at least had lost her prestige.

Another Cycle-10 ending date, which differs from the preceding in that it is almost surely contemporaneous, is that on Stela 11 at Seibal,

---

[1] This excludes Stela C, which has two Initial Series (see figs. 68 and 77), though neither of them, as explained on p. 175, footnote 1, records the date of this monument. The true date of this monument is declared by the Period-ending date figured in pl. 21, *H*, which is 9.17.0.0.0 **6 Ahau 13 Kayab**. (See p. 226.)

[2] See Maudslay, 1889-1902: II, pl. 44, west side, glyphs G4 H4, F5.

the latest of the great southern sites.[1]   This is figured in plate 22, *D*.
Glyphs 1 and 2 show very clearly the date **7 Ahau 18 Zip,** and glyph
3 declares this to be "at the end of Cycle 10." [2]   Compare the ending-
sign superfix in glyph 3 with figure 37, *a–h*.   This glyph is followed
by 1 katun in 4, which in turn is followed by the date **5 Ahau 3 Kayab**
in 5 and 6.   Finally, glyph 7 declares "The end of Katun 1."   Counting forward 1 katun from 10.0.0.0.0 **7 Ahau 18 Zip,** the date reached
will be **5 Ahau 3 Kayab,** as recorded by 5 and 6, and the Initial Series
corresponding to this date will be 10.1.0.0.0 **5 Ahau 3 Kayab,** as
declared by glyph 7.   See below:

$$10.0.0.0.0 \quad \textbf{7 Ahau 18 Zip}$$
$$1.0.0.0$$
$$10.1.0.0.0 \quad \textbf{5 Ahau 3 Kayab}$$

End of Katun 1.

This latter date is found also on Stelæ 8, 9, and 10, at the same
city.

Another Cycle-10 ending date which was probably "prophetic", like
the one on Zoömorph G at Quirigua, is figured on Altar S at Copan
(see fig. 81).   In the first glyph on the left appears an Initial-series
introducing glyph; this is followed in glyphs 1–3 by the Initial-
series number 9.15.0.0.0, which the student will find leads to the
terminal date **4 Ahau 13 Yax** recorded in glyph 4.   This whole
Initial Series reads, therefore, 9.15.0.0.0 **4 Ahau 13 Yax.**   In glyph
6a is recorded 5 katuns and in glyph 7 the date **7 Ahau 18 Zip,** in
other words, a Secondary Series.[3]   Reducing the number in glyph
6a to units of the first order, we have:

$$6a = 5 \times 7,200 = 36,000$$
$$\text{Not recorded} \begin{cases} 0 \times & 360 = & 0 \\ 0 \times & 20 = & 0 \\ 0 \times & 1 = & 0 \end{cases}$$

$$\overline{36,000}$$

Counting this number forward from the date **4 Ahau 13 Yax,** the
terminal date reached will be found to agree with the date recorded
in glyph 7, **7 Ahau 18 Zip.**   But turning to our text again, we find
that this date is declared by glyph 8a to be at the end of Cycle 10.
Compare the ending sign, which appears as the superfix in glyph 8a,
with figure 37, *a–h*.   Therefore the Secondary-series date **7 Ahau 18**

---

[1] The dates 10.2.5.0.0 **9 Ahau 18 Yax** and 10.2.10.0.0 **2 Ahau 13 Chen** on Stelæ 1 and 2, respectively, at
Quen Santo, are purposely excluded from this statement.   Quen Santo is in the highlands of Guatemala
(see pl. 1) and is well to the south of the Usamacintla region.   It rose to prominence probably after the
collapse of the great southern cities and is to be considered as inaugurating a new order of things, if not
indeed a new civilization.

[2] See Maler, 1908 a: IV, No. 1, pl. 9, glyphs E2, F2, A3, and A4.

[3] The student will note that the lower periods (the tun, uinal, and kin signs) are omitted and consequently
are to be considered as having the coefficient 0.

Zip, there recorded, closed Cycle 10. The same fact could have been determined by adding the Secondary-series number in glyph 6a to the Initial-series number of the starting point **4 Ahau 13 Yax** in glyphs 1–3:

$$9.15.0.0.0 \quad \textbf{4 Ahau 13 Yax}$$
$$5.(0.0.0)$$
$$10.\ 0.0.0.0 \quad \textbf{7 Ahau 18 Zip}$$

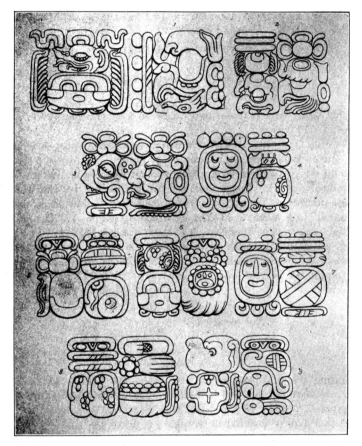

FIG. 81.   The Initial Series, Secondary Series, and Period-ending date on Altar S, Copan.

The "end of Cycle 10" in glyph 8a is merely redundancy. The writer believes that 9.15.0.0.0 **4 Ahau 13 Yax** indicates the present time of Altar S rather than 10.0.0.0.0 **7 Ahau 18 Zip,** and that consequently the latter date was "prophetic" in character, as was the same date on Zoömorph G at Quirigua. One reason which renders this prob-

PLATE 23

INITIAL SERIES, SECONDARY SERIES, AND PERIOD-
ENDING DATES ON STELA 3, PIEDRAS NEGRAS

able is that the sculpture on Altar S very closely resembles the sculpture on Stelæ A and B at Copan, both of which date from 9.15.0.0.0 **4 Ahau 13 Yax**. A possible explanation of the record of Cycle 10 on this monument is the following: On the date of this monument, 9.15.0.0.0 **4 Ahau 13 Yax**, just three-fourths of Cycle 9 had elapsed. This important fact would hardly have escaped the attention of the old astronomer-priests, and they may have used this monument to point out that only a quarter cycle, 5 katuns, was left in Cycle 9. This concludes the discussion of Cycle-10 Period-ending dates.

The student will note in the preceding example (fig. 81) that Initial-series, Secondary-series, and Period-ending dating have all been used together in the same text, glyphs 1–4 recording an Initial-series date, glyphs 6a and 7, a Secondary-series date, and glyphs 7 and 8a, a Period-ending date. This practice is not at all unusual in the inscriptions and several texts illustrating it are figured below.

TEXTS RECORDING INITIAL SERIES, SECONDARY SERIES, AND PERIOD ENDINGS

In plate 23 is shown the inscription on Stela 3 at Piedras Negras. The introducing glyph appears in A1 and is followed by the Initial-series number 9.12.2.0.16 in B1–B3. This number reduced to units of the first order and counted forward from its starting point will be found to reach the terminal date **5 Cib 14 Yaxkin**, which the student will readily recognize in A4–B7; the "month-sign indicator" appearing very clearly in A7, with the coefficient 9 affixed to it. Compare the day sign in A4 with figure 16, *z*, and the month sign in B7 with figure 19, *k, l*. The Initial Series recorded in A1–A4, B7 reads, therefore, 9.12.2.0.16 **5 Cib 14 Yaxkin**. In C1 D1 is recorded the number 0 kins, 10 uinals, and 12 tuns; that is, 12.10.0, the first of several Secondary Series in this text. Reducing this to units of the first order and counting it forward from the terminal date of the Initial Series, **5 Cib 14 Yaxkin**, the terminal date of the Secondary Series will be found to be **1 Cib 14 Kankin**, which the student will find recorded in C2b D2a. The Initial-series value of this latter date may be calculated as follows:

$$9.12\ \ 2.\ 0.16 \quad \textbf{5 Cib 14 Yaxkin}$$
$$12.10.\ 0$$
$$9.12.14.10.16 \quad \textbf{1 Cib 14 Kankin}$$

Following along the text, the next Secondary-series number appears in D4–C5a and consists of 10 kins,[1] 11 uinals, 1 tun, and 1 katun; that

---

[1] The usual positions of the uinal and kin coefficients in D4a are reversed, the kin coefficient 10 standing *above* the uinal sign instead of at the left of it. The calculations show, however, that 10, not 11, is the kin coefficient.

is, 1.1.11.10. Reducing this number to units of the first order and counting it forward from the date next preceding it in the text, that is, **1 Cib 14 Kankin** in C2b D2a, the new terminal date reached will be **4 Cimi 14 Uo**, which the student will find recorded in D5–C6. Compare the day sign in D5 with figure 16, *h*, *i*, and the month sign in C6 with figure 19, *b*, *c*. The Initial-series value of this new date may be calculated from the known Initial-series value of the preceding date:

$$9.12.14.10.16 \quad \textbf{1 Cib 14 Kankin}$$
$$1.\ 1.11.10$$
$$9.13.16.\ 4.\ 6 \quad \textbf{4 Cimi 14 Uo}$$

The third Secondary Series appears in E1 and consists of 15 kins,[1] 8 uinals, and 3 tuns, or 3.8.15. Reducing this number to units of the first order and counting it forward from the date next preceding it in the text, **4 Cimi 14 Uo**, in D5–C6, the new terminal date reached will be **11 Imix 14 Yax**, which the student will find recorded in E2 F2. The day sign in E2 appears, as is very unusual, as a head variant of which only the headdress seems to show the essential element of the day sign **Imix**. Compare E2 with figure 16, *a*, *b*, also the month sign in F2 with figure 19, *q*, *r*. The Initial Series of this new terminal date may be calculated as above:

$$9.13.16.\ 4.\ 6 \quad \textbf{4 Cimi 14 Uo}$$
$$3.\ 8.15$$
$$9.13.19.13.\ 1 \quad \textbf{11 Imix 14 Yax}$$

The fourth and last Secondary Series in this text follows in F6 and consists of 19 kins and 4 uinals, that is, 4.19. Reducing this number to units of the first order and counting it forward from the date next preceding it in the text, **11 Imix 14 Yax** in E2 F2, the new terminal date reached will be **6 Ahau 13 Muan**, which the student will find recorded in F7–F8. Compare the month sign in F8 with figure 19, *a' b'*. But the glyph following this date in F9 is very clearly an ending sign; note the hand, tassel-like postfix, and subfixial element showing the curl infix, all of which are characteristic ending elements (see figs. 37, *l–q*, and 54). Moreover, in F10 is recorded "the end of Katun 14." Compare the ending prefix in this glyph with figure 37, *a–h*. This would seem to indicate that the date in F7–F8, **6 Ahau 13 Muan**, closed Katun 14 of Cycle 9 of the Long Count. Whether this be true or not may be tested by finding the Initial-series value corresponding to **6 Ahau 13 Muan**, as above:

$$9.13.19.13.\ 1 \quad \textbf{11 Imix 14 Yax}$$
$$4.19$$
$$9.14.\ 0.\ 0.\ 0 \quad \textbf{6 Ahau 13 Muan}$$

---

[1] In this number also the positions of the uinal and kin coefficients are reversed.

PLATE 24

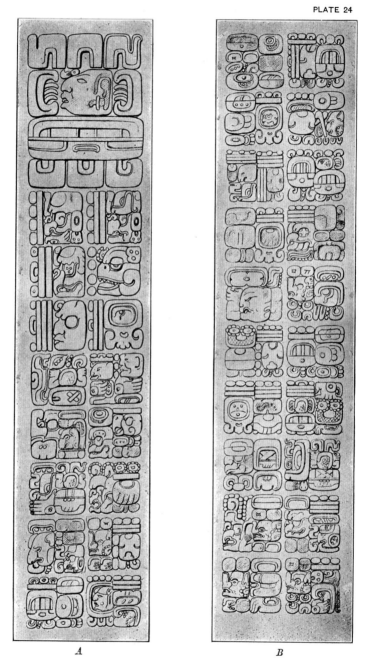

A   B

INITIAL SERIES, SECONDARY SERIES, AND PERIOD-ENDING DATES
ON STELA E (WEST SIDE), QUIRIGUA

This shows that the date **6 Ahau 13 Muan** closed Katun 14, as glyphs F9–F10 declare. This may also be verified by changing "the end of Katun 14" recorded in F9–F10 into its corresponding Initial-series value, 9.14.0.0.0, and solving for the terminal date. The day reached by these calculations will be **6 Ahau 13 Muan**, as above. This text, in so far as it has been deciphered, therefore reads:

9.12. 2. 0.16	**5 Cib 14 Yaxkin**	A1–A4, B7
12.10. 0		C1 D1
9.12.14.10.16	**1 Cib 14 Kankin**	C2b D2a
1. 1.11.10		D4–C5a
9.13.16. 4. 6	**4 Cimi 14 Uo**	D5–C6
3. 8.15		E1
9.13.19.13. 1	**11 Imix 14 Yax**	E2 F2
4.19		F6
9.14. 0. 0. 0	**6 Ahau 13 Muan**	F7–F8
End of Katun 14		F9–F10

The inscription just deciphered is worthy of special note for several reasons. In the first place, all its dates and numbers are not only exceedingly clear, thus facilitating their identification, but also unusually regular, the numbers being counted forward from the dates next preceding them to reach the dates next following them in every case; all these features make this text particularly well adapted for study by the beginner. In the second place, this inscription shows the three principal methods employed by the Maya in recording dates, that is, Initial-series dating, Secondary-series dating, and Period-ending dating, all combined in the same text, the example of each one being, moreover, unusually good. Finally, the Initial Series of this inscription records identically the same date as Stela 1 at Piedras Negras, namely, 9.12.2.0.16 **5 Cib 14 Yaxkin**. Compare plate 23 with plate 17. Indeed, these two monuments, Stelæ 1 and 3, stand in front of the same building. All things considered, the inscription on Stela 3 at Piedras Negras is one of the most satisfactory texts that has been found in the whole Maya territory.

Another example showing the use of these three methods of dating in one and the same text is the inscription on Stela E at Quirigua, illustrated in plate 24 and figure 82.[1] This text begins with the Initial Series on the west side. The introducing glyph appears in A1–B3 and is followed by the Initial-series number 9.14.13[2].4.17 in A4–A6. Reducing this number to units of the first order, remembering the correction in the tun coefficient in A5 noted below, and applying the rules previously given for solving Initial Series, the terminal date

---

[1] For the full text of this inscription, see Maudslay, 1889–1902: II, pls. 28–32.

[2] The student will note that 12, not 13, tuns are recorded in A5. As explained elsewhere (see pp. 247, 248), this is an error on the part of the ancient scribe who engraved this inscription. The correct tun coefficient is 13, as used above.

reached will be **12 Caban 5 Kayab**. This the
student will readily recognize in B6–B8b,
the form in B8a being the "month sign
indicator," here shown with a head-variant
coefficient 10.   Compare B6 with figure
16, *a'*, *b'*, and B8b with figure 19, *d'–f'*.
This Initial Series therefore should read
as follows: 9.14.13.4.17 **12 Caban 5 Kayab.**
Following down the text, there is reached
in B10b–A11a, a Secondary-series number
consisting of 3 kins, 13 uinals, and 6 tuns,
that is, 6.13.3.   Counting this number forward from the date next preceding it in
the text, **12 Caban 5 Kayab**, the date
reached will be **4 Ahau 13 Yax**, which the
student will find recorded in B11.   Compare the month form in B11b with figure
19, *q, r*.   But since the Initial-series value
of **12 Caban 5 Kayab** is known, the Initial-
series value of **4 Ahau 13 Yax** may be calculated from it as follows:

9.14.13. 4.17   **12 Caban 5 Kayab**
6.13. 3
9.15. 0. 0. 0   **4 Ahau 13 Yax**

The next Secondary-series number appears in B12, plate 24, *B*, and consists of
6 kins, 14 uinals, and 1 tun, that is, 1.14.6.[1]
The student will find that all efforts to
reach the next date recorded in the text,
6 Cimi 4 Tzec in A13b B13a, by counting
forward 1.14.6 from **4 Ahau 13 Yax** in B11,
the date next preceding this number, will
prove unsuccessful.   However, by counting *backward* 1.14.6 from **6 Cimi 4 Tzec**, he
will find the date from which the count
proceeds is **10 Ahau 8 Chen**, though this
latter date is nowhere recorded in this text.
We have seen elsewhere, on Stela F for example (pl. 19, *A, B*), that the date **6 Cimi
4 Tzec** corresponded to the Initial-series
number 9.15.6.14.6; consequently, we may
calculate the position of the unrecorded

FIG. 82. The Initial Series on Stela E
(east side), Quirigua.

[1] This Secondary-series number is doubly irregular. In the
first place, the kin and uinal coefficients are reversed, the latter
standing to the left of its sign instead of above, and in the second place, the uinal coefficient, although it is
14, has an ornamental dot between the two middle dots.

date **10 Ahau 8 Chen** in the Long Count from this known Initial Series, by subtracting [1] 1.14.6 from it:

$$9.15.6.14.6 \quad\quad \textbf{6 Cimi 4 Tzec}$$
$$1.14.6$$
$$9.15.5.\ 0.0 \quad\quad \textbf{10 Ahau 8 Chen}$$

We now see that there are 5 tuns, that is, 1 hotun, not recorded here, namely, the hotun from 9.15.0.0.0 **4 Ahau 13 Yax,** to 9.15.5.0.0 **10 Ahau 8 Chen,** and further, that the Secondary-series number 1.14.6 in B12 is counted from the unexpressed date **10 Ahau 8 Chen** to reach the terminal date **6 Cimi 4 Tzec** recorded in A13b B13a.

The next Secondary-series number appears in A14b B14 and consists of 15 kins, 16 uinals, 1 tun, and 1 katun, that is, 1.1.16.15. As in the preceding case, however, all efforts to reach the date following this number, **11 Imix 19 Muan** in A15b B15a, by counting it forward from **6 Cimi 4 Tzec,** the date next preceding it in the text, will prove unavailing. As before, it is necessary to count it *backward* from **11 Imix 19 Muan** to determine the starting point. Performing this operation, the starting point will be found to be the date **7 Cimi 9 Zotz.** Since neither of these two dates, **11 Imix 19 Muan** and **7 Cimi 9 Zotz,** occurs elsewhere at Quirigua, we must leave their corresponding Initial-series values indeterminate for the present.

The last Secondary Series in this text is recorded in A17b B17a and consists of 19 kins,[2] 4 uinals, and 8 tuns. Reducing this number to units of the first order and counting it forward from the date next preceding it in the text, **11 Imix 19 Muan** in A15b B15a, the terminal date reached will be **13 Ahau 18 Cumhu,** which the student will find recorded in A18. Compare the month sign with figure 19, *g'*, *h'*. But immediately following this date in B18a is Katun 17 and in the upper part of B18b the hand-denoting ending. These glyphs A18 and B18 would seem to indicate, therefore, that Katun 17 came to an end on the date **13 Ahau 18 Cumhu.** That they do, may be proved beyond all doubt by changing this period ending into its corresponding Initial-series number 9.17.0.0.0 and solving for the terminal date. This will be found to be **13 Ahau 18 Cumhu,** which is recorded in A18. This latter date, therefore, had the following position in the Long Count: 9.17.0.0.0 **13 Ahau 18 Cumhu.** But having determined the position of this latter date in the Long Count, that is, its Initial-series value, it is now possible to fix the positions of the two dates **11 Imix 19 Muan** and **7 Cimi 9 Zotz,** which we were obliged to leave indeterminate above. Since the date **13 Ahau 18 Cumhu** was derived

---

[1] Since we counted *backward* 1.14.6 from **6 Cimi 4 Tzec** to reach **10 Ahau 8 Chen,** we must *subtract* 1.14.6 from the Initial-series value of **6 Cimi 4 Tzec** to reach the Initial-series value of **10 Ahau 8 Chen.**

[2] It is obvious that the kin and uinal coefficients are reversed in A17b since the coefficient above the uinal sign is very clearly 19, an impossible value for the uinal coefficient in the inscriptions, 19 uinals *always* being written 1 tun, 1 uinal. Therefore the 19 must be the kin coefficient. See also p. 110, footnote 1.

by counting forward 8.4.19 from **11 Imix 19 Muan**, the Initial-series value of the latter may be calculated by subtracting 8.4.19 from the Initial-series value of the former:

$$9.17.\ 0.\ 0.\ 0 \quad \textbf{13 Ahau 18 Cumhu}$$
$$8.\ 4.19$$
$$9.16.11.13.\ 1 \quad \textbf{11 Imix 19 Muan}$$

And since the date **11 Imix 19 Muan** was reached by counting forward 1.1.16.15 from **7 Cimi 9 Zotz**, the Initial-series value of the latter may be calculated by subtracting 1.1.16.15 from the now known Initial-series value of the former:

$$9.16.11.13.\ 1 \quad \textbf{11 Imix 19 Muan}$$
$$1.\ 1.16.15$$
$$9.15.\ 9.14.\ 6 \quad \textbf{7 Cimi 9 Zotz}$$

Although this latter date is not recorded in the text, the date next preceding the number 1.1.16.15 is **6 Cimi 4 Tzec**, which corresponded to the Initial Series 9.15.6.14.6 **6 Cimi 4 Tzec**, as we have seen, a date which was exactly 3 tuns earlier than **7 Cimi 9 Zotz**, 9.15.9.14.6–9.15.6.14.6 = 3.0.0.

The inscription on the west side closes then in A18 B18 with the record that Katun 17 ended on the date **13 Ahau 18 Cumhu**. The inscription on the east side of this same monument opens with this same date expressed as an Initial Series, 9.17.0.0.0 **13 Ahau 18 Cumhu**. See figure 82, A1–A6, A7,[1] and A10.

The reiteration of this date as an Initial Series, when its position in the Long Count had been fixed unmistakably on the other side of the same monument by its record as a Period-ending date, together with the fact that it is the latest date recorded in this inscription, very clearly indicates that it alone designated the contemporaneous time of Stela E, and hence determines the fact that Stela E was a hotun-marker. This whole text, in so far as deciphered, reads as follows:

West side: 9.14.13.[2] 4.17	**12 Caban 5 Kayab**	Plate 24, *A*, A1–B6, B8b
6.13. 3		Plate 24, *A*, B10b–A11a
9.15. 0. 0. 0	**4 Ahau 13 Yax**	Plate 24, *A*, B11
[5. 0. 0]		Undeclared
9.15. 5. 0. 0	**10 Ahau 8 Chen**	"
1.14. 6		Plate 24, *B*, B12
9.15. 6.14. 6	**6 Cimi 4 Tzec**	Plate 24, *B*, A13b B13a
[3. 0. 0]		Undeclared

---

[1] The first glyph of the Supplementary Series, B6a, very irregularly stands between the kin period glyph and the day part of the terminal date.

[2] Incorrectly recorded as 12. See pp. 247, 248.

9.15. 9.14. 6	7 Cimi 9 Zotz	Undeclared
1. 1.16.15		Plate 24, *B*, A14b B14
9.16.11.13. 1	11 Imix 19 Muan	Plate 24, *B*, A15b B15a
8. 4.19		Plate 24, *B*, A17b B17a
9.17. 0. 0. 0	13 Ahau 18 Cumhu	Plate 24, *B*, A18
End of Katun 17		Plate 24, *B*, B18
East side: 9.17. 0. 0. 0	13 Ahau 18 Cumhu	Figure 82, A1–A6, A7, A10

Comparing the summary of the inscription on Stela E at Quirigua, just given, with the summaries of the inscriptions on Stelæ J and F, and Zoömorph G, at the same city, all four of which are shown side by side in Table XVII,[1] the interrelationship of these four monuments appears very clearly.

TABLE XVII. INTERRELATIONSHIP OF DATES ON STELÆ E, F, AND J AND ZOÖMORPH G, QUIRIGUA

Date		Stela J	Stela F	Stela E	Zoömorph G
9.14.13. 4.17	12 Caban 5 Kayab	x	x	x	x
9.15. 0. 0. 0	4 Ahau 13 Yax	–	x	x	–
9.15. 5. 0. 0	10 Ahau 8 Chen	x	–	x	–
9.15. 6.14. 6	6 Cimi 4 Tzec	x	x	x	x
9.15. 9.14. 6	7 Cimi 9 Zotz	–	–	x	–
9.15.10. 0. 0	3 Ahau 3 Mol	–	x	–	–
9.16. 5. 0. 0	**8 AHAU 8 ZOTZ**	x	–	–	–
9.16.10. 0. 0	**1 AHAU 3 ZIP**	–	x	–	–
9.16.11.13. 1	11 Imix 19 Muan	–	–	x	–
9.17. 0. 0. 0	**13 AHAU 18 CUMHU**	–	–	x	–
9.17.15. 0. 0	**5 AHAU 3 MUAN**	–	–	–	x

In spite of the fact that each one of these four monuments marks a different hotun in the Long Count, and consequently dates from a different period, all of them go back to the same date, 9.14.13.4.17 **12 Caban 5 Kayab**, as their original starting point (see above). This date would almost certainly seem, therefore, to indicate some very important event in the annals of Quirigua. Moreover, since it is the earliest date found at this city which can reasonably be regarded as having occurred during the actual occupancy of the site, it is not improbable that it may represent, as explained elsewhere, the time at which Quirigua was founded.[2]   It is necessary, however, to cau-

---

[1] In this table the numbers showing the distances have been omitted and all dates are shown in terms of their corresponding Initial-series numbers, in order to facilitate their comparison. The contemporaneous date of each monument is given in bold-faced figures and capital letters, and the student will note also that this date not only ends a hotun in each case but is, further, the latest date in each text.

[2] The Initial Series on the west side of Stela D at Quirigua is 9.16.13.4.17 **8 Caban 5 Yaxkin**, which was just 2 katuns later than 9.14.13.4.17 **12 Caban 5 Kayab**, or, in other words, the second katun anniversary, if the term anniversary may be thus used, of the latter date.

tion the student that the above explanation of the date 9.14.13.4.17
12 Caban 5 Kayab, or indeed any other for that matter, is in the
present state of our knowledge entirely a matter of conjecture.

Passing on, it will be seen from Table XVII that two of the monuments, namely, Stelæ E and F, bear the date 9.15.0.0.0 **4 Ahau 3
Yax,** and two others, Stelæ E and J, the date 9.15.5.0.0 **10 Ahau 8
Chen,** one hotun later. All four come together again, however,
with the date 9.15.6.14.6 **6 Cimi 4 Tzec,** which is recorded on each.
This date, like 9.14.13.4.17 **12 Caban 5 Kayab,** designates probably
another important event in Quirigua history, the nature of which,
however, again escapes us: After the date 9.15.6.14.6 **6 Cimi 4 Tzec,**
these monuments show no further correspondences, and we may pass
over the intervening time to their respective closing dates with but
scant notice, with the exception of Zoömorph G, which records a
half dozen dates in the hotun that it marks, 9.17.15.0.0 **5 Ahau 3
Muan.**   (These latter are omitted from Table XVII.)

This concludes the presentation of Initial-series, Secondary-series,
and Period-ending, dating, with which the student should be sufficiently familiar by this time to continue his researches independently.

It was explained (see p. 76) that, when a Secondary-series date
could not be referred ultimately to either an Initial-series date
or a Period-ending date, its position in the Long Count could
not be determined with certainty, and furthermore that such a date
became merely one of the 18,980 dates of the Calendar Round and
could be fixed only within a period of 52 years. A few examples of
Calendar-round dating are given in figure 83 and plate 25. In
figure 83, *A*, is shown a part of the inscription on Altar M at Quirigua.[1]
In A1 B1 appears a number consisting of 0 kins, 2 uinals, and 3 tuns,
that is, 3.2.0, and following this in A2b B2, the date **4 Ahau 13 Yax,**
and in A3b B3 the date **6 Ahau 18 Zac.** Compare the month glyphs
in B2 and B3 with *q* and *r*, and *s* and *t*, respectively, of figure 19.
This has every appearance of being a Secondary Series, one of the
two dates being the starting point of the number 3.2.0, and the
other its terminal date. Reducing 3.2.0 to units of the first order,
we have:

$$B1 = 3 \times 360 = 1,080$$
$$A1 = 2 \times 20 = 40$$
$$A1 = 0 \times 1 = 0$$
$$\overline{\ 1,120}$$

Counting this number forward from **4 Ahau 13 Yax,** the nearest date
to it in the text, the terminal date reached will be found to be **6 Ahau
18 Zac,** the date which, we have seen, was recorded in A3b B3. It

---

[1] For the full text of this inscription, see Maudslay, 1889–1902: II, pl. 50.

PLATE 25

CALENDAR-ROUND DATES ON ALTAR 5, TIKAL

is clear, therefore, that this text records the fact that 3.2.0 has been counted forward from the date **4 Ahau 13 Yax** and the date **6 Ahau 18 Zac** has been reached, but there is nothing given by means of which the position of either of these dates in the Long Count can be determined; consequently either of these dates will be found recurring like any other Calendar-round date, at intervals of every 52 years. In such cases the first assumption to be made is that one of the dates recorded the close of a hotun, or at least of a tun, in Cycle 9 of the Long Count. The reasons for this assumption are quite ob-

A   B

FIG. 83.   Calendar-round dates: *A*, Altar M, Quirigua; *B*, Altar Z, Copan.

vious. The overwhelming majority of Maya dates fall in Cycle 9, and nearly all inscriptions have at least one date which closed some hotun or tun of that cycle. Referring to Goodman's Tables, in which the tun endings of Cycle 9 are given, the student will find that the date **4 Ahau 13 Yax** occurred as a tun ending in Cycle 9, at 9.15.0.0.0 **4 Ahau 13 Yax**, in which position it closed not only a hotun but also a katun. Hence, it is probable, although the fact is not actually recorded, that the Initial-series value of the date **4 Ahau 13 Yax** in this text is 9.15.0.0.0 **4 Ahau 13 Yax**, and if this is so the Initial-series value of the date **6 Ahau 18 Zac** will be:

9.15.0.0.0   **4 Ahau 13 Yax**
3.2.0
9.15.3.2.0   **6 Ahau 18 Zac**

In the case of this particular text the Initial-series value 9.15.0.0.0 might have been assigned to the date **4 Ahau 13 Yax** on the ground that this Initial-series value appears on two other monuments at Quirigua, namely, Stelæ E and F, with this same date.

In figure 83, *B*, is shown a part of the inscription from Altar Z at Copan.[1] In A1 B1 appears a number consisting of 1 kin, 8 uinals, and 1 tun, that is, 1.8.1, and following this in B2–A3 is the date **13 Ahau 18 Cumhu**, but no record of its position in the Long Count. If **13 Ahau 18 Cumhu** is the terminal date of the number 1.8.1, the starting point can be calculated by counting this number backward, giving the date **12 Cauac 2 Zac**. On the other hand, if **13 Ahau 18 Cumhu** is the starting point, the terminal date reached by counting 1.8.1 forward will be **1 Imix 9 Mol**. However, since an ending prefix appears just before the date **13 Ahau 18 Cumhu** in A2 (compare fig. 37, *a–h*), and since another, though it must be admitted a very unusual ending sign, appears just after this date in A3 (compare the prefix of B3 with the prefix of fig. 37, *o*, and the subfix with the subfixes of *l–n* and *q* of the same figure), it seems probable that **13 Ahau 18 Cumhu** is the terminal date and also a Period-ending date. Referring to Goodman's Tables, it will be found that the only tun in Cycle 9 which ended with the date **13 Ahau 18 Cumhu** was 9.17.0.0.0 **13 Ahau 18 Cumhu**, which not only ended a hotun but a katun as well.[2] If this is true, the unrecorded starting point **12 Cauac 2 Zac** can be shown to have the following Initial-series value:

> 9.17. 0.0. 0   **13 Ahau 18 Cumhu**
> 1.8. 1   Backward
> 9.16.18.9.19   **12 Cauac 2 Zac**

In each of the above examples, as we have seen, there was a date which ended one of the katuns of Cycle 9, although this fact was not recorded in connection with either. Because of this fact, however, we were able to date both of these monuments with a degree of probability amounting almost to certainty. In some texts the student will find that the dates recorded did not end any katun, hotun, or even tun, in Cycle 9, or in any other cycle, and consequently such dates can not be assigned to their proper positions in the Long Count by the above method.

The inscription from Altar 5 at Tikal figured in plate 25 is a case in point. This text opens with the date **1 Muluc 2 Muan** in glyphs 1 and 2 (the first glyph or starting point is indicated by the star).

---

[1] For the full text of this inscription, see Maudslay, 1889–1902: I, pl. 112.

[2] Every fourth hotun ending in the Long Count was a katun ending at the same time, namely:

> 9.16. 0.0.0   **2 Ahau 13 Tzec**
> 9.16. 5.0.0   **8 Ahau 8 Zotz**
> 9.16.10.0.0   **1 Ahau 3 Zip**
> 9.16.15.0.0   **7 Ahau 18 Pop**
> 9.17. 0.0.0   **13 Ahau 18 Cumhu**
>   etc.

Compare glyph 1 with figure 16, *m*, *n*, and glyph 2 with figure 19, *a'*, *b'*. In glyphs 8 and 9 appears a Secondary-series number consisting of 18 kins, 11 uinals, and 11 tuns (11.11.18). Reducing this number to units of the first order and counting it forward from the date next preceding it in the text, **1 Muluc 2 Muan** in glyphs 1 and 2, the terminal date reached will be **13 Manik 0 Xul**, which the student will find recorded in glyphs 10 and 11. Compare glyph 10 with figure 16, *j*, and glyph 11 with figure 19, *i*, *j*. The next Secondary-series number appears in glyphs 22 and 23, and consists of 19 kins, 9 uinals, and 8 tuns (8.9.19). Reducing this to units of the first order and counting forward from the date next preceding it in the text, **13 Manik 0 Xul** in glyphs 10 and 11, the terminal date reached will be **11 Cimi 19 Mac**, which the student will find recorded in glyphs 24 and 25. Compare glyph 24 with figure 16, *h*, *i*, and glyph 25 with figure 19, *w*, *x*. Although no number appears in glyph 26, there follows in glyphs 27 and 28 the date **1 Muluc 2 Kankin**, which the student will find is just three days later than **11 Cimi 19 Mac**, that is, one day **12 Manik 0 Kankin**, two days **13 Lamat 1 Kankin**, and three days **1 Muluc 2 Kankin**.

In spite of the fact that all these numbers are counted regularly from the dates next preceding them to reach the dates next following them, there is apparently no glyph in this text which will fix the position of any one of the above dates in the Long Count. Moreover, since none of the day parts show the day sign **Ahau**, it is evident that none of these dates can end any uinal, tun, katun, or cycle in the Long Count, hence their positions can not be determined by the method used in fixing the dates in figure 83, *A* and *B*.

There is, however, another method by means of which Calendar-round dates may sometimes be referred to their proper positions in the Long Count. A monument which shows only Calendar-round dates may be associated with another monument or a building, the dates of which are fixed in the Long Count. In such cases the fixed dates usually will show the positions to which the Calendar-round dates are to be referred.

Taking any one of the dates given on Altar 5 in plate 25, as the last, **1 Muluc 2 Kankin**, for example, the positions at which this date occurred in Cycle 9 may be determined from Goodman's Tables to be as follows:

9. 0.16. 5.9	**1 Muluc 2 Kankin**
9. 3. 9. 0.9	**1 Muluc 2 Kankin**
9. 6. 1.13.9	**1 Muluc 2 Kankin**
9. 8.14. 8.9	**1 Muluc 2 Kankin**
9.11. 7. 3.9	**1 Muluc 2 Kankin**
9.13.19.16.9	**1 Muluc 2 Kankin**
9.16.12.11.9	**1 Muluc 2 Kankin**
9.19. 5. 6.9	**1 Muluc 2 Kankin**

Next let us ascertain whether or not Altar 5 was associated with any other monument or building at Tikal, the date of which is fixed unmistakably in the Long Count. Says Mr. Teobert Maler, the discoverer of this monument:[1] "A little to the north, fronting the north side of this second temple and very near it, is a masonry quadrangle once, no doubt, containing small chambers and having an entrance to the south. In the middle of this quadrangle stands Stela 16 in all its glory, still unharmed, *and in front of it, deeply buried in the earth, we found Circular Altar 5,* which was destined to become so widely renowned." It is evident from the foregoing that the altar we are considering here, called by Mr. Maler "Circular Altar 5," was found in connection with another monument at Tikal, namely, Stela 16. But the date on this latter monument has already been deciphered as "**6 Ahau 13 Muan** ending Katun 14" (see pl. 21, *D;* also p. 224), and this date, as we have seen, corresponded to the Initial Series 9.14.0.0.0 **6 Ahau 13 Muan.**

Our next step is to ascertain whether or not any of the Initial-series values determined above as belonging to the date **1 Muluc 2 Kankin** on Altar 5 are near the Initial Series 9.14.0.0.0 **6 Ahau 13 Muan,** which is the Initial-series date corresponding to the Period-ending date on Stela 16. By comparing 9.14.0.0.0 with the Initial-series values of **1 Muluc 2 Kankin** given above the student will find that the fifth value, 9.13.19.16.9, corresponds with a date **1 Muluc 2 Kankin,** which was only 31 days (1 uinal and 11 kins) earlier than 9.14.0.0.0 **6 Ahau 13 Muan.** Consequently it may be concluded that 9.13.19.16.9 was the particular day **1 Muluc 2 Kankin** which the ancient scribes had in mind when they engraved this text. From this known Initial-series value the Initial-series values of the other dates on Altar 5 may be obtained by calculation. The texts on Altar 5 and Stela 16 are given below to show their close connection:

Altar 5

9.12.19.12. 9	**1 Muluc 2 Muan**	glyphs 1 and 2
11.11.18		glyphs 8 and 9
9.13.11. 6. 7	**13 Manik 0 Xul**	glyphs 10 and 11
8. 9.19		glyphs 22 and 23
9.13.19.16. 6	**11 Cimi 19 Mac**	glyphs 24 and 25
(3)	undeclared	
9.13.19.16. 9	**1 Muluc 2 Kankin**	glyphs 27 and 28
(1.11)	(Time between the two monuments, 31 days.)	

Stela 16

| 9.14.0.0.0 | **6 Ahau 13 Muan** | A1–A4 |

---

[1] Maler, 1911: No. 1, p. 40.

Sometimes, however, monuments showing Calendar-round dates stand alone, and in such cases it is almost impossible to fix their dates in the Long Count. At Yaxchilan in particular Calendar-round dating seems to have been extensively employed, and for this reason less progress has been made there than elsewhere in deciphering the inscriptions.

ERRORS IN THE ORIGINALS

Before closing the presentation of the subject of the Maya inscriptions the writer has thought it best to insert a few texts which show

FIG. 84. Texts showing actual errors in the originals: *A*, Lintel, Yaxchilan; *B*, Altar Q, Copan; *C*, Stela 23, Naranjo.

actual errors in the originals, mistakes due to the carelessness or oversight of the ancient scribes.

Errors in the original texts may be divided into two general classes: (1) Those which are revealed by inspection, and (2) those which do not appear until after the indicated calculations have been made and the results fail to agree with the glyphs recorded.

An example of the first class is illustrated in figure 84, *A*. A very cursory inspection of this text—an Initial Series from a lintel at Yaxchilan—will show that the uinal coefficient in C1 represents an impossible condition from the Maya point of view. This glyph as it stands unmistakably records 19 uinals, a number which had no existence in the Maya system of numeration, since 19 uinals are always recorded as 1 tun and 1 uinal.[1] Therefore the coefficient in C1 is incorrect on its face, a fact we have been able to determine before proceeding with the calculation indicated. If not 19, what then was the coefficient the ancient scribe should have engraved in its place? Fortunately the rest of this text is unusually clear, the Initial-series number 9.15.6.?.1 appearing in B1–D1, and the terminal date which it reaches, **7 Imix 19 Zip**, appearing in C2 D2. Compare C2 with figure 16, *a*, *b*, and D2 with figure 19, *d*. We know to begin with that the uinal coefficient must be one of the eighteen numerals 0 to 17, inclusive. Trying 0 first, the number will be 9.15.6.0.1, which the student will find leads to the date **7 Imix 4 Chen**. Our first trial, therefore, has proved unsuccessful, since the date recorded is **7 Imix 19 Zip**. The day parts agree, but the month parts are not the same. This month part **4 Chen** is useful, however, for one thing, it shows us how far distant we are from the month part **19 Zip**, which is recorded. It appears from Table XV that in counting forward from position **4 Chen** just 260 days are required to reach position **19 Zip**. Consequently, our first trial number 9.15.6.0.1 falls short of the number necessary by just 260 days. But 260 days are equal to 13 uinals; therefore we must increase 9.15.6.0.1 by 13 uinals. This gives us the number 9.15.6.13.1. Reducing this to units of the first order and solving for the terminal date, the date reached will be **7 Imix 19 Zip**, which agrees with the date recorded in C2 D2. We may conclude, therefore, that the uinal coefficient in C1 should have been 13, instead of 19 as recorded.

Another error of the same kind—that is, one which may be detected by inspection—is shown in figure 84, *B*. Passing over glyphs 1, 2, and 3, we reach in glyph 4 the date **5 Kan 13 Uo**. Compare the upper half of 4 with figure 16, *f*, and the lower half with figure 19, *b*, *c*. The coefficient of the month sign is very clearly 13, which represents an impossible condition when used to indicate the position of a day whose name is **Kan**; for, according to Table VII, the only positions which the day **Kan** can ever occupy in any division of the year are 2, 7, 12, and 17. Hence, it is evident that we have detected an error in this text before proceeding with the calculations indicated. Let us endeavor to ascertain the coefficient which should have been used with the month sign in glyph 4 instead of the 13 actually recorded. These glyphs present seemingly a regular Secondary Series, the starting point being given in 1 and 2, the number in 3, and the terminal date in 4. Counting this number 3.4 forward from the starting point, **6 Ahau 13 Kayab**, the terminal date reached will be **5 Kan 12 Uo**. Comparing this with the terminal date actually recorded, we find that the two agree except for the month coefficient. But since the date recorded represents an impossible condition, as we

---

[1] For a seeming exception to this statement, in the codices, see p. 110, footnote 1.

have shown, we are justified in assuming that the month coefficient which should have been used in glyph 4 was 12, instead of 13.   In other words, the craftsman to whom the sculpturing of this inscription was intrusted engraved here 3 dots instead of 2 dots, and 1 ornamental crescent, which, together with the 2 bars present, would have given the month coefficient determined by calculation, 12.   An error of this kind might occur very easily and indeed in many cases may be apparent rather than real, being due to weathering rather than to a mistake in the original text.

Some errors in the inscriptions, however, can not be detected by inspection, and develop only after the calculations indicated have been performed, and the results are found to disagree with the glyphs recorded.   Errors of this kind constitute the second class mentioned above.   A case in point is the Initial Series on the west side of Stela E at Quirigua, figured in plate 24, *A*.   In this text the Initial-series number recorded in A4–A6 is very clearly 9.14.12.4.17, and the terminal date in B6–B8b is equally clearly **12 Caban 5 Kayab**.   Now, if this number 9.14.12.4.17 is reduced to units of the first order and is counted forward from the same starting point as practically all other Initial Series, the terminal date reached will be **3 Caban 10 Kayab**, not **12 Caban 5 Kayab**, as recorded.   Moreover, if the same number is counted forward from the date **4 Ahau 8 Zotz**, which may have been another starting point for Initial Series, as we have seen, the terminal date reached will be **3 Caban 10 Zip**, not **12 Caban 5 Kayab**, as recorded.   The inference is obvious, therefore, that there is some error in this text, since the number recorded can not be made to reach the date recorded.   An error of this kind is difficult to detect, because there is no indication in the text as to which glyph is the one at fault.   The first assumption the writer makes in such cases is that the date is correct and that the error is in one of the period-glyph coefficients.   Referring to Goodman's Table, it will be found that the date **12 Caban 5 Kayab** occurred at the following positions in Cycle 9 of the Long Count:

9. 1. 9.11.17	12 Caban 5 Kayab
9. 4. 2. 6.17	12 Caban 5 Kayab
9. 6.15. 1.17	12 Caban 5 Kayab
9. 9. 7.14.17	12 Caban 5 Kayab
9.12. 0. 9.17	12 Caban 5 Kayab
9.14.13. 4.17	12 Caban 5 Kayab
9.17. 5.17.17	12 Caban 5 Kayab
9.19.18.12.17	12 Caban 5 Kayab

An examination of these values will show that the sixth in the list, 9.14.13.4.17, is very close to the number recorded in our text, 9.14.12.4.17.   Indeed, the only difference between the two is that the former has 13 tuns while the latter has only 12.   The similarity between these two numbers is otherwise so close and the error in this event would be so slight—the record of 2 dots and 1 ornamental crescent instead of 3 dots—that the conclusion is almost inevitable that the error here is in the tun coefficient, 12 having been recorded instead of 13. In this particular case the Secondary Series and the Period-ending date, which follow the Initial-series number 9.14.12.4.17, prove that the above reading of 13 tuns for the 12 actually recorded is the one correction needed to rectify the error in this text.

Another example indicating an error which can not be detected by inspection is shown in figure 84, *C*. In glyphs 1 and 2 appears the date **8 Eznab 16 Uo** (compare glyph 1 with fig. 16, *c'*, and glyph 2 with fig. 19, *b*, *c*). In glyph 3 follows a number consisting of 17 kins and 4 uinals (4.17). Finally, in glyphs 4 and 5 is recorded the date **2 Men 13 Yaxkin** (compare glyph 4 with fig. 16, *y*, and glyph 5 with fig. 19, *k*, *l*). This has every appearance of being a Secondary Series, of which **8 Eznab 16 Uo** is the starting point, 4.17, the number to be counted, and **2 Men 13 Yaxkin** the terminal date. Reducing 4.17 to units of the first order and counting it forward from the starting point indicated, the terminal date reached will be **1 Men 13 Yaxkin**. This differs from the terminal date recorded in glyphs 4 and 5 in having a day coefficient of 1 instead of 2. Since this involves but a very slight change in the original text, we are probably justified in assuming that the day coefficient in glyph 4 should have been 1 instead of 2, as recorded.

One more example will suffice to show the kind of errors usually encountered in the inscriptions. In plate 26 is figured the Initial Series from Stela N at Copan. The introducing glyph appears in A1 and is followed by the Initial-series number 9.16.10.0.0 in A2–A6, all the coefficients of which are unusually clear. Reducing this to units of the first order and solving for the terminal date, the date reached will be **1 Ahau 3 Zip**. This agrees with the terminal date recorded in A7–A15 except for the month coefficient, which is 8 in the text instead of 3, as determined by calculation. Assuming that the date recorded is correct and that the error is in the coefficient of the period glyphs, the next step is to find the positions in Cycle 9 at which the date **1 Ahau 8 Zip** occurred. Referring to Goodman's Tables, these will be found to be:

9. 0. 8.11.0	**1 Ahau 8 Zip**
9. 3. 1. 6.0	**1 Ahau 8 Zip**
9. 5.14. 1.0	**1 Ahau 8 Zip**
9. 8. 6.14.0	**1 Ahau 8 Zip**
9.10.19. 9.0	**1 Ahau 8 Zip**
9.13.12. 4.0	**1 Ahau 8 Zip**
9.16. 4.17.0	**1 Ahau 8 Zip**
9.18.17.12.0	**1 Ahau 8 Zip**

PLATE 26

INITIAL SERIES ON STELA N, COPAN, SHOWING
ERROR IN MONTH COEFFICIENT

The number in the above list coming nearest to the number recorded in this text (9.16.10.0.0) is the next to the last, 9.16.4.17.0. But in order to reach this value of the date **1 Ahau 8 Zip** (9.16.4.17.0) with the number actually recorded, two considerable changes in it are first necessary, (1) replacing the 10 tuns in A4 by 4 tuns, that is, changing 2 bars to 4 dots, and (2) replacing 0 uinals in A5 by 17 uinals, that is, changing the 0 sign to 3 bars and 2 dots. But these changes involve a very considerable alteration of the original, and it seems highly improbable, therefore, that the date here *intended* was 9.16.4.17.0 **1 Ahau 8 Zip**. Moreover, as any other number in the above list involves at least three changes of the number recorded in order to reach **1 Ahau 8 Zip**, we are forced to the conclusion that the error must be in the terminal date, not in one of the coefficients of the period glyphs. Let us therefore assume in our next trial that the Initial-series number is correct as it stands, and that the error lies somewhere in the terminal date. But the terminal date reached in counting 9.16.10.0.0 forward in the Long Count will be **1 Ahau 3 Zip**, as we have seen on the preceding page, and this date differs from the terminal date recorded by 5—1 bar in the month coefficient. It would seem probable, therefore, that the bar to the left of the month sign in A15 should have been omitted, in which case the text would correctly record the date 9.16.10.0.0 **1 Ahau 3 Zip**.

The student will note that in all the examples above given the errors have been in the numerical coefficients, and not in the signs to which they are attached; in other words, that although the numerals are sometimes incorrectly recorded, the period, day, and month glyphs never are.

Throughout the inscriptions, the exceptions to this rule are so very rare that the beginner is strongly advised to disregard them altogether, and to assume when he finds an incorrect text that the error is in one of the numerical coefficients. It should be remembered also in this connection that errors in the inscriptions are exceedingly rare, and a glyph must not be condemned as incorrect until every effort has been made to explain it in some other way.

This concludes the presentation of texts from the inscriptions. The student will have noted in the foregoing examples, as was stated in Chapter II, that practically the only advances made looking toward the decipherment of the glyphs have been on the chronological side. It is now generally admitted that the relative ages [1] of most Maya monuments can be determined from the dates recorded upon them, and that the final date in almost every inscription indicates the time at or near which the monument bearing it was erected, or at least formally dedicated. The writer has endeavored to show, moreover,

---

[1] That is, the age of one compared with the age of another, without reference to their actual age as expressed in terms of our own chronology.

that many, if indeed not most, of the monuments, were "time markers" or "period stones," in every way similar to the "period stones" which the northern Maya are known to [1] have erected at regularly recurring periods. That the period which was used as this chronological unit may have varied in different localities and at different epochs is not at all improbable. The northern Maya at the time of the Spanish Conquest erected a "period stone" every katun, while the evidence presented in the foregoing texts, particularly those from Quirigua and Copan, indicates that the chronological unit in these two cities at least was the hotun, or quarter-katun period. Whatever may have been the chronological unit used, the writer believes that the best explanation for the monuments found so abundantly in the Maya area is that they were "period stones," erected to commemorate or mark the close of successive periods.

That we have succeeded in deciphering, up to the present time, only the calendric parts of the inscriptions, the chronological skeleton of Maya history as it were, stripped of the events which would vitalize it, should not discourage the student nor lead him to minimize the importance of that which is already gained. Thirty years ago the Maya inscriptions were a sealed book, yet to-day we read in the glyphic writing the rise and fall of the several cities in relation to one another, and follow the course of Maya development even though we can not yet fill in the accompanying background. Future researches, we may hope, will reconstruct this background from the undeciphered glyphs, and will reveal the events of Maya history which alone can give the corresponding chronology a human interest.

---

[1] See Chapter II for the discussion of this point and the quotations from contemporary authorities, both Spanish and native, on which the above statement is based.

Chapter VI

THE CODICES

The present chapter will treat of the application of the material presented in Chapters III and IV to texts drawn from the codices, or hieroglyphic manuscripts; and since these deal in great part with the tonalamatl, or sacred year of 260 days, as we have seen (p. 31), this subject will be taken up first.

Texts Recording Tonalamatls

The *tonalamatl*, or 260-day period, as represented in the codices is usually divided into five parts of 52 days each, although tonalamatls of four parts, each containing 65 days, and tonalamatls of ten parts, each containing 26 days, are not at all uncommon. These divisions are further subdivided, usually into unequal parts, all the divisions in one tonalamatl, however, having subdivisions of the same length.

So far as its calendric side is concerned,[1] the tonalamatl may be considered as having three essential parts, as follows:

1. A column of day signs.

2. Red numbers, which are the coefficients of the day signs.

3. Black numbers, which show the distances between the days designated by (1) and (2).

The number of the day signs in (1), usually 4, 5, or 10, shows the number of parts into which the tonalamatl is divided. Every red number in (2) is used *once* with every day sign in (1) to designate a day which is reached in counting one of the black numbers in (3) forward from another of the days recorded by (1) and (2). The most important point for the student to grasp in studying the Maya tonalamatl is the fundamental difference between the use of the red numbers and the black numbers. The former are used only as day coefficients, and together with the day signs show the days which begin the divisions and subdivisions of the tonalamatl. The black numbers, on the other hand, are exclusively *time counters*, which show only the distances between the dates indicated by the day signs and their corresponding coefficients among the red numbers. They show in effect the lengths of the periods and subperiods into which the tonalamatl is divided.

---

[1] As explained on p. 31, tonalamatls were probably used by the priests in making prophecies or divinations. This, however, is a matter apart from their composition, that is, length, divisions, dates, and method of counting, which more particularly concerns us here.

Most of the numbers, that is (2) and (3), in the tonalamatl are presented in a horizontal row across the page or pages [1] of the manuscript, the red alternating with the black. In some instances, however, the numbers appear in a vertical column or pair of columns, though in this case also the same alternation in color is to be observed. More rarely the numbers are scattered over the page indiscriminately, seemingly without fixed order or arrangement.

It will be noticed in each of the tonalamatls given in the following examples that the record is greatly abbreviated or skeletonized. In the first place, we see no month signs, and consequently the days recorded are not shown to have had any fixed positions in the year. Furthermore, since the year positions of the days are not fixed, any day could recur at intervals of every 260 days, or, in other words, any tonalamatl with the divisions peculiar to it could be used in endless repetition throughout time, commencing anew every 260 days, regardless of the positions of these days in succeeding years. Nor is this omission the only abbreviation noticed in the presentation of the tonalamatl. Although every tonalamatl contained 260 days, only the days commencing its divisions and subdivisions appear in the record, and even these are represented in an abbreviated form. For example, instead of repeating the numerical coefficients with each of the day signs in (1), the coefficient was written once above the column of day signs, and in this position was regarded as belonging to each of the different day signs in turn. It follows from this fact that all the main divisions of the tonalamatl begin with days the coefficients of which are the same. Concerning the beginning days of the subdivisions, a still greater abbreviation is to be noted. The day signs are not shown at all, and only their numerical coefficients appear in the record. The economy of space resulting from the above abbreviations in writing the days will appear very clearly in the texts to follow.

In reading tonalamatls the first point to be determined is the name of the day with which the tonalamatl began. This will be found thus:

Rule 1. To find the beginning day of a tonalamatl, prefix the first red number, which will usually be found immediately above the column of the day signs, to the uppermost [2] day sign in the column.

From this day as a starting point, the first black number in the text is to be counted forward; and *the coefficient* of the day reached will be the second red number in the text. As stated above, the *day signs* of the beginning days of the subdivisions are always omitted. From the second red number, which, as we have seen, is the coeffi-

---

[1] The codices are folded like a screen or fan, and when opened form a continuous strip sometimes several yards in length. As will appear later, in many cases one tonalamatl runs across several pages of the manuscript.

[2] If there should be two or more columns of day signs the topmost sign of the left-hand column is to be read first.

cient of the beginning day of the second *subdivision* of the first division, the *second black number* is to be counted forward in order to reach the third red number, which is the coefficient of the day beginning the *third subdivision* of the first division. This operation is continued until the last black number has been counted forward from the red number just preceding it and the last red number has been reached.

This last red number will be found to be the same as the first red number, and the day which the count will have reached will be shown by the first red number (or the last, since the two are identical) used with the *second day sign* in the column. And this latter day will be the beginning day of *the second division* of the tonalamatl. From this day the count proceeds as before. The black numbers are added to the red numbers immediately preceding them in each case, until the last red number is reached, which, together with *the third day sign* in the column, forms the beginning day of *the third division* of the tonalamatl. After this operation has been repeated until the last red number in the last division of the tonalamatl has been reached—that is, the 260th day—the count will be found to have reentered itself, or in other words, the day reached by counting forward the last black number of the last division will be the same as the beginning day of the tonalamatl.

It follows from the foregoing that the sum of all the black numbers multiplied by the number·of day signs in the column—the number of main divisions in the tonalamatl—will equal exactly 260.   If any tonalamatl fails to give 260 as the result of this test, it may be regarded as incorrect or irregular.

The foregoing material may be reduced to the following:

Rule 2. To find the coefficients of the beginning days of succeeding divisions and subdivisions of the tonalamatl, add the black numbers to the red numbers immediately preceding them in each case, and, after subtracting all the multiples of 13 possible, the resulting number will be the coefficient of the beginning day desired.

Rule 3. To find the day signs of the beginning days of the succeeding divisions and subdivisions of the tonalamatl, count forward in Table I the black number from the day sign of the beginning day of the preceding division or subdivision, and the day name reached in Table I will be the day sign desired. If it is at the beginning of one of the *main divisions* of the tonalamatl, the day sign reached will be found to be recorded in the column of day signs, but if at the beginning of a *subdivision* it will be unexpressed.

To these the test rule above given may be added:

Rule 4. The sum of all the black numbers multiplied by the number of day signs in the column of day signs will equal exactly 260 if the tonalamatl is perfectly regular and correct.

In plate 27 is figured page 12 of the Dresden Codex. It will be noted that this page is divided into three parts by red division lines; after the general practice these have been designated *a*, *b*, and *c*, *a* being applied to the upper part, *b* to the middle part, and *c* to the lower part. Thus "Dresden 12b" designates the middle part of page 12 of the Dresden Codex, and "Dresden 15c" the lower part of page 15 of the same manuscript. Some of the pages of the codices are divided into four parts, or again, into two, and some are not divided at all. The same description applies in all cases, the parts being lettered from top to bottom in the same manner throughout.

The first tonalamatl presented will be that shown in Dresden 12b (see the middle division in pl. 27). The student will readily recognize the three essential parts mentioned on page 251: (1) The column of day signs, (2) the red numbers, and (3) the black numbers. Since there are five day signs in the column at the left of the page, it is evident that this tonalamatl has five main divisions. The first point to establish is the day with which this tonalamatl commenced. According to rule 1 (p. 252) this will be found by prefixing the first red number to the topmost day sign in the column. The first red number in Dresden 12b stands in the regular position (above the column of day signs), and is very clearly 1, that is, one red dot. A comparison of the topmost day sign in this column with the forms of the day signs in figure 17 will show that the day sign here recorded is **Ix** (see fig. 17, *t*), and the opening day of this tonalamatl will be, therefore, **1 Ix**. The next step is to find the beginning days of the succeeding subdivisions of the first main division of the tonalamatl, which, as we have just seen, commenced with the day **1 Ix**. According to rule 2 (p. 253), the first black number—in this case 13, just to the right of and slightly below the day sign **Ix**—is to be added to the red number immediately preceding it—in this case 1—in order to give the coefficient of the day beginning the next subdivision, all 13s possible being first deducted from the resulting number. Furthermore, this coefficient will be the red number next following the black number.

Applying this rule to the present case, we have:

1 (first red number) + 13 (next black number) = 14. Deducting all the 13s possible, we have left 1 (14 − 13) as the coefficient of the day beginning the next subdivision of the tonalamatl. This number 1 will be found as the red number immediately following the first black number, 13. To find the corresponding day sign, we must turn to rule 3 (p. 253) and count forward in Table I this same black number, 13, from the preceding day sign, in this case **Ix**. The day sign reached will be **Manik**. But since this day begins only a *subdivision* in this tonalamatl, not one of the *main divisions*, its day sign will not be recorded, and we have, therefore, the day **1 Manik**,

PLATE 27.

PAGE 12 OF THE DRESDEN CODEX, SHOWING
TONALAMATLS IN ALL THREE DIVISIONS

of which the 1 is expressed by the second red number and the name part **Manik** only indicated by the calculations.

The beginning day of the next subdivision of the tonalamatl may now be calculated from the day **1 Manik** by means of rules 2 and 3 (p. 253). Before proceeding with the calculation incident to this step it will be necessary first to examine the next black number in our tonalamatl. This will be found to be composed of this sign (*), to which 6 (1 bar and 1 dot) has been affixed. It was explained on page 92 that in representing tonalamatls the Maya had to have a sign which by itself would signify the number 20, since numeration by position was impossible. This special character for the number 20 was given in figure 45, and a comparison of it with the sign here under discussion will show that the two are identical. But in the present example the number 6 is attached to this sign thus: (**), and the whole number is to be read $20+6=26$. This number, as we have seen in Chapter IV, would ordinarily have been written thus (†): 1 unit of the second order (20 units of the first order) $+6$ units of the first order $=26$. As explained on page 92, however, numeration by position—that is, columns of units— was impossible in the tonalamatls, in which many of the numbers appear in a horizontal row, consequently some character had to be devised which by itself would stand for the number 20.

Returning to our text, we find that the "next black number" is 26 $(20+6)$, and this is to be added to the red number 1 next preceding it, which, as we have seen, is an abbreviation for the day **1 Manik** (see rule 2, p. 253). Adding 26 to 1 gives 27, and deducting all the 13s possible, namely, two, we have left 1 $(27-26)$; this number 1, which is the coefficient of the beginning day of the next *subdivision*, will be found recorded just to the right of the black 26.

The day sign corresponding to this coefficient 1 will be found by counting forward 26 in Table I from the day name **Manik**. This will give the day name **Ben**, and **1 Ben** will be, therefore, the beginning day of the next subdivision (the third subdivision of the first main division).

The next black number in our text is 13, and proceeding as before, this is to be added to the red number next preceding it, 1, the abbreviation for **1 Ben**. Adding 13 to 1 we have 14, and deducting all the 23s possible, we obtain 1 again (14–13), which is recorded just to the right of the black 13 (rule 2, p. 253).[1] Counting forward 13 in Table I from the day name **Ben**, the day name reached will be **Cimi**, and the day **1 Cimi** will be the beginning day of the next part of the tonalamatl. But since 13 is the last black number, we should have reached in **1 Cimi** the beginning day of the *second main division* of

---

[1] In the original this last red dot has disappeared. The writer has inserted it here to avoid confusing the beginner in his first acquaintance with a tonalamatl.

the tonalamatl (see p. 253), and this is found to be the case, since the day sign **Cimi** is *the second* in the column of day signs to the left. Compare this form with figure 17, *i, j*. The day recorded is therefore **1 Cimi**.

The first division of the tonalamatl under discussion is subdivided, therefore, into three parts, the first part commencing with the day **1 Ix,** containing 13 days; the second commencing with the day **1 Manik,** containing 26 days; and the third commencing with the day **1 Ben,** containing 13 days.

The second division of the tonalamatl commences with the day **1 Cimi,** as we have seen above, and adding to this the first black number, 13, as before, according to rules 2 and 3 (p. 253), the beginning day of the next subdivision will be found to be **1 Cauac.** Of this, however, only the 1 is declared (see to the right of the black 13). Adding the next black number, 26, to this day, according to the above rules the beginning day of the next subdivision will be found to be **1 Chicchan.** Of this, however, the 1 again is the only part declared. Adding the next and last black number, 13, to this day, **1 Chicchan,** according to the rules just mentioned the beginning day of the next, or third, main division will be found to be **1 Eznab.** Compare the third day sign in the column of day signs with the form for **Eznab** in figure 17, *z, a'.* The second division of this tonalamatl contains, therefore, three parts: The first, commencing with the day **1 Cimi,** containing 13 days; the second, commencing with the day **1 Cauac,** containing 26 days; and the third, commencing with the day **1 Chicchan,** containing 13 days.

Similarly the third division, commencing with the day **1 Eznab,** could be shown to have three parts, of 13, 26, and 13 days each, commencing with the day **1 Eznab, 1 Chuen,** and **1 Caban,** respectively. It could be shown, also, that the fourth division commenced with the day **1 Oc** (compare the fourth sign in the column of day signs with figure 17, *o*), and, further, that it had three subdivisions containing 13, 26, and 13 days each, commencing with the days **1 Oc, 1 Akbal,** and **1 Muluc,** respectively. Finally, the fifth and last division of the tonalamatl will commence with the day **1 Ik.** Compare the last day sign in the column of day signs with figure 17, *c, d*; and its three subdivisions of 13, 26, and 13 days each with the days **1 Ik, 1 Men,** and **1 Imix,** respectively. The student will note also that when the last black number, 13, has been added to the beginning day of the *last subdivision* of the *last division*, the day reached will be **1 Ix,** the day with which the tonalamatl commenced. This period is continuous, therefore, reentering itself immediately on its conclusion and commencing anew.

There follows below an outline [1] of this particular tonalamatl:

	1st Division	2d Division	3d Division	4th Division	5th Division
1st part, 13 days, beginning with day.............	1 Ix	1 Cimi	1 Eznab	1 Oc	1 Ik
2d part, 26 days, beginning with day.............	1 Manik	1 Cauac	1 Chuen	1 Akbal	1 Men
3d part, 13 days, beginning with day.............	1 Ben	1 Chicchan	1 Caban	1 Muluc	1 Imix
Total number of days	52	52	52	52	52

Next tonalamatl: 1st Division, 1st part, 13 days, beginning with the day 1 Ix, etc.

We may now apply rule 4 (p. 253) as a test to this tonalamatl. Multiplying the sum of all the black numbers, $13 + 26 + 13 = 52$, by the number of day signs in the column of day signs, 5, we obtain 260 (52×5), which proves that this tonalamatl is regular and correct.

The student will note in the middle division of plate 27 that the pictures are so arranged that one picture stands under the first sub-divisions of all the divisions, the second picture under the second subdivisions, and the third under the third subdivisions. It has been conjectured that these pictures represent the gods who were the patrons or guardians of the subdivisions of the tonalamatls, under which each appears. In the present case the first god pictured is the Death Deity, God A (see fig. 3). Note the fleshless lower jaw, the truncated nose, and the vertebræ. The second deity is unknown, but the third is again the Death God, having the same characteristics as the god in the first picture. The cloak worn by this deity in the third picture shows the crossbones, which would seem to have been an emblem of death among the Maya as among us. The glyphs above these pictures probably explain the nature of the periods to which they refer, or perhaps the ceremonies peculiar or appropriate to them. In many cases the name glyphs of the deities who appear below them are given; for example, in the present text, the second and sixth glyphs in the upper row [2] record in each case the fact that the Death God is figured below.

The glyphs above the pictures offer one of the most promising problems in the Maya field. It seems probable, as just explained, that the four or six glyphs which stand above each of the pictures in a tonalamatl tell the meaning of the picture to which they are appended, and any advances made, looking toward their decipher-ing, will lead to far-reaching results in the meaning of the nonnu-

[1] This and similar outlines which follow are to be read down in columns.
[2] The fifth sign in the lower row is also a sign of the Death God (see fig. 3). Note the eyelashes, suggesting the closed eyes of the dead.

merical and noncalendric signs. In part at least they show the name glyphs of the gods above which they occur, and it seems not unlikely that the remaining glyphs may refer to the actions of the deities who are portrayed; that is, to the ceremonies in which they are engaged. More extended researches along this line, however, must be made before this question can be answered.

The next tonalamatl to be examined is that shown in the lower division of plate 27, Dresden 12c. At first sight this would appear to be another tonalamatl of five divisions, like the preceding one, but a closer examination reveals the fact that the last day sign in the column of day signs is like the first, and that consequently there are only four different signs denoting four divisions. The last, or fifth sign, like the last red number to which it corresponds, merely indicates that after the 260th day the tonalamatl reenters itself and commences anew.

Prefixing the first red number, 13, to the first day sign, **Chuen** (see fig. 17, *p*, *q*), according to rule 1 (p. 252), the beginning day of the tonalamatl will be found to be **13 Chuen**. Adding to this the first black number, 26, according to rules 2 and 3 (p. 253), the beginning day of the next subdivision will be found to be **13 Caban.** Since this day begins only a subdivision of the tonalamatl, however, its name part **Caban** is omitted, and merely the coefficient 13 recorded. Commencing with the day **13 Caban** and adding to it the next black number in the text, again 26, according to rules 2 and 3 (p. 253), the beginning day of the next subdivision will be found to be **13 Akbal,** represented by its coefficient 13 only. Adding the last black number in the text, 13, to **13 Akbal,** according to the rules just mentioned, the beginning day of the next part of the tonalamatl will be found to be **13 Cib.** And since the black 13 which gave this new day is the last black number in the text, the new day **13 Cib** will be the beginning day of the next or *second division* of the tonalamatl, and it will be recorded as the second sign in the column of day signs. Compare the second day sign in the column of day signs with figure 17, *v*, *w*.

Following the above rules, the student will have no difficulty in working out the beginning days of the remaining divisions and subdivisions of this tonalamatl. These are given below, though the student is urged to work them out independently, using the following outline simply as a check on his work. Adding the last black number, 13, to the beginning day of the last subdivision of the last division, **13 Eznab,** will bring the count back to the day **13 Chuen** with which the tonalamatl began:

	1st Division	2d Division	3d Division	4th Division
1st part, 26 days, beginning with day....................	13 Chuen	13 Cib	13 Imix	13 Cimi
2d part, 26 days, beginning with day....................	13 Caban	13 Ik	13 Manik	13 Eb
3d part, 13 days, beginning with day....................	13 Akbal	13 Lamat	13 Ben	13 Eznab
Total number of days	65	65	65	65

Next tonalamatl: 1st division, 1st part, 26 days, beginning with the day **13 Chuen**, etc.

Applying the test rule to this tonalamatl (see rule 4, p. 253), we have: $26+26+13=65$, the sum of the black numbers, and 4 the number of the day signs in the column of day signs,[1] $65 \times 4 = 260$, the exact number of days in a tonalamatl.

The next tonalamatl (see the upper part of pl. 27, that is, Dresden 12a) occupies only the latter two-thirds of the upper division, the black 12 and red 11 being the last black and red numbers, respectively, of another tonalamatl.

The presence of 10 day signs arranged in two parallel columns of five each would seem at first to indicate that this is a tonalamatl of 10 divisions, but it develops from the calculations that instead there are recorded here two tonalamatls of five divisions each, the first column of day signs designating one tonalamatl and the second another quite distinct therefrom.

The first red numeral is somewhat effaced, indeed all the red has disappeared and only the black outline of the glyph remains. Its position, however, above the column of day signs, seems to indicate its color and use, and we are reasonably safe in stating that the first of the two tonalamatls here recorded began with the day **8 Ahau**. Adding to this the first black number, 27, the beginning day of the next subdivision will be found to be **9 Manik**, neither the coefficient nor day sign of which appears in the text. Assuming that the calculation is correct, however, and adding the next black number, 25 (also out of place), to this day, **9 Manik**, the beginning day of the next part will be **8 Eb**. But since 25 is the last black number, **8 Eb** will be the beginning day of the next main division and should appear as the second sign in the first column of day signs. Comparison of this form with figure 17, *r*, will show that **Eb** is recorded in this place.

---

[1] The last sign **Chuen,** as mentioned above, is only a repetition of the first sign, indicating that the tonalamatl has re-entered itself.

In this manner all of the beginning days could be worked out as below:

	1st Division	2d Division	3d Division	4th Division	5th Division
1st part, 27 days, beginning with day..................	8 Ahau	8 Eb	8 Kan	8 Cib	8 Lamat
2d part, 25 days, beginning with day..................	9 Manik	9 Cauac	9 Chuen	9 Akbal	9 Men
Total number of days........	52	52	52	52	52

The application of rule 4 (p. 253) to this tonalamatl gives: $5 \times 52 = 260$, the exact number of days in a tonalamatl. As previously explained, the second column of day signs belongs to another tonalamatl, which, however, utilized the same red 8 as the first and the same black 27 and 25 as the first. The outline of this tonalamatl, which began with the day **8 Oc,** follows:

	1st Division	2d Division	3d Division	4th Division	5th Division
1st part, 27 days, beginning with day..........	8 Oc	8 Ik	8 Ix	8 Cimi	8 Eznab
2d part, 25 days, beginning with day..........	9 Caban	9 Muluc	9 Imix	9 Ben	9 Chicchan
Total number of days in...	52	52	52	52	52

The application of rule 4 (p. 253) to this tonalamatl gives: $5 \times 52 = 260$, the exact number of days in a tonalamatl. It is interesting to note that the above tonalamatl, beginning with the day **8 Oc,** commenced just 130 days later than the first tonalamatl, which began with the day **8 Ahau.** In other words, the first of the two tonalamatls in Dresden 12a was just half completed when the second one commenced, and the second half of the first tonalamatl began with the same day as the first half of the second tonalamatl, and vice versa.

The tonalamatl in plate 28, upper division, is from Dresden 15a, and is interesting because it illustrates how certain missing parts may be filled in. The first red number is missing and we can only say that this tonalamatl began with some day **Ahau.** However, adding the first black number, 34, to this day? **Ahau,** the day reached will be **13 Ix,** of which only 13 is recorded. Since **13 Ix** was reached by counting 34 forward from the day with which the count must have started, by counting back 34 from **13 Ix** the starting point will be

PLATE 28

PAGE 15 OF THE DRESDEN CODEX, SHOWING
TONALAMATLS IN ALL THREE DIVISIONS

found to be **5 Ahau**, and we may supply a red bar above the column
of the day signs. Adding the next black number, 18, to this day
13 Ix, the beginning day of the next *division* will be found to be **5 Eb**,
which appears as the second day sign in the column of day signs.

The last red number is 5, thus establishing as correct our restoration of a red 5 above the column of day signs. From here this tonalamatl presents no unusual features and it may be worked as follows:

	1st Division	2d Division	3d Division	4th Division	5th Division
1st part, 34 days, beginning with day.................	**5 Ahau**	**5 Eb**	**5 Kan**	**5 Cib**	**5 Lamat**
2d part, 18 days, beginning with day.................	13 Ix	13 Cimi	13 Eznab	13 Oc	13 Ik
Total number of days........	52	52	52	52	52

Applying rule 4 (p. 253), we have: $5 \times 52 = 260$, the exact number
of days in a tonalamatl. The next tonalamatl (see lower part of pl.
28, that is, Dresden 15c) has 10 day signs arranged in two parallel
columns of 5 each. This, at its face value, would seem to be divided
into 10 divisions, and the calculations confirm the results of the preliminary inspection.

The tonalamatl opens with the day **3 Lamat**. Adding to this the
first black number, 12, the day reached will be **2 Ahau**, of which only
the 2 is recorded here. Adding to **2 Ahau** the next black number,
14, the day reached will be **3 Ix**. And since 14 is the last black number, this new day will be the beginning of the next division in the
tonalamatl and will appear as the upper day sign in the second column.[1] Commencing with **3 Ix** and adding to it the first black number 12, the day reached will be **2 Cimi**, and adding to this the next
black number, 14, the day reached will be **3 Ahau**, which appears as
the second glyph in the first column. This same operation if carried
throughout will give the following outline of this tonalamatl:

	1st Division	2d Division	3d Division	4th Division	5th Division
1st part, 12 days, beginning with day.................	**3 Lamat**	**3 Ix**	**3 Ahau**	**3 Cimi**	**3 Eb**
2d part, 14 days, beginning with day.................	2 Ahau	2 Cimi	2 Eb	2 Eznab	2 Kan
Total number of days.......	26	26	26	26	26

[1] As previously stated, the order of reading the glyphs in columns is from left to right and top to bottom.

(Concluded)

	6th Division	7th Division	8th Division	9th Division	10th Division
1st part, 12 days, beginning with day................	3 Eznab	3 Kan	3 Oc	3 Cib	3 Ik
2d part, 14 days, beginning with day.................	2 Oc	2 Cib	2 Ik	2 Lamat	2 Ix
Total number of days.......	26	26	26	26	26

Applying rule 4 (p. 253) to this tonalamatl, we have: $10 \times 26 = 260$, the exact number of days in a tonalamatl.

The tonalamatl which appears in the middle part on plate 28—that is, Dresden 15b—extends over on page 16b, where there is a black 13 and a red 1. The student will have little difficulty in reaching the result which follows: The last day sign is the same as the first, and consequently this tonalamatl is divided into four, instead of five, divisions:

	1st Division	2d Division	3d Division	4th Division
1st part, 13 days, beginning with day...................	1 Ik	1 Manik	1 Eb	1 Caban
2d part, 31 days, beginning with day...................	1 Men	1 Ahau	1 Chicchan	1 Oc
3d part, 8 days, beginning with day	6 Cimi	6 Chuen	6 Cib	6 Imix
4th part, 13 days, beginning with day	1 Ix	1 Cauac	1 Kan	1 Muluc
Total number of days...........	65	65	65	65

Applying rule 4 (p. 253) to this tonalamatl, we have: $4 \times 65 = 260$, the exact number of days in a tonalamatl. The tonalamatls heretofore presented have all been taken from the Dresden Codex. The following examples, however, have been selected from tonalamatls in the Codex Tro-Cortesianus. The student will note that the workmanship in the latter manuscript is far inferior to that in the Dresden Codex. This is particularly true with respect to the execution of the glyphs.

The first tonalamatl figured from the Codex Tro-Cortesianus (see pl. 29) extends across the middle part of two pages (Tro-Cor. 10b, 11b). The four day signs at the left indicate that it is divided into four divisions, of which the first begins with the day **13 Ik**.[1] Adding to this the first black number 9, the day **9 Chuen** is reached, and proceeding in this manner the tonalamatl may be outlined as follows:

---

[1] The right-hand dot of the 13 is effaced.

PLATE 29

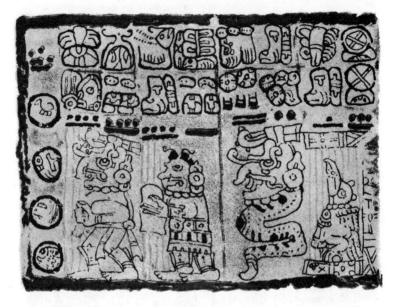

MIDDLE DIVISIONS OF PAGES 10 AND 11 OF THE CODEX
TRO-CORTESIANO, SHOWING ONE TONALAMATL
EXTENDING ACROSS THE TWO PAGES

PLATE 30

PAGE 113 OF THE CODEX TRO-CORTESIANO, SHOWING
TONALAMATLS IN THE LOWER THREE SECTIONS

MORLEY] INTRODUCTION TO STUDY OF MAYA HIEROGLYPHS 263

	1st Division	2d Division	3d Division	4th Division
1st part, 9 days, beginning with day..................	13 Ik	13 Manik	13 Eb	13 Caban
2d part, 9 days, beginning with day..................	9 Chuen	9 Cib	9 Imix	9 Cimi
3d part, 10 days, beginning with day..................	5 Ahau	5 Chicchan	5 Oc	5 Men
4th part, 6 days, beginning with day..................	2 Oc	2 Men	2 Ahau	2 Chicchan
5th part, 2 days, beginning with day..................	8 Cib	8 Imix	8 Cimi	8 Chuen
6th part, 10 days, beginning with day..................	10 Eznab	10 Akbal	10 Lamat	10 Ben
7th part, 5 days, beginning with day..................	7 Lamat	7 Ben	7 Eznab	7 Akbal
8th part, 7 days, beginning with day..................	12 Ben	12 Eznab	12 Akbal	12 Lamat
9th part, 7 days, beginning with day..................	6 Ahau [1]	6 Chicchan[1]	6 Oc [1]	6 Men [1]
Total number of days..........	65	65	65	65

[1] The manuscript has incorrectly 7.

Applying rule 4 (p. 253) to this tonalamatl, we have: $4 \times 65 = 260$, the exact number of days in a tonalamatl.

Another set of interesting tonalamatls is figured in plate 30, Tro-Cor., 102.[1] The first one on this page appears in the second division, 102b, and is divided into five parts, as the column of five day signs shows. The order of reading is from left to right in the pair of number columns, as will appear in the following outline of this tonalamatl:

	1st Division	2d Division	3d Division	4th Division	5th Division
1st part, 2 days, beginning with day........	4 Manik	4 Cauac	4 Chuen	4 Akbal	4 Men
2d part, 7 days, beginning with day........	6 Muluc	6 Imix	6 Ben	6 Chicchan	6 Caban
3d part, 2 days, beginning with day........	13 Cib	13 Lamat	13 Ahau	13 Eb	13 Kan
4th part, 10 days, beginning with day........	2 Eznab	2 Oc	2 Ik	2 Ix	2 Cimi
5th part, 9 days, beginning with day........	12 Lamat	12 Ahau	12 Eb	12 Kan	12 Cib
6th part, 22 days, beginning with day........	8 Caban	8 Muluc	8 Imix	8 Ben	8 Chicchan
Total number of days....	52	52	52	52	52

[1] In the title of plate 30 the page number should read 102 instead of 113.

Applying rule 4 (p. 253) to this tonalamatl, we have: $5 \times 52 = 260$, the exact number of days in a tonalamatl. The next tonalamatl on this page (see third division in pl. 29, that is, Tro-Cor., 102c) is interesting chiefly because of the fact that the pictures which went with the third and fourth parts of the five divisions are omitted for want of space. The outline of this tonalamatl follows:

	1st Division	2d Division	3d Division	4th Division	5th Division
1st part, 17 days, beginning with day................	4 Ahau	4 Eb	4 Kan	4 Cib	4 Lamat
2d part, 13 days, beginning with day................	8 Caban	8 Muluc	8 Imix	8 Ben	8 Chicchan
3d part, 10 days, beginning with day................	8 Oc	8 Ik	8 Ix	8 Cimi	8 Eznab
4th part, 12 days, beginning with day..........	5 Ahau	5 Eb	5 Kan	5 Cib	5 Lamat
Total number of days	52	52	52	52	52

Applying rule 4 (p. 253) to this tonalamatl, we have: $5 \times 52 = 260$, the exact number of days in a tonalamatl. The last tonalamatl in plate 29, Tro-Cor., 102d, commences with the same day, **4 Ahau**, as the preceding tonalamatl and, like it, has five divisions, each of which begins with the same day as the corresponding division in the tonalamatl just given, **4 Ahau, 4 Eb, 4 Kan, 4 Cib**, and **4 Lamat**. Tro-Cor. 102d differs from Tro-Cor. 102c in the number and length of the parts into which its divisions are divided.

Adding the first black number, 29, to the beginning day, **4 Ahau**, the day reached will be **7 Muluc**, of which only the 7 appears in the text. Adding to this the next black number, 24, the day reached will be **5 Ben**. An examination of the text shows, however, that the day actually recorded is **4 Eb**, the last red number with the second day sign. This latter day is just the day before **5 Ben**, and since the sum of the black numbers in this case does not equal any factor of 260 $(29 + 24 = 53)$, and since changing the last black number from 24 to 23 would make the sum of the black numbers equal to a factor of 260 $(29 + 23 = 52)$, and would bring the count to **4 Eb**, the day actually recorded, we are justified in assuming that there is an error in our original text, and that 23 should have been written here instead of 24. The outline of this tonalamatl, corrected as suggested, follows:

	1st Division	2d Division	3d Division	4th Division	5th Division
1st part, 29 days, beginning with day..............	4 Ahau	4 Eb	4 Kan	4 Cib	4 Lamat
2d part, 23 [1] days, beginning with day	7 Muluc	7 Imix	7 Ben	7 Chicchan	7 Caban
Total number of days	52	52	52	52	52

[1] The manuscript incorrectly has 24.

Applying rule 4 (p. 253) to this tonalamatl, we have: $52 \times 5 = 260$, the exact number of days in a tonalamatl.

The foregoing tonalamatls have been taken from the pages of the Dresden Codex or those of the Codex Tro-Cortesiano. Unfortunately, in the Codex Peresianus no complete tonalamatls remain, though one or two fragmentary ones have been noted.

No matter how they are divided or with what days they begin, all tonalamatls seem to be composed of the same essentials:

1. The calendric parts, made up, as we have seen on page 251, of (a) the column of day signs; (b) the red numbers; (c) the black numbers.

2. The pictures of anthropomorphic figures and animals engaged in a variety of pursuits, and

3. The groups of four or six glyphs above each of the pictures.

The relation of these parts to the tonalamatl as a whole is practically determined. The first is the calendric background, the chronological framework, as it were, of the period. The second and third parts amplify this and give the special meaning and significance to the subdivisions. The pictures represent in all probability the deities who presided over the several subdivisions of the tonalamatls in which they appear, and the glyphs above them probably set forth their names, as well as the ceremonies connected with, or the prognostications for, the corresponding periods.

It will be seen, therefore, that in its larger sense the meaning of the tonalamatl is no longer a sealed book, and while there remains a vast amount of detail yet to be worked out the foundation has been laid upon which future investigators may build with confidence.

In closing this discussion of the tonalamatl it may not be out of place to mention here those whose names stand as pioneers in this particular field of glyphic research. To the investigations of Prof. Ernst Förstemann we owe the elucidation of the calendric part of the tonalamatl, and to Dr. Paul Schellhas the identification of the gods and their corresponding name glyphs in parts (2) and (3), above. As pointed out at the beginning of this chapter, the most promising line of research in the codices is the groups of glyphs above the pictures, and from their decipherment will probably come the determination of the meaning of this interesting and unusual period.

TEXTS RECORDING INITIAL SERIES

Initial Series in the codices are unusual and indeed have been found, up to the present time, in only one of the three known Maya manuscripts, namely, the Dresden Codex. As represented in this manuscript, they differ considerably from the Initial Series heretofore described, all of which have been drawn from the inscriptions. This difference, however, is confined to unessentials, and the system of counting and measuring time in the Initial Series from the inscriptions is identical with that in the Initial Series from the codices.

The most conspicuous difference between the two is that in the codices the Initial Series are expressed by the second method, given on page 129, that is, numeration by position, while in the inscriptions, as we have seen, the period glyphs are used, that is, the first method, on page 105. Although this causes the two kinds of texts to appear very dissimilar, the difference is only superficial.

Another difference the student will note is the absence from the codices of the so-called Initial-series "introducing glyph." In a few cases there seems to be a sign occupying the position of the introducing glyph, but its identification as the Initial-series "introducing glyph" is by no means sure, and, moreover, as stated above, it does not occur in all cases in which there are Initial Series.

Another difference is the entire absence from the codices of Supplementary Series; this count seems to be confined exclusively to the monuments. Aside from these points the Initial Series from the two sources differ but little. All proceed from identically the same starting point, the date **4 Ahau 8 Cumhu,** and all have their terminal dates or related Secondary-series dates recorded immediately after them.

The first example of an Initial Series from the codices will be found in plate 31 (Dresden 24), in the lower left-hand corner, in the second column to the right. The Initial-series number here recorded is 9.9.16.0.0, of which the zero in the 2d place (uinals) and the zero in the 1st place (kins) are expressed by red numbers. This use of red numbers in the last two places is due to the fact that the zero sign in the codices is *always red.*

The student will note the absence of all period glyphs from this Initial Series and will observe that the multiplicands of the cycle, katun, tun, uinal, and kin are fixed by the positions of each of the corresponding multipliers. By referring to Table XIV the values of the several positions in the second method of writing the numbers will be found. and using these with their corresponding coefficients

PLATE 31

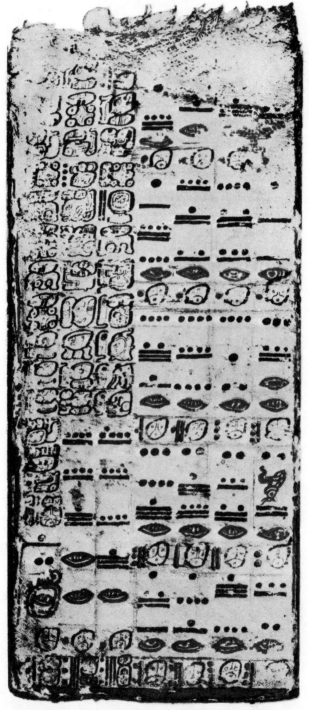

PAGE 24 OF THE DRESDEN CODEX, SHOWING
INITIAL SERIES

in each case the Initial-series number here recorded may be reduced to units of the 1st order, as follows:

$$9 \times 144,000 = 1,296,000$$
$$9 \times 7,200 = 64,800$$
$$16 \times 360 = 5,760$$
$$0 \times 20 = 0$$
$$0 \times 1 = 0$$

$$1,366,560$$

Deducting from this number all the Calendar Rounds possible, 72 (see Table XVI), it may be reduced to zero, since 72 Calendar Rounds contain exactly 1,366,560 units of the first order. See the preliminary rule on page 143.

Applying rules 1, 2, and 3 (pp. 139, 140, and 141) to the remainder, that is, 0, the terminal date of the Initial Series will be found to be **4 Ahau 8 Cumhu**, exactly the same as the starting point of Maya chronology. This must be true, since counting forward 0 from the date **4 Ahau 8 Cumhu**, the date **4 Ahau 8 Cumhu** will be reached. Instead of recording this date immediately below the last period of its Initial-series number, that is, the 0 kins, it was written below the number just to the left. The terminal date of the Initial Series we are discussing, therefore, is **4 Ahau 8 Cumhu**, and it is recorded just to the left of its usual position in the lower left-hand corner of plate 31. The coefficient of the day sign, 4, is effaced but the remaining parts of the date are perfectly clear. Compare the day sign **Ahau** with the corresponding form in figure 17, *c'*, *d'*, and the month sign **Cumhu** with the corresponding form in figure 20, *z–b'*. The Initial Series here recorded is therefore 9.9.16.0.0 **4 Ahau 8 Cumhu**. Just to the right of this Initial Series is another, the number part of which the student will readily read as follows: 9.9.9.16.0. Treating this in the usual way, it may be reduced thus:

$$9 \times 144,000 = 1,296,000$$
$$9 \times 7,200 = 64,800$$
$$9 \times 360 = 3,240$$
$$16 \times 20 = 320$$
$$0 \times 1 = 0$$

$$1,364,360$$

Deducting from this number all the Calendar Rounds possible, 71 (see Table XVI), it may be reduced to 16,780. Applying to this number rules 1, 2, and 3 (pp. 139, 140, and 141, respectively), its terminal date will be found to be **1 Ahau 18 Kayab**; this date is recorded just to the left below the kin place of the *preceding* Initial

Series. Compare the day sign and month sign of this date with figures 17, c', d', and 20, x, y, respectively. This second Initial Series in plate 31 therefore reads 9.9.9.16.0 **1 Ahau 18 Kayab.** In connection with the first of these two Initial Series, 9.9.16.0.0 **4 Ahau 8 Cumhu,** there is recorded a Secondary Series. This consists of 6 tuns, 2 uinals, and 0 kins (6.2.0) and is recorded just to the left of the first Initial Series from which it is counted, that is, in the left-hand column.

It was explained on pages 136–137 that the almost universal direction of counting was forward, but that when the count was backward in the codices, this fact was indicated by a special sign or symbol, which gave to the number it modified the significance of "backward" or "minus." This sign is shown in figure 64, and, as explained on page 137, it usually is attached only to the lowest period. Returning once more to our text, in plate 31 we see this "backward" sign—a red circle surmounted by a knot—surrounding the 0 kins of this Secondary-series number 6.2.0, and we are to conclude, therefore, that this number is to be counted backward from some date.

Counting it backward from the date which stands nearest it in our text, **4 Ahau 8 Cumhu,** the date reached will be **1 Ahau 18 Kayab.** But since the date **4 Ahau 8 Cumhu** is stated in the text to have corresponded with the Initial-series value 9.9.16.0.0, by deducting 6.2.0 from this number we may work out the Initial-series value for this date as follows:

9.9.16. 0.0	**4 Ahau 8 Cumhu**
6. 2.0	Backward
9.9. 9.16.0	**1 Ahau 18 Kayab**

The accuracy of this last calculation is established by the fact that the Initial-series value 9.9.9.16.0 is recorded as the second Initial Series on the page above described, and corresponds to the date **1 Ahau 18 Kayab** as here.

It is difficult to say why the terminal dates of these two Initial Series and this Secondary Series should have been recorded to the *left* of the numbers leading to them, and not just *below* the numbers in each case. The only explanation the writer can offer is that the ancient scribe wished to have the starting point of his Secondary-series number, **4 Ahau 8 Cumhu,** recorded as near that number as possible, that is, just below it, and consequently the Initial Series leading to this date had to stand to the right. This caused a displacement of the corresponding terminal date of his Secondary Series, **1 Ahau 18 Kayab,** which was written under the Initial Series 9.9.16.0.0; and since the Initial-series value of **1 Ahau 18 Kayab** also appears to the right of 9.9.16.0.0 as 9.9.9.16.0, this causes a displacement in its terminal date likewise.

Two other Initial Series will suffice to exemplify this kind of count in the codices. In plate 32 is figured page 62 from the Dresden Codex. In the two right-hand columns appear two black numbers. The first of these reads quite clearly 8.16.15.16.1, which the student is perfectly justified in assuming is an Initial-series number consisting of 8 cycles, 16 katuns, 15 tuns, 16 uinals, and 1 kin. Moreover, above the 8 cycles is a glyph which bears considerable resemblance to the Initial-series introducing glyph (see fig. 24,*f*). Note in particular the trinal superfix. At all events, whether it is an Initial Series or not, the first step in deciphering it will be to reduce this number to units of the first order:

$$
\begin{array}{rcl}
8 \times 144,000 &=& 1,152,000 \\
16 \times 7,200 &=& 115,200 \\
15 \times 360 &=& 5,400 \\
16 \times 20 &=& 320 \\
1 \times 0 &=& 1 \\
\hline
& & 1,272,921
\end{array}
$$

Deducting from this number all the Calendar Rounds possible, 67 (see Table XVI), it may be reduced to 1,261. Applying rules 1, 2, and 3 (pp. 139, 140, and 141, respectively) to this remainder, the terminal date reached will be **4 Imix 9 Mol**. This is not the terminal date recorded, however, nor is it the terminal date standing below the next Initial-series number to the right, 8.16.14.15.4. It would seem then that there must be some mistake or unusual feature about this Initial Series.

Immediately below the date which stands under the Initial-series number we are considering, 8.16.15.16.1, is another number consisting of 1 tun, 4 uinals, and 16 kins (1.4.16). It is not improbable that this is a Secondary-series number connected in some way with our Initial Series. The red circle surmounted by a knot which surrounds the 16 kins of this Secondary-series number (1.4.16) indicates that the whole number is to be counted *backward* from some date. Ordinarily, the first Secondary Series in a text is to be counted from the terminal date of the Initial Series, which we have found by calculation (if not by record) to be **4 Imix 9 Mol** in this case. Assuming that this is the case here, we might count 1.4.16 *backward* from the date **4 Imix 9 Mol**.

Performing all the operations indicated in such cases, the terminal date reached will be found to be **3 Chicchan 18 Zip**; this is very close to the date which is actually recorded just *above* the Secondary-series number and just below the Initial-series number. The date here recorded is **3 Chicchan 13 Zip**, and it is not improbable that the ancient scribe intended to write instead **3 Chicchan 18 Zip**, the date indicated by the calculations. We probably have here:

$$8.16.15.16.\ 1 \quad (\textbf{4 Imix 9 Mol})$$
$$1.\ 4.16 \quad \text{Backward}$$
$$8.16.14.11.\ 5 \quad \textbf{3 Chicchan 18}^{1}\ \textbf{Zip}$$

In these calculations the terminal date of the Initial Series, **4 Imix 9 Mol**, is suppressed, and the only date given is **3 Chicchan 18 Zip**, the terminal date of the Secondary Series.

Another Initial Series of this same kind, one in which the terminal date is not recorded, is shown just to the right of the preceding in plate 32. The Initial-series number 8.16.14.15.4 there recorded reduces to units of the first order as follows:

$$
\begin{aligned}
8 \times 144,000 &= 1,152,000 \\
16 \times 7,200 &= 115,200 \\
14 \times 360 &= 5,040 \\
15 \times 20 &= 300 \\
4 \times 1 &= 4 \\
\hline
&1,272,544
\end{aligned}
$$

Deducting from this number all the Calendar Rounds possible, 67 (see Table XVI), it will be reduced to 884, and applying rules 1, 2, and 3 (pp. 139, 140, and 141, respectively) to this remainder, the terminal date reached will be **4 Kan 17 Yaxkin**. This date is not recorded. There follows below, however, a Secondary-series number consisting of 6 uinals and 1 kin (6.1). The red circle around the lower term of this (the 1 kin) indicates that the whole number, 6.1, is to be counted *backward* from some date, probably, as in the preceding case, from the terminal date of the Initial Series above it. Assuming that this is the case, and counting 6.1 backward from 8.16.14.15.4 **4 Kan 17 Yaxkin**, the terminal date reached will be **13 Akbal 16 Pop**, again very close to the date recorded immediately above, **13 Akbal 15 Pop**. Indeed, the date as recorded, **13 Akbal 15 Pop**, represents an impossible condition from the Maya point of view, since the day name **Akbal** could occupy only the first, sixth, eleventh, and sixteenth positions of a month. See Table VII. Consequently, through lack of space or carelessness the ancient scribe who painted this book failed to add one dot to the three bars of the month sign's coefficient, thus making it 16 instead of the 15 actually recorded. We are obliged to make some correction in this coefficient, since, as explained above, it is obviously incorrect as it stands. Since the addition of a single dot brings the whole date into harmony with the date determined by calculation, we are probably justified

---

[1] Incorrectly recorded as 13 in the text.

in making the correction here suggested. We have recorded here therefore:

$$8.16.14.15.4 \quad \textbf{(4 Kan 17 Yaxkin)}$$
$$6.1 \quad \text{Backward}$$
$$8.16.14.\ 9.3 \quad \textbf{13 Akbal 16}^{\,1}\ \textbf{Pop}$$

In these calculations the terminal date of the Initial Series, **4 Kan 17 Yaxkin**, is suppressed and the only date given is **13 Akbal 16 Pop**, the terminal date of the Secondary Series.

The above will suffice to show the use of Initial Series in the codices, but before leaving this subject it seems best to discuss briefly the dates recorded by these Initial Series in relation to the Initial Series on the monuments. According to Professor Förstemann[2] there are 27 of these altogether, distributed as follows:

Page 24:	9. 9.16. 0. 0 [3]		Page 58:	9.12.11.11. 0
Page 24:	9. 9. 9.16. 0		Page 62:	8.16.15.16. 1
Page 31:	8.16.14.15. 4		Page 62:	8.16.14.15. 4
Page 31:	8.16. 3.13. 0		Page 63:	8.11. 8. 7. 0
Page 31:	10.13.13. 3. 2 [4]		Page 63:	8.16. 3.13. 0
Page 43:	9.19. 8.15. 0		Page 63:	10.13. 3.16. 4 [9]
Page 45:	8.17.11. 3. 0		Page 63:	10.13.13. 3. 2
Page 51:	8.16. 4. 8. 0 [5]		Page 70:	9.13.12.10. 0
Page 51:	10.19. 6. 1. 8 [6]		Page 70:	9.19.11.13. 0
Page 52:	9.16. 4.11.18 [7]		Page 70:	10.17.13.12.12
Page 52:	9.19. 5. 7. 8 [8]		Page 70:	10.11. 3.18.14
Page 52:	9.16. 4.10. 8		Page 70:	8. 6.16.12. 0
Page 52:	9.16. 4.11. 3		Page 70:	8.16.19.10. 0
Page 58:	9.18. 2. 2. 0			

There is a wide range of time covered by these Initial Series; indeed, from the earliest 8.6.16.12.0 (on p. 70) to the latest, 10.19.6.1.8 (on p. 51) there elapsed more than a thousand years. Where the difference between the earliest and the latest dates is so great, it is a matter of vital importance to determine the contemporaneous date of the manuscript. If the closing date 10.19.6.1.8 represents the time at which the manuscript was made, then the preceding dates reach back

---

[1] Incorrectly recorded as 15 in the text.

[2] *Bull. 28, Bur. Amer. Ethn.*, p. 400.

[3] The terminal dates reached have been omitted, since for comparative work the Initial-series numbers alone are sufficient to show the relative positions in the Long Count.

[4] The manuscript incorrectly reads 10.13.3.13.2; that is, reversing the position of the tun and uinal coefficients.

[5] The manuscript incorrectly reads 8.16.4.11.0. The uinal coefficient is changed to an 8, above.

[6] The manuscript incorrectly reads 10.19.6.0.8. The uinal coefficient is changed to 1, above.

[7] The manuscript incorrectly reads 9.16.4.10.18. The uinal coefficient is changed to 11, above.

[8] The manuscript incorrectly reads 9.19.8.7.8. The tun coefficient is changed to 5, above.

[9] The manuscript incorrectly reads 10.8.3.16.4. The katun coefficient is changed to 13, above. These corrections are all suggested by Professor Förstemann and are necessary if the calculations he suggests are correct, as seems probable.

for more than a thousand years. On the other hand, if 8.6.16.12.0 records the present time of the manuscript, then all the following dates are prophetic. It is a difficult question to answer, and the best authorities have seemed disposed to take a middle course, assigning as the contemporaneous date of the codex a date about the middle of Cycle 9. Says Professor Förstemann (*Bulletin 28*, p. 402) on the subject:

In my opinion my demonstration also definitely proves that these large numbers [the Initial Series] do not proceed from the future to the past, but from the past, through the present, to the future. Unless I am quite mistaken, the highest numbers among them seem actually to reach into the future, and thus to have a prophetic meaning. Here the question arises, At what point in this series of numbers does the present lie? or, Has the writer in different portions of his work adopted different points of time as the present? If I may venture to express my conjecture, it seems to me that the first large number in the whole manuscript, the 1,366,560 in the second column of page 24 [9.9.16.0.0 **4 Ahau 8 Cumhu**, the first Initial Series figured in plate 31], has the greatest claim to be interpreted as the present point of time.

In a later article (*Bulletin 28*, p. 437) Professor Förstemann says: "But I think it is more probable that the date farthest to the right (1 Ahau, 18 Zip . . .) denotes the present, the other two [namely, 9.9.16.0.0 **4 Ahau 8 Cumhu** and 9.9.9.16.0 **1 Ahau 18 Kayab**] alluding to remarkable days in the future." He assigns to this date **1 Ahau 18 Zip** the position of 9.7.16.12.0 in the Long Count.

The writer believes this theory to be untenable because it involves a correction in the original text. The date which Professor Förstemann calls **1 Ahau 18 Zip** actually reads **1 Ahau 18 Uo**, as he himself admits. The month sign he corrects to **Zip** in spite of the fact that it is very clearly **Uo**. Compare this form with figure 20, *b, c*. The date **1 Ahau 18 Uo** occurs at 9.8.16.16.0, but the writer sees no reason for believing that this date or the reading suggested by Professor Förstemann indicates the contemporaneous time of this manuscript.

Mr. Bowditch assigns the manuscript to approximately the same period, selecting the second Initial Series in plate 31, that is, 9.9.9.16.0 **1 Ahau 18 Kayab**: "My opinion is that the date 9.9.9.16.0 **1 Ahau 18 Kayab** is the present time with reference to the time of writing the codex and is the date from which the whole calculation starts."[1] The reasons which have led Mr. Bowditch to this conclusion are very convincing and will make for the general acceptance of his hypothesis.

Although the writer has no better suggestion to offer at the present time, he is inclined to believe that both of these dates are far too early for this manuscript and that it is to be ascribed to a very much later period, perhaps to the centuries following immediately the colonization of Yucatan. There can be no doubt that very early dates appear in the Dresden Codex, but rather than accept one so early as

---

[1] Bowditch, 1909: p. 279.

PLATE 32

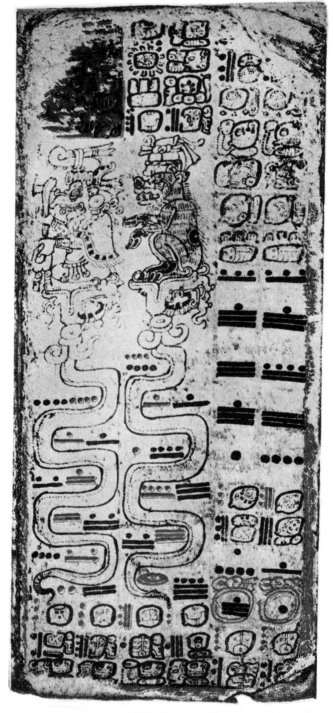

PAGE 62 OF THE DRESDEN CODEX, SHOWING THE
SERPENT NUMBERS

9.9.9.16.0 or 9.9.16.0.0 as the contemporaneous date of the manuscript the writer would prefer to believe, on historical grounds, that the manuscript now known as the Dresden Codex is a copy of an earlier manuscript and that the present copy dates from the later Maya period in Yucatan, though sometime before either Nahuatl or Castilian acculturation had begun.

Texts Recording Serpent Numbers

The Dresden Codex contains another class of numbers which, so far as known, occur nowhere else. These have been called the Serpent numbers because their various orders of units are depicted between the coils of serpents. Two of these serpents appear in plate 32. The coils of each serpent inclose two different numbers, one in red and the other in black. Every one of the Serpent numbers has six terms, and they represent by far the highest numbers to be found in the codices. The black number in the first, or left-hand serpent in plate 32, reads as follows: 4.6.7.12.4.10, which, reduced to units of the first order, reads:

$$
\begin{array}{rll}
4 \times 2,880,000 & = & 11,520,000 \\
6 \times 144,000 & = & 864,000 \\
7 \times 7,200 & = & 50,400 \\
12 \times 360 & = & 4,320 \\
4 \times 20 & = & 80 \\
10 \times 1 & = & 10 \\
\hline
& & 12,438,810
\end{array}
$$

The next question which arises is, What is the starting point from which this number is counted? Just below it the student will note the date **3 Ix 7 Tzec**, which from its position would seem almost surely to be either the starting point or the terminal date, more probably the latter. Assuming that this date is the terminal date, the starting point may be calculated by counting 12,438,810 *backward* from **3 Ix 7 Tzec**. Performing this operation according to the rules laid down in such cases, the starting point reached will be **9 Kan 12 Xul**, but this date is not found in the text.

The red number in the first serpent is 4.6.11.10.7.2, which reduces to—

$$
\begin{array}{rll}
4 \times 2,880,000 & = & 11,520,000 \\
6 \times 144,000 & = & 864,000 \\
11 \times 7,200 & = & 79,200 \\
10 \times 360 & = & 3,600 \\
7 \times 20 & = & 140 \\
2 \times 1 & = & 2 \\
\hline
& & 12,466,942
\end{array}
$$

Assuming that the date below this number, **3 Cimi 14 Kayab**, was its terminal date, the starting point can be reached by counting backward. This will be found to be **9 Kan 12 Kayab**, a date actually found on this page (see pl. 32), just above the animal figure emerging from the second serpent's mouth.

The black number in the second serpent reads 4.6.9.15.12.19, which reduces as follows:

$$
\begin{aligned}
4 \times 2,880,000 &= 11,520,000 \\
6 \times 144,000 &= 864,000 \\
9 \times 7,200 &= 64,800 \\
15 \times 360 &= 5,400 \\
12 \times 20 &= 240 \\
19 \times 1 &= 19 \\
\hline
& 12,454,459
\end{aligned}
$$

Assuming that the date below this number, **13 Akbal 1 Kankin**, was the terminal date, its starting point can be shown by calculation to be just the same as the starting point for the previous number, that is, the date **9 Kan 12 Kayab**, and as mentioned above, this date appears above the animal figure emerging from the mouth of this serpent.

The last Serpent number in plate 32, the red number in the second serpent, reads, 4.6.1.9.15.0 and reduces as follows:

$$
\begin{aligned}
4 \times 2,880,000 &= 11,520,000 \\
6 \times 144,000 &= 864,000 \\
1 \times 7,200 &= 7,200 \\
9 \times 360 &= 3,240 \\
15 \times 20 &= 300 \\
0 \times 1 &= 0 \\
\hline
& 12,394.740
\end{aligned}
$$

Assuming that the date below this number, **3 Kan 17 Uo**,[1] was its terminal date, its starting point can be shown by calculation to be just the same as the starting point of the two preceding numbers, namely, the date **9 Kan 12 Kayab**, which appears above this last serpent.

It will be seen from the foregoing that three of the four Serpent dates above described are counted from the date **9 Kan 12 Kayab**, a date actually recorded in the text just above them. The all-important question of course is, What position did the date **9 Kan 12 Kayab** occupy in the Long Count? The page (62) of the Dresden Codex we

---

[1] The manuscript has incorrectly **16 Uo**. It is obvious this can not be correct, since from Table VII **Kan** can occupy only the 2d, 7th, 12th, or 17th position in the months. The correct reading here, as we shall see, is probably **17 Uo**. This reading requires only the addition of a single dot.

are discussing sheds no light on this question.   There are, however, two other pages in this Codex (61 and 69) on which Serpent numbers appear presenting this date, **9 Kan 12 Kayab,** under conditions which may shed light on the position it held in the Long Count.   On page 69 there are recorded 15 katuns, 9 tuns, 4 uinals, and 4 kins (see fig. 85); these are immediately followed by the date **9 Kan 12 Kayab.** It is important to note in this connection that, unlike almost every other number in this codex, this number is expressed by the first method, the one in which the period glyphs are used.   As the date **4 Ahau 8 Cumhu** appears just above in the text, the first supposition is that 15.9.4.4 is a Secondary-series number which, if counted forward from **4 Ahau 8 Cumhu,** the starting point of Maya chronology, will reach **9 Kan 12 Kayab,** the date recorded immediately after it.

Proceeding on this assumption and performing the operations indicated, the terminal date reached will be **9 Kan 7 Cumhu,** not **9 Kan 12 Kayab,** as recorded. The most plausible explanation for this number and date the writer can offer is that the whole constitutes a Period-ending date.   On the west side of Stela C at Quirigua, as explained on page 226, is a Period-ending date almost exactly like this (see pl. 21, *H*). On this monument 17.5.0.0 **6 Ahau 13 Kayab** is recorded, and it was proved by calculation that 9.17.5.0.0 would lead to this date if counted forward from the starting point of Maya chronology.   In effect, then, this 17.5.0.0 **6 Ahau 13 Kayab** was a Period-ending date, declaring that Tun 5 of Katun 17 (of Cycle 9, unexpressed) ended on the date **6 Ahau 13 Kayab.**

FIG. 85. Example of first method of numeration in the codices (part of page 69 of the Dresden Codex).

Interpreting in the same way the glyphs in figure 85, we have the record that Kin 4 of Uinal 4 of Tun 9 of Katun 15 (of Cycle 9, unexpressed) fell (or ended) on the date **9 Kan 12 Kayab.**   Changing this Period-ending date into its corresponding Initial Series and solving for its terminal date, the latter date will be found to be **13 Kan 12 Ceh,** instead of **9 Kan 12 Kayab.**   At first this would appear to be even farther from the mark than our preceding attempt, but if the reader will admit a slight correction, the above number can be made to reach the date recorded.   The date **13 Kan 12 Ceh** is just 5 uinals earlier than **9 Kan 12 Kayab,** and if we add one bar to the four dots of the uinal coefficient, this passage can be explained in the above manner, and yet agree in all particulars.   This is true since 9.15.9.9.4 reaches the date **9 Kan 12 Kayab.**   On the above grounds the writer is inclined to believe that the last three Serpent numbers on plate 32, which were shown to have proceeded from a date **9 Kan 12 Kayab,** were counted from the date 9.15.9.9.4 **9 Kan 12 Kayab.**

TEXTS RECORDING ASCENDING SERIES

There remains one other class of numbers which should be described before closing this chapter on the codices. The writer refers to the series of related numbers which cover so many pages of the Dresden Codex. These commence at the bottom of the page and increase toward the top, every other number in the series being a multiple of the first, or beginning number. One example of this class will suffice to illustrate all the others.

In the lower right-hand corner of plate 31 a series of this kind commences with the day 9 Ahau.[1] Of this series the number 8.2.0 just above the 9 Ahau is the first term, and the day 9 Ahau the first terminal date. As usual in Maya texts, the starting point is not expressed; by calculation, however, it can be shown to be 1 Ahau [2] in this particular case.

Counting forward then 8.2.0 from 1 Ahau, the unexpressed starting point, the first terminal date, 9 Ahau, will be reached. See the lower right-hand corner in the following outline, in which the Maya numbers have all been reduced to units of the first order:

151,840 [3]	113,880 [3]	75,920 [3]	37,960 [3]
1 Ahau	1 Ahau	1 Ahau	1 Ahau
185,120	68,900	33,280	9,100
1 Ahau	1 Ahau	1 Ahau	1 Ahau
35,040	32,120	29,200	26,280
6 Ahau	11 Ahau	3 Ahau	8 Ahau
23,360	20,440	17,520	14,600
13 Ahau	5 Ahau	10 Ahau	2 Ahau
11,680 [4]	8,760	5,840	2,920
7 Ahau	12 Ahau	4 Ahau	9 Ahau

(Unexpressed starting point, 1 Ahau.)

In the above outline each number represents the total distance of the day just below it from the unexpressed starting point, 1 Ahau, *not* the distance from the date immediately preceding it in the series. For example, the second number, 5,840 (16.4.0), is not to be counted forward from 9 Ahau in order to reach its terminal date, 4 Ahau, but from the unexpressed starting point of the whole series, the day 1 Ahau. Similarly the third number, 8,760 (1.4.6.0), is not to be counted forward from 4 Ahau in order to reach 12 Ahau, but from 1 Ahau instead, and so on throughout the series.

---

[1] In the text the coefficient appears to be 8, but in reality it is 9, the lower dot having been covered by the marginal line at the bottom.

[2] Counting backward 8.2.0 (2,920) from 9 Ahau, 1 Ahau is reached.

[3] Professor Förstemann restored the top terms of the four numbers in this row, so as to make them read as given above.

[4] The manuscript reads 1.12.5.0, which Professor Förstemann corrects to 1.12.8.0; in other words, changing the uinal from 5 to 8. This correction is fully justified in the above calculations.

Beginning with the number 2,920 and the starting point **1 Ahau**, the first twelve terms, that is, the numbers in the three lowest rows, are the first 12 multiples of 2,920.

$$
\begin{array}{ll}
2,920 = 1 \times 2,920 & 20,440 = 7 \times 2,920 \\
5,840 = 2 \times 2,920 & 23,360 = 8 \times 2,920 \\
8,760 = 3 \times 2,920 & 26,280 = 9 \times 2,920 \\
11,680 = 4 \times 2,920 & 29,200 = 10 \times 2,920 \\
14,600 = 5 \times 2,920 & 32,120 = 11 \times 2,920 \\
17,520 = 6 \times 2,920 & 35,040 = 12 \times 2,920 \\
\end{array}
$$

The days recorded under each of these numbers, as mentioned above, are the terminal dates of these distances from the starting point, **1 Ahau**. Passing over the fourth row from the bottom, which, as will appear presently, is probably an interpolation of some kind, the thirteenth number—that is, the right-hand one in the top row—is 37,960. But 37,960 is 13×2,920, a continuation of our series the twelfth term of which appeared in the left-hand number of the third row. Under the thirteenth number is set down the day **1 Ahau**; in other words, not until the thirteenth multiple of 2,920 is reached is the terminal day the same as the starting point.

With this thirteenth term 2,920 ceases to be the unit of increase, and the thirteeth term itself (37,960) is used as a difference to reach the remaining three terms on this top line, all of which are multiples of 37,960.

$$
\begin{array}{l}
37,960 = 1 \times 37,960 \text{ or } 13 \times 2,920 \\
75,920 = 2 \times 37,960 \text{ or } 26 \times 2,920 \\
113,880 = 3 \times 37,960 \text{ or } 39 \times 2,920 \\
151,840 = 4 \times 37,960 \text{ or } 52 \times 2,920 \\
\end{array}
$$

Counting forward each one of these from the starting point of this entire series, **1 Ahau**, each will be found to reach as its terminal day **1 Ahau**, as recorded under each. The fourth line from the bottom is more difficult to understand, and the explanation offered by Professor Förstemann, that the first and third terms and the second and fourth are to be combined by addition or subtraction, leaves much to be desired. Omitting this row, however, the remaining numbers, those which are multiples of 2,920, admit of an easy explanation.

In the first place, the opening term 2,920, which serves as the unit of increase for the entire series up to and including the 13th term, is the so-called Venus-Solar period, containing 8 Solar years of 365 days each and 5 Venus years of 584 days each. This important period is the subject of extended treatment elsewhere in the Dresden Codex (pp. 46–50), in which it is repeated 39 times in all, divided into three equal divisions of 13 periods each. The 13th term of our series 37,960 is, as we have seen, 13×2,920, the exact number of days treated of in the upper divisions of pages 46–50 of the Dresden Codex. The 14th term (75,920) is the exact number of days treated of in the first two divisions, and finally, the 15th, or next to the last term (113,880), is the exact number of days treated of in all three divisions of these pages.

This 13th term (37,960) is the first in which the tonalamatl of 260 days comes into harmony with the Venus and Solar years, and as such must have been of very great importance to the Maya. At the same time it represents two Calendar Rounds, another important chronological count. With the next to the last term (113,880) the Mars year of 780 days is brought into harmony with all the other periods named. This number, as just mentioned, represents the sum of all the 39 Venus-Solar periods on pages 46–50 of the Dresden Codex. This next to the last number seems to possess more remarkable properties than the last number (151,840), in which the Mars year is not contained without a remainder, and the reason for its record does not appear.

The next to the last term contains:

438 Tonalamatls of 260 days each
312 Solar years of 365 days each
195 Venus years of 584 days each
146 Mars years of 780 days each
39 Venus-Solar periods of 2,920 days each
6 Calendar Rounds of 18,980 days each

It will be noted in plate 31 that the concealed starting point of this series is the day **1 Ahau,** and that just to the left on the same plate are two dates, **1 Ahau 18 Kayab** and **1 Ahau 18 Uo,** both of which show this same day, and one of which, **1 Ahau 18 Kayab,** is accompanied by its corresponding Initial Series 9.9.9.16.0. It seems not unlikely, therefore, that the day **1 Ahau** with which this series commences was **1 Ahau 18 Kayab,** which in turn was 9.9.9.16.0 **1 Ahau 18 Kayab** of the Long Count. This is rendered somewhat probable by the fact that the second division of 13 Venus-Solar periods on pages 46–50 of the Dresden Codex also has the same date, **1 Ahau 18 Kayab,** as its terminal date. Hence, it is not improbable (more it would be unwise to say) that the series of numbers which we have been discussing was counted from the date 9.9.9.16.0. **1 Ahau 18 Kayab.**

The foregoing examples cover, in a general way, the material presented in the codices; there is, however, much other matter which has not been explained here, as unfitted to the needs of the beginner. To the student who wishes to specialize in this field of the glyphic writing the writer recommends the treatises of Prof. Ernst Förstemann as the most valuable contribution to this subject.

INDEX

A CATALOGUE OF SELECTED DOVER BOOKS
IN ALL FIELDS OF INTEREST

A CATALOGUE OF SELECTED DOVER BOOKS
IN ALL FIELDS OF INTEREST

THE DEVIL'S DICTIONARY, Ambrose Bierce. Barbed, bitter, brilliant witticisms in the form of a dictionary. Best, most ferocious satire America has produced. 145pp. 20487-1 Pa. $1.50

ABSOLUTELY MAD INVENTIONS, A.E. Brown, H.A. Jeffcott. Hilarious, useless, or merely absurd inventions all granted patents by the U.S. Patent Office. Edible tie pin, mechanical hat tipper, etc. 57 illustrations. 125pp. 22596-8 Pa. $1.50

AMERICAN WILD FLOWERS COLORING BOOK, Paul Kennedy. Planned coverage of 48 most important wildflowers, from Rickett's collection; instructive as well as entertaining. Color versions on covers. 48pp. 8¼ x 11. 20095-7 Pa. $1.35

BIRDS OF AMERICA COLORING BOOK, John James Audubon. Rendered for coloring by Paul Kennedy. 46 of Audubon's noted illustrations: red-winged blackbird, cardinal, purple finch, towhee, etc. Original plates reproduced in full color on the covers. 48pp. 8¼ x 11. 23049-X Pa. $1.35

NORTH AMERICAN INDIAN DESIGN COLORING BOOK, Paul Kennedy. The finest examples from Indian masks, beadwork, pottery, etc. — selected and redrawn for coloring (with identifications) by well-known illustrator Paul Kennedy. 48pp. 8¼ x 11. 21125-8 Pa. $1.35

UNIFORMS OF THE AMERICAN REVOLUTION COLORING BOOK, Peter Copeland. 31 lively drawings reproduce whole panorama of military attire; each uniform has complete instructions for accurate coloring. (Not in the Pictorial Archives Series). 64pp. 8¼ x 11. 21850-3 Pa. $1.50

THE WONDERFUL WIZARD OF OZ COLORING BOOK, L. Frank Baum. Color the Yellow Brick Road and much more in 61 drawings adapted from W.W. Denslow's originals, accompanied by abridged version of text. Dorothy, Toto, Oz and the Emerald City. 61 illustrations. 64pp. 8¼ x 11. 20452-9 Pa. $1.50

CUT AND COLOR PAPER MASKS, Michael Grater. Clowns, animals, funny faces ... simply color them in, cut them out, and put them together, and you have 9 paper masks to play with and enjoy. Complete instructions. Assembled masks shown in full color on the covers. 32pp. 8¼ x 11. 23171-2 Pa. $1.50

STAINED GLASS CHRISTMAS ORNAMENT COLORING BOOK, Carol Belanger Grafton. Brighten your Christmas season with over 100 Christmas ornaments done in a stained glass effect on translucent paper. Color them in and then hang at windows, from lights, anywhere. 32pp. 8¼ x 11. 20707-2 Pa. $1.75

THE FITZWILLIAM VIRGINAL BOOK, edited by J. Fuller Maitland, W.B. Squire. Famous early 17th century collection of keyboard music, 300 works by Morley, Byrd, Bull, Gibbons, etc. Modern notation. Total of 938pp. 8⅜ x 11.
ECE 21068-5, 21069-3 Pa., Two vol. set $12.00

COMPLETE STRING QUARTETS, Wolfgang A. Mozart. Breitkopf and Härtel edition. All 23 string quartets plus alternate slow movement to K156. Study score. 277pp. 9⅜ x 12¼.
22372-8 Pa. $6.00

COMPLETE SONG CYCLES, Franz Schubert. Complete piano, vocal music of Die Schöne Müllerin, Die Winterreise, Schwanengesang. Also Drinker English singing translations. Breitkopf and Härtel edition. 217pp. 9⅜ x 12¼.
22649-2 Pa. $4.00

THE COMPLETE PRELUDES AND ETUDES FOR PIANOFORTE SOLO, Alexander Scriabin. All the preludes and etudes including many perfectly spun miniatures. Edited by K.N. Igumnov and Y.I. Mil'shteyn. 250pp. 9 x 12.
22919-X Pa. $5.00

TRISTAN UND ISOLDE, Richard Wagner. Full orchestral score with complete instrumentation. Do not confuse with piano reduction. Commentary by Felix Mottl, great Wagnerian conductor and scholar. Study score. 655pp. 8⅛ x 11.
22915-7 Pa. $10.00

FAVORITE SONGS OF THE NINETIES, ed. Robert Fremont. Full reproduction, including covers, of 88 favorites: Ta-Ra-Ra-Boom-De-Aye, The Band Played On, Bird in a Gilded Cage, Under the Bamboo Tree, After the Ball, etc. 401pp. 9 x 12.
EBE 21536-9 Pa. $6.95

SOUSA'S GREAT MARCHES IN PIANO TRANSCRIPTION: ORIGINAL SHEET MUSIC OF 23 WORKS, John Philip Sousa. Selected by Lester S. Levy. Playing edition includes: The Stars and Stripes Forever, The Thunderer, The Gladiator, King Cotton, Washington Post, much more. 24 illustrations. 111pp. 9 x 12.
USO 23132-1 Pa. $3.50

CLASSIC PIANO RAGS, selected with an introduction by Rudi Blesh. Best ragtime music (1897-1922) by Scott Joplin, James Scott, Joseph F. Lamb, Tom Turpin, 9 others. Printed from best original sheet music, plus covers. 364pp. 9 x 12.
EBE 20469-3 Pa. $6.95

ANALYSIS OF CHINESE CHARACTERS, C.D. Wilder, J.H. Ingram. 1000 most important characters analyzed according to primitives, phonetics, historical development. Traditional method offers mnemonic aid to beginner, intermediate student of Chinese, Japanese. 365pp.
23045-7 Pa. $4.00

MODERN CHINESE: A BASIC COURSE, Faculty of Peking University. Self study, classroom course in modern Mandarin. Records contain phonetics, vocabulary, sentences, lessons. 249 page book contains all recorded text, translations, grammar, vocabulary, exercises. Best course on market. 3 12" 33⅓ monaural records, book, album.
98832-5 Set $12.50

THE BEST DR. THORNDYKE DETECTIVE STORIES, R. Austin Freeman. The Case of Oscar Brodski, The Moabite Cipher, and 5 other favorites featuring the great scientific detective, plus his long-believed-lost first adventure — 31 New Inn — reprinted here for the first time. Edited by E.F. Bleiler. USO 20388-3 Pa. $3.00

BEST "THINKING MACHINE" DETECTIVE STORIES, Jacques Futrelle. The Problem of Cell 13 and 11 other stories about Prof. Augustus S.F.X. Van Dusen, including two "lost" stories. First reprinting of several. Edited by E.F. Bleiler. 241pp. 20537-1 Pa. $3.00

UNCLE SILAS, J. Sheridan LeFanu. Victorian Gothic mystery novel, considered by many best of period, even better than Collins or Dickens. Wonderful psychological terror. Introduction by Frederick Shroyer. 436pp. 21715-9 Pa. $4.00

BEST DR. POGGIOLI DETECTIVE STORIES, T.S. Stribling. 15 best stories from EQMM and The Saint offer new adventures in Mexico, Florida, Tennessee hills as Poggioli unravels mysteries and combats Count Jalacki. 217pp. 23227-1 Pa. $3.00

EIGHT DIME NOVELS, selected with an introduction by E.F. Bleiler. Adventures of Old King Brady, Frank James, Nick Carter, Deadwood Dick, Buffalo Bill, The Steam Man, Frank Merriwell, and Horatio Alger — 1877 to 1905. Important, entertaining popular literature in facsimile reprint, with original covers. 190pp. 9 x 12. 22975-0 Pa. $3.50

ALICE'S ADVENTURES UNDER GROUND, Lewis Carroll. Facsimile of ms. Carroll gave Alice Liddell in 1864. Different in many ways from final Alice. Handlettered, illustrated by Carroll. Introduction by Martin Gardner. 128pp. 21482-6 Pa. $1.50

ALICE IN WONDERLAND COLORING BOOK, Lewis Carroll. Pictures by John Tenniel. Large-size versions of the famous illustrations of Alice, Cheshire Cat, Mad Hatter and all the others, waiting for your crayons. Abridged text. 36 illustrations. 64pp. 8¼ x 11. 22853-3 Pa. $1.50

AVENTURES D'ALICE AU PAYS DES MERVEILLES, Lewis Carroll. Bué's translation of "Alice" into French, supervised by Carroll himself. Novel way to learn language. (No English text.) 42 Tenniel illustrations. 196pp. 22836-3 Pa. $2.00

MYTHS AND FOLK TALES OF IRELAND, Jeremiah Curtin. 11 stories that are Irish versions of European fairy tales and 9 stories from the Fenian cycle — 20 tales of legend and magic that comprise an essential work in the history of folklore. 256pp. 22430-9 Pa. $3.00

EAST O' THE SUN AND WEST O' THE MOON, George W. Dasent. Only full edition of favorite, wonderful Norwegian fairytales — Why the Sea is Salt, Boots and the Troll, etc. — with 77 illustrations by Kittelsen & Werenskiöld. 418pp. 22521-6 Pa. $3.50

PERRAULT'S FAIRY TALES, Charles Perrault and Gustave Doré. Original versions of Cinderella, Sleeping Beauty, Little Red Riding Hood, etc. in best translation, with 34 wonderful illustrations by Gustave Doré. 117pp. 8⅛ x 11. 22311-6 Pa. $2.50

HOUDINI ON MAGIC, Harold Houdini. Edited by Walter Gibson, Morris N. Young. How he escaped; exposés of fake spiritualists; instructions for eye-catching tricks; other fascinating material by and about greatest magician. 155 illustrations. 280pp. 20384-0 Pa. $2.50

HANDBOOK OF THE NUTRITIONAL CONTENTS OF FOOD, U.S. Dept. of Agriculture. Largest, most detailed source of food nutrition information ever prepared. Two mammoth tables: one measuring nutrients in 100 grams of edible portion; the other, in edible portion of 1 pound as purchased. Originally titled Composition of Foods. 190pp. 9 x 12. 21342-0 Pa. $4.00

COMPLETE GUIDE TO HOME CANNING, PRESERVING AND FREEZING, U.S. Dept. of Agriculture. Seven basic manuals with full instructions for jams and jellies; pickles and relishes; canning fruits, vegetables, meat; freezing anything. Really good recipes, exact instructions for optimal results. Save a fortune in food. 156 illustrations. 214pp. 6⅛ x 9¼. 22911-4 Pa. $2.50

THE BREAD TRAY, Louis P. De Gouy. Nearly every bread the cook could buy or make: bread sticks of Italy, fruit breads of Greece, glazed rolls of Vienna, everything from corn pone to croissants. Over 500 recipes altogether. including buns, rolls, muffins, scones, and more. 463pp. 23000-7 Pa. $3.50

CREATIVE HAMBURGER COOKERY, Louis P. De Gouy. 182 unusual recipes for casseroles, meat loaves and hamburgers that turn inexpensive ground meat into memorable main dishes: Arizona chili burgers, burger tamale pie, burger stew, burger corn loaf, burger wine loaf, and more. 120pp. 23001-5 Pa. $1.75

LONG ISLAND SEAFOOD COOKBOOK, J. George Frederick and Jean Joyce. Probably the best American seafood cookbook. Hundreds of recipes. 40 gourmet sauces, 123 recipes using oysters alone! All varieties of fish and seafood amply represented. 324pp. 22677-8 Pa. $3.00

THE EPICUREAN: A COMPLETE TREATISE OF ANALYTICAL AND PRACTICAL STUDIES IN THE CULINARY ART, Charles Ranhofer. Great modern classic. 3,500 recipes from master chef of Delmonico's, turn-of-the-century America's best restaurant. Also explained, many techniques known only to professional chefs. 775 illustrations. 1183pp. 6⅝ x 10. 22680-8 Clothbd. $17.50

THE AMERICAN WINE COOK BOOK, Ted Hatch. Over 700 recipes: old favorites livened up with wine plus many more: Czech fish soup, quince soup, sauce Perigueux, shrimp shortcake, filets Stroganoff, cordon bleu goulash, jambonneau, wine fruit cake, more. 314pp. 22796-0 Pa. $2.50

DELICIOUS VEGETARIAN COOKING, Ivan Baker. Close to 500 delicious and varied recipes: soups, main course dishes (pea, bean, lentil, cheese, vegetable, pasta, and egg dishes), savories, stews, whole-wheat breads and cakes, more. 168pp. USO 22834-7 Pa. $1.75

CONSTRUCTION OF AMERICAN FURNITURE TREASURES, Lester Margon. 344 detail drawings, complete text on constructing exact reproductions of 38 early American masterpieces: Hepplewhite sideboard, Duncan Phyfe drop-leaf table, mantel clock, gate-leg dining table, Pa. German cupboard, more. 38 plates. 54 photographs. 168pp. 8⅜ x 11¼. 23056-2 Pa. $4.00

JEWELRY MAKING AND DESIGN, Augustus F. Rose, Antonio Cirino. Professional secrets revealed in thorough, practical guide: tools, materials, processes; rings, brooches, chains, cast pieces, enamelling, setting stones, etc. Do not confuse with skimpy introductions: beginner can use, professional can learn from it. Over 200 illustrations. 306pp. 21750-7 Pa. $3.00

METALWORK AND ENAMELLING, Herbert Maryon. Generally conceded best all-around book. Countless trade secrets: materials, tools, soldering, filigree, setting, inlay, niello, repoussé, casting, polishing, etc. For beginner or expert. Author was foremost British expert. 330 illustrations. 335pp. 22702-2 Pa. $3.50

WEAVING WITH FOOT-POWER LOOMS, Edward F. Worst. Setting up a loom, beginning to weave, constructing equipment, using dyes, more, plus over 285 drafts of traditional patterns including Colonial and Swedish weaves. More than 200 other figures. For beginning and advanced. 275pp. 8¾ x 6⅜. 23064-3 Pa. $4.00

WEAVING A NAVAJO BLANKET, Gladys A. Reichard. Foremost anthropologist studied under Navajo women, reveals every step in process from wool, dyeing, spinning, setting up loom, designing, weaving. Much history, symbolism. With this book you could make one yourself. 97 illustrations. 222pp. 22992-0 Pa. $3.00

NATURAL DYES AND HOME DYEING, Rita J. Adrosko. Use natural ingredients: bark, flowers, leaves, lichens, insects etc. Over 135 specific recipes from historical sources for cotton, wool, other fabrics. Genuine premodern handicrafts. 12 illustrations. 160pp. 22688-3 Pa. $2.00

THE HAND DECORATION OF FABRICS, Francis J. Kafka. Outstanding, profusely illustrated guide to stenciling, batik, block printing, tie dyeing, freehand painting, silk screen printing, and novelty decoration. 356 illustrations. 198pp. 6 x 9. 21401-X Pa. $3.00

THOMAS NAST: CARTOONS AND ILLUSTRATIONS, with text by Thomas Nast St. Hill. Father of American political cartooning. Cartoons that destroyed Tweed Ring; inflation, free love, church and state; original Republican elephant and Democratic donkey; Santa Claus; more. 117 illustrations. 146pp. 9 x 12.
22983-1 Pa. $4.00
23067-8 Clothbd. $8.50

FREDERIC REMINGTON: 173 DRAWINGS AND ILLUSTRATIONS. Most famous of the Western artists, most responsible for our myths about the American West in its untamed days. Complete reprinting of *Drawings of Frederic Remington* (1897), plus other selections. 4 additional drawings in color on covers. 140pp. 9 x 12.
20714-5 Pa. $3.95

SLEEPING BEAUTY, illustrated by Arthur Rackham. Perhaps the fullest, most delightful version ever, told by C.S. Evans. Rackham's best work. 49 illustrations. 110pp. 7⅞ x 10¾.   22756-1 Pa. $2.00

THE WONDERFUL WIZARD OF OZ, L. Frank Baum. Facsimile in full color of America's finest children's classic. Introduction by Martin Gardner. 143 illustrations by W.W. Denslow. 267pp.   20691-2 Pa. $2.50

GOOPS AND HOW TO BE THEM, Gelett Burgess. Classic tongue-in-cheek masquerading as etiquette book. 87 verses, 170 cartoons as Goops demonstrate virtues of table manners, neatness, courtesy, more. 88pp. 6½ x 9¼.
                                                           22233-0 Pa. $1.50

THE BROWNIES, THEIR BOOK, Palmer Cox. Small as mice, cunning as foxes, exuberant, mischievous, Brownies go to zoo, toy shop, seashore, circus, more. 24 verse adventures. 266 illustrations. 144pp. 6⅝ x 9¼.   21265-3 Pa. $1.75

BILLY WHISKERS: THE AUTOBIOGRAPHY OF A GOAT, Frances Trego Montgomery. Escapades of that rambunctious goat. Favorite from turn of the century America. 24 illustrations. 259pp.   22345-0 Pa. $2.75

THE ROCKET BOOK, Peter Newell. Fritz, janitor's kid, sets off rocket in basement of apartment house; an ingenious hole punched through every page traces course of rocket. 22 duotone drawings, verses. 48pp. 6⅞ x 8⅜.   22044-3 Pa. $1.50

PECK'S BAD BOY AND HIS PA, George W. Peck. Complete double-volume of great American childhood classic. Hennery's ingenious pranks against outraged pomposity of pa and the grocery man. 97 illustrations. Introduction by E.F. Bleiler. 347pp.   20497-9 Pa. $2.50

THE TALE OF PETER RABBIT, Beatrix Potter. The inimitable Peter's terrifying adventure in Mr. McGregor's garden, with all 27 wonderful, full-color Potter illustrations. 55pp. 4¼ x 5½.   USO 22827-4 Pa. $1.00

THE TALE OF MRS. TIGGY-WINKLE, Beatrix Potter. Your child will love this story about a very special hedgehog and all 27 wonderful, full-color Potter illustrations. 57pp. 4¼ x 5½.   USO 20546-0 Pa. $1.00

THE TALE OF BENJAMIN BUNNY, Beatrix Potter. Peter Rabbit's cousin coaxes him back into Mr. McGregor's garden for a whole new set of adventures. A favorite with children. All 27 full-color illustrations. 59pp. 4¼ x 5½.
                                                        USO 21102-9 Pa. $1.00

THE MERRY ADVENTURES OF ROBIN HOOD, Howard Pyle. Facsimile of original (1883) edition, finest modern version of English outlaw's adventures. 23 illustrations by Pyle. 296pp. 6½ x 9¼.   22043-5 Pa. $2.75

TWO LITTLE SAVAGES, Ernest Thompson Seton. Adventures of two boys who lived as Indians; explaining Indian ways, woodlore, pioneer methods. 293 illustrations. 286pp.   20985-7 Pa. $3.00

JEWISH GREETING CARDS, Ed Sibbett, Jr. 16 cards to cut and color. Three say "Happy Chanukah," one "Happy New Year," others have no message, show stars of David, Torahs, wine cups, other traditional themes. 16 envelopes. 8¼ x 11.
23225-5 Pa. $2.00

AUBREY BEARDSLEY GREETING CARD BOOK, Aubrey Beardsley. Edited by Theodore Menten. 16 elegant yet inexpensive greeting cards let you combine your own sentiments with subtle Art Nouveau lines. 16 different Aubrey Beardsley designs that you can color or not, as you wish. 16 envelopes. 64pp. 8¼ x 11.
23173-9 Pa. $2.00

RECREATIONS IN THE THEORY OF NUMBERS, Albert Beiler. Number theory, an inexhaustible source of puzzles, recreations, for beginners and advanced. Divisors, perfect numbers. scales of notation, etc. 349pp.
21096-0 Pa. $2.50

AMUSEMENTS IN MATHEMATICS, Henry E. Dudeney. One of largest puzzle collections, based on algebra, arithmetic, permutations, probability, plane figure dissection, properties of numbers, by one of world's foremost puzzlists. Solutions. 450 illustrations. 258pp.
20473-1 Pa. $2.75

MATHEMATICS, MAGIC AND MYSTERY, Martin Gardner. Puzzle editor for Scientific American explains math behind: card tricks, stage mind reading, coin and match tricks, counting out games, geometric dissections. Probability, sets, theory of numbers, clearly explained. Plus more than 400 tricks, guaranteed to work. 135 illustrations. 176pp.
20335-2 Pa. $2.00

BEST MATHEMATICAL PUZZLES OF SAM LOYD, edited by Martin Gardner. Bizarre, original, whimsical puzzles by America's greatest puzzler. From fabulously rare Cyclopedia, including famous 14-15 puzzles, the Horse of a Different Color, 115 more. Elementary math. 150 illustrations. 167pp.
20498-7 Pa. $2.00

MATHEMATICAL PUZZLES FOR BEGINNERS AND ENTHUSIASTS, Geoffrey Mott-Smith. 189 puzzles from easy to difficult involving arithmetic, logic, algebra, properties of digits, probability. Explanation of math behind puzzles. 135 illustrations. 248pp.
20198-8 Pa. $2.00

BIG BOOK OF MAZES AND LABYRINTHS, Walter Shepherd. Classical, solid, and ripple mazes; short path and avoidance labyrinths; more — 50 mazes and labyrinths in all. 12 other figures. Full solutions. 112pp. 8⅛ x 11.
22951-3 Pa. $2.00

COIN GAMES AND PUZZLES, Maxey Brooke. 60 puzzles, games and stunts — from Japan, Korea, Africa and the ancient world, by Dudeney and the other great puzzlers, as well as Maxey Brooke's own creations. Full solutions. 67 illustrations. 94pp.
22893-2 Pa. $1.25

HAND SHADOWS TO BE THROWN UPON THE WALL, Henry Bursill. Wonderful Victorian novelty tells how to make flying birds, dog, goose, deer, and 14 others. 32pp. 6½ x 9¼.
21779-5 Pa. $1.00

EGYPTIAN MAGIC, E.A. Wallis Budge. Foremost Egyptologist, curator at British Museum, on charms, curses, amulets, doll magic, transformations, control of demons, deific appearances, feats of great magicians. Many texts cited. 19 illustrations. 234pp. USO 22681-6 Pa. $2.50

THE LEYDEN PAPYRUS: AN EGYPTIAN MAGICAL BOOK, edited by F. Ll. Griffith, Herbert Thompson. Egyptian sorcerer's manual contains scores of spells: sex magic of various sorts, occult information, evoking visions, removing evil magic, etc. Transliteration faces translation. 207pp. 22994-7 Pa. $2.50

THE MALLEUS MALEFICARUM OF KRAMER AND SPRENGER, translated, edited by Montague Summers. Full text of most important witchhunter's "Bible," used by both Catholics and Protestants. Theory of witches, manifestations, remedies, etc. Indispensable to serious student. 278pp. 6⅝ x 10. USO 22802-9 Pa. $3.95

LOST CONTINENTS, L. Sprague de Camp. Great science-fiction author, finest, fullest study: Atlantis, Lemuria, Mu, Hyperborea, etc. Lost Tribes, Irish in pre-Columbian America, root races; in history, literature, art, occultism. Necessary to everyone concerned with theme. 17 illustrations. 348pp. 22668-9 Pa. $3.50

THE COMPLETE BOOKS OF CHARLES FORT, Charles Fort. Book of the Damned, Lo!, Wild Talents, New Lands. Greatest compilation of data: celestial appearances, flying saucers, falls of frogs, strange disappearances, inexplicable data not recognized by science. Inexhaustible, painstakingly documented. Do not confuse with modern charlatanry. Introduction by Damon Knight. Total of 1126pp.
23094-5 Clothbd. $15.00

FADS AND FALLACIES IN THE NAME OF SCIENCE, Martin Gardner. Fair, witty appraisal of cranks and quacks of science: Atlantis, Lemuria, flat earth, Velikovsky, orgone energy, Bridey Murphy, medical fads, etc. 373pp. 20394-8 Pa. $3.00

HOAXES, Curtis D. MacDougall. Unbelievably rich account of great hoaxes: Locke's moon hoax, Shakespearean forgeries, Loch Ness monster, Disumbrationist school of art, dozens more; also psychology of hoaxing. 54 illustrations. 338pp. 20465-0 Pa. $3.50

THE GENTLE ART OF MAKING ENEMIES, James A.M. Whistler. Greatest wit of his day deflates Wilde, Ruskin, Swinburne; strikes back at inane critics, exhibitions. Highly readable classic of impressionist revolution by great painter. Introduction by Alfred Werner. 334pp. 21875-9 Pa. $4.00

THE BOOK OF TEA, Kakuzo Okakura. Minor classic of the Orient: entertaining, charming explanation, interpretation of traditional Japanese culture in terms of tea ceremony. Edited by E.F. Bleiler. Total of 94pp. 20070-1 Pa. $1.25